The Politics of Flexibility

The Politics of Flexibility
Restructuring State and Industry in Britain, Germany and Scandinavia

Editors

Bob Jessop
University of
Lancaster UK

Hans Kastendiek
University of
Giessen Germany

Klaus Nielsen
Roskilde University
Center Denmark

Ove K. Pedersen
Roskilde University
Center Denmark

Edward Elgar

Published by
Edward Elgar Publishing Limited
Gower House
Croft Road
Aldershot
Hants GU11 3HR
England

Edward Elgar Publishing Company
Old Post Road
Brookfield
Vermont 05036
USA

Reprinted 1994

A CIP catalogue record for this book is available from the British Library

ISBN 1 85278 548 9

Printed in Great Britain by Ipswich Book Co. Ltd., Ipswich,
Suffolk

Contents

Part 3. Germany: The Neo-Corporatist Road Beyond Flexi-Fordism

Part 4. Scandinavia: Negotiated Economy and Bargained Flexibility

Preface

During the 1980s western European economic and political debates on economics and politics shifted their focus from crises and crisis management to issues of structural change. A search for new answers replaced the failed attempts to use the old remedies. Restructuring became the order of the day.

The need for greater flexibility is a generally accepted premiss in current discourses on restructuring. Most of these are centred around state and industry. In relation to the state old themes are reformulated and new themes are introduced. The old critiques of public bureaucracies and the welfare state have been rephrased. The problems are now seen as consequences of inflexible rules, rigid behaviour and rigidities in the provision of services. More important, increased flexibility is also seen as a required response to recent development trends in industry. Flexibilization of public programmes and structures is demanded to facilitate efforts to increase flexibility in the organization of production and labour markets.

Flexibility has also become a dominant concern in relation to discourses on industry and work. The need for more flexible forms of organizing production and labour processes to take advantage of the new technologies is one of the prominent themes. The need for more flexibility in relation to wage formation, mobility of workers, hire-and-fire rules and other regulations of labour markets is another.

Discourses on flexibility are by no means restricted to these areas. Other central issues are the corporate structure, inter-firm relations and localization of enterprises. Moreover, as even a cursory glance at the news cannot fail to reveal, flexibility has become a prominent catchword in recent economic and political debates more generally.

The need for flexibilization is often seen as part of the international economic modernization race. The struggle to develop industrial activities using the new technologies (microelectronics, biotechnology, etc.) leads to efforts to remove a lot of institutional hindrances such as established norms, rules and regulations as well as some vested interests. Furthermore, the new technologies seem to generate more flexibility in themselves. Modern telecommunication and computer-aided manufacturing make it possible to adapt more flexibly to consumer demand, allow flexible changes in flows of input and make small batch production profitable. Flexible automation or flexible specialization is used to designate these new forms of production which demand another set of labour skills and qualifications and forms of organization and management which differ from traditional forms of production. This in turn seems to challenge the established forms of industrial relations, education and welfare provision.

These tendencies are strengthened by the structural changes in international economic exchange. The shift from fixed to flexible exchange rates in the beginning of the 1970s combined with a thorough liberalization and deregulation of international financial flows has created an environment which forces economic and political agents alike to adapt quickly to change in the international economy.

The attempts to increase flexibility might be interpreted as means to secure a better 'match' between techno-economic restructuring and socio-political reorganization. In these terms they might be directed against rigidities hampering techno-economic modernization. Alternatively, they might aim to impede or slow down societal disturbances created by economic changes. Or, again, they might be aimed at shaping the direction of techno-economic changes by means of a reformed socio-political institutional framework.

Whatever the ideas behind such 'matching' endeavours might be, it is obvious that the need for increased flexibility in various areas of society is generally accepted. But, it is not unchallenged. Some consider it a purely discursive construct without sufficient reference to actually emergent phenomena. Others question the real novelty of the concern. In any case, the implications are certainly controversial. Does flexibilization involve major reorganization or merely incremental adaptation within the existing institutional set-up? What are the constraints on the direction and the eventual outcome of the restructuring process? How wide is the scope for strategic choice? Such questions are subject to heated theoretical disputes. The answers probably vary considerably across national contexts.

This book is about the discourses of flexibility, the theoretical approaches to the phenomenon, and the political responses to the preceived need for flexibility. The theme of this book is not flexibility as such. It does not focus on flexibility in the organization of production or the labour market, nor in any other area in particular. It is about the politics of flexibility and the strategies for flexibilization in state and industry.

Politics is used here as a dimension rather than a specific level of analysis. It is about 'the politics of production' (Burawoy, 1985), and even to a certain extent the politics of 'daily life', as well as about corporatism, pluralism, local politics, party politics, state programmes and administrative decision-making. The political dimension involves not only the various forms of representation and coordination of interests but also the efforts of the actors to mobilize support for their preferred formulation of the collective interest and their own collective identity. In other terms: this book is about discourses on flexibility as well as about conflicts, actions and strategies at all levels of decision-making in relation to the perceived need for flexibilization.

We have chosen to relate this to Britain, Germany and Scandinavia on two grounds. Firstly, these countries are sufficiently similar in level of development and culturally to warrant a comparison; and, yet, secondly, they are very different in their approach to flexibility. The most obvious difference is, of course, between Britain and the other countries. Britain represents a neo-liberal approach while Germany and the Scandinavian countries are normally (together with Austria) considered the 'model' neo-corporatist countries. Thatcherism is the 'model' case of state driven liberalism while conservatism and social democracy characterize the development in Germany and Scandinavia. Some see the neo-liberal strategy as the most successful and the only one to secure prosperity in the long run. Others maintain that the neo-corporatist countries are the ones best equipped to develop 'offensive' strategies of flexibilization because of their capacity for involvement of workers.

Below this high level of abstraction the common stamp of Germany and the Scandinavian countries disappear. A closer look reveals different industrial structures, labour market institutions, state apparatuses, norms and cultural values, etc. All the Scandinavian countries have resemblances which make them different from Germany in relation to the structure and development of the welfare state, smallness and openness to world markets, labour law, traditional dominance of the Social Democracy and egalitarian values, etc. But nor is Scandinavia a uniform set of countries. Its nations differ widely as far as their industrial profiles and insertion into the international economy are concerned (Mjøset, 1987). Their institutional set-up are also significantly different. In this book reference is mainly made to Sweden and Denmark which constitute in several aspects opposite cases in the Scandinavian context. The Swedish institutions of labour market policy and solidaristic wage policy are internationally renowned and Sweden is generally considered the 'success story' of neo-corporatism - or, as Swedes prefer to see it, democratic class struggle between organized labour and big capital. Denmark, on the other hand, appears more backward, pluralist, almost 'ungovernable', in deep economic trouble and non-Scandinavian in its inability, or even reluctance, to give priority to full employment in its economic policy.

The national differences influence the interpretations of the need for increased flexibility as well as the initiatives taken to implement flexibilization. The collection of country studies in this book makes it possible to compare not only neo-liberal and neo-corporatist responses to the challenge of flexibility but also different neo-corporatist attempts to develop offensive strategies for flexibilization.

The book includes three parts with country studies. That on Britain includes chapters on Thatcherism and industrial relations, a comparison of two central industrial sectors, and a chapter on public law. The part on Germany (actually West Germany as the impacts of the reunification are not included) includes chapters on industrial relations, work organization, and neo-conservative political strategies. The Scandinavian part includes a comparative study of Nordic welfare states, and chapters on political strategies in Denmark and industrial relations in Sweden.

In addition to the parts on Britain, Germany and Scandinavia this book also includes a part ('Myths and Realities') with theoretical, comparative and historical contributions about selected areas of flexibilization or about flexibility in general.

Even if the book is rather long and contains a faily large number of contributions, it is true that the coverage of the general theme of the book is scattered and incomplete. This is probably unavoidable considering the comprehensiveness of the theme. Not all areas of flexibilization are covered, not even some of the most important ones, in the British, the German or the Scandinavian parts. Nor does the book include a thorough presentation and critique of the main theoretical approaches to flexibility. The introductory chapter is meant to compensate somewhat for these flaws. It is a survey of the main theories as well as the discourses and strategies of flexibility related to the labour market, industrial organization, and so on. Instead of the usual editorial strategy in collections of this sort of merely stringing together a series of abstracts of individual papers, the introductory overview is an attempt to present the major theoretical and empirical issues in their own right and on their own terms. Nevertheless, for the convenience of the readers, we have included a section in front of the book with simple abstracts of the chapters that follow.

This book has been long in the making. Almost half of the chapters are revised versions of papers that were first presented in April 1988 at a conference in Roskilde, Denmark: 'Strategies for flexibilization. Techno-economic and socio-political restructuring in western Europe in the 1980s'. (Other conference papers have been published in Scandinavian Political Studies no. 4, 1989.) The other half of the chapters have been collected from various other sources. Most of the chapters were prepared early or mid 1990.

The dominant interpretations of flexibility may have changed during the last few years but flexibilization is still very much on the political agenda. This can be expected to last for years to come, although one can already see a tendency that the need for flexibility has become less controversial and entered into the public opinion as a unquestionable virtue. This does not reduce the importance of an informed and critical debate. Hopefully, this book will make a small contribution to inform the debate.

We are indebted to several institutions that have sponsored the preparation of this book. First of all, the Danish Social Science Research Council, which sponsored the initial conference in Denmark and part of the editorial work. Also the National Bank of Denmark and the Center for Public Organization and Management at Copenhagen Business School have contributed to the financing of the work. Last but not least, we are indebted to people who have delivered invaluable assistance during the process of preparing the book. We want to express our gratitude to Jan P. Windmüller, Dorthe Johnson and, in particular, Henrik Kjær Hansen without whom the technicalities of the editorial work would have proven an insurmountable obstacle.

Klaus Nielsen

Contributors

Robert Boyer : Research officer at *CEPREMAP* in Paris and Professor of Economics in Paris 1.

Martin Börjeson : Research officer at the Department of Technology and Social Change at the *University of Linköping*.

Noelle Burgi : CNRS research officer at *University of Lille* and teacher at the Sorbonne.

Mark Elam : Research officer at the Department of Technology and Social Change at the *University of Linköping*.

Joachim Hirsch : Professor of Sociology at the *University of Frankfurt*.

Kurt Hübner : Wissenschaftliche assistent in Political Economy at the *Free University of Berlin*.

Richard Hyman : Professor in Industrial Relations at the Industrial Relations Research Unit, *University of Warwick*.

Otto Jacobi : Research officer at the *Institute for Social Research in Frankfurt*.

Bob Jessop : Professor of Sociology at the *University of Lancaster*.

Björn Johnson : Associated professor at the *University of Ålborg*.

Ulrich Jürgens : Research officer at the *Wissenschaftszentrum Berlin*.

Hans Kastendiek : Professor in Anglistik at the *University of Grießen*.

Pekka Kosonen : Associated professor at the *University of Helsinki*.

Norman Lewis : Professor of Public Law, *University of Sheffield*.

Bengt Åke Lundvall : Associated professor in Economics at the *University of Ålborg*.

Klaus Nielsen : Associated professor at the *University of Roskilde* and research officer at the *Center for Public Organization and Management* in Copenhagen.

Ove K. Pedersen : Associated professor at the *University of Roskilde* and research officer at the *Center for Public Organization and Management* in Copenhagen.

Hans-Joachim Schabedoth : Research officer and cooperating staff member of the department for principal matters in the *IG Metall executive board* in Frankfurt.

Abstracts

Towards a Flexible Future - Theories and Politics
Klaus Nielsen

This introductory article reviews some of the theoretical and empirical issues involved in the discourses of flexibility and the strategies for flexibilization. Flexibility entered the political agenda when the 'euro-sclerosis' diagnosis gained dominance. Institutional rigidities were seen as responsible for the relatively mediocre performance of western Europe in the early stages of the crisis and flexibility was seen as the cure. This reflects a neoclassical conception of flexibility. Other theoretical approaches analyse flexibility in a historical perspective: flexible specialization, the neo-Schumpeterian approach, and the French regulation school. They all see the search for more flexibility as part of the dynamics initiated by the crisis of Fordism but they differ in their analysis of this process. The neoclassical conception of flexibility and neo-liberal or neo-conservative strategies dominated most of the 1980s. But lately more nuanced conceptions of flexibility and more consensual approach to flexibilization have gained prominence.

Flexibility and Institutional Learning
Björn Johnson and Bengt Åke Lundvall

This article discusses the neo-liberal programme for institutional design in relation to the process of innovation. When the economy is viewed more as a process of learning than as a system of allocation, its innovativeness becomes the most important aspect of its flexibility. Learning, growth of knowledge and innovations are shaped by the institutional set-up of the economy which calls for an institutionalist rather than a general equilibrium perspective. When viewed from such a perspective, the current state of the economy requires more flexibility in the broader sense, but the kind of institutional reform needed is radically different from the neo-liberal recommendations. Reference is made to a recent comparative study of the US and Japan which calls for such institutional change. Markets are seen as too pure, competition too dominating, and corporatism and cooperative behaviour too weakly developed in the US economy.

Flexibilization and Autonomization of World Money Markets: Obstacles for a New Long Expansion?
Kurt Hübner

Since the beginning of the 1970s, the dollar standard has been replaced by a regime of multi-currency standards with flexible exchange rates between regional currency blocks. This article analyses the reasons for the demise of the Bretton Woods System and the extensive flexibilization of the world monetary markets since then. It is argued that the transition to a flexible exchange rate regime has propelled the autonomization of monetary and financial transactions and produced more new instabilities than it disposed of the old. An ever growing portion of the earned profits flow into financial investments, and interest earnings constitute an ever increasing portion of the cash flow. Consequently, growth rates in the real sphere of the economy keep below their potential and the expansion of the world economy is based on financial instabilities. It is concluded that a new long expansion requires a reduction in the degree of current flexibility at the international level and this can only be achieved by coordinated action of the advanced capitalist countries.

From the Fordist to the Post-Fordist State
Joachim Hirsch

Along with the Fordist accumulation regime, the Fordist political form, i.e. the bureaucratic-corporative Keynesian welfare state, has also entered into crisis. As the old structures break down and the associated political and social struggles continue the outlines of the post-Fordist state are still indistinct. This article presents in general terms the dominant tendencies of the emerging post-Fordist state. This involves a steady decomposition of the Fordist pattern of integrating encompassing and corporatively structured material interests into the political apparatus. The big parties change from mass integrative to explicitly ideological parties; trade unions are being weakened through the flexibilization of the labour process; and new social movements are growing in significance alongside or against the parties. The fragmentation of the social structure and the declining mass integrative capacity of parties and interest organizations give a new push towards a repressively controlling 'security state'.

The Welfare State in the Transition from Fordism to Post-Fordism
Bob Jessop

This article considers how current changes in capitalism affect possible resolutions of the welfare state crisis. The crisis of Fordism exerted a 'scissors' effect on welfare state finances as the tax-base was reduced and the demand for expenditure increased. Moreover, the rational-legal form of the welfare state itself is seen to have caused some of its own problems: bureaucratization, juridification of social relations, political empire-building, centralization, clientelism, and intensification of personal dependence, etc. The article considers the general implications of the transition to post-Fordism for the welfare state and possible neo-liberal, neo-corporatist and neo-statist solutions to the crisis are analysed. The implications of the introduction of post-Fordist techniques into the welfare state are far-reaching. Information technology offers opportunities to raise productivity in the welfare state and make it more flexible. In addition, new products could radically change the mix of waged service labour, machinery and unpaid labour in ways analogous to those which have already happened in the private service sector.

The Eighties: The Search for Alternatives to Fordism
Robert Boyer

Traditionally the analyses of the Regulation Approach have been retrospective and comparative, not much prospective or comparative. This article is devoted to the challenge of assessing the likelihood of various future alternatives to Fordism. Boyer distinguishes between four different visions of the process of structural change: the Schumpeterian vision; democracy at the workplace; flexible specialization; and a new international regime. They are seen to derive from specific interpretations which overemphasize one or another feature of the crisis of Fordism. An alternative composite model is suggested: towards a new stage in flexible mass production. In addition, a new research agenda including international comparisons is outlined.

Thatcherism and Flexibility: The White Heat of a Post-Fordist Revolution
Bob Jessop

Thatcherism involves a major break with key features of postwar politics. The article links the rise of Thatcherism to two interrelated shifts: the growth and crisis of Britain's flawed Fordism and an emergent crisis of the state; economic rigidities combine with state incapacities. Thatcherism is seen as an attempt to prepare a path to post-Fordism by reorganizing the state and enhancing state capacities used to remove institutional rigidities. The article includes an analysis of the implementation of the neo-liberal strategy for securing economic flexibility and, in particular, the endeavours to change the British state. The conclusion outlines the achievements and promises as well as the risks and contradictions. Thatcherism has reorganized the terrain of British politics but its forward march is likely to be blocked. Its preferred road to post-Fordist is undermining its own room of manoeuvre, its long-run impact on the competitiveness of the British economy is dubious, and its increasing concern with redistribution and partisan advantage fail to grasp the nature of flexibility required in a post-Fordist era.

The Fetishism of Flexibility: The Case of British Rail
Richard Hyman

This article includes a critical discussion of flexibilization and deregulation as features of employer strategies and state policy. It examines, in particular, the case of British Rail where management in the past decades has embraced commercial priorities in anticipation of eventual privatization. It is concluded that flexibility is not a coherent managerial strategy but rather a piecemeal set of initiatives linked by a politically driven rhetoric which perhaps misleads managers themselves even as it alarms the workforce. Flexibilization is seen as one more instance in the attempt to strengthen management's ability to direct and manipulate labour, an attempt however constrained by management's dependence on worker's unforced initiative. It is generally concluded that governments, employers and academics alike have tended to fetishize the notion of flexibility.

Flexibilization and State Strategies: Coal and the City
Noelle Burgi and Bob Jessop

The coal industry and the City played crucial roles in Britain's industrialization and her rise to economic predominance in the world economy. Both sectors experienced a gradual decline which turned into structural crises in the 1960s. They represent different poles in the changing balance of economic forces and are tied to opposite poles in the changing balance of political forces. Both sectors have been subject to state sponsored restructuring as well as the discipline of market forces. And, more recently, both sectors have undergone reorganization and flexibilization - promoted in both cases through neo-liberal state strategies. This article relates coal and the City to the postwar settlement, describes the forms and timing of their respective structural crises and looks at the state's changing policies to make them profitable and/or more flexible. It is concluded that the Thatcherite neo-liberal strategy in each case has shown an increasing capacity for continuous adaptation of policies to changing circumstances.

Changes in Socio-Legal Structures: The British Case
Norman Lewis

Recent years have seen remarkable changes in the modes and styles of government in Britain: neo-corporatism has been dismantled; local government has been enervated by legislative and administrative measures; managers and professionals have been given more influence at the expense of politics; the prime minister has been given enormous power and leverage at the expense not only of parliament but also the cabinet, etc. The flexible constitutional arrangements in Britain is part of the reason for these changes. Few formal impediments stand in the way of a government which has a clear philosophy and a burning commitment to change. It is concluded that the British constitution has been too flexible for its own good and is in need of reform.

Neo-Conservatism and Modernization Policy in West Germany
Hans-Joachim Schabedoth

This article describes the neo-conservative modernization project which has become hegemonic in West Germany at the national level and partly at the regional level as well. The land of Badem-Württenberg is seen as the model case of neo-conservatism. The central concern of the neo-conservative project is the subjugation of individuals and collective agents to the requirements of international competition. This is associated with a new set of values such as individualism, flexibility and differentiation. Other important concerns are: unrestricted promotion of new technologies, real world applications of research and education and integration of the arts and the enterprises. Trade unions are accepted but are also expected voluntarily to accept subordination to the overall modernization project.

Departures from Taylorism and Fordism: New Forms of Work in the Automobile Industry
Ulrich Jürgens

The focus of this article is on the changing patterns of labour deployment and management control over the labour process in the automobile industry. During the 1980s work reforms have turned away from the traditional Tayloristic-Fordist paradigm for regulation of labour. The international automobile industry, in general, is characterized by an unfinished process of development in which differing configurations of the Tayloristic-Fordist regulation mode and its negation forms are visible. The national systems of industrial relations and labour policy institutions influence the forms of rationalization. The 'German model' is a skilled worker orientated form of rationalization. It is contrasted with the Japanese model of group orientated labour regulation which is the other model for future development in the automobile industry.

Debureaucratization and Flexibility
Otto Jacobi

One aspect in the present debate on flexibilization refers to the rearrangements of traditionally hierarchic management structures. These involve tendencies towards debureaucratization through the downward transfer of responsibilities. These trends might lead to the establishment of company-based micro-corporatism. However, management faces the risk of losing control and unions risk to be alienated from the workers and their representative, and the overall outcome remains uncertain. This article reviews the debate and gives a brief overview of current research. It distinguishes between genuine decentralization, as in the metal industry, and fictious decentralization as in banking.

Flexibilization and the Alternatives of the Nordic Welfare States
Pekka Kosonen

Since the mid 1970s, the welfare state has often been seen as an obstacle to growth or even as a source of crisis; some kind of restructuring or flexibilization is seen as necessary. The Nordic countries have unusually large public sectors which makes them good objects for an analysis of these phenomena. This article outlines the growth of the welfare states in the Nordic countries and its attendant difficulties. Some cuts, changes in criteria of entitlements and fee-for-services have been introduced, particularly in Denmark and also to some extent in Norway. However, the institutional pillars of the Nordic welfare states are still intact. Analyses show that the economic crisis is not primarily caused by the welfare state and it is not possible to speak of a political crisis of the welfare state; its legitimacy is not lost. It is argued that neo-corporatist and participatory strategies of flexibilization are more effective in the Nordic context than the neo-liberal kind of flexibilization.

Learning to Manage the Supply-Side: Flexibility and Stability in Denmark
Klaus Nielsen

Danish Fordism can best be interpreted as 'demand-side Fordism'. On the supply-side there was almost no evidence of Fordist structures while the demand-side was Fordist as in few other countries. In the present era there is a pressure for the adoption of appropriate forms of supply-side management to replace the established methods of demand management. This is a particularly tough challenge in the Danish case with its non-interventionist state. This article describes the Danish mode of development, the political development, the Danish response to the crisis of Fordism and, in particular, the troublesome process of learning to manage the supply-side. It is argued that some of the features in Danish society which have been seen as backward in the Fordist era might be turned into future advantages: the flexible forms of production and particularly the flexible forms of representation, coordination and consensus formation ('the negotiated economy') which have emerged in this multi-centred structure where big capital and big labour never became as dominant as in other industrialized countries. Denmark might develop a 'flexible corporatism' but this requires dismantling of a set of blockages, not the least in relation to supply-side management.

Workplace Reform and the Stabilization of Flexible Production in Sweden
Mark Elam and Martin Börjeson

This paper focuses on the process of formulating a new shared language of workplace reform in Sweden at the national level and in two different industrial sectors: steel and printing. It is assumed that the new hegemonic language of reform plays an important role in the constitution of flexible production in Sweden. Gradually, a new language of workplace reform has appeared around a rhetorical anti-Taylorism with demands for more challenging jobs to well-educated individuals. Intense cooperation between labour and capital is meant to ensure the simultaneous achievement of a good working life and enhanced business efficiency. The language apparently paves the way for a new 'business unionism' comparable to the brand of company unionism visible in Japan. However, this is an awesome task and the newly conceived Swedish Model of working life may yet prove to be stillborn.

Introduction

1. Towards a Flexible Future - Theories and Politics

Klaus Nielsen

Discourses and Theories

The theme of this book is the discourses of flexibility as well as the various conflicts, decision-making processes and strategies involved in pursuit of increased flexibility. These issues are examined in greater detail in later chapters. The present introduction briefly reviews some more general theoretical and empirical issues.

It was the 'euro-sclerosis' diagnosis which made flexibility such a prominent issue on the political agenda. The institutional set-up was held to have caused rigidities which calcify the veins of the modern economy: and increased flexibility was seen as the cure. This approach prevailed at least until the late 1980s.

The 'euro-sclerosis' diagnosis of the economic problems of Western Europe is based on a conception of the economy inspired by neoclassical economic theory which sees responsiveness to price signals as the sole mechanism governing economic behaviour. This is clearly unsatisfactory and a more comprehensive approach is called for. This includes the issues of technological and socio-institutional innovation and flexibility is interpreted in a historical context.

The sequence of presentation is the following: Firstly, I look at the 'euro-sclerosis' diagnosis, the neo-liberal cure, and the neo-classical conception of flexibility. Secondly, and this is the main part of the article, I discuss three different theories. All of them analyse flexibility in a historical context and they all focus on the relationship between technological, economic and socio-institutional change: flexible specialization; the neo-Schumpeterian approach; and the French regulation school. They all see the search for more flexible forms of accumulation and institutions as part of the dynamics initiated by the crisis of 'Fordism', or Fordist mass production, but they differ in their analysis of this process.

The Cure to Euro-sclerosis?

There is a particular European dimension to the politics of flexibility. In the

3

early and mid 1980s euro-pessimism prevailed. The European OECD-countries had low growth and high unemployment, compared with Japan and USA, and also seemed to fall behind in the development of high technology. These problems were seen to originate from various rigidities ('euro-sclerosis' or 'institutional sclerosis'). The OECD was particularly active among the agents who propagated this view.

Special emphasis was put on high unemployment and the lack of job creation in Europe relative to USA (Grahl and Teague, 1989; McDowell, 1990). Between the mid 1970s and mid 1980s the member states of the European Community suffered a net loss of three million jobs while, in the same period, the US had a net increase of 18 million jobs. The better performance was attributed to the highly flexible nature of its labour market. By contrast, numerous rigidities in labour markets were seen as responsible for Europe's relatively weak performance in job creation. Wages were seen as too high and too rigid, wage differentials as too small, and legally based labour rights, employment protection schemes, and social security systems as taken too far. The consequences were seen to be that workers priced themselves out of jobs; labour mobility, and thus structural adjustment, was hindered; and hiring of workers was discouraged while voluntary unemployment was encouraged.

Other rigidities were seen as responsible for the poor performance in high technology sectors and the inability to move swiftly into new growth areas (Drouin et al, 1987). Inflexibilities in capital markets and government regulations were said to discourage risk-taking and implied a bias against the small entrepreneur and venture capitalist who had difficulty obtaining funds. Likewise, high government expenditures and high marginal income taxes were seen to imply disincentives and risk-aversion.

Promotion of flexibility was presented as the cure - especially in relation to the labour market. It also implied deregulation of capital markets, lowering of tax rates and a general slimming of the state. Revitalization and accelerated integration of the European Community were also seen as part of the cure.

The diagnosis was made in accordance with recommendations from contemporary mainstream economists who had developed new faith in unfettered market forces after the breakdown of Keynesianism. Flexibility was seen in relation to the ideal of competitive markets. Institutions and behaviour which hamper such an 'ideal' flexibility were considered rigidities, i.e. suitable objects for flexibilization. The western industrialized countries were in general seen to suffer from a high degree of calcification of the mechanism which was characterized as the major systemic merit of capitalist market economies: the capacity for fast and flexible response to changing circumstances through price signals (Scitovsky, 1980). The industrialized countries were also, in general, seen to be marked by strong growth of interest group organizations and the formation of strong distributional coalitions which, according to Olson (1982), constitute institutional rigidities hampering economic growth.

This diagnosis is vulnerable to various forms of criticism. The evidence is not as easy to interpret as it might appear at first sight. The better job creation performance in USA springs to a high degree from the expansionist economic policy of the Reagan government after 1982. Furthermore, the majority of the new jobs in USA were low-wage service jobs with low productivity, and productivity growth was lower in USA than in Europe, also in manufacturing. In other words, USA traded jobs against productivity gains.

Flexibility and Innovation

Another kind of criticism concerns the theoretical foundation of the cure (see also Johnson and Lundvall in this book). It reflects a neoclassical conception of the economy. Market agents are seen to adapt their behaviour in response to movements in prices which are supposed to inform the agents in a sufficient way about the changes in preferences, relative scarcities and technology. In an ideal-type market economy it is not just agents who are supposed to adapt smoothly to changes mediated by price signals. Systems, i.e. the structural and institutional features of the economy, are supposed to adapt through the same processes as well. Price movements constitute the necessary and sufficient impulses for structural reallocation of resources from declining to growing branches. They are also supposed to erode the foundation of obsolete institutions and to initiate the emergence of new 'organic' economic institutions.

Neoclassical theory does recognize that obsolete structures and institutions might prevail in the short run[1]. Inertia and vested interests imply that institutions and structures do not adapt as smoothly as is desirable. Political intervention might then be necessary in order to combat obsolete institutions, to design new ones, to facilitate reallocation of resources between branches and between the public and the private sectors, and to initiate other forms of restructuring.

The neoclassical approach accords with the common meaning of flexibility as adaptability to changes in external circumstances. In a stimulus-response model, flexibility refers to the response side of the model, i.e. to those properties of the context and of the actors that make for slow or fast adjustment. However, neoclassical theory conceptualizes only one form of response, i.e. responsiveness to price signals. It ignores responses to other signals and responses transmitted through other forms of social interaction than market exchange. It also ignores the innovative aspects of the economic process.

The limitations of the neoclassical approach to flexibility can be seen from Figure 1[2]. For both agents and systems, flexibility is seen as a quality attached to the re-active adaptation process. Agents are flexible in as far as they react to price movements; systems flexibility is similarly derived from the adaptation to changing relative prices. Thus flexibilization measures are directed towards removing features that hamper the reactive qualities of the ideal market. All such features are by definition 'rigidities' which originate either from deficiences in the formation of prices or from inadequate response of agents or systems to price movements. Indeed, apart from the legal arrangements necessary to guarantee market exchange and property rights all other institutions are basically considered rigidities impeding the ideal flexibility of the market.

Such an approach ignores the fact that some of the perceived rigidities are essential to make markets work at all. Institutions are necessary to produce 'price norms' (Skouras, 1981), to reduce uncertainty, to guide expectations, and to generate a minimum of trust (Hodgson, 1988).

Furthermore, neoclassical economics do not allow for pro-active behaviour by agents, i.e. forms of action which are independent of price signals but spring instead from the creative imagination of individual agents (technological innovation) or collective agents (socio-political innovation).

Neoclassical economics cannot conceptualize technological innovation in a satisfactory way. Technology remains basically an exogenous variable. Technological change through price signals merely involves shifting combinations of already existing factors and products while product innovation is unexplained. Schumpeter recognized this and stressed the importance of entrepreneurship and creative destruction.

Figure 1. Forms of flexibility and innovation

	re-active	pro-active
agents	individual flexibility	technological innovation
systems	structural flexibility	socio-political innovation

Others stress the institutional preconditions for innovation (Johnson and Lundvall, in this book). Firms are seen as more than production functions. They are also units capable of learning independently of the development of prices. Knowledge of technical opportunities and the needs of potential users are acquired through non-price interaction between R&D and marketing and through relations with external users.

Socio-political institutions seldom adapt smoothly to price signals in accordance with the normative prescriptions of neoclassical theory - and for good reasons. Institutions 'think' (Douglas, 1986). They do not just react to environmental changes in a quasi-mechanical way but also innovate as part of an institutional learning process. This reflects the character of social behaviour as a double stranded process (Hodgson, 1988). The one strand is cognitive: the demand for perceived order and coherence. The other is transactional: the use of available means to attain the perceived ends. Socio-political innovations involve both cognitive and transactional aspects in coherent processes: the development of conceptions of society (meaning), the perception of ends, and the design of institutions to direct action in accordance with the perceived ends and the perceived conceptions of society. Socio-economic innovations are different from simple inertia or institutional 'lagging behind' as a result of tradition or vested interests. To emphasize socio-economic innovations is to recognize that ideas and power matter.

Socio-political innovations have taken different forms in different nations reflecting different national trajectories, structures and processes. For instance, the role of interest organizations vary according to the accumulation of socio-political innovations in different countries. In some countries organized interests are paralysed in a 'prisoners' dilemma' situation while this potential dilemma is overcome in other countries through accumulated mutual trust and common conceptions of economic reality, and the procedures for regulation of conflicts and mediation of disputes.

Thus, if we move beyond the limitations of the neoclassical theory another view of institutional 'rigidities' as preconditions for a flexible economy emerges. Firstly, institutions are needed to reduce uncertainty and guide expectations in order to make individual adaptation possible. Secondly, technological innovation requires institutions for learning. Thirdly, institutions not only adapt but are innovative in the continuous search for cognitive as well as transactional improvement.

Flexibility and Stability

Flexibility is often used as a quasi-objective concept and in a prescriptive way. But both flexibility and rigidity are controversial concepts (see for critical discussion of the concept of flexibility, and the way it is used, Grahl and Teague (1989), Sayer (1989), Salvati (1988), Boyer (1987) and Hyman in this book). Flexibility is a complex, multidimensional, and hard-to-capture concept. Over 50 different terms for various types of flexibility can be found in the manufacturing literature, alone; and even more if economic and organizational aspects are included (Sethi and Sethi, 1990). Clarity of definition involves narrowing and is often bought at the expense of relevance: it may well be, for example, that a rigidity in one segment of the economic system is compensated, or, indeed, overcompensated by a flexibility elsewhere in the system (Salvati, 1988).

Identifying a need for increased flexibility in specific fields is always a discursive phenomenon which often tends to overlook the institutional environment essential to the overall functioning of the flexible units. Yet, flexibility is an empty concept if unrelated to a set of specific rigidities. Not all areas can be flexible. An omni-flexible world would be so uncertain as to make action completely impossible. Flexibility in one area requires rigidities (or stability) in many other areas.

Thus, it is not a sensible strategy to promote flexibility everywhere. Any institution or organization is always more or less flexible in relation to a specific range of problems or perturbations and its relative flexibility depends on the presence of stability in other institutional or organizational features and procedures. The existence of flexibility depends on a specific combination of flexibility in some areas and rigidity in others. Or, to phrase it in another way: flexibility requires a foundation of institutional stability.

Obviously, these remarks are abstract and formal. They can, however, be illustrated through various successful combinations of flexibility and stability. One is the specific Japanese combination of a high degree of flexibility in production and investment and a high degree of stability or rigidity in employer-employee and user-producer relationships. Dore (1985) has described the basic features of this successful model under the illustrative heading: 'Flexible Rigidities'. Florida and Kenney (1989) make a similar point: they distinguish between 'structured flexibility', which characterizes the organization of high technology industries in Japan, and the 'simple flexibility' of the same industries in USA.

Small countries in Western Europe (Scandinavia, Benelux, Austria and Switzerland) constitute other successful combinations of flexible adjustment and political stability - at least according to Katzenstein (1985). The stability of the basic institutional set-up ('democratic corporatism') has made possible a smooth and continuous adaptation of economic and industrial policies to the ever-changing conditions on the world market.

In all these cases rigidities or stability at the micro level seem to be preconditions for flexibility at the macro level. Short-term flexibility on the supply-side of the economy, as presupposed in Keynesian economics, likewise, depends on rigidities at the firm level, i.e. planning of capacity and staff from longrun rather than short-term considerations (Bruno, 1987): earlier, Keynesianism worked because of excess capacity in the firms which made real responses to rising demand possible but the increased micro-flexibility during the last decades implies less excess capacity ('just-in-time') and therefore the short-term responses to increases in demand have become monetary instead of real.

It is also possible to identify a variety of institutional rigidities which are preconditions for flexibility at the firm level. 'Rigid' inter-firm linkages of a collaborative kind which ignore short-term price fluctuations are preconditions not only for innovation but also for smooth functioning of daily transactions. Another example concerns the decision of employers to hire skilled workers. The qualifications of individual workers are most easily and reliably assessed by potential employers in a strict, formalized system of certification by measured level of knowledge and experience; but such a system implies the reservation of certain types of work for the holders of specific qualifications. The flexible functioning of labour markets for skilled workers is dependent on this form of institutional rigidity (Grahl and Teague, 1989, p. 93).

The strategy for flexibilization inspired by the 'euro-sclerosis' diagnosis appears to ignore the importance of a foundation of stability and the intricacies of the relationship of flexibility and rigidity. Or, at least, it did so in the early and mid 1980s. Since the late 1980s there has been an increasing awareness of the importance of stability, security and consensus as preconditions for increased flexibility. The promotion of a 'social dimension' within the European Community represents a major reorientation of discursive focus. It is also remarkable how the need to strike a balance between flexibility and security is stressed in recent OECD reports on labour market flexibility (cf. OECD, 1989, 1990a).

This seems to represent a shift in the dominant perception of flexibility. Until recently, flexibility was contrasted with rigidity and seen as purely positive. Now, the attention has apparently shifted to trade-offs between flexibility and stability. This conceptual shift reflects a development from a focus on the problems of the past to a situation where the creation of the future institutional structure is on the agenda; from flexibilization as a means to remove rigidities, which were seen as causes for the disease, to flexibility as a quality of specific units or areas in a new structure of rigidities. Future prosperity does not require full-scale flexibilization but rather reorganization of the balance of flexibility and rigidity - removal of some old rigidities by flexibilization combined with the creation of new rigidities.

This interpretation implies that the attraction of the neo-liberal approach to flexibility was due to a specific historical situation. It also suggests that neo-liberalism may have been instrumental in the destructive phase but has little value in the creative phase in the process of 'creative destruction' between the outdated past and the new stability. We now turn to theories which look at flexibility in such a historical context.

Flexibility in a Historical Context: Three Approaches

The reductionist conception of flexibility in the 'euro-sclerosis' diagnosis followed from its theoretical basis in neoclassical economics. Classical political economy had a fundamentally different perspective. It analysed long run economic development as the combined outcome of technological development on the one hand and socio-institutional factors on the other. Typical examples are Ricardo's analysis of the 'corn laws' and Marx's analysis of the long run dynamics of the relationship between the forces of production and the relations of production (Fagerberg, 1988). The neoclassical revolution in economics shifted perspective from long run development to the conditions for short-term equilibrium. Neoclassical economics sees the economy as a system of perfectly informed, rational and short-term optimizing individuals. Technological and socio-institutional development is to a large extent excluded from the theoretical perspective. In relation to flexibility this implies an exclusive focus on the left part of Figure 1, while the right part is ignored.

Other recent theories attempt to analyse short-term phenomena in a historical context as did classical political economy. They see the interaction between technological and socio-institutional development as primary and so treat flexibility/rigidity in a way quite different from the 'euro-sclerosis' argument.

Three such theoretical approaches merit special interest: (a) flexible specialization; (b) the neo-Schumpeterian 'techno-economic paradigms'; and (c) regulation theory. All three are frequently mentioned in the other contributions of this book. All three distinguish between periods of growth with relatively stable regimes of mutually reinforcing techno-economic structures and socio-political institutions, and periods of crisis with an absence of such regimes. They also have common features in their interpretation of the present era. They all identify a crisis of the former regime which they designate mass production or 'Fordism'; and they all see the last two decades as a period of transition to something else. They differ, however, in two respects. First, they have different views of the causes and the dynamics of the crisis and, second, they have different interpretations of the ('Post-Fordist') future.

Elam (1989) has termed the three approaches neo-Smithian, neo-Schumpeterian and neo-Marxian respectively. The adjectives point at essential differences in the basic arguments. The 'flexible specialization' approach is termed neo-Smithian because it places the changing face of markets at the centre of the historical stage. The contemporary crisis is seen as caused by the instability, uncertainty and fragmentation of core markets in the major capitalist economies. This is assumed to have far-reaching consequences for the choice of technique and the organization of production: mass production will be replaced by flexible specialization. The 'techno-economic paradigm' approach regards basic technological change as the decisive dynamic force. Full scale implementation of information technology represents the new 'techno-economic paradigm'. In 'regulation' theory, on the contrary, the dynamics of change are double-sided. Besides the techno-economic forces the importance of a largely autonomous sphere of political and institutional forces is also stressed.

Regulationists are hesitant to give the new era of capitalist development a name. The perspective leaves much to be decided by social struggle and historical contingency.

While the neo-Schumpeterian and neo-Smithian perspectives tend to see the information technology paradigm and flexible specialisation as pervasive ready-made disciplines for the post-Fordist era; the regulation perspective sees the new rule book of capitalist life as only partially written with room for many more co-authors (Elam, 1989).

Below I shall present the three approaches in more detail and especially focus on the differences in how they perceive the dynamics of the crisis and their notions of the new or coming combinations of flexibility and stability (see also Boyer in this volume). I stress the differences even if they appear to me less clear-cut than signalled above; they have all thrived from mutual inspiration, and attempts to draw from all sources or even to make syntheses appear reasonable. Anyhow, the differences are important because each approach typically still functions as an exclusive frame of discussion. Better knowledge of the other approaches may improve the terms of the debate and prevent some frequent misunderstandings. In addition, several important differences do exist and, for example, much of the critique of Piore and Sabel's conception of Fordism and flexible specialization is wide off the mark in relation to similar conceptions within the other two approaches.

All three approaches give primacy to the periodic stability of the institutional forms of capitalism succeeded by periods of crisis. Other theoretical trends in political economy, similarly, identify stages of development but they use other concepts and alternative criteria for periodization than Fordist/post-Fordist. According to Lash and Urry (1987), a new era of 'disorganized capitalism' has replaced 'organized capitalism', as it was originally conceptualized by

Hilferding. Bromley (1988) identifies seven alternative periodizations, for example those of Mandel in 'Late Capitalism' and Fine and Harris in 'Rereading Capital', and points out that they are ignored in the present debate with little argument as to the superior merits of the Fordism/post-Fordism typology.

Others criticize the periodization in itself and see the present changes as nothing but capitalism as usual. Some consider the talk of a transition from Fordism to post-Fordism as pure and simple 'flexi-talk', i.e. as part of the ideological struggle to undermine the defensive power of the labour movement (Pollert, 1989). Others insist on the primacy of the class struggle over the institutional forms of capitalism and reject the relevance of concepts such as Fordism (Holloway, 1988; Clarke; 1988). They see the postwar institutions as nothing more than the particular institutional embodiment of the postwar class compromise with no explanatory value in their own terms (cf. Jessop, 1989b).

Flexible Specialization

Piore and Sabel (1984) base their argument on a simple conceptual distinction between two opposite types of industrial production: mass production and flexible specialization. 'Mass production' involves the use of special purpose (product specific) machines and of semi-skilled workers to produce standardized goods while 'flexible specialization', or craft production, is based on skilled workers who produce a variety of customized goods.

Mass production and flexible specialization are seen as two types of production which co-exist in different combinations throughout the modern period. They can be historically realized as dominant types - regionally, nationally or internationally. However, there are only rare moments of choice when the path of technological development is at issue. Piore and Sabel claim that throughout the nineteenth century the two types were in collusion until the first 'industrial divide' when the emergence of mass production technology limited the growth of less rigid production techniques which prior to that existed in various industrial districts in Europe. After the first 'divide' mass production became dominant internationally, in all the leading countries and in all leading industries. Its was dominance reinforced by the introduction of Keynesianism as a means to stabilize demand which is considered the crucial regulation problem in an economy dominated by mass production.

Elements of flexible specialization persisted but they were clearly subordinate to mass production. Some firms in all industries and almost all firms in some industries continued to apply craft principles of production. This was so because some demands will always be too small or too irregular to justify mass production. The specific combinations of mass production and flexible specialization were seen to depend on national or regional traditions. This explains, for instance, according to Piore and Sabel, the differences between the USA and countries like West Germany and Japan in relation to shop floor control over the work process; while in the USA mass production systems were implemented with highly authoritarian forms of control, West Germany and Japan retained important elements of an alternative craft system of shop floor control.

The 'second industrial divide' is contemporary and dates from the stagnation of the international economy in the 1970s. As in the nineteenth century the choice is again supposed to be between mass production and flexible specialization. The causes and the dynamics of the current general crisis of the industrial system are seen to spring mainly from the demand side of the economy. Not only did total demand stagnate and become more uncertain due to external shocks such as the oil price rises and the breakdown of the Bretton Woods system. More fundamental were the structural problems with the level and composition of demand in relation to mass production. One problem is the saturation of markets for a lot of traditional consumer durables in advanced economies. Another is the fragmentation of mass markets for standardized goods caused by the growing diversity of tastes.

These market trends constitute a problem for mass production and an opportunity for flexible specialization. Furthermore, current trends in manufacturing technology are seen to reinforce the advantage of flexible specialization in meeting such demand. Small batch production will be more profitable as flexible machinery becomes more widespread and the relative disadvantage of small firms will tend to disappear.

Piore and Sabel see a potential for small firms proliferating using the new technology to compete in market niches both sectorally and geographically. This is seen to cause the emergence of new industrial districts consisting of networks of small firms similar to the nineteenth-century districts prior to the first 'divide'.

Flexible specialization in networks of small firms in industrial districts is seen to offer possibilities for upgrading of skills. It requires reorganization of the labour process and industrial relations totally different from under mass production. The ideal-type model has been termed 'Proudhonist'. The model is one of groups of semi-independent, generally skilled employees operating machinery that is capable of reacting without delay or excessive costs to changes in the nature of products and the volume of demand. Workers are given much more responsibility, and wage formation and labour relations must be organized in ways that secure much greater involvement.

Under flexible specialization management of total demand is not considered a major regulation problem as firms have learnt to adapt to shifting levels. However, institutional reform is needed to secure a framework for permanent innovation. History shows that this can be achieved in many ways (Piore and Sabel, 1984, p. 31). But, generally, it is presumed that permanent innovation in industrial districts can be mobilized only if wages and labour conditions are removed from competition, if relations of trust and mutual support develop in networks of firms instead of cut-throat competition between individual firms, and in case of political and social consensus for the development of the local economy.

Piore and Sabel identify such regional islands of prosperity built on flexible specialization which have already challenged mass production as the paradigm and provide us with models for the future. The 'Third Italy' and Silicon Valley were the model cases in Piore and Sabel (1984). A more comprehensive survey of such industrial districts is presented in Sabel (1989, pp. 9-11) with further examples from Denmark, Sweden, West Germany, France, USA and Japan.

However, Piore and Sabel do not see any necessity in the shift from mass production to flexible specialization as the dominant type of economy. The outcome is seen to depend on the exercise of political and economic power. They insist that a revival of Keynesianism at the international level might stabilize demand and provide renewed prosperity based on mass production as an alternative to future dominance of flexible specialization. The outcome is seen to depend on political struggle and economic power, just like the situation of the first industrial 'divide'.

Even if 'international Keynesianism' might stabilize total demand it is obvious that it does not provide any solution to the 'break up of mass markets for standardized goods'. The apparent openness has been characterized by critics as false. The outcome on the other side of the divide seems pregiven if you accept the stated premises. The apparent stress on political and institutional forces and exercises of economic power in the analysis of the 'industrial divides' is seen as a mere decoration. Market trends are the determining force, anyhow (Williams et al. 1987, p. 412).

The 'flexible specialization' approach has been criticized in many ways[3]. One line of criticism concerns its conceptual ambiguity and theoretical unclarity. Is it an empirical phenomenon, an ideal type or a normative claim? (Haslam et al. 1987; Walker, 1989). What does it mean that one or another type of production is dominant? and how is it possible to identify particular enterprises or industries as instances of mass production or flexible specialization? (Williams et al. 1987). Flexible technology, flexible work practices, output diversification, organizational restructuring and flexible labour markets are neither equivalent nor necessarily interrelated as implicitly presumed by Piore and Sabel (Sayer, 1989; Sorge and Streek, 1987). Vertical disintegration does not necessarily imply decentralization of economic power (Amin and Robins, 1990). Moreover, the dichotomy of flexibility and 'rigid' Fordism is treated too literally (Wood, 1988).

Another line of criticism is directed against the empirical premisses of the second 'divide'. The fundamental premiss of saturation and fragmentation of markets is said to rest on weak empirical evidence (Williams et al. 1987, pp. 424-429). It has further been noted that if markets do become fragmented this does not necessarily favour small-scale producers. Established large-scale producers have shown capacity for introducing a high degree of variety and flexibility into mass production (Gough, 1986). Today, Japanese industry, in particular, has proved that previously unimagined degrees of product variety can be achieved within mass production enterprises (Haslam et al. 1987).

Moreover, it is not evident that vertical disintegration is actually accompanied by decentralization of economic control. On the contrary, corporate power is becoming increasingly centralized: the locus of strategic control is extending beyond the formal boundaries of the firm; and a heightened degree of cooperation between oligopolists is occurring (Amin and Dietrich, 1990). It has been proposed to designate this development quasi-integration instead of vertical disintegration (Leborgne and Lipietz, 1988).

Neither is it self-evident that the emergent new technologies imply the resurgence of flexible specialization. Computer-integrated manufacturing systems, for instance, do not necessarily require any return to semi-independent, generally skilled craftsmen or any re-creation of the 'craft model of shop floor control' (Williams et al. 1987, pp. 429-34).

The shining face of flexible specialization with its benefits for labour have been criticized, particularly on the left, for looking only at a part of the economy while ignoring the peripheral groups as well as the strength of corporate measures to retain control. Furthermore, the data on new industrial districts are deemed suggestive at best and, more fundamentally, flexible specialization is seen as a purely defensive measure to cope with the unpredictability of the crisis rather than a means to overcome the crisis itself (see Boyer in this volume).

In a more recent work, Sabel (1989) has clarified his position in a way to take account of some of the criticism. He has, for instance, developed a more sophisticated analysis of the responses of large and small firms to the challenges of the second 'divide'. He identifies a double convergence of large- and small-firm structures. Large firms try to recreate among their specialized units the collaboration characteristic of relations between firms in the 'flexible specialization' economy. Small firms, simultaneously, organize in collaboration centralized laboratories, marketing agencies and technology consultancies inspired by the large-firm model. Another new observation concerns the reorganization of the multinational firms; they have begun to organize production along the lines of flexible specialization without repudiating the mass production model. Product lines are being concentrated in single operating units which have been given increased authority to organize their own sales, subcontracting and even research. Furthermore, flexible large firms and small firms form alliances or networks which effectively blur the familiar distinctions between large and small firms.

Piore and Sabel's sharply focused account of the contemporary economic transition has been subject to much attention and controversy. Much of the criticism, however, can be countered by correction and elaboration of the initial positions as has already, to a certain extent, been done by Sabel and others. The new methods of production can be seen as contingently connected to conditions of employment (Scott, 1988). The romanticism of small flexible firms, the ignorance of the continued degradation of work in parts of the economy as well as the ignorance of the capacity for large firms to reorganize in order to retain corporate power, do not necessarily follow from the approach. Neither does the implicit determinacy as far as future trajectories are concerned. The alternative to flexible specialization, international Keynesianism, does not appear illusionary if you take into account the utilization of flexible specialization 'proxies' in mass production. However, even more sophisticated versions of 'flexible specialization' have several conceptual and empirical weaknesses. The perspective is from the start too narrow to give rise to a fruitful research programme. It gives too little guidance about the direction of capitalist development and makes for poor history.

Even so, it has received a great deal of attention in contemporary political debate, and more so than the other two approaches presented here. The clear message, the suggestive line of argument and the optimistic vision is part of reason why.

..everywhere it strikes comforting and responsive chords. Thus in Britain, Piore and Sabel's work provides a rationale for the local initiatives and plans for socialism in one municipality which have been increasingly popular over the past decade (Haslam, 1987, p. 438).

It also provides a rationale for the much wanted new 'offensive' strategy in countries where the power of the left is less defensively rooted than in Britain. However, the dangers are obvious if the chosen guide to the future industrial world is overly optimistic and ignores important preconditions and side-effects.

Information Technology as
Techno-economic Paradigm

The slow-down in the growth of the world economy from the mid 1970s was followed by a renewed interest in long-cycle or long-wave theories and particularly in the Schumpeter's theory of business cycles. Some of the important early contributions to this debate are Mensch (1979), Mandel (1980). Contemporary neo-Schumpeterian theory includes a variety of approaches. Most of them give only modest attention to socio-institutional innovation and are of little interest in this connection. It is otherwise with Dosi, Freeman, Perez and other writers associated with SPRU, (Dosi et al. (1988) is a major collection of works within this tradition).

The works of Freeman and Perez (Freeman and Perez, 1984, 1988; Freeman, 1983; Freeman and Soete, 1987; Freeman, Clark and Soete, 1982; Perez, 1983) are among the most influential contributions to the neo-Schumpeterian debate in the last decade. They represent a significant extension and refinement of Schumpeter's original formulations. Their interpretation of the process of 'creative destruction' is broader than most other neo-Schumpeterians. They do not only focus at the swarming of investments and innovations and their economic effects. They emphasize the importance of the interrelationship between technological changes and wider economic and socio-institutional transformations.

They have identified five so-called 'Kondratiev' long waves (Freeman and Perez, 1988, pp. 50-57). They interpret the long waves as increasing degrees of 'match' between the techno-economic subsystem and the socio-institutional framework in the upswing followed by increasing degrees of 'mismatch' in the downswing. Situations of 'mismatch' arise because the two subsystems have very different rates of change. The socio-institutional framework changes much slower than the techno-economic subsystem as institutions are supposed to 'suffer from a high degree of natural inertia, strengthened by past successes and upheld by pressure from the main benieficiary groups' (Freeman and Perez, 1984, p. 9).

The fundamental reason for these periods of 'match' and 'mismatch' are successive techno-economic paradigms. The central idea can be summarized in the following way: 'certain types of technological change - defined as changes in 'techno-economic paradigm' - have such widespread consequences for all sectors of the economy that their infusion is accompanied by major structural crises of adjustment, in which social and institutional changes are necessary to bring about a better 'match' between the new technology and the system of social management of the economy' (Freeman and Perez, 1988, p.

38).

A 'techno-economic paradigm' is a cluster of innovations, whose advantages are to be found not only in a range of new products. It involves completely new forms of work, new models of management, new locational patterns and new high growth sectors. It influences the relative cost structure of all possible inputs to production and introduces a new set of 'common-sense' principles into capitalist production. Each techno-economic paradigm hinges on a particular input or set of inputs, which may be described as the 'key factor' of the paradigm. This input has the following characteristics: it involves clearly perceived low and descending relative costs; it is in unlimited supply for all practical purposes; and it is possible to use it in many products and processes throughout the economic system. Freeman and Perez maintain that this combination of characteristics holds today for microelectronics (Freeman and Perez, 1984, pp. 10-11; Freeman and Perez, 1988, pp. 50-55).

The previous long wave - 'Fordist mass production' - was based on low cost oil and energy intensive materials. Its 'ideal type' of production was the continuous-flow assembly line to turn out massive quantities of standardized goods. Today, with cheap microelectronics widely available, and consequently low cost information handling, energy and materials intensity is no longer 'common sense'. The current 'ideal type' of production turns out a flexible output of information intensive, rapidly changing, products and services. Diversity and flexibility at all levels substitute standardization and massification as 'common-sense' best practice.

The new techno-economic paradigm based on information technology offers solutions to the limitations of the previous paradigm. Diseconomies of scale and the inflexibility of dedicated assembly-lines might be overcome by flexible manufacturing systems, networking and 'economies of scope'. Limitations of energy and materials intensity might, likewise, be overcome by electronic control systems. The new paradigm is associated with new forms of intra- and inter-firm relationship: 'networks of large and small firms based increasingly on computer networks and close co-operation in technology, quality, control, training, investment planning and production planning (just-in-time) etc.' (Freeman and Perez, 1988, p. 53).

This will not be achieved, however, by merely introducing new technology. It is not possible to reap all the potential productivity increase at the firm level without transforming the whole organization. Similarly, it will not be possible at the societal level to yield all the growth potential of a new paradigm until the socio-institutional framework is fully adapted to its requirements.

At present there are deep structural problems involved in the change of paradigm all around the world (Freeman and Perez, 1988, p. 61-65). Acute and persistent shortage of skills associated with the new paradigm co-exist with high levels of unemployment. The leading-edge industries experience tempestuous growth interrupted by periodic crises of over-supply. The old, 'smokestack', energy-intensive industries have persistent surplus supply; and all sectors experience difficult periods of adjustment, involving a kind of cultural revolution as well as a need for major re-equipment.

Freeman and Perez stress the vast scope of needed institutional change.

It will involve enormous changes in the pattern of skills ... ; in management and labour attitudes; the pattern of industrial relations and worker participation; in working arrangements; in the pattern of consumer demand; in the conceptual framework of economists, accountants and governments, and in social, political and legislative priorities (Freeman and Perez, 1984, p. 12).

The 'necessity' of such changes has initiated

a growing search for new social and political solutions in such areas as flexible working time, shorter working hours, re-education and retraining systems, regional policies based on creating favourable conditions for information technology (rather than tax incentives to capital-intensive mass production industries), new financial systems, possible decentralisation of management and government, and access to data banks and networks at all levels and new telecommunication systems (Freeman and Perez, 1988, p. 61).

So far, however, only minor changes have taken place. The needed socio-institutional innovations are of a magnitude and pervasiveness like the Keynesian revolution and the profound institutional transformations in the postwar period such as the development of the welfare state. Freeman and Perez have a rather pessimistic view of this socio-political innovative process. The present era is seen to resemble the 1930s and a similar crisis cannot be excluded. Their pessimism is due to the lack of coordinating mechanisms at the international level.

It appears that Freeman and Perez are not guilty of exclusively emphasizing the importance of technology as is sometimes true of other neo-Schumpeterians. Indeed, they are well aware of the complexity of socio-institutional change. 'The socio-institutional framework always influences and may sometimes facilitate and sometimes retard processes of technical and structural change, coordination and dynamic adjustment' (Freeman, 1988b, p. 2).

The importance of the socio-institutional framework is reflected in their account of the spatial dimension of the long waves. It is argued that the diffusion of innovations is highly dependent on attitudes, institutions, policy etc. in different spaces. Freeman, Clark and Soete (1982) present several cases - for instance, the growth of the US automobile industry after the Second World War and, recently, the Japanese electronics industry - where the location and growth of the new industries depended on the socio-institutional framework to such a degree as actually to offset an early technological leadership of other countries.

'National systems of innovation' is a relatively recent concept and a promising new field of inquiry within the neo-Schumpeterian perspective (Andersen and Lundvall, 1988; Freeman, 1988a). It highlights unequal national capacities to generate and assimilate new technology and the qualitatively different impacts of the same techno-economic paradigm in time and space.

Nonetheless, one can justly criticize this approach of technological determinism. The history of capitalism remains one where 'new' techno-economic forces always initiate the changes while the 'old' socio-institutional frameworks always react. They influence, facilitate or retard, but never fundamentally form, the technology-induced changes. The 'socio-institutional' is clearly perceived as subordinate to the 'techno-economic'. The approach strongly resembles the 'regulation' theories. The main differences concern the view of the future trajectories and the extent of autonomous influence of socio-institutional features. Recently, attempts have been made to integrate the two approaches (Roobeek, 1987). Freeman himself has introduced new terms such as 'regime of regulation' and seems to embrace the idea of building an original synthesis of the two 'complementary' approaches (Freeman, 1988b).

The ideas of Freeman and Perez and other neo-Schumpeterians have been rather influential in academic circles, particularly among economists. Their influence in political discourse is perhaps less evident, or at least more indirect, than the influence of the 'flexible specialization' approach. They have, however, been very influential, or even dominant, in connection with the re-orientation of industrial policies and the emergence of technology policy programmes in recent years; both at the national level and at the level of international organizations such as OECD (see *STI Review*, Nos. 7 and 8, 1990) and the European Community.

Regulation Theories

The regulation approach was developed in France during the 1970s. During the 1980s, general interest in regulation theories grew fast and the literature is already extensive[4]. Jessop (1989a) has identified seven contemporary regulationist schools[5], and divergent approaches exist even within the core group of regulationists in Paris: e.g. the value-theoretical approach of Aglietta and Lipietz versus the price-theoretical approach of Boyer (Hübner, 1989). The key concepts of the regulation school have become common academic currency but the original methodological principles are now generally ignored

The common core of regulation theories is often simply identified with a specific language of Fordism and post-Fordism.

Although this 'language' is the central object of interest here. I shall, firstly, summarize the major concepts and ideas of the regulation approach including how the research programme relates to other theoretical approaches. I shall base this brief summary on recent attempts by Boyer (1988a, b), Lipietz (1985, 1989) and Delorme (1990) to present the ideas of the (Paris) regulation school in a synthetic way.

It was the emergence of the general crisis of capitalism in the early 1970s that triggered the research. It was seen as a genuine crisis but also one quite different from earlier crises such as that in the 1930s. It took the economic form of inflation and stagnation instead of deflation and decline. The ambition was to understand the form and the dynamic of the contemporary crisis in a long-term perspective. Three general questions were asked: How can we explain the transition from periods of high and relatively regular growth to periods of relative stagnation and instability? Why do crises take different directions over time? Why do growth and crises assume significantly different national forms?

The attention was directed at the capacity of capitalism for fundamental reorganization during periods of crisis. Capitalism was seen, not as a system of immutable social relations and a set of eternal laws and behaviour rules, but as a sequence of historical constructs formed through the economic and social dynamics of the crises. Between these major crises a great compromise is accepted between the different social classes including the acceptance of a 'pattern of development'. Each such period of compromise is characterized by a given configuration of social relations, forms and structures which makes it possible to identify regularities in the behaviour of economic agents.

The objects of analysis of the approach are these 'regulation' mechanisms, and the transition from one such mechanism to another in a long-term perspective. The concept of regulation has to be complemented by its twin: that of (structural) crisis. Crises are either cyclical or structural. Cyclical crises are the usual business cycles which are normal features of any stabilized form of regulation. Structural crises, on the other hand, are '(episodes) during which the very functioning of regulation comes into contradiction with existing institutional forms, which are then abandoned, destroyed or bypassed' (Boyer, 1988c, p. 76).

> The regulation approach is an attempt to elaborate a continuum of concepts from the more abstract ones (for example that of production modes) to the observed regularities in the behaviour of economic agents ... (These) intermediate notions (are based on) the conclusions of long-run historical studies and point in the direction of a new theoretical framework which would combine a critique of Marxian orthodoxy, and an extension of Kaleckian and Keynesian macroeconomic ideas, in order to rejuvenate a variant or earlier institutional or historical theory (Boyer, 1988b, p. 127).

The regulation approach 'is basically built upon a critique of the mechanical and catastrophic interpretations of Marx' (Boyer, 1988c, p. 70). Of particular importance is the critique of 'structuralism' and Althusserian Marxism with its focus on quasi-mechanic mechanisms of reproduction instead of crises and change.

It also presents itself as an alternative to neoclassical general equilibrium theory. The regulation approach rejects the existence of general laws based on an abstract price mechanism. The economic process is seen as dependent on the structural forms and institutional mechanisms specific of each historical period. Each period has its own 'general' laws and regularies of behaviour dependent on the specific structural and institutional framework. Keynes, Kalecki and Kaldor are seen as economists who delivered major contributions to the understanding of the specific '(general) economic laws' of the 'Fordist' period. However, such 'laws' break down in periods of transition from one form of regulation to another[6].

The regulationists stress the importance of the specificity of national contexts. Thus the concepts and theories developed from each case study are not to be directly applied in other cases. The tendencies to generalize the results of the pioneer case studies of the regulation school (such as Aglietta's work on USA) are not in accordance with the methodological core of the approach. These studies are to be considered as provisional stages in a permanent, iterative process of theoretical elaboration based on analyses of different cases (Hübner, 1989, pp. 14-15).

The key concepts are accumulation regime and mode of regulation (for more detailed definitions, see Boyer in this volume).

The 'accumulation regime' is defined as a set of regularities at the level of the whole economy, enabling a more or less coherent process of capital accumulation. Macroeconomic models can be built along these lines.

The 'mode of regulation' refers to the institutional ensemble (laws, agreements, etc.) and the complex of cultural habits and norms which secures capitalist reproduction as such. It consists of a set of formal or informal 'rules' that codify the main social relationships.

Other widely used concepts among regulationists are: industrial paradigm, mode of growth, mode of development and mode of societalization.

The 'industrial paradigm' is defined as a pattern of productive organization within firms which determines the way workers relate to the means of production. Some regulationists include this as a part of an accumulation regime while others (Lipietz, Delorme, etc.) treat it as a distinct category.

Some regulationists use the concept of a mode of growth to refer to an accumulation regime in its national context. The 'mode of growth' comprises the regularities at the level of a national economy considered in terms of its role in the international division of labour.

In addition, Lipietz, Delorme and others use the concept 'mode of development' (or 'model of development') to refer to the total pattern of development of an economy which is based on (a) its dominant industrial paradigm, (b) its accumulation regime, and (c) its mode of regulation.

'Mode of societalization' is a key concept in the German branch of the regulation school and is also used by Jessop and others. It is defined as a pattern of mass integration and social cohesion. When societalization is successful, there is both an 'historical bloc' and a 'hegemonic' bloc, in Gramsci's terms (Jessop, 1990, pp. 43-44).

The historical studies within the regulation approach have uncovered two regimes of accumulations: extensive versus intensive accumulation. The former regime corresponds to 'competitive regulation' where the economic activities are regulated ex post by demand and supply. The latter regime corresponds to 'monopolistic regulation' where the regulation is ex ante as market forces have to a large extent been replaced by institutionalized rules (such as mark-up pricing and productivity-related collective wage-bargaining) or regulation by the government).

During the 1920s and 1930s a mixture of extensive and intensive forms of accumulation prevailed. Monopolistic regulation was introduced in embryonic forms in democracies (for instance Ford's five dollar-day), and in authoritarian ways in Fascist countries (Siegel, 1988). In the postwar period, however, more or less coherent forms of monopolistic regulation were established in all major capitalist countries. The concept of 'Fordism' is used to characterize this 'golden age' of intensive accumulation and monopolistic regulation.

Several attempts have been made to describe the ideal-type Fordism (see for example Jessop, 1990; Boyer, 1988d; Lipietz, 1985, 1989). It can be identified at four levels of analysis: industrial paradigm (or labour proces), accumulation regime, mode of regulation and mode of societalization (see the section on 'The Nature of Fordism' in Jessop's chapter on Thatcherism in this book).

Very few national economies come close to ideal-type Fordism. On every level of analysis each case represent different combinations of Fordist and non-Fordist features. Various national 'Fordisms' can be identified; for instance 'flawed Fordism' in Britain and 'flexi Fordism' in Germany (Jessop, 1989a), 'demand-side Fordism' in Denmark (Nielsen in this book) and different types of 'peripheral Fordism' (Lipietz, 1988, 1989). The differences are due to such variables as the industrial profiles, the institutional preconditions, the political alliances, and the relative strength of the social forces. During the heyday of Fordism, the deviations were often interpreted as different degrees of backwardness as progress was seen as linked to the diffusion of Fordism from its homeland in USA to other advanced economies. A comparative study organized by Boyer seem to confirm this hypothesis. Macroeconomic achievements (low unemployment and inflation rates, external and budget equilibria) appeared as strictly correlated with the degree of implementation of the Fordist model: the various European economies ranged from the German, French and Italian so-called 'miracles' to the 'British disease' (Boyer, 1988a). However, the evidence is not as clear if data from the small, open economies is included. Many of those countries have achieved good macroeconomic results and rising standards of mass consumption by filling non-Fordist niches (small batch capital goods, luxury consumer goods, shipping or financial services, agricultural goods, and/or raw materials) in the international division of labour. 'Where an economy is not itself predominantly Fordist ... its mode of growth must complement the dominant Fordist logic. In this way it can still be involved in the Fordist growth dynamic rather than being (increasingly) excluded from it' (Jessop, 1990, p. 8). In any case, this is now history as the 'golden age' of Fordism have come to an end. The regulation school dates the outbreak of its crisis from the early 1970s. In this respect it is not different from the 'flexible specialization' and 'techno-economic-paradigm' approaches.

However, the regulationist perspective on the dynamics of the crisis is clearly different from that of the other two approaches.

The following four tendencies have led to the structural crisis (Boyer, 1988a, pp. 199-203, see also Boyer in this volume): Firstly, productivity gains decreased as a result of the social and technical limits of Fordism (worker resistance to the Fordist organization of work and increasing difficulties in 'balancing' ever longer and more rigid production lines). Secondly, the expansion of mass production led to an increasing globalization of economic flows which made national economic management increasingly difficult. Thirdly, Fordism led to growing social expenditure (the relative costs of collective consumption increased, because of the inapplicability of mass production methods in this area, leading to inflationary pressures and distributional conflicts). Fourthly, the consumption pattern has gradually changed towards a greater variety of use values (the new demands are at odds with standardization, the basis of economies of scale, and cannot easily be satisfied through mass production methods).

The fourth tendency resembles the saturation and fragmentation of markets emphasized by Piore and Sabel but it is here considered a part of a more comprehensive set of determinants.

The 'socio-institutional framework' plays a more autonomous role in the regulation perspective compared with the neo-Schumpeterian approach of

Freeman and Perez. The motor in the history of mankind is seen to be not only the development of the productive forces. It is just as much the struggle over control of the process of production and reproduction and even the development of habits and conventions (Lipietz, 1985). The social content of the concepts is always emphasized as, for example, in the first of the above-mentioned four tendencies. The productivity problems are not only seen as technical. They also reflect the 'social' limits of the Fordist organization of the labour process.

In the regulation approach the emergence of new technologies is not seen as the decisive factor in the dynamics of the crisis. Neither is information technology seen as offering a ready-made way out. Technology might point at an exit from the crisis but the key can only be found through social processes. The outcome is not pre-given. Social processes are supposed not only to hamper or facilitate the application of new technology. They influence in a fundamental way the forms of technical and social change. Lipietz (1988) emphasizes, for example, the relative openness of application and the significance of strategic choice in relation to recent innovations within microelectronics.

The regulation perspective sees the peculiarities of national capitalisms as significant features in the process of crisis and transformation. They stress the importance of analyses of the historically-specific conditions under which the crisis of Fordism evolves, in order to uncover the conjuncture of general and particular determinants in the process.

The assumed openness of historical process implies that much more importance is attached to politics and strategies. Strategic resistance against what might appear as 'imperatives' of new technology and market forces is not interpreted as necessarily useless or a cause for postponement of inevitable changes. It might be an essential component in the process towards a new period of stable capitalist growth.

The regulation school offers a challenging and complex research programme (for a general critique, see Hübner (1989) and Jessop (1989a)). Its theory of crisis and development is hard to criticize and this is exactly one of its problems. Is it after all just a reformulation of the theory of the relationship between the productive forces and the mode of production or between basis and superstructure? Or does it represent a far-reaching elasticity and openness in the analysis of social relations and social development? (Becker, 1989, p. 231). Both views are reflected in the applause and in the critique as well. Meegan (1988) and Elam (1989) praise the regulation approach for exactly opposite reasons. Likewise, the regulation school is criticized for being too functionalistic and deterministic by some (for example Becker, 1989) and as too open and indeterministic by others (for example Salvati, 1988; Hirsch,

1988; Harvey, 1989). 'he latter line of critique seems more to the point than the former one.

Hirsch (1988) sees the regulationist theory of crisis as characterized by a certain degree of vagueness and eclecticism. The theory is characterized as strictly anti-functionalistic and the modes of regulation are treated as merely 'objects found'. 'The lack of any precise specification of the underlying theoretical conceptualisation of crises makes it extremely difficult to provide more than a descriptive analysis of the causes, conditions and possibilities for transformation processes' (Hirsch, 1988, p. 4). Harvey, similarly, claims that 'there is, within the regulation school, little or no attempt to provide any detailed understanding of the mechanisms and logic of transitions' (Harvey, 1989, p. 179). Both resort to the Marxian theory of the underlying logic of capitalism, in general, for a solution. Hirsch has developed his own version of the contemporary transformation process which gives priority the law of the falling rate of profit in his theory of the dynamics of crises (Hirsch and Roth, 1986). The value-theoretical branch of the Parisian regulation school, likewise, refer to this Marxian law in its theory of crisis (Lipietz, 1988) but the differences between the two approaches are obvious; Lipietz stresses the contingency of the evolving modes of regulations while Hirsch stresses an element of necessity.

Salvati (1988) compares the Marxian and the regulationist vision of history. He considers the regulation approach much richer and more sophisticated, but also much weaker. Whereas the Marxist vision involves a theory (although a crude one) of historical development, the regulation approach is 'simply a succession of ideal-types of regulation - self-reproducing patterns of system-integration - separated by periods of crisis and transition' (Salvati, 1988, p. 26).

Neo-Fordism, Post-Fordism, or Just 'Après'-Fordism

The regulation approach has its strength in the analysis of the 'self-producing patterns of system-integration' and not in its theoretical conception or the logic of tranformation. This is reflected in its treatment of the future era or the way out of the contemporary crisis.

The regulation school has not given a real name to the new era of capitalist development to replace Fordism. Usually, the names actually used just indicates a relation to its predecessor. 'Neo-Fordism' stresses a strong element of continuity in relation to the basic traits of Fordism. Others use the concept of 'post-Fordism' by adding a simple chronological prefix. This is probably meant to indicate that the new era is something entirely different from Fordism but yet not so clearly visible or predictable as to give it a real name.

Jessop points out that 'a serious analysis of post-Fordism cannot rest content with noting that it occurs after Fordism but must establish how it relates to the specific developmental tendencies and crises of Fordism' (Jessop, 1990, pp. 27-28). If this proves impossible, it would be better to use the term 'non-Fordism'.

Useful analyses of post-Fordism do exist but a lot of speculative 'newspeak' also uses this increasingly popular heading. Considering the difficulties involved in distinguishing within such an open perspective between traces of a new order and transitory phenomena it is hard to avoid an element of speculation in such an exercise. To avoid this speculative flavour some has retreated to the original usage of the term in French (*après fordisme*) which was apparently meant simply to designate the period after Fordism rather than the new subsequent era.

Aglietta (1979a) was the one who introduced the concept of neo-Fordism. The concept is related to his analysis of US capitalism and his focus on the international dimension of Fordism. A renewal of US capitalism to sustain hegemony of USA in the world economy is said to involve 'neo-Fordism' which is defined as a new regime of intensive accumulation. Neo-Fordism involves a deepening as well as a widening of the range of intensive accumulation. It involves 'the transformation of the totality of the conditions of existence of the wage-earning class' (Aglietta, 1979a, p. 168). An essential aspect is the application of Fordist methods of production to welfare services and other non-Fordist areas, such as leisure activities. Another element in the new regime is a new organization of the labour process to increase the intensity of work by means of new information technology, automatic control of production, autonomous work groups, etc. It also involves globalization of firms, utilizing the new information technology.

Neo-Fordism represents a vision of the consequences of the application of new information technology which is entirely different from the vision of craft production in a network of small firms:

> (neo-Fordism) reconstitutes the totality of the production process through the use of electronic information systems and computer programming. This enables a fully integrated and self-correcting machine system to be introduced (Perrons, 1981).

Aglietta considers neo-Fordism as the only durable solution to the crisis but this does not imply that he believes it will necessarily materialize. He presents four possible scenarios of the late twentieth-century world economy (Aglietta, 1982). Neo-Fordism is the first. The second is a vision of a more troubled world economy segmented in the 'triad' parts. The other two scenarios are more gloomy: general stagflation, and financial collapse and fragmentation.

Recent Parisian contributions refer to neo-Fordism less often. Sometimes post-Fordism is used as a mere heuristic device but often general reference to 'ways out of the crisis of Fordism' is preferred. The prospective analyses of the Parisian regulation school often involve presentation, comparison, criticism and reformulation of the major other interpretations including flexible specialization and information technology as new techno-economic paradigm. They tend to argue for 'mixed' solutions; they discuss various possible solutions instead of pointing at probable or even deterministic solutions; and they often emphasize the different national ways of the crisis. Typical examples are Boyer (1988a), Leborgne and Lipietz (1988, 1989) and the chapter of Boyer in this book.

Boyer (1988a, pp. 268-273) presents a set of possible (post-Fordist) developments in wage/labour relations in response to the challenge of flexibility and shows the different prospects of each of the national economies included in the comparative study of labour market flexibility. He identifies five possible scenarios: the two alternatives included in Piore and Sabel (flexible specialization and international Keynesianism); competitive flexibility (the neo-liberal model); a multi-tier system based on highly segmented labour markets; and negotiated involvement of unions in attempts to promote offensive flexibility (training and acquisition of new skills, rapid introduction of new machinery). The prospects appear highly dependent on historically inherited features in each country's system of wage/labour relations. Each of the five scenarios represent a possible (post-Fordist) model dependent on the national context.

In his article in this book, Boyer assesses four possible new accumulation regimes, including 'information technology as techno-economic paradigm' and 'flexible specialization'. He concludes that a composite model is likely: flexible mass production in modern high-tech industries, flexible specialization in declining sectors, and old Fordist methods exported to the periphery and applied in traditional services.

Leborgne and Lipietz (1988) discuss labour process, industrial organization and its spatial consequences and identify three possible ways out of the crisis: the 'neo-Taylorist', the 'Californian' (the Silicon Valley model of local production systems, no unions, flexible wages, involvement of workers through corporate culture), and the 'Saturnian' model (Japanese and Swedish forms of negotiated involvement, collective bargaining and rigid wages). Future development is supposed to be determined by social struggle and different national solutions is to be expected. In all cases, however, they see acute dangers of exclusion (dual or segmented labour markets and welfare systems).

In a later work, Leborgne and Lipietz (1989) confine themselves to two 'possible capital/labour relations at the end of the crisis of Fordism'. The first is the 'offensive' strategy of flexibility: advanced compromises with negotiated involvement of workers in the labour process, skilled jobs, welfare benefits, and strong labour contracts. The second is the 'defensive' strategy of flexibility; low and flexible wages (direct and indirect), no involvement and precarious status of workers.

Other regulationists are less hesitant to give names to the future. Hirsch is one of them. He has developed an elaborate vision of the post-Fordist future (Hirsch and Roth, 1986; Hirsch, 1985a; Hirsch, in this volume). His outline of 'the new face of capitalism' is based partly on his conception of the causes for the crisis of Fordism and partly on an extrapolation of already visible changes. He identifies some rather bleak social consequences of the 'new face': individualization, polarization, segmentation, increased inequalities, and authoritarianism. He stresses the following features: (1) new flexible combinations of man and machine in time and space, i.e. systematic individualization of the labour process; (2) new forms of consumption based on microelectronic technology, i.e. 'hyper-industrialization' and 'self-service'; (3) polarization of the labour force and a segmented corporatist structure; (4) reorganization of the welfare state, i.e. selective privatization and new inequalities; and (5) authoritarian étatism with increased repression and supervision. He emphasizes, like the Parisian regulationists, how the crisis takes specific national forms, and his 'new face of capitalism' is deliberately presented as the German one (Hirsch and Roth, 1986, p. 106).

However, it is not at all clear how the ideal-type of German post-Fordism is developed. The methodological remarks are vague and no references are made to any data. It remains unclear how Hirsch has handled the basic difficulties in such exercises: the contemporary trends are necessarily a confusing mixture of features; and the responses to the crisis, and even the successful attempts to remove the obstacles of the former era, do not constitute any direct links into the future (cf. Boyer's chapter in this book).

While Hirsch presents a rather detailed account of various features of post-Fordism including its 'mode of societalization' most regulationists limit themselves to the post-Fordist economic institutions. Jessop, for example, assumes that post-Fordism will be 'based on the dominance of flexible forms of production in combination with non-standardized consumption patterns' (Jessop, 1990, p. 28). He considers it justified to talk about post-Fordist labour processes but finds it premature to talk of post-Fordist ideal-types in other societal spheres.

Among self-proclaimed regulationists it is customary to go further than that although not as far as Hirsch. For example, Harvey (1989), Schoenberger (1988) and Allen and Massey (1988), who talk of 'flexible accumulation' instead of post-Fordism, seem to represent the contemporary 'consensus view'. Flexible accumulation is supposed to develop directly from the attempts to confront the rigidities of Fordism. Its defining quality is flexibility with respect to labour processes, labour markets, products and patterns of consumption, coupled with wide-scale application of the new information technologies. However, the increased flexibility at the microeconomic level is not merely seen as an aggregation of the decentralized responses to the crises. It is supposed to be supported and reinforced by new rigidities, i.e. a new regime of accumulation and a new mode of regulation.

Notes

1. Or rather, what has been called the 'neo-Marshallian' approach to institutions does so, while the 'neo-Walrasian' approach (Mirowski, 1981).

2. A slightly different version can be found in Johnson (1985). See also Johnson and Lundvall in this volume.

3. Williams et al. (1987) is a comprehensive review article. Gertler (1988) is a typical critique. For an enthusiastic enthuastic review, see Murray (1985).

4. The pioneer work was done by Aglietta (1974, 1979a). Other important early contributions are Boyer and Mistral (1982), Lipietz (1979), and Delorme and Andre (1983). Useful reviews of the regulation school are found in Jessop (1989a, 1990), Hübner (1989), Noel (1987), Boyer (1986c, 1988c), Mjøset (1985a) and de Vroey (1984).

5. Other important groups are the GRREC team in Grenoble (see, for example, de Bernis, 1988); the West German school (for reviews, see Jessop (1988); and Hübner and Mahnkopf (1988) and the North American 'social structure of accumulation approach' (see, for example, Gordon, Edwards and Reich, 1982; for as review, see Mehrwert no. 20, 1986).

6. The Kaldor-Verdoorn law summarizes a lot of evidence about a positive correlation between growth and productivity. This correlation now appears as a direct consequence of the organization of production under Fordism. Since 1973 there has been no systematic relationship between growth and productivity (Boyer, 1988d). The breakdown of the relatively stable relation between unemployment and inflation (the 'Phillips curve') can likewise be seen as an effect of the crisis of 'Fordism'.

Part 1. Myths and Realities

2. Flexibility and Institutional Learning

Björn Johnson and Bengt-Åke Lundvall

The 'Institutional Sclerosis' Hypothesis

Flexibility is not a well-defined concept in economic theory. Usually, it refers to two different kinds of abilities to react to exogenous changes (Scitovsky, 1980). First, there is the flexibility of the individual actors in the economic system, i.e. the ability of firms and households to react upon price changes and adjust their product mix, and their structure of consumption, respectively. Second, there is the flexibility of the system as a whole: its ability to shift focus and centre of gravity and reallocate incomes and wealth in favour of those who respond to, and cope best with, a new situation.

According to mainstream economics, in a capitalist economy both these kinds of flexibility reflect the workings of the market mechanism. If tastes or technologies change, the market economy responds by reallocating resources, so that production always tends to be effective and consumer tastes catered to. Actually, flexibility is often seen as one of the great merits of capitalism. It may not always score high on equity issues, but when it comes to flexibility, it is supposed to be the champion of economic systems.

According to conventional economic wisdom, capitalism works when it is flexible and runs into trouble when it is not. So, in periods when it is obvious that the economic system does not work satisfactorily, for example when there is a drawn-out economic crisis, it is tempting to conclude that the market mechanism has been undermined. Something or someone has interfered with the market, and prevents it from working freely as an allocation and incentive system. Thus, the long period of widespread production and productivity growth slow-down, high unemployment and balance of payments disturbances up through the 1970s and 1980s led many mainstream economists to conclude that there was something wrong with the central institution of the capitalist economy, i.e. the market.

In this way, the 'institutional sclerosis' hypothesis was born (Johnson, 1981). In a series of publications from the OECD and other international economic organizations in the late 1970s it was argued that due to political processes, leading to growing government sectors and trade union powers, severe rigidities had been built into the economic systems of the industrialized western world, reducing its responsiveness to price signals. At the same time, however, the need for flexible economic systems was assumed to be more pressing than ever. International interdependence was increasing and there was a strong need for adaptations to radically changing circumstances, as for example the rise in energy prices, the increasing exports from NIC countries and the new technological opportunities. A growing conflict between an increasing need for change and a decreasing flexibility was assumed to lie behind the observed, less than satisfactory, macroeconomic performance.

To some extent, the diagnosis of institutional sclerosis had built into itself the cure of the disease; a movement towards flexibility was assumed to demand the restoration of an institutional framework closer to the ideal of the pure, and perfectly competitive, market economy. To approach this ideal was defined as the most important task for economic policy in many countries[1]. At the practical level, it usually meant efforts to reduce the size of the public sector through budget cuts and privatizations, less government regulation of private industries, and less trade union power. This can be characterized as a neo-liberal programme for institutional design. As the program is based, mainly, on standard neoclassical general equilibrium theory, and as this theory, except for the assumption of pure and perfectly competitive markets, largely, neglects the role of the institutional set-up, it was a bold and daring enterprise to develop and present recommendations for practical policies on this basis. Luckily for the functionality of the whole system, and unsurprisingly, it has only been possible to implement the programme to a very limited degree. There has been a clear difference between the neo-liberal rhetorics and the policies actually pursued.

Thus, it doesn't seem to have been any strong efforts, in any country, to remove or reduce 'private' obstacles to perfect competition, like highly concentrated product and financial markets, multinational companies, and so on. Public support of private interests has been redirected rather than reduced. Deregulation has, actually, often meant increased government powers, and so on. But also this limited neo-liberal institutional redesign activity may have caused more harm than good to the flexibility properties of the market economies. Its most serious consequence might have come from the fact that it focused the attention of policy makers on the wrong questions.

Active Versus Reactive Flexibility

One fundamental problem with this project of 'neo-liberal' institutional design is that it reflects quite a narrow understanding of 'flexibility'. Rational, but essentially passive and mechanical, firms and households are assumed, only, to react upon external changes. They never seem to act wilfully, and there is not much 'animal spirit' around. In relation to technical change, for example, firms make choices between existing blueprints according to rules for profit maximization. But given a perfectly competitive environment the outcomes of these choices are predetermined and there is no room for uncertainty or for context shaping initiatives. This way of thinking about flexibility follows, naturally, from the way neoclassical economics poses the problem of allocation of given scarce resources, as the main economic problem, and from the way it treats tastes, technologies and institutions as exogenous to the analysis.

This kind of reactive, passive flexibility is, undoubtedly, important in many situations. From the point of view of individual firms and households, most changes are external and, also, for the small nation changes often emanate from worldmarkets. But as already suggested a long time ago:

> ... it is the characteristic of man to do something, not simply to suffer pleasures and pains through the impact of suitable forces. He is not simply a bundle of desires that are to be saturated by being placed in the path of forces of the environment, but rather a coherent structure of propensities and habits which seeks realisation and expression in an unfolding activity (Veblen, 1898).

The clear-cut distinction between changed circumstances (regarded as exogenous), and responses (assumed to reflect rational behaviour of individual agents), is quite misleading even as an abstraction. If we change the focus of the analysis from a fictitious, semistationary, world to one where creative agents engage in innovative activities, where uncertainty rules, and where learning is of strategic importance, the distinction crumbles away.

The point may be illustrated by the distinction made in innovation theory between the first introduction of a new process, or product, by a specific firm, i.e. the innovation as such, and the subsequent spread of the innovation throughout the economy, i.e. the diffusion of the innovation. Recent research has shown that this separation between the innovation as an isolated event and a subsequent phase of diffusion gives a distorted picture of the actual process of innovation (Dosi, 1988). Especially at the early stage of the diffusion process, the innovation is redefined in different ways and the rate of diffusion will reflect these redefinitions. Specifications are made, quality and design is improved, new fields of application are discovered, the organization of production processes are changed, etc. Innovation and diffusion are mutually dependent and parts of the same process. The same is true for consumption, where consumers, while expressing their preferences in their choice between alternatives, learn, at the same time, to consume new products and change their own preferences.

Even incremental changes in technical knowledge will give rise not only to passive adjustments to the new conditions (flexibility in the narrow sense) but also trigger acts and deeds aiming at, actively, changing and improving the situation. To react is to act. And, when it comes to more radical innovations, uncertainties about future prices and possibilities are great and it is often impossible to define, in advance, what a rational response should be. Results will depend more on the innovative capability and creativity of the firm than on its neoclassical flexibility. In short, then, in a dynamic, long run, perspective, the ability to improve technologies and organizations, the ability to change a given situation to your own advantage, and the capacity to produce and utilize unexpected novelty, is more important than the ability to receive and react upon external price signals.

Thus when the economy is viewed more as a process of learning - as an unfolding sequence - than as a system of allocation, its innovativeness becomes the most important aspect of its flexibility. This calls for an evolutionary rather than a general equilibrium perspective. In this article we shall show that, viewed from such a perspective, the current state of the economy calls for more flexibility in this broader sense but that the kind of institutional design needed is of a kind radically different from the neoliberal recommendations. Actually, some of the cornerstones of this ideology (the pure market and competitive behaviour) are now under strong attack in United States and even OECD, a strong advocate for the neoliberal credo a decade ago, has begun to broaden its understanding of the kind of institutional change needed[2].

Our argument is presented in two steps. First, we demonstrate that, in general, an institutional perspective is of fundamental importance to the understanding of the process of innovation. Second, we refer to a recent comparative study of the USA and Japan, made by MIT-experts, pointing to the need for institutional change and social innovation in order to strengthen the innovativeness and flexibility of the US economy (Dertouzos, Lester and Solow, 1989). Finally, we note that the new programme for institutional design implied by this study tends to go in a direction opposite the original neoliberal programme at crucial points. Actually, it implies that markets are too pure, competition too dominating, and corporatism and cooperative behaviour too weakly developed in the US economy.

Innovation as a Cumulative Process Rooted in Learning

In some versions of innovation theory innovation is regarded as single and isolated event, reflecting the ingenuity and creativity of single individuals. This perspective has its background in Schumpeter's early and classical contribution to innovation theory, putting the entrepreneur at the centre of the process of economic development (Schumpeter, 1919). Later he revised his model of economic development, and took into account that innovations had gradually become the concern of big firms and organized in collective R&D-laboratories but still the emphasis was upon the discontinuity of innovation and innovation was assumed to emanate from activities within single economic units (Schumpeter, 1928, 1942).

It is true that innovations, by definition, are discontinuous and sometimes they will represent radical breaks with the past practice of the agents developing and adopting them. But at the same time it is important to emphasize that they are also cumulative and based upon learning going on in the routine activities in the economy. In this context it is instructive to use another Schumpeterian concept refering to innovations as 'new combinations'. Most innovative activities represent new combinations of already existing knowledge. Sometimes the combination is easy to find and takes little effort and creativity, sometimes it might take the continuous effort of large teams and the extreme originality of individuals but all the same the final result will be 'a new combination' rather than a pure revelation.

We assume the routine economic activities of producing, selling and buying to give rise to important inputs to the process of innovation. One kind of input is new items, entered on the agenda for innovative efforts. Problems encountered, and bottle-necks registered, in the production, sales and procurement departments, will affect the direction and intensity of innovative efforts. Another kind of input is learning through everyday experience. It involves learning to produce a set of products more efficiently - called learning-by-doing in Arrow (1962) - learning to use new products and systems more efficiently - called learning-by-using in Rosenberg (1982) - and, finally, learning through combining the experiences of customers and suppliers - called learning-by-interacting in Lundvall (1988).

We shall now proceed to show why this perspective on the process of innovation makes an institutional perspective important when it comes to understand what constitutes the innovativeness, and flexibility, of firms and national economies.

The Importance of Institutions

Institutions are central in a perspective of economic change, because they set preconditions for learning and innovation processes, which are important engines of change in modern economies. Learning, growth of knowledge and innovations are shaped by the institutional set-up of the economy. Veblen actually defines institutions as 'habits of thought'. He underlines the interaction between institutional and technical change, and he considers all economic change, in the last resort, to be a change in habits of thought:

This is true even of changes in the mechanical processes of industry. A given contrivance for effecting certain material ends becomes a circumstance which affects the further growth of habits of thought - habitual methods of procedure - and so becomes a point of departure for further development of the methods of compassing the ends sought and for the further variation of ends that are sought to be compassed. (Veblen, 1898)

The concept of 'institutions' has been defined in many ways. In the institutionalist tradition in economic theory, however, the common idea has been that societies are characterized by regularities of behaviour, and that these are specific to time and place. Behaviour is thus instituted, not because of some universal human characteristics, but rather through a process of enculturation (Mayhew, 1987). The role of culture in shaping human cognitions and actions is emphasized. This was described by Commons (1931) as 'collective control of individual action' and by Veblen as 'habits of use and wont'.

The simplest forms of behaviour regularities are habits. In order to deal with the complexity of everyday life, habits are formed; they provide us with a means of retaining a pattern of behaviour without engaging in global rational calculations involving a vast amount of complex information (Hodgson, 1988). Habits are important in economic analysis, because they relate to a large set of routinized behaviour in the economy. The importance of routines in economic processes is, increasingly, recognized in economic theory, in large part thanks to the work by Nelson and Winter (1982). Beside habits and routines there are other types of reasons for regularities of behaviour such as laws, formal rules on different levels and moral norms.

The central point, common to the different kinds of regularities of behaviour, is that institutions, in this respect, are informational devices which reduce uncertainties. They make it unnecessary to start life from scratch every day. Every possible action in relation to other people does not have to be reflected on; we act in accordance with norms, rules, habits, etc. widely accepted as guidelines for social life, regardless of whether each member of society accepts them ideologically or politically. Thereby, institutions make purposeful action possible by making other people's and organization's actions more predictable. In this sense, institutions actually provide information. They are 'signposts' for the relation between people and people (Lachman, 1970). However, it should be observed in this connection that institutions need not be politically neutral in any way. They also signal established power relationships between people. Nor should one be misled to believe that institutions have to be efficient, or optimal, in any meaningful sense. But without regularities of behaviour, i.e. without institutions, society would be impossible.

The preceding paragraphs motivate the following broad definition of the concept of institutions: institutions are sets of habits, routines, rules, norms, and laws, which, by reducing the amount of information necessary for individual and collective action, make reproduction and change of society possible. To avoid misunderstandings, it should perhaps be mentioned that post offices, trade unions, government agencies and other tangible organizations, referred to as 'institutions' in everyday speech, are institutions, also, under the present definition. They may be referred to as 'formal institutions'. To say that a bank is a financial institution means that the already institutionalized acts of borrowing and lending, according to certain rules (keeping reserves, and so on), have been formalized and organized by the creation of a bank.

Institutions, Stability and Change

Institutions survive because they serve some functions. Empty institutions cannot exist in the long run. At the most general level, the function of institutions is, as we have seen, the informational 'signpost' function. This can be further divided into different sub-functions. Institutions reduce uncertainties, mediate conflicts, and provide incentive systems. By serving in these functions institutions provide the stability necessary for the reproduction of society. They hold images stable enough for communication to be possible. Therefore, there are also important limits to how fast they themselves can change without disrupting society. Inertia is thus a basic feature of institutions. At the same time, they are important for change in society. Institutions provide frames of references within which change can be understood and implemented. They provide the stability necessary for change.

Institutions provide this stability for different kinds of change. First, a certain amount of stability is required for 'incremental innovation' to go on. Incremental innovation along established technological trajectories, i.e. the activity of technological progress along the economic and technological trade-offs defined by a paradigm (Dosi, 1988), may be regarded as an activity involving both institutionalized elements and elements of change. The fact that engineers and business men tend to agree upon dimensions in which technology should be enhanced and further developed makes possible a more concentrated effort and more rapid progress. Incremental innovation is, thus, based on an institutionally provided stability.

Even the process bringing forward radical innovations will encompass elements of institutionalized routine behaviour. The formalized and informal rules for scientific experimenting might be regarded as meta-routines, setting free resources for creative activities and for activities aiming at radical inventions and innovations.

Generally, we find that, in a sense, every institution may be characterized

as a 'rigidity'. Its basic function is to introduce stability in an unstable world
and to make change, without chaos, possible in such a world. According to
the neo-liberal programme for institutional design, using neoclassical general
equilibrium theory as its norm and ideal, all institutions except the poorly
defined competitive markets should be banned from the economic scene. The
realization of this programme in its most radical form, would certainly result
in a chaotic and unstable world, making sustained technical progress
impossible.

This does not mean that the existing institutional set-up, at any certain point
of time, is promoting technical and social progress. Heuristics in relation to
incremental technical change are often embodied in organizational routines
and, even, in higher level procedures to alter these routines when needed
(Dosi, 1988). But this means also that there are continuous tensions between
incremental technical change, along established trajectories, on the one hand,
and the capability of doing radically new things, on the other. Radical
innovations cannot be fully accounted for in terms of the gradual learning
processes, and, often, implies routines of incremental innovation to be broken
and new routines to be established. The stability needed for incremental
innovation is in conflict with major shifts in the technological base of the
economy.

Especially in periods of a shift in technological paradigms, such a conflict
can be costly for the economy in terms of stagnation and unemployment. In
such situations, however, it is not a good idea to rely on 'competitive
markets', as the sole furnisher of flexibility, as implied by the crude version
of the 'institutional sclerosis' hypothesis. The existing set of institutions is
always stubbornly, and thoroughly, weaved into the 'market economy' (as
routines inside firms, as established patterns of user-producer relationships,
and as generally accepted rules and norms, forming the behaviour
economy-wide of management, workers and engineers). To break these
patterns, without very long delays, will, as a rule, take conscious political
efforts by different agents and groups of agents rather than just more markets
and more purified markets. Sometimes, social conflict, resulting in a new
'social contract', is the only way to realize such an institutional
transformation.

And, of course, an institutional set-up, well-suited to promote growth and
employment in the OECD countries, may have catastrophic consequences for
third world countries, in terms of impoverishment, and it might bring us
closer to ecological breakdowns. Institutional learning, bringing the
institutional set-up closer to one promoting justice and long-term ecological
viability, seems to be a slow process indeed, often involving major set-backs.
But neither in this context should we expect much help from the neo-liberal

institutional design. In order to promote such 'non economic' goals we must weaken, rather than strengthen, the logic and the limited rationality of the market.

Institutions and Learning

We have argued that the innovative capability of an economy is an important aspect of its flexibility. Futhermore, we have showed that innovation, in turn, is a cumulative process which depends on growth of knowledge and application of new knowledge in the economy. Knowledge doesn't fall like manna from heaven, as technical change is assumed to do in neoclassical growth theory. It has its origin in different forms of learning. The learning capacity of an economy is thus crucial to its innovativeness and flexibility.

We also argued above that institutions not only provide stability to society, and make its reproduction possible, though this may be their most obvious function, but that they also set the preconditions for different forms of change and make orderly change, i.e. change without disruption, possible. The most important way in which institutions influence change may be through their impacts on learning. Institutions influence learning in many ways and at many levels. In fact, it is rather difficult and may be impossible for an individual to think and act freely in any specific field of application without being influenced by the institutional set-up[3].

Institutions influence all aspects of the cognitive process. The information communicated through institutions is not transmitted raw. It is affected by those institutions themselves. Information is selected, arranged and perceived through institutions which thus influence cognition in its most basic aspects (Hodgson, 1987). This is one reason why institutions cannot be reduced to rigidities and hindrances in the process of economic change. As long as information is not perfect and costless, the individual's perception of the world matters. There is a possible difference between the world as it is and the way it is perceived, and it can be perceived differently between individuals, and between groups and classes. Institutions are informational devices and they govern these perceptions.

This is well formulated in a recent book by Mary Douglas (1988). 'Institutions think', she says. We recognize, classify, remember and forget in accordance with institutions. Particular ideas and ideals dominate in particular institutional and cultural configurations. Going back to Weber, Durkheim and Fleck, she discusses how a 'thought style' sets the preconditions of any cognition for the members of a 'thought collective' or in a 'thought world'. Douglas' discussion of these concepts show some similarities with Perez' (1985) idea of a 'techno-economic paradigm', governing the ways decision-makers think about technical and economic problems.

The point is, that institutions through governing the cognitive process, in a fundamental way, influence the learning processes in society. Not only is learning different in different historical epochs, and culturally divergent societies with radically different institutional settings, but it also differs between communities in the same period and even in the same society. An 'instituted community', which could be a firm or a network of firms, or maybe the 'enterprise community' of a certain country, also has a profound influence on what kind of learning is going on inside it:

As we have already seen, institutions survive by harnessing all information processes to the task of establishing themselves. The instituted community blocks personal curiosity, organizes public memory, and heroically imposes certainty on uncertainty. In making its own boundaries it affects all lower level thinking, so that persons realize their own identities and classify each other through community affiliation. Since it uses the division of labour as a source of metaphors to affirm itself, the community's self-knowledge and knowledge of the world must undergo change when the organization of work changes. (Douglas, 1987, p.102)

Facts don't speak for themselves. Raw observation of the world doesn't, automatically, transform itself into knowledge. Information only becomes knowledge through a social process of learning and this process is, inevitably, influenced by institutions.

Interactive Learning

Summing up, learning - here conceived both as a process leading to new knowledge and as a process putting old knowledge into new heads - is a fundamental aspect of economic change. It affects the knowledge base of the economy, and can result in an increased innovative capability in firms and organizations, thus increasing the flexibility of the economy (in its broad sense). If capitalists have positive expectations regarding prospective demand and profits, this capability will be transformed into technical, and organizational, innovations affecting production and employment. The whole of this learning process, from the growth of knowledge to its application and diffusion in the system of production, is affected by the institutional set-up of the economy.

Of course, there are different forms of learning, but most of it involves different degrees of social interacting, which, of course, is one reason why institutions matter. Undoubtedly, there is some individual and isolated imprinting of immediate experiences on the memory, but this is certainly not the most important form. There is also rote learning, i.e. learning through repetition, when it is not necessary to understand what you are doing. This, normally, involves observing and learning from other people and thus involves more human interaction than simple imprinting. A lot of learning is done by feedback, which involves still more interacting. We do, say or try something and get a response from other people, who directly or through their behaviour tell us something about our first action, and so on[4].

Finally, there is active, systematic and organized searching for new knowledge, with learning as a professionalized activity and with specific organizations aiming, explicitly, at the creation or gathering of new knowledge. This is characteristic for the modern industrialized society, with its universities, research institutes, R&D departments and so on, and it involves intense and complicated forms of interacting inside the research community, as well as between this community and other communities and individuals in the economy.

Generally, the more complex and systemic the innovations, the more complicated communication processes they require. In modern, technically advanced firms, innovations often require combinations of different kinds of knowledge and experience. Often, the knowledge of people from other firms and organizations have to be consulted. The way production is organized affects the character of the interaction and communication going on, and hence the learning processes and innovative capabilities of the firms. In the same way, learning is affected by the relations between different firms. Not only firms, but also markets are often organized, and the information flows between firms are not limited to price-type information. The communication and interaction between firms provide important inputs to the innovation process. This is why it is often more relevant to analyse innovation as a process involving pairs, groups, or networks of firms, rather than as unique events emanating from the single firm in isolation.

We suggest that the flexibility of an economy is very much dependent on its innovativeness and, hence, its learning capabilities. We also suggest that most learning, in the economic sphere of society, i.e. in relation to accumulation, production and distribution, is interactive and that the interaction and communication have tended to become more complex as production has become more science-based and systemic. In order to understand what constitutes innovativeness and flexibility in this context, we must put the focus upon how the institutional set-up changes, and upon the relationship between technical innovation and institutional learning and social innovation.

Technical Innovation and Institutional Change

In a historical perspective, the creation of new private institutions like the joint-stock company, and, later, the multidivisional form of organization, and the R&D departments, have played an important role in shaping the institutional set-up surrounding technical innovation. Of even greater importance was the non-formalized institutions, i.e. the routines and trajectories connected to the Fordist regime (labour saving and energy intensive innovations and mass production and mass consumption as the norm) and together they formed the basis for rapid and ordered change.

In the modern industrial firm, there is, normally, a close connection between organizational and technical change. Product innovation usually interacts with process innovation and reorganizations and, conversely, increases in productivity at the level of the production line normally goes hand in hand with redesigns of the product (Eliasson, 1987). The communication pattern between different departments, for example procurement, production, sales, and R&D departments has an important impact on process as well as product innovations, etc. (Aoki, 1986; Freeman, 1987).

Also, change in government institutions like the public educational infrastructure, including engineering schools and universities, and the communication system, for example will be crucial to the innovative capability of the economy in certain periods. The more the knowledge base of the economy matters - the more growth by innovation means, compared with growth by accumulation - the more important institutional and organizational change becomes. Thus, when the economy is viewed as a process its capability of institutional learning, and its social innovativeness, become as important as its technical innovativeness. They are interrelated, and in a dynamic perspective, they are both important parts of the flexibility of the economy. The interaction between technical and institutional innovations is a fundamental feature of modern economic growth and development.

But the need for rapid institutional learning and for social innovations becomes more important in some historical periods than in others. As we shall argue, we are now in a period where stagnation and unemployment will prevail, until a new institutional set-up has been developed, and diffused, in the economic system. In order to illustrate our point we shall refer some of the main results from an interesting, fresh analysis of the US national system of production and innovation.

Made in America - An Alternative Programme for Institutional Design

In the summer 1989 a group of MIT Scholars presented their analysis of the US system of production (Dertouzos, Lester and Solow, 1989). All through the report, 'Made in America', comparisons are made with the Japanese system and the analysis gives an interesting understanding of the institutional differences between the two countries.

There are several reasons why the MIT study is interesting in our context. First, the juxtaposition of the US and the Japanese systems shows, clearly, the importance of the institutional set-up and the analysis presents itself as an application of an institutional perspective to the problems of flexibility and innovativeness. Second, we believe the MIT study to be of importance for the prospects of alternative European 'flexibilization strategies'. Even if the US-hegemony may be faltering in certain dimensions, the transfer of ideological gadgets and new economic ideas to Europe, sometimes through OECD and other international organizations, and sometimes through the academic community, seems still to be a forceful process. The fact that highly esteemed academics, including Robert M. Solow, mainstream macroeconomist and Noble Prize Winner, from one of the most prestigious universities in the USA, have produced a document of this kind may, actually, signal new turns also for the European flexibilization debate.

One conclusion of the analysis, which is based upon nine different industry-wide case studies, is that the USA has a real problem in terms of structural competitiveness and innovative capability. It also points to a number of mutually interdependent factors giving rise to this problem. A fundamental result is the negative role played by the weak tradition for cooperation at all levels of the US system. The emphasis upon individualist, competitive and conflictual, behaviour, at all levels of the economic and social system, is presented as a serious hindrance for adopting a best-practice economic organization. Related to this cultural characteristic are a short-term financial perspective on investment and the tendency to regard workers only as a cost factor, rather than as human resources to be further developed.

Cooperative behaviour is lacking inside the firm where the R&D department tend to design new products, without involving the expertise in the production department and where experts get frozen into narrow specialties, without experience and understanding of the other kinds of expertise in the firms.

The relationships between workers and management are predominantly antagonistic and it reflects that management has very limited expectations to the capability of workers and that workers respond by being passive and negative to change.

In the USA, vertical interfirm relationships are of the arm's length type. Professional users try to get cheap products from their suppliers and do not establish any enduring relationships, aiming at cooperation towards better quality and innovation. Possibilities to obtain short-term profits by exchanging the supplier firms or by squeezing their profit are always exploited.

Horizontal relationships are difficult to establish in the USA both because of the anti-trust legislation, and because of mutual distrust between the parties. Even when a common effort would be necessary in order to keep ahead in technological terms, as in the semiconductor industry, it has been very difficult to coordinate the efforts of competing firms.

According to the MIT analysis, the current institutions of the US economy reflect decades of very successful economic development. This development had, at its core, the Fordist combination of mass consumption and mass production as well as the Taylorist principles for work organization. The US economy, with its vast home market, developed this model to its extreme and, now, the very success it once had makes the institutional set-up difficult to change.

But, according to the MIT experts, it must change if the US economy shall not fall back in the international competitive race. New techno-economic conditions have made a cooperative mode to the best practice mode of management. This reflects several different interdependent trends. First, the volatility of demand, and its increasingly diversified character, reflecting a movement towards customer-designed products and systems, calls for a flexibility at the supply side, making it possible for firms swiftly to switch between products without too many extra costs. Second, the increasingly systemic character of technologies requires more cooperation between experts inside firms, and more cooperation between firms, in coordinated R&D projects. Also, a more rapid rate of technical change - as reflected in the shortening of product life cycles - requires a new, and more intimate, kind of cooperation between different departments inside the firm, as well as between user firms and suppliers.

Some Implications of the MIT-Study

First it is interesting to note that the main conclusion of the MIT study is that the most pressing need is not for technical innovation per se, but rather for institutional change and social innovation. The study does not give many and detailed prescriptions for how its more or less implicit programme for institutional design should be put into practice. (Actually, one of the most specified recommendations is a reform of the education system at MIT, including attempts to teach students to work in groups, and towards common goals.) But it is obvious that the MIT programme points in directions quite different from those of the neo-liberal programme for institutional design.

As a matter of fact, the MIT study attacks the basic assumptions behind the neo-liberal programme. Instead of pure competitive markets, it recommends a movement towards organized markets, and lasting relationships between users and producers. Instead of 'rational behaviour', aiming at individual gain, it wants to strengthen cooperation and collective responsibility. Instead of weakening the trade unions, the MIT report recommends a strengthening of the position of workers in order to establish the basis for some kind of corporatist cooperation.

Also, the concept of flexibility gets a broader and very different meaning in the MIT report than it has in the neo-liberal context. It reflects the capacity of organizations, individually or in cooperation, not only to adjust, but also to act wilfully, as a response to changes in an increasingly volatile environment. And, actually, the tendency among agents to react too rapidly on short-term changes in relative prices, and on monetary stimuli, is presented as a problem. What makes for flexibility in the neo-liberal analysis, pure market and ready responses on changes in relative prices, appears as institutionalized handicaps and rigidities in behaviour in the MIT analysis.

It is also interesting to note the differences in origin of the two programmes. The neo-liberal programme was developed mainly by theoretical macroeconomists with little interest in the details of production and technology. The MIT programme is based upon detailed empirical work engaging scholars from many different disciplines. On this background, it is tempting to regard the neo-liberal scheme mainly as an ideological offensive reflecting vested interests, which could find their rationalization in standard 'neoclassical' reactions among economists, with general equilibrium as their main theoretical reference point.

The Limits of the MIT Approach to Flexibility and Institutional Learning

We believe many of the conclusions reached in the MIT study regarding the direction of change of the new best practice and regarding the diagnosis of why the US manufacturing stagnates to be correct. We also believe that some of them may be transferred the European scene. But there are also some important flaws in the analysis.

First, its focus is almost exclusively upon manufacturing and little is said about the much bigger and growing service sector. In spite of its arguments for giving priority to the manufacturing sector, a closer look at the service sector might be needed. The service sector is often even more closely dependent on specific national, formal as well as informal, institutions, and the process of internationalization will result in quite contradictory developments in this sector, sometimes with a strong impact on economic growth and international competitiveness.

Second, the stylization of the Japanese system of production and innovation which is at the basis of the analysis of the US system tends to idealize the Japanese system. We get a simplified dual picture where the Japanese firms tend to do the things in the correct way and the American in the wrong way. More comparative work analysing countries closer in terms of culture and historical background might give a somewhat more complex but also a more realistic map of the problems and opportunities currently facing different national systems of innovation.

At present, such comparisons are developing in the context of the Nordic countries. In a recent preliminary study it was found that the institutional differences between national systems of innovation, as close in terms of geography, historical experience and culture, as Denmark and Sweden, are considerable. This preliminary study indicates that the way technology is developed differs; Sweden tends to base its innovative processes on systematic R&D while Danish firms tend to build much more upon practical skills, and upon interaction with users. The focus of innovative activities differs also; in Sweden the focus is upon process technology while it is more upon incremental product innovations in Denmark (Edquist and Lundvall, 1989).

Third, the MIT analysis is focused exclusively upon the industrial growth and competitiveness of the USA. The permanent problem of the impoverished countries in the third world, and the more and more serious threat of a global ecological disaster are not reflected at all in the programme for institutional design. An interesting and fundamental question is, for example, if a stronger element of cooperation inside national systems of innovation, aiming at promoting national economic strength, makes these systems better prepared to develop cooperative institutions at the global level. In the not to distant future, the institutional set-up at the national level must be designed so that it can also contribute to the solution of the fundamental global problems. The real test of the flexibility of the capitalist system will be its capacity to engage in institutional learning and social innovation, establishing global institutions, able to produce an acceptable degree of equality at the global level and viability in relation to the global ecological system.

Notes

1. Obviously, this is in sharp conflict with one of the main propositions of institutional economic theory - that pure markets are not a viable setting. As Polanyi (1957) has argued, a completely free market economy, with totally unregulated goods, labour, land, and money markets would tend to over-exploit and destroy the labour power and the environment and destabilize the money and credit system. Therefore the free market experiment was, according to Polanyi, only a brief period in history, and new institutions which stabilized the pure market institutions were quickly established.

2. At OECD parts of the organization have always been sceptical to the neo-liberal offensive. What seems to have happened in the last few years is that the whole organization has been forced to recognize the importance of 'active flexibility' and innovativeness. The Technology and Economic Policy Program (TEP) to be realized in 1989-90 involves all sections of OECD and at the first TEP seminar in Paris, June 1989, which was on the global productivity slow-down, institutional perspectives played quite an important role in the discussions.

3. Again it is relevant to quote Veblen discussing the development of economics from such a perspective:
   'Like other men the economist is an individual with but one intelligence. He is a creature of habits and propensities given through the antecedents, hereditary and cultural, of which he is an outcome; and the habits of thought formed in any other line of experience affect his thinking in any other. Methods of observation and of handling facts that are familiar through habitual use in general range of knowledge, gradually assert themselves in any special range of knowledge'. (Veblen, 1898)

4. These three forms of learning are discussed in Boulding (1985).

3. Flexibilization and Autonomization of World Money Markets: Obstacles for a New Long Expansion?

Kurt Hübner

Introduction

'Flexibilization' appears as the new magic word whenever the topic turns to the creation and description of ways out of the 'crisis of Fordism'. Many authors share the opinion that the developed capitalist countries have long since embarked upon the road to a 'regime of flexible accumulation'. The contours of a new, post-Fordist regime of accumulation, they say, are no longer waiting on the horizon, but are palpably near. 'The new regime', asserts Harvey (1987, p. 109) with regard to the US,

> which was set into motion during the deep recession of 1973-75 and consolidated through the equally violent Reagan recession of 1981-82 is distinguished by a surprising flexibility in relation to labour markets, work processes and commodity and consumption patterns ... At the same time, rapid shifts in branch as well as regional patterns of distribution have emerged - a process which was also supported by the creation of fully new financial systems and markets.

More exact analyses point out that indeed a range of new flexible structures have emerged, but not all forms of flexibilization themselves create a coherent accumulation regime. Within the context of overcoming the crisis, Boyer and Coriat (1987), for example, differentiate between flexible specialization and flexible automation. Flexible specialization alludes to the mass production of a number of products by using flexible manufacturing systems. These products have until now either been confined to production by the Fordist small batch production method, or have been manufactured as rigidly standardized products. According to Boyer and Coriat, this strategy of flexible specialization - which implies product differentiation and consumer market segmentation - ultimately represents only an adjustment to slackened growth rates and stagnating markets: without accompanying radical changes in consumption norms, this strategy will merely lead to a redistribution process which will benefit suppliers first to introduce flexible specialization production methods, i.e. producers who earn 'pioneer profits' due to initial cost reductions involved in this strategy. Flexible automation, by contrast, alludes not only to new production processes but to new products in the form of new consumption goods. The crux of this strategy lies not in the segmentation of existing markets, but in the creation of new markets. The argument holds that a resulting change in the 'demand function' could stimulate a new productivity-growth nexus which may provide the key to a new long phase of expansion.

In the following essay I would like to develop arguments which at the least problematize such concepts of flexibilization regarding their potential function in overcoming crisis. I will discuss the concept of flexibilization in a realm of the capitalist world economy, or, more specifically, the world monetary market. The choice of the level of discussion is not arbitrary. Within the framework of the regulation theory, to which many theorists actually refer, four criteria have been formulated which a new development model must contain if it is to count as being potentially capable of overcoming the 'crisis of Fordism'. They are: (a) a new form of work process; (b) a new macroeconomic model, i.e. a new accumulation regime; (c) a new series of institutionalized rules, i.e. a new mode of regulation and (d) a new 'international configuration' (Leborgne and Lipietz, 1988, p. 1). Until now, discussions of flexibilization have revolved exclusively around criteria (a)-(c) (see for example the contributions in *Labor and Society*, 1987). In light of the developed structure of the capitalist world economy and the high degree of integration of developed capitalist nations into the same, an analysis which focuses atttention on factor (d) seems much more than warranted. What follows should also make clear that a strong flexibilization-based argument for this level of analysis exists: the capitalist world economy - understood here as the realm in which the regulation of international economic relationships is economically reproduced and politically organized - has itself been the object of strong flexibilization tendencies since the early 1970s.

The Basic Argument

Flexibilization effects are no strangers to economic theory. If one generally understands flexibilization as the degree to which quantities and prices of individual economic actors are able to adjust to sectoral or aggregate economic quantity and price signals, then the neoclassical market model embodies a flexibilization concept of the purest form. The neoclassical market model and its genuine equilibrum characteristics - themselves a result of presupposed flexibilities - is indeed a theoretical fiction. This becomes apparent as soon as one replaces the premise of logical-continual time with that of intertemporal decision constellations, that is, decisions met along past, present and future. A dynamic model of price building, the so-called Cobweb model, credibly disproves the neoclassical model in this way by demonstrating how price changes within a production period can lead to quantity-price movements which result in cumulative disequilibria. Such processes became famous as 'Hanauer Pig Cycles'. Producers base their breeding decisions upon pork prices given at a specific point in time. Because of the long incubation period involved in pig breeding, the later selling price may vary considerably from the price given at the time production desicions were met. This means that at the time of finished production, quantity-price incongruencies have been created which, through inevitable adjustment reactions, become dynamically reproduced and generate disequilibria.

When dynamically approached then, a fully flexible ideal-typical market with unlimited price flexibility conceals high risks of instability. This Cobweb theorem can be in some sense applied to the relation between highly sensitive and flexible international money markets and the real sphere of accumulation. In international money markets, not especially long but - quite the contrary - extremely short incubation periods between 'production decisions' and 'executions' create instabilities. In the wake of the technological 'revolution' of electronic banking, transaction periods have dwindled drastically. Because of this prices in individual markets can change with lightning speed and so bring about extreme price deflections in both directions. This is the hour for margin dealings, securitization and also speculative operations. Money as capital which is dealt with in these markets exhibits no neutrality as some theories suggest. The price for money capital is an important variable within the calculus for money capital holders, i.e. if the interest rate is higher than the average and expected rate of profit then they will invest their money capital in the national and international money markets. Moreover, if the interest rate shows a high degree of fluctuations the investment decisions of the entrepreneurs will be irritated. The result will be a slackening of accumulation. The higher the degree of monetary flexibilization the higher the negative impacts for the 'real sphere'.

In the 'real world' (Davidson), such price swings are a part of everyday life. This is especially true for international market transactions where exchanges are made not only between commodities and money, but simultaneously between national and foreign money. That means that the circulation figure C - M - C gains a simultaneous correspondence in the figure M - M*. The scene of transactions are commodity and currency markets: the actors are buyers and sellers of both commodities (C) and currencies (M and M*). Only when the transformation from foreign money into national money has been completed does the individual producer know if the obtained price is sufficient to cover costs and grant high enough additional profits. Prices on the commodity markets and prices on the currency markets are determined by different factors. The exchange rate is determined by factors which not only go far beyond the concrete conditions of individual production and price determination, but actually incorporate the aggregate comparative national economic power of buyers and producers. For the development of the exchange rate then, the decisive factor is not the individual's productivity and cost structure, but the productivity and cost structure of the entire economy. Also, depending upon the degree to which interest-earning capital is internationalized, decisions and developments of individual actors outside of the real economic sphere may exert strong influence upon the exchange rate. In short, in the case of international commodity transactions, unpredicted exchange rate variations may lead to wide deviations between prices given at the moment production begins or is expanded, t1, and price at the moment of sale, t2. Dynamically considered, this implies the risk of cumulative instabilities in the world economy.

The capitalist world economy had historically been organized in such a way that specific regulations reduced potentials for instabilities. Here I am referring to various world currency systems or regimes, each of which reduced potentials for instabilities in their own specific manner. The gold standard and gold-currency standard achieved this through a relatively high degree of regulation and rule-making. The gold-currency standard - or better: the dollar standard - for example, was tied to a system of fixed exchange rates whereby national central banks were obliged to intervene in the currency market when the market exchange rate deviated above or below predetermined margins. In this way, national producers were fully protected against exchange rate risks - at least within foreseeable periods: redeemed currencies could be exchanged for national money at politically guaranteed rates.

Since the beginning of the 1970s, the dollar standard - meaning the structure of the world currency system as it was established at Bretton Woods after World War II - has been replaced by an extensive flexible currency regime. This flexible system renounced strict regulation and fixed parities and entrusted itself once again to the capacity for self-regulation. The transition from a world currency system to a world currency regime was accompanied by a wide range of structural innovations which may be interpreted as the substitution of political forms of regulation by market forms of regulation. I will further illustrate these developments and, in doing so, attempt to develop my central thesis. My thesis holds that the increase in international economic instabilities and, consequently, national economic instabilities is unquestionably tied to the transition from political to marketforms of regulations, the latter being embodied by an increase in flexible institutions. I do not, however, view the principle dysfunctionality of market regulation itself as being responsible for instabilities. Much more, I would like to argue that the transition to a flexible exchange rate regime produced a high need for

protection against previously politically mediated risks. This, in turn, created
an institutional environment that propelled the autonomization of monetary and
financial transactions. If this thesis can be convincingly developed, one must
logically conclude that - at least on an international level - a new long phase
of expansion requires a reduction in the degree of current flexibility.

The Rise and Demise of Bretton Woods

The success of the developed capitalist nations's postwar boom rested upon
the high degree to which economic relations within national as well as
international space were regulated. In retrospect, more than representing
simply an 'international configuration' of national Fordist reproduction
models, as Lipietz and Leborgne (1988) assume, the development of postwar
international economic relations was actually the building up of an 'Atlantic
Fordism': Only after an international economic space for commodity
circulation, and the norms and rules governing commodity and money
exchange had been established, could the dominant production conditions of
the Fordist 'forerunner' USA enforce themselves the central motor of
accumulation in the world economy. Mediated by competition between
capitals, the dominant US conditions of production enforced tendencies
towards the equalization of production processes, that is, the assimilation of
'national Fordism'. In light of this, the implementation of national 'Fordism'
could only be realized upon the basis of corresponding world economic
structures. It comes as no surprise, that at the close of the West European
reconstruction phase in the late 1950s, the growth rate of world trade had
already far exceeded the growth rate of world industrial production, a pattern
which was strengthened until well into the 1970s (Aglietta, 1979b, p. 70).
Without the explicit creation of a world economic space, at least the Western
European nations would have probably in no way been able to imitate the
Fordist model of accumulation: the masss production lines and economies of
scale-technologies inherent to the Fordist regime would have been neither
capable of generating productivity gains nor of creating distribution margins
responsible for the virtuous circle of the past, had they been confined to the
barriers posed by the relatively small European internal markets.

The reconstruction of the capitalist world economy after World War II was
a political project whose intended form was discussed and finally set down in
writing at the conference of Bretton Woods in 1944 (de Cecco, 1979). What
arose after the World War II was a regime of 'embedded liberalism' (Ruggie,
1982). In the centre of this regime stood the hegemonical power USA and the
international currency system of Bretton Woods which has its base in the
dollar. It was agreed upon that exchange rates remain fixed and national

currencies remain convertible: only in the case of a 'fundamental disequilibrium' in the balance of payments, and after international agreement had been reached, could national exchange rates be adjusted. The institution of the International Monetary Fund (IMF) was created for the purpose of financing short-term balance of payment deficits. If the need arose, the IMF was to provide necessary amounts of international liquidity. The dollar was able to establish its position as leading currency and was defined in a fixed parity to gold. The USA furthermore obliged itself to change dollars into gold. All other national currencies were therefore tied to the dollar which now functioned as the new world money.

Potential contradictions were imbedded in this system of regulation from the very start. In the early 1960s contradictions already became apparent which would later lead to the break-up of the Bretton Woods System in the early 1970s. The central problem proved to be the dollar's double function as national and world money. The only source of international liquidity in the capitalist world market was a permanent US balance of payments deficit. In face of continual US trade balance surpluses - themselves rooted in the comparative superiority of US conditions of production - this liquidity flow necessitated capital exports of considerably large amounts. The monetary equivalents of US direct investment and credits at first flowed back into the USA in the form of export earnings. This brought about an internal growth spurt. Under increasing pressure from US competition and fed by US capital exports, however, this cycle became more and more unstable. 'The successful financing of European reconstruction by the United States', summarizes Wachtel (1986, p. 61),

made their products competitive with ours and reduced dollar repatriation via American exports. No longer did Europe need to import as much from the United States. In fact, they could begin to sell us some of their products that were becoming preferable to American-produced goods. When the repatriation of foreign-held dollars through the United States' trade surpluses diminished, the United States had to underwrite the Bretton Woods system by the sale of its relative fixed gold stock.

In face of incongruencies between externally accumulated dollars and national gold reserves, the US government was neither willing nor capable of performing this task.

The dollars which did not flow back into the United States as either goods purchased abroad, direct foreign investment or actual dollar exchanges from gold, developed an independent economic life of their own in the so-called Eurodollar markets. Dollars traded in these markets no longer functioned only as a means of transaction or payment but were searching for valorization in the realm of world financial markets. Supported by US economic and bank policy, these markets have become increasingly important since the late 1960s. In comparison with national money and credit markets the Euromarkets have several advantages of which missing regulations and the absence of an official minimum reserve are the most prominent.

The volume of US dollars circulating outside the USA is momentous compared with the stock of monetary gold with the result that the speculative pressure against the dollar grows. As the USA were forced to admit to its first trade balance deficit in 1971, signalling that the phase of US productive superiority belonged to the past, it became clear that the days of the gold standard and fixed-rate system were numbered.The pillars supporting the Bretton Woods System had crumbled. Responsibility for the breakdown of Bretton Woods rested a shift in relations between official and private international liquidity, each of which functions according to different 'logics'. Official liquidity is subjected to politically institutionalized controls which functions according to criteria set by monetary and currency policy. Private liquidity, on the other hand, obeys the valorization calculus of its owner. The emergence of a transnational money market against the background of a crisis-inducing process of assimilation of conditions producing profit within developed capitalist countries, that is the successful enforcement of Atlantic Fordism, wrested the basis from the international system of regulation.

Paradoxically, one may summarize, it was the success of the international postwar order which led to its downfall: the security of stable international exchange relationships and monetary transactions propelled the accumulation and growth process as well as equalized conditions for the production of profit in developed capitalist countries, and so caused the institutional breakdown of Bretton Woods. The crisis of the international system of regulation and the crisis of the hegemonical power USA went hand in hand.

Flexibilization and the Construction of an International Credit Economy

The fixed-rate system and with it, the position of the dollar as leading currency were replaced by a regime of multi-currency standards with flexible exchange rates between regional currency blocks. Events leading up to this were the termination of the dollar-gold parity in 1971 and consequent floating of exchange rates in 1973. Japan, the USA, Canada and to a certain extent Great Britain allowed their currencies to float; all other currencies remained in some way fixed, either to another currency unit or to a currency basket, i.e. a synthetic clearing unit. Even in the case of the latter, fixed internal parities, as it the case with the European Currency System, stood in contrast to flexible external parities.

Globally considered, movements of real effective exchange rates between 1973 and the early 1980s were not especially large. Using the parities of

March 1973 as a basis, the dollar fluctuated during this period within a range of 12 per cent, the German Mark approximately 14 per cent, and the Japanese Yen within a considerably higher range of 30 per cent calculated on a quarterly basis (Cooper, 1987, p.17). Starting in the third quarter of 1980 the real exchange rate climbed to a height until 1985 and then again sank to the level of 1974 when the real exchange rate reached its deepest level after World War II. If we look at the changes of the nominal exchange rates we see that the short-term variability for the seven major currencies was about six times greater than during the last decade of adjustable par values. These exchange rate fluctuations reveal nothing, however, about the extreme daily fluctuations which accompanied the transition to a flex-rate regime. Daily fluctuations are those of most importance to economic actors. The dollar experienced veritable roller-coaster movements: between the second week of April and the second week of May 1986, the values of the DM, the Swiss Frank and Japanese Yen increased by 60 per cent in relation to the dollar (using exchange rates of the preceeding 15 months as a basis). In the second week of May 1986 the dollar revalued on an average of 8 per cent against these currencies, only to devalue once again by almost 13 per cent between the beginning of June and the end of August (BIS, 1987, p. 166). This tendency of rapid exchange rate movements is unbroken in the second half of the 1980s. These fluctuations generated both a growing need among economic actors for protection against risks as well as an explosion in speculative operations.

One direct consequence of the transition to a flex-rate regime then was the enormous increase in the volume of currency transactions on the international foreign exchange markets - a volume which multiplied several times within only a few years (Strange, 1985, p. 11). Meanwhile, more than 200 billion dollars are being exchanged daily on the foreign exchange markets, a sum which far exceeds the amount necessary to finance total international commodity exchanges and direct investments. The New York Federal Reserve estimates that daily transaction volumes on the international financial markets alone approach one trillion dollars.

Within the fix-rate system, a firm's financial department would trade in foreign markets in foreign exchange to protect itself from potential interest rate differentials between bond claims and obligations in varying currencies. Within the flex-rate regime it became necessary to establish safeguards against daily fluctuations. National Central Banks therefore passed on exchangerate risks of international transactions onto private actors. The emergence or, more appropriately, the massive expansion of secondary markets within which safety nets against these risks were established was a direct consequence of this risk privatization (Strange, 1985, p. 12).

The decisive consequence of the transition to a flex-rate regime was not, then, the scale of exchange rate fluctuations as above all the Keynesian school would argue (Herr, 1987). Much more, it was the emergence and explosive growth of a wide variety of financial transactions and operations which were directed either at safeguarding currency and interest rate risks, purely speculative in nature, or were operations directed at real valorization of capital. The establishment of the flex-rate regime decisively propagated the expansion of the world money market. It also speeded up the separation of the monetary sphere from the real economic sphere of the world market. The separation between these two spheres becomes especially obvious when one looks at the nature of transactions conducted in the Eurodollar market: transactions in Eurodollar markets increased by an annual average of 25 per cent during the 1970s. World trade, in contrast, grew by an annual average of only 4 per cent. Even when one includes the volume of direct investment in the calculation, one hardly changes the fact that the monetary and real economic sphere disjoined[1]. This separation expresses that the accumulation of money capital can proceed rather independently from the accumulation of real capital as Marx has shown in Volume III of *Capital*. Indeed, this separation is not absolute. Analytically it can be shown that there exists a maximum limit for this separation. Take a closed system and assume (a) accelerating rates of accumulation in the form of money capital which outrun those of real capital and don't serve for productive purposes and (b) assume further a strict separation between money capitalists as lenders and industrial capitalists as debtors. This system in operation tends to diminish the surplus value in that the relatively faster growing interest claims run out the profit claims. In the course of such a process the reproduction of the whole system comes to a halt. In the 1980s we have not reached this maximum limit but are faced with rising claims of interest payments against the surplus value. In this respect the separation between monetary and real accumulation seems to be an obstacle for efficient strategies of modernizations to improve the international competitiveness.

The crystallization of a multi-currency standard combined with a flex-rate system proved to be an economic milieu predestined for speculative currency deals. The Keynesian interpretations of this new constellation concentrate in general only at one moment of the new valorization structure (Tobin, 1984; Herr, 1986). According to this view, in the absence of a stable medium of international liquidity, the money holder is veritably forced into constantly shifting his/her portfolio, which of course increases world-wide economic instabilities. But the world money market is not merely a place where portfolios are optimized: since the late seventies, the money market itself has become a genuine realm for the valorization of capital. This indicates a drastic increase in liquidity preference of industrial capital as well as of money capital holders, releasing a massive switch from productive to financial assets. The main cause for this shift was the decline of the profit rate which inhibits rising uncertainty in the production sectors, and makes a higher flexibility necessary. Money and capital transactions no longer solely serve for investment purposes in the productive realm. The historical task of the credit system, Marx has spoken of, is no longer the anchor of the system. A host of new valorization possibilities for profit-seeking money capital have been created within international money markets during the past, which even financial experts have a hard time keeping track of (de Cecco, 1987). 'Financial engineering' has not only created new valorization possibilities in the form of financial innovations, but has speeded up the mobility of money capital between investment spheres. Deregulation of the world currency system and the reversion to flexible markets did not, as the orthodox economists predicted, lead to the creation of frictionlessness and equilibrium including money and capital markets. It is more so the case that the emergence of a network of various markets produced a situation within which price signals from one market are immediately recorded and intensified by another market. That is, the reflexibilization of international currency and credit relationships produced more new instabilities than it disposed of the old.

One should in no way confuse between the causes and effects, or between the sufficient and necessary prereguisities for such processes. The new currency and credit regime did indeed provide the institutional environment for these transactions. The actual driving force of the rapid expansion of the world money market, however, was delivered by real economic accumulation processes. The enormous increase in international liquidity embodies the converse side of a secular crisis of overaccumulation within developed capitalist countries. Since the 1960s, a trend of decreasing national profit rates has been diagnosed in developed capitalist countries. This trend towards sinking profit rates is a process mediated by the world market. Its source lies in the equalization of the material and value-type conditions of the production of profit which limited the possibilities for the production of extra-profit first in the USA and, soon after, in the economies of the Fordist latecomers. This combined with a simultaneously occuring cyclical drop in profit rates ultimately triggered the world economic crisis of 1974-75 (Altvater, Hoffmann and Semmler, 1979; Altvater, Hübner and Stanger, 1983).

Table 1

Gross Rates of Return[2]

Manufacturing

	1960	1973	1982	Trend
USA	18.9	18.5	10.6	-2.7
Japan	33.3	32.4	20.7	-4.9
Germany	26.2	16.5	11.7	-3.0
France	15.6	18.2	13.8	-2.7

(Source: Chan-Lee and Sutch, 1985, p. 41)

The accumulation crisis (which was induced by the synchronized fall in national profit rates), led to a build-up of a 'Plethora of Capital' (Marx). Declining marginal profit rates induced widespread pessimism regarding future profit expectations, meaning that this 'Plethora of Capital' found no productive sphere of valorization. Profit quotas also joined this trend until the beginning of the 1980s. Chan-Lee and Sutch observe, however, that profit quotas declined much less than profit rates (1985, p. 142). Private firms in every capitalist country succeeded in considerably raising their profit quotas after taxes by reducing the wage quota[3]. One indicator of this new accumulation behaviour of private enterprise is the reduced proportion of net investment to entrepreneurial profits (net to accumulation quota): in the Federal Republic of Germany, this quota dropped from 39.9 per cent in 1973 to 25.6 per cent in 1982; in the USA from 30.5 per cent to 11.5 per cent within the same period and in Great Britain from 31.5 per cent to 10.6 per cent (Altvater and Hübner, 1986, p. 34). The growth of the world money market since the 1970s can consequently be interpreted as a 'reflex' to the build-up of surplus liquidity in the real economic accumulation process which was not productively invested due to existing conditions of valorization.

There is indeed no simple circulatory relationship between world money markets and real economic accumulation. The valorization of money capital in the productive sphere of accumulation (measured as profit rates) competes against the valorization of money capital in the monetary sphere of accumulation (measured as interest rates). The cause of the accumulation crisis of the 1980s has thus been determined by the conflict between profit and interest earners over the distribution of surplus value. If the surplus liquidity of the real sector is to 'translate' into growth of the monetary sector, valorization conditions in the monetary sector must be comparatively advantageous for valorization-seeking money capital. The so-called Tobin q represents one measurement of comparative conditions of valorization. It is generally defined as the expected profit rate on supply prices of productive capital. The Tobin q can be empirically measured as the ratio of the market value of a firm to the replacement cost of its net reproducible capital. When q > 1, it's worth to invest productively. When q < 1, financial investments promise to make better economic sense. Empirical research conducted by the OECD (1983a, p. 10) demonstrates how between 1970 and 1980-84, the Tobin q in all developed countries fell below the value of one. The Federal Republic of Germany is the exception to the rule in that the 'relative earning rate' indeed fell, but always remained slightly above the value of one. In total, these data point to the fact that comparatively favourable valorization conditions were offered by financial sectors during this period.

When one uses this definition of the Tobin q as a basis, the monetary sphere can offer more favourable valorization opportunities as soon as the profit rates on productive capital and profit expectations of firms decrease. The combination of a fall in the rate of profit and continuous underutilization of productive capacity in the early eighties was most likely responsible for the worsening of relative earning rates. According to analyses of the OECD (1986c), however, since 1984 profit rates have risen once again. The world money market has nevertheless continued its unbroken pattern of growth. The BIS (Bank of International Settlements) reports that banks' foreign activities in 1986 grew by more than 650 billion US dollars. This is by far the greatest annual increase ever recorded (BIS, 1987, p. 97). Some authors (e.g. Hickel, 1987) will attribute this to unreasonably high profit demands of private enterprises which could not be satisfied. This does not strike me as a convincing argument. Enterprises demand high profits only because alternative money-capital investment possibilities exist which offer comparatively better and far less risky means of getting profit. A reason must be provided, which explains why valorization rates on money capital in the international money market are so high that productive investments are either better avoided, or reduced to the bare reproductive essentials.

The answer to this question may be found, once again, in the transition to a flex-rate regime. Since the 1970s a trend towards the polarization of national current accounts has been observed. Contrary to the expectations of flex-rate advocates, instead of reversing itself, this trend has actually strengthened. The consequences have been twofold. First, an extremely high demand for capital and for money as means of payment arose in the world economy. This led to the creation of an international debt economy. Both, the steep rise and the persistence of high interest rates have their base in the dynamic involved in this creation of a international debt economy.

Japan, the Federal Republic of Germany and Great Britain were able to realize surpluses in their current accounts;[4] the losers of the world economic transformation includes the countries of the Third World and, especially, the USA. In the period 1978-87 the first mentioned group accumulated a surplus of 350 billion US dollars, the second group a deficit 900 billion US dollars (IMF, 1987, p. 171). Above all else different national positions in the international economic competitiveness hierarchy explain this polarization process. This seems especially true for the US economy. Between 1982 and 1987 the US clearly lost its competitive position in relation to Japan, the FRG, and even a number of NICs. The US thus amassed a deficit of the trade balance of approximately 700 billion US dollars. The overvaluation of the dollar during the first phase of the Reagan administration explains only one part in the deficit. Various empirical studies attribute the deficit much more to the fact that many sectors of US industry simply fell out of the international restructuring competition (e.g. Kremp and Mistral, 1985). The group of Third World countries suffering under structural current account deficits on the other hand, owe their deficit to skyrocketing net interest payments on credits amassed since the early 1970s (Altvater 1987; Altvater and Hübner, 1987).

In each case a structural demand for capital imports emerged out of the need to remedy structural deficits in current accounts. This international demand for money capital could only be satisfied on the supply-side if valorization conditions on money capital in surplus countries levelled off to such a degree that investors chose to engage in such transactions. The creditization of structural current accounts deficits became a lucrative activity within the private banking system. The IMF had indeed transformed from a currency to a political credit institution, yet its financial resources were by far too meagre to set the needed volume of credit in motion. The new international debt economy was built by private credit flowing through the international banking system.

Favourable conditions of valorization for money capital, i.e. high (nominal and real) interest rates emerged first at the beginning of this decade. In the mid 1970s long-term real interest rates in the advanced capitalist countries were still extremely low. In some countries real interest rates were even negative in several years. During the first phase of the world economic crisis, starting in 1973, private enterprises' financial strategies were characterized by a real balance approach. They invested surplus liquidity in international finance and credit markets even when the valorization rates within these markets were low. The reason behind this behaviour was most probably the fall in national rates of profit. In the face of underutilized productive capacities and uncertainty concerning potential new areas of profitable productive investments, the common strategy was to abstain from new investments and instead modernize existing production lines. The result was that new investments sank while replacement investments rose. Surplus funds were built up in this phase - preferably in the form of near-money assets which are available when the need rose. An impression of high liquidity flows was thus created which motivated actors in financial markets to go on a deregulation and liberalization offensive: their goal was to create new valorization fields for this money capital.

The 'overliquidity' situation begans to decompose at the beginning of the 1980s when, next to the big debtors of the Third World, of the camp of real existing socialism and some Western European countries, the USA emerged as the largest capital importer on the markets. International capital flows could only be drawn into the USA through an further improvement of valorization rates on money capital. It was, however, also of utmost necessity to regain the trust of the international community in the US currency; the dollar's external value had hit rock bottom in 1979. For the Reagan administration the flex-rate regime revealed itself as a political resource conducive to achieving this goal:

> In an unregulated foreign exchange market the only effective weapon a country has to defend its currency is the interest rate offered to a currency dealer on its money. An interest rate higher than a competitor's encourages currency speculators to buy a nation's currency, thereby strengthening its value in the free play of unregulated markets (Wachtel, 1987, p. 30).

The US prime rate rose in the wake of the US interest rate offensive[5].

This strategy by no means minimized the polarization between surplus and deficit national accounts structures. On the contrary, it actually fostered the creation of an international debt economy which benefited a sector of supra-national money mandarins (Wachtel) who financed and consolidated this structure of polarization. The resulting negative effects on real economic accumulation processes are thus clear:

> Considerable high real earnings on short-term investments can be detrimental to production in that the acquisition of liquid financial assets in place of consumer expenditures or stock pile investments by private enterprises is promoted. In actuality these high real earnings on money holdings offer an explanation for the fact that... real income growth within the Group of 10 ... did not fully transfer into higher expenditures (BIS, 1987, p. 71).

The process of real accumulation is thus blocked by the monetary side of the valorization process. Interest claims on the surplus value fund structurally increased with the autonomization of world money markets. Enterprise in the productive sphere have adjusted to this new structure of valorization in that an ever-growing portion of earned profits flow into financial investments, and interest earnings constitute an ever-increasing portion of the cash flow. The consequences of the transformation of capital valorization structures are twofold: growth and accumulation rates in the real sphere keep below their potential while the expansion of the capitalist world economy is based on financial instabilities.

Final Remarks

It is incontestable that a wide discrepancy has developed between the need for regulation and the regulative capacities within the world money and financial markets. This scissor effect cannot be remedied merely by returning to the good old times of Bretton Woods. The transition from a fix-rate system to a flex-rate regime represents more than a simple substitution of political regulation by market forms of regulation. The flex-rate regime created the ground upon which ubiquitous market transactions could be enacted and, with them, new spheres of investment for money capital developed. This makes any pretence of return to the strictly regulative system of Bretton Woods impossible. When compared with the international monetary and credit structures of the late 1960s, the structure of world money markets in the 1980s are historically unprecedented.

Instabilities within the capitalist world economy and obstacles preventing a new long phase of expansion comparable to the long upswing of the 1950s and 1960s are not genuinely produced by the flexibilization of international currency and credit relationships itself. What the flex-rate regime did was to create the institutional prerequisites for the autonomization of world money markets from the real sphere of accumulation and so the build-up of a valorization circle of its own. This, in turn, brought the intercapitalist distribution struggle over the surplus value funds to its peak. In the 1980s, the distribution struggle between wage labour and capital has been eclipsed by the competition between profit earners and interest earners. Real economic accumulation is trapped by an interest squeeze which thus prevents the start of a new long phase of expansion.

There seems to be no question that these transformations reduced the sovereignty of national economic policy. From a political-economic point of view it seems to be a third best strategy if some theorists and also politicians consider the supremacy of money capital as reason to assign national economies and economic policy the position of an independent variable, whose duty it is to adjust optimally to the 'external' data represented by the world economy and its financial sphere. In this light Scharpf (1987), for example, recommends that suitable 'Keynesian Supply Side oriented' economic measures be implemented to raise national rates of profits to such high levels that the rate of relative earning clearly exceeds the amount one. That is, that once again productive investments be given priority over financial investments. In reality this means nothing less than using wages as a variable buffer against investors' interest expectations and against the tendencies of world financial markets: the higher the interest rate expectations are in relation to the surplus value funds, the more (real) wages must be cut. Such socio-economic flexibilization strategies pregnantly illustrate the defensive position actually taken by West German Socialdemocrats against the constraints of the world market in that they concentrate solely upon the problem how to compete in a most flexible way in a highly uncertain world economy. One can label such a strategy as concealing helplessness in analytical terms.

It seems evident that successful economic policies must be directed at reducing the claims of the new money mandarins and consequently expand the distributionary field between labour and capital. But what may be evident could only be realized when national obstacles are put aside. Due to the existing Prisoner's Dilemma the reduction of interest claims in a world of international money and capital mobility could only be achieved by coordinated action of the advanced capitalist countries. Maybe it is only wishful thinking that the risks of international financial instabilities are an incentive to act in this direction. Although this would only be a first step to regain regulative supremacy, it would be a very important one.

Notes

1. The OECD also has dealt with the enormous growth of eurocurrency banking (1983a, p. 12). The documented data show an annual average growth rate of eurocurrency banking of almost 30 per cent between 1961 and 1981; in contrast the volume of world trade expanded by approximately 15 per cent and the GNP of the OECD countries by 11 per cent. When one considers that world trade hardly expanded between the mid 1970s and the early 1980s, then these calculations offer sign of a (relative) separation between real and monetary accumulation.

2. 'The gross rate of return is defined as the ratio of the gross operating surplus (P) to the gross stock of fixed reproducible assets' (Chan-Lee and Sutch, 1985, p. 141).

3. The same OECD study shows with convincing plausibility that the trend of falling rates of profit was due first and foremost to a decline in capital productivity, i.e. to a rise in the capital coefficient (Chan-Lee and Sutch, 1985, p. 144).

4. Great Britain represents a 'special case' within this successful group because, first, the high earnings from the sales of North Sea oil makes the deficit in the trade balance less bad, and second, because net interest earnings on foreign British monetary investments

reached considerable sums due to the regained strength of London as one of the worldwide money market centres.

5. In theoretical terms it seems to be important that this offensive of the FED could only be successful due to the international high demand for new credits.

4. From the Fordist to the Post-Fordist State

Joachim Hirsch

Introduction

The crisis of Fordist capitalism which has been developing since the 1970s
has involved a restructuring of the accumulation regime and mode of
regulation. This is expressed not least in the changed structure and functioning
of the state. The capitalist state certainly has a number of basic general
features which persist throughout its history but its concrete configuration,
i.e. its inner structure and the mutual relation of its apparatuses, its activities
and class relations, will nonetheless change significantly with the transition to
a new capitalist formation. In turn this will also change the conditions, forms,
actors and institutional terrain of politics. Along with the Fordist accumulation
regime, the Fordist political form, i.e. the bureaucratic-corporative 'welfare
state', has also entered into crisis. As the old structures break down and the
associated political and social struggles continue the outlines of the
post-Fordist state are still indistinct, for the new accumulation and regulation
model is in no way fully developed and, indeed, is strongly contested; and,
at the same time, the crisis of Fordism and the decline of US hegemony has
led to a significant pluralization of regional and national development models.
Thus, whilst one could speak of an overarching type of 'Fordist' state despite
significant national differences, this is no longer possible in relation to the
latest trends. Indeed significant national and regional differences seem to be
a defining feature of the post-Fordist state (Lash and Bagguley, 1988). To
present these differences as well as the common features of the advanced
capitalist countries is not possible here. At most I can present in general terms
some of the often contradictory and counteracting dominant tendencies.

The Crisis of the Fordist State

It was the 'Keynesian welfare state' which marked the political structure of
the developed capitalist countries in the period of Fordism - to a varying
extent to be sure but nonetheless as the determining tendency. It was based
on an era which involved a high growth rate, the expansion of mass
consumption, an accelerated penetration of capitalist forms throughout society

(especially as regards the reproduction of labour power) and a vigorous expansion of wage labour (at the expense of agrarian and craft production as well as domestic services: hence the aptness of the phrase 'internal colonization' (Lutz, 1984)). The development of a society based on mass employment permitted the growth of overarching and encompassing trade union organizations, the achievement of general rules for labour contracts, and hence the standardization and normalization of labour relations. And it also permitted a strengthening of the ever more bureaucratic and statist social democratic-reformist workers' parties. The extensive penetration of the capital relation into society and the dissolution of traditional social milieus, family structures and forms of subsistence encouraged a gradual bureaucratization and statization of society. Thus, influenced by the expanding capitalist wage relation with its associated processes of social disintegration and individualization and under the pressure of reformist parties and unions, the welfare state (in the sense of an ever more encompassing system of bureaucratic care) developed. The reproduction of wage labour and the regulation of the labour process and wage relation became more and more the product of the interplay of state administration and large union and employers' organizations (Poulantzas, 1978, p. 161). As a result the class relations inside the state changed fundamentally. The development of reformist, mass-integrative 'people's' parties (*Volksparteien*) and the emergence of corporative political structures based on social partnership implied a 'passive' integration of the working class into the state. This had the dual effect of bureaucratically laying to rest the class struggle and also politicizing it in a new, etatist form. Thus the establishment of the Fordist state also implied the end of the workers' movement in its historic form.

The material basis of the Fordist 'class compromise' was state-sponsored full employment policy, the construction of the welfare state, mass consumption and state-reformist redistributive policies based on a high growth rate. Together these offered workers the prospect of a continuous improvement in their living conditions. Incomes policies based on social partnership and other corporative arrangements were charged with making compatible the material demands of workers who now enjoyed a certain political and social power with the reproduction requirements of the overall economic system, i.e. the valorization conditions of capital under the prevailing accumulation regime. Admittedly this was only possible in a very contradictory and conflictual fashion and led to an ever-stronger inflationary outcome. In any event, under this economic and institutional arrangement, it seemed possible to overcome the opposition between the interests of capital and wage-earners and to pursue income and social security measures which would benefit workers and also stimulate capitalist expansion. In this sense it seemed one could equate 'workers' interests' and the national interest (Buci-Glucksmann and Therborn, 1982, p. 118).

Thus Fordist capitalism developed into a standardized, normalized, and individualized, bureaucratically articulated mass society; it seemed that its conflicts had been transcended within the state apparatus. Its mode of regulation was 'monopolistic' in the broad sense that it linked a highly concentrated and organized capital with the expanded social and interventionist state as well as with the bureaucratized and centralized parties and union apparatuses into a complex, institutional nexus. The state apparatus became an ever more integral part of the social and economic reproduction process - not only involved in the material reproduction and training of labour power but also engaged in a growing range of infrastructural, industrial and technology policies.

The Fordist class compromise was based on a 'Keynesian' hegemonic project. This defined social progress in terms of unlimited economic growth; individualism characterized by labour discipline, standardization of conduct, and consumerism; emancipation through wage labour; statist social reform; bureaucratically realized egalitarianism; the limitless exploitability of natural resources; and a belief in the powers of science and technology. Social democratic parties and related reformist 'people's' parties became the decisive political supports of this class compromise (Buci-Glucksmann and Therborn, 1982). The accumulation regime and mode of regulation of the capitalist metropoles rested on a 'neo-colonial' relation to the periphery, which forced the latter into becoming an extremely exploited source of labour power and a supplier of cheap raw materials and simple semi-finished and finished goods. The dominating mode of regulation was strictly based on the nationstate in the sense that guaranteeing the state reformist organized class compromise and expansion of national capital under the umbrella of US hegemony was the unambiguous priority of the nation state. One consequence of this was that balance of payments deficits and international currency and financial crises became ever more severe.

Seen in historical perspective, then, Fordism involved a forceful shift within a developmental tendency which is fundamentally rooted in the capitalist production relation: namely, continuing monopolization and capitalization, market-conforming individualization and bureaucratization, generalization of wage labour (including new forms of segmentation and stratification such as female labour, the multinationalization of the labour force, an increase in office work, expansion of the new middle classes), the growing penetration of science into the production and reproduction process, and the predominance of instrumental rationality in social consciousness. It was in the framework of this pattern of societalization and class structure that there developed the special form of the Keynesian-Fordist state. Admittedly this was not a product of some objective logic but resulted from political and social struggles which had their roots in the crisis of pre-Fordist capitalism up to the end of the World War II. The establishment of Fordist political structures, 'social democratic' reformism, the welfare state, and centrally administered corporatism also secured an essential presupposition of the full realization and success of the Fordist accumulation regime and the national growth and development models which were based thereon.

The crisis which broke out in the 1970s also signified the end of the Keynesian-corporative welfare state and the emergence of a 'secular' crisis of capitalism with economic, political and ideological dimensions (Hirsch and Roth, 1986, p. 78). The economically decisive factor was the striking world market integration and associated internationalization of capital: this increasingly undermined the basis for an economic and social policy conducted within national boundaries. At the same time the room for manoeuvre provided by productivity and growth in the Fordist accumulation regime now proved too narrow to continue to support the state reformist class compromise with its distinctive institutionalized relations of force and interest dynamic. The capital valorization process thus collided with the institutions of the mode of regulation. As growth rates declined and world market integration expanded Keynesian full employment and redistributive policies could no longer be maintained. The welfare state with its inbuilt expansionary dynamic changed from a prop to a fetter on capitalist valorization: the corporative, social partnership compromise with its institutional forms (social contracts, 'concerted action') broke down. The effects of unlimited exploitation of nature and destruction of the environment became more and more problematic. The dangers of an apparently autonomous technical development expanded. There was also growing criticism of bureaucratic despotism and controls, the new forms of the gender division of labour and patriarchal domination introduced by Fordism, growing social isolation, and a concept of progress orientated to performance and consumption. The ideological crisis of the Fordist hegemonic project intensified the political crisis of the institutions supporting it; the regulation nexus based on *Volksparteien* and bureaucratic and statized unions lost not only its economic basis but also proved incapable of taking account of the new interests and value orientations generated by Fordism itself and of giving them political expression. Many kinds of new social movements began to question the traditional political pattern and weakened its supporting institutions - especially the (social democratic) people's parties. In turn the economic, political and ideological crisis of social democracy signified the end of the welfare state based on bureaucratic, corporatist, statist reformism.

Post-Fordist Society

The basis of the post-Fordist state seems to be a new accumulation regime which rests on a range of new technologies, such as those involved in information, communication, or biological and genetic engineering; on a radical uprooting of Fordist labour relations, the class structures, consumption norms, and societalization forms (Hirsch and Roth, 1986, p. 104; Lash and Urry, 1987). This does not mean that a 'post-industrial society' is emerging but that there is a new industrialization drive which is subjecting fields which previously were more dominated by craft production (e.g. machine and equipment construction), agricultural production, and, above all, the expanding sector of business services to a forced mechanization and rationalization process (Hack, 1987). Thus the emerging accumulation regime is not so much characterized by 'tertiarization' in the classic sense as it is by a hyperindustrialization, i.e. a renewed wave of industrial capitalization of production and reproduction. The social and class structure is changing under the impact of a further strong increase in white-collar jobs at the cost of traditional industrial employment and is also experiencing new stratification and differentiation processes. To name just a few typical tendencies: there are growing differences in qualifications; individualization and flexibilization of work relations; multinationalization of the labour force as well as an expansion in various forms of unprotected and peripheral employment to the disadvantage of the core workforce which was a major force in Fordism. Thus general wage negotiation agreements are losing their significance in the light of tendencies towards more flexibility and heterogeneity and instead we find a growing importance for plant-level and individual agreements. The uncoupling of growth and employment, which is linked to new possibilities for rationalization, creates a lasting, structural type of mass unemployment. Moreover, under the impact of these changed wage and work relations, the stable social blocs which once formed the basis of the Fordist mode of regulation are now crumbling. The development of Fordist capitalism was marked by the dominance of regulation at the level of the nation state which operated under the hegemony of the USA. Nonetheless there was gradual improvement in transport and communication conditions and a steady global coordination and internationalization of production. This internationalization of capital as well the dispersion and decentralization of production and circulation processes made possible by new technologies significantly reduced capital's spatial dependence and enabled it to exploit ever more flexibly various political social locational advantages (worldwide sourcing). The intensification of world competition associated with the crisis of Fordism and the decline of US hegemony reacted back on nation states in two ways: they suffered from a narrowing of their freedom to pursue independent economic and social policies, i.e. materially to underwrite class compromises, and, in addition, the competition to attract and keep investment intensified as capital became ever more mobile.

This increases the pressures for economic and social structural adaptation and also threatens to break up the coherence between national accumulation and regulation (Lipietz, 1988, p. 28). In turn this has strengthened the tendency to use coercive means to implement restructuring measures which conform to the changing demands of valorization and are orientated to both nature and labour. The scope for effective regulation on the national state level is also shrinking by virtue of internal spatial restructuring and the uneven regional development which accompanies this (Esser and Hirsch, 1987). This is characterized by the attempts of regional and local political forces to advance their own 'locational policy' strategies directly orientated to the worldmarket. In West Germany, for example, this is happening through an outbreak of 'partial states' with their own models of regulation and development (e.g. *'Späth-kapitalismus'*) and/or the development of so-called 'world cities' which are also directly orientated to the world market. Consequently the social and economic homogeneity and coherence of society viewed in spatial terms declines and ever sharper regional disparities emerge (prosperous vs declining regions, 'sun-belt' vs 'frost-belt', 'north-south divides', etc.). This tendential disintegration of the historic bloc formed at the level of the nation state by the accumulation and regulation nexus increases the level of political and social conflict on both the national and international planes. In this way it undermines the regulative capacity of the inherited political and social institutions and stimulates openly forcible forms of exercising domination and pursuing social conflicts.

Overall the post-Fordist social structure seems to involve the development of cross-cutting cleavages and antagonisms relative to class relations in forms and to a degree not previously seen. The material situation of classes are overlain with socially threatening conditions which arise from new technological developments. These certainly have their roots in the capitalist reproduction and valorization process but also have aspects unrelated to class (Beck, 1986, p. 46). Decisive sectors of capital are becoming global and firms operating on a world scale enter into differing connections within the newly multipolar structure of metropolitan capital. The flexibilization of work organization, the dismantling of collective bargaining and welfare state measures of social security and social protection, unemployment and growing income differentials are reinforcing a shift towards individualization (Beck, 1986). In turn this is partially breaking the linkages between normalization and standardization characteristic of Fordism and it is encouraging a 'pluralization of lifestyles' which is based on consumerism and relativizes social structural contrasts. In everyday consciousness individual 'performance', achievement capacities on the market, and the 'fate and fortune' which these shape are becoming more decisive than social and economic class and stratum membership.

The Post-Fordist State

This is connected to a politics which is not only motivated by labour market and technology policy considerations (such as job creation or the promotion of risk-taking innovators) but is also concerned to further the newly independent and small businessmen. It is also concerned to create new strata who will support the process of post-Fordist modernization (Jessop, this volume). Regarding the social differentiation and heterogenization processes there are also strong tendencies to a 'refeudalization' at the plant level. These tendencies are rooted in the technologically conditioned creation of highly qualified cores of workers with strong bonds to the enterprise - both among white-collar employees and skilled workers. This core is stabilized through a selective, supportive personnel policy and is set off against the multiply segmented marginal sectors (Baethge and Overbeck, 1985; Hack and Hack; 1986). There is certainly much evidence to suggest that the preconditions for a centralized, corporative form of institutionalized class compromise and the Fordist form of monopolistic regulation are disappearing. This is occurring not only because of the narrowing scope for national regulation as the valorization conditions of capital change but also due to changes in the social and class structure. Thus the economic and social conditions are missing for a Fordist 'Deal' which embraces the big social blocks. This means that finding a new social compromise relation is now on the agenda: the only question is by whom, with whom, and against whom.

In the wake of the crisis of the Fordist state the neo-liberal conception is dominant in all capitalist metropoles. Programmatically it aims to roll back state intervention, cut bureaucracy, deregulate and emancipate market forces. In practice it is more a question of fundamentally reorganizing the fields of state activity as well as class relations. This does not so much involve 'less state' as a new form of state. In the context of a national locational policy orientated to the world market, the industrial, technological and infrastructural involvement of the state undergoes further increase and state monopolistic, administrative-industrial complexes become more dense. At the same time state strategy is orientated to revitalizing the market by promoting small business, reforming environmental protection measures so that they are more in line with market needs, and, above all, by ever more extensive liberation of wage and working conditions from the limitations entailed in past legislation and collective bargaining. The dismantling of the corporatist-bureaucratic regulation of the work relation by means of market-conforming 'flexibilization' is accompanied by a restructuring of the welfare state which is pushing towards greater privatization of the risks borne by the wage earner and which is adapting the bureaucratic system to the new pressures for flexibility and mobility. This is occurring through reinforced stratification and segmentation of the reserve army of labour, through rotation of the reserve army through work creating and vocational retraining measures, through promoting part-time work, creating or encouraging spurious forms of self-employment (such as the 'lump' in the building trades) and short-time working arrangements which fall outside the rules of the social security system (Jessop, 1986; Jessop, this volume).

Thus the transition from Fordism to post-Fordism involves an extra ordinarily contradictory process of autonomization of the state. Its dependence on the development of the world market, international economic regulatory institutions (e.g. in the framework of the European Community) as well as the deepening of state monopoly complexes in the field of new technologies goes hand in hand with an exclusion of previously institutionalized interest relations, especially those involving the working class. The pressure deriving from the world market to reorder the wage relation and working conditions, to step up the exploitation of nature, and to dismantle social security and the pressure to push ahead with technology development which is dictated by the international competition - these tend to raise the conflict potential between the state and large parts of the population. At the same time the disciplining and normalizing effect of the Fordist work and consumption model operates less widely. Also in decline are the mass integrative capacity and the control effects once enjoyed by the big parties and interest organizations which influenced how interests came to be perceived and represented affected. This is giving a new push and changing the significance of developments towards a repressively controlling 'security state' (Hirsch, 1986; Poulantzas, 1980). This is characterized by the ever stronger re-equipping of the police against 'internal disorder, preventive interventions into various social and political milieus, an ever wider system of judicial and secret security 'struggle against terrorism'. Linked to this is the expansion of the available legal sanctions (cf. the successive versions of the 'security laws' in Germany since the end of the 1960s) and the perfecting of highly developed supervision and control systems based on information technology.

Overall the autonomization of the administrative state is connected to its uncoupling from significant social interests and its subordination to the alleged facts of life entailed in valorization conditioned by the world market. It is accompanied by a narrowing of the scope for action enjoyed by the nation state and by growing regional inequalities (Esser and Hirsch, 1987). The state which is emerging in the transition from Fordism to post-Fordism thus seems much stronger, more repressive, and controlling. But it is standing at the same time on feet of clay.

The Transformation of Parties and Interest Associations

The transformation of class relations institutionalized in and through the state is particularly clear in the field of interest organizations and parties. Trade unions are being weakened not only through mass unemployment but also, and more seriously, through the tertiarization, flexibilization, and heterogenization processes at work in the labour relation, the tendencies towards plant-level unions, and the divisions opened up thereby within the working class. They are increasingly losing their claim to represent the working class as a whole and are politically torn by significant internal conflicts over the changed accumulation regime. A similar development is evident in farmers' organizations, which are confronted by massive internal divisions among their clientele owing to the rapid industrialization and restructuring of the agricultural economy. This process can also be seen at work in employers' and commercial organizations under the impact of the steady internationalization and monopolization of capital.

Parties are also affected. This is especially true of the mass integrative type of *Volkspartei*, which had been able to compensate under the conditions of Fordism for its reduced ties to class and and other social milieus by stepping up its bureaucratization, statization, tactical social state redistributive policies, and corporative interest arrangements. This now sees itself under pressure as its scope for redistributive policy declines, it is affected by economic and social restructuring pressures, and as society becomes more individualized and heterogeneous. In short, it faces real problems of survival. The stable and corporatively organized social groups on whose support it had relied are decomposing, party loyalties are growing weaker and more volatile, membership figures are falling as does their share of the vote. The monopolistic system of the Fordist Volks-partei is eroding and it is ever more difficult to bind together the diverging social and economic interests and 'life styles' through party political measures. The party system is becoming more pluralistic and 'new' social movements ranged alongside and against the parties are growing in significance. The parties are reacting to the break-up of their social basis with stronger bureaucratization, centralization and statization (evident in the rapid expansion of state finance for parties) and a displacement of their politics from material interest integration towards more selective politics directed towards diverging promotional groups, towards ever stronger symbolic, discursive strategies relying on mass media techniques (Häusler and Hirsch, 1987). This is leading in turn to an autonomization of party political personnel and a strengthening of careerism and corruption.

The crisis of the parties should not be seen merely in terms of their weakening but should be understood as an expression of their changing position within the institutionalized system of regulation (Poulantzas, 1980). On the one hand, they are no longer so significant in mediating between the capitalist 'power bloc' and the bureaucratically homogenized and institutionally highly organized social field occupied by the 'popular masses'. And, on the other hand, they are acquiring new roles. In particular they are becoming bureaucratic and etatized 'communication nodal points' which deploy various discursive strategies to articulate pluralized 'life styles', interest orientations, and milieus. In pursuing these strategies they seek to make these different forces amenable to the restructuring imperatives imposed by the world market; and to make them accessible to a politics based on tactical vote maximizing ('culturalization' and 'mediatization' of politics). The party system operates less and less to mediate reciprocally between administrative decisions taken under the pressure of economic system constraints and the interests of those affected by such measures (Poulantzas, 1980). Instead its role is to uncouple politics and material interests and administer the resulting system.

Conflicts over the attitudes and 'values' which should guide society are growing once again following the collapse of the Fordist hegemonic project. This is shifting the character of parties from 'mass integrative' to explicitly 'ideological' parties. This involves the risk that fundamental material interests, such as secure jobs, acceptable living conditions, or a functioning system of health care, will no longer be major themes in party political discourse. However, since they are not easily talked out of existence, they will find political expression in other ways. This could well occur outside the established parties.

How the Post-Fordist State
Institutionalizes Class Relations

Regarding the form of institutionalizing class relations a dual shift seems to be occurring in the post-Fordist state. There is a steady decomposition of the Fordist pattern of integrating encompassing and corporatively structured material interests into the political apparatus. And this is accompanied by a growing heterogenization, individualization and privatization of interests. These latter processes are not simply rooted in social and economic changes but are also being actively created and reproduced in and through political activities. If the Fordist state represented a form of centralized institutionalization of the capitalist class relation, then the post-Fordist state operates by reinforcing its social and economic disorganization through political and ideological means.

One cannot yet speak - even on a national level - of a fully developed post-Fordist capitalism. Indeed the long duration of the crisis is precisely due to the fact that the conflictual tendencies towards economic, social and political restructuring have not yet crystallized into a new social formation which could facilitate a long-term renewal of capitalist expansion on the basis of a coherent articulation between an accumulation regime and a corresponding mode of regulation. Nonetheless one can discern possible basic features of a mode of regulation which could give some structure and form to the post-Fordist accumulation regime based on new technologies and working relations.

Among these basic features is the development of new, decentralized corporative structures. These would be socially more selective in so far as they involve tight links between state and capital but fail to integrate unions at all or do so only on condition that interest representation is restricted to privileged groups of workers. Social heterogenization, individualization, and pluralization make it possible to replace the corporatively anchored Fordist 'class deal' with a kind of 'gentrification deal'. This would be more selective and tougher than before and would include only privileged parts of the wage earning class and the newly independent ('yuppies' and the 'boutique bourgeoisie'). It could also have its institutional base in the restructured post-Fordist party system. The party system, once deprived to a significant extent of its social anchorage and links to traditional milieus, can become a thoroughly flexible mediating factor for fluctuating, situationally specific coalitions. Given the post-Fordist shift towards 'individualization' (Beck, 1986) and the pluralization of lifestyles which this entails, such a role becomes quite probable.

The political and social exclusion processes which have this institutional structure both as their precondition and their consequence produce their own forms of 'regulation of marginality'. In addition to immediate state repression and supervision, which are directed towards an increasingly obscure and incalculable field of deviant individuals, 'scenes' and 'marginal groups', there are new forms of administratively and politically mediated institutionalization of oppositional movements and milieus. This can occur in and through the party form - as in the case of the West German 'Greens', who have effected a selective re-integration of individuals and interests which were excluded from the Fordist system of monopolistic regulation. Another form is the control-intensive administrative support of social self-help projects and/or small alternative businesses. Thus the post-Fordist mode of regulation is proving much more particularistic, decentralized and complex than the Fordist mode. It involves a changed form of state penetration of the social order. Compared with Fordism this is less based on centralized bureaucratic processes and instead reorganizes the relation between administration and market, state and society. Thus, given that 'civil society' has undergone changes in its institutional forms, we are also witnessing a reordering of the relationship between 'state' and 'civil society'.

Whatever concrete form the post-Fordist mode of regulation will assume, it will be characterized by a structural lability. This results from a heightened inner-societal conflict potential, hegemonial instabilities on the world market, and the increased dependence of national politics on global economic processes. The scope for building social compromises on a national state level will therefore be significantly restricted. The absence of an international economic regulation due to the decline of US hegemony and the tripolarization of metropolitan capitalism (USA, Japan, Europe) as well as the sharpening of international competition on the world market will probably last for some time. The resulting problems will be made more acute still by the economic and social crisis in the Third World, the frontyard and backyard of the developed metropoles. Hence a reasonably consistent and global post-Fordist hegemonic project, which could lend the new accumulation regime and mode of regulation coherence and form, is scarcely in sight. As regards the viability of national strategies, such as those expressed in 'Reagonomics' in the USA, Thatcherism in Britain, or the conservatively inclined liberalism on the Continent of Europe, this too has been cast into doubt.

The marked growth of authoritarian-populist currents in almost all the capitalist metropoles results from the economic, political and ideological crisis of Fordism and the restructing processes which this has prompted. This is also proving to be a major factor of lability in the transition to post-Fordism. The origins of this development do not just lie in the intrusive processes of marginalization and division which are rapidly increasing the number of victims of modernization. Just as important are the restricted scope for national politics and above all the bureaucratization and social uncoupling of parties and interest organizations. In particular the traditional 'Volksparteien' are rapidly losing their integrative force in relation to significant parts of their erstwhile traditional committed voters. This is reinforced by the nationalist and chauvinist rhetoric which has increased remarkably after the neo-conservative *'Wende'* (turn) in West Germany. The reactivation of nationalist syndromes can be seen to a certain extent as the other side of the trend towards internationalization and the closely related weakening of nation states. It also has a more important material base in the sharpened competition over where capital will locate. This is articulated under the slogan that everyone, even wage-earners, depend first and last on the capitalist investment in 'their' locality and must, therefore, in the face of growing international competition, conduct themselves aggressively towards those 'outside', whilst being ready to make concessions at home. As a result, however, classes become, if not submerged by national and ethnic oppositions, at least visibly relativized as just one interest constellation among others.

Given the transformation of parties into tactical vote maximizing machines, the institutionalization of right-wing radicalism and authoritarian populism in the party form - which has occurred in West Germany in the guise of the 'Republicans' - acquires its own dynamic. This is rooted in the reaction of the 'Volksparteien' to the radical right when they find themselves confronted with a significant loss of votes. Since they lack a more encompassing social-political project and are primarily orientated in a discursive-tactical manner to the demands of particular 'attitudinal groups', such parties openly or covertly reproduce the arguments of those whom they should be politically contesting. This could seriously disrupt the dominant cartel of parties committed to capitalist modernization parties (to which the Greens meanwhile also belong up to a point) and therefore orientated to rapid technical development, integration into the world market, and economic-political liberalism. This would occur not so much through the threat of a more powerful right-wing competitor party but through their own adaptation to the emergence of the radical right. This is especially clear in the West German case. For here the previously dominant strategy of economic and political integration into the West has been put at risk by the collapse of Soviet empire and the dramatic changes this has occasioned in East Europe (above all, of course, in East Germany) as well as the tendencies towards pluralization on the world market and the decline of US hegemony. The transition to post-Fordism in West Germany would also be characterized by much greater socio-economic ruptures than we have seen before.

Future Prospects for the Post-Fordist Regime

The crude development of reactionary-nationalist and authoritarian populist patterns of domination nonetheless stands opposed to another important but perhaps more regressive trend. For we are also witnessing an internationalization of capital (significant parts of which long ago jumped the national 'ship') and mounting pressure to create an overarching economic space which would overlay the inherited national state system. Nor should we forget the enduring cross-national mobility of labour power which is still essential for capital. Thus there is something to be said for the argument that a post-Fordist hegemonic project cannot simply replace the etatist-bureaucratic form of dealing with class antagonisms by a chauvinist or authoritarian populist strategy of reactionary politicization. More and more the dominant trends appear to assume the form of a 'depoliticization' of the social. This is expressed in privatized possessive individualism, repressive individualization, intense status competition as one aspect of the pluralization of lifestyles, and the explosion of splintered corporative interests. A little bit of right-wing radicalism is not out of place here so long as it does not become a dominant 'movement'. Only the highly differentiated and pervasive complex of political social control and supervision apparatuses remain as an important guarantee that political mobilization processes will be blocked - including, up to a point, the mobilization of the right. A renewed drive in the direction of capitalist penetration of society, commercialization of social relations (tertiarization), and the divergence of lifestyles and consumption norms is certainly creating the conditions for this depoliticization of the social. So too is the expansion and restructuring of the culture industry on the basis of new information and communication technologies. This is especially likely if the trend towards a 'repoliticization of the social' (Buci-Glucksmann, 1982b, p. 19) which occurred as the new social movements resisted the corporative-bureaucratic institutionalization of class conflict can be successfuly absorbed into a new mode of regulation and thereby gets to be defused politically. Were this to happen, the claim, advanced by the extra-institutional protest movements generated by the crisis of Fordism, that 'the private is political' would then have changed into its opposite. For, given the extensive transformation of the political system, the dynamic of these protest movements would itself ensure their depoliticization. All that would remain is a 'culturalist' veneer for an 'economic' state, largely deprived of its social dimensions, obscured by an individualism whose implausibility is self-evident in the light of continuing monopolization and the concentration of power. This culminates in the decline of the Fordist values of equality, bureaucratic security, and collective emancipation and their replacement with an emphasis on individual capacities for self-realization, natural inequality and performance on the market. If the post-Fordist mode of regulation is to replace the institutional class compromise through a struggle of each against all which cross-cuts classes, then this requires above all the development of a strong state. Since the foundations of the strong state are becoming ever more problematic on the national level, however, this means that a potential for social coercion is being released which is far removed from the customary Fordist forms of normalization and integration.

5. The Welfare State in the Transition from Fordism to Post-Fordism

Bob Jessop

It is a commonplace that the welfare state is in crisis. If this involves a crisis in the welfare state, piecemeal reforms and/or more radical restructuring could restore its role in societal reproduction without changing its basic forms of organization and intervention. If there is a crisis of the welfare state, however, a new system of social reproduction would be necessary. This paper considers how current changes in capitalism affect possible resolutions of the welfare state crisis. This does not mean that the welfare state is somehow determined in the 'last instance' by the dynamic of the capitalist economy. For, although this dynamic is certainly a crucial determinant, others, such as the changing nature of the modern state, also matter. Thus I will consider how the circuit of capital and the modern state together shape the forms of struggle among different class and non-class forces and also constitute terrains favouring some strategies over others in the struggle among these forces.

The Forms and Functions of Welfare States

The welfare state is a peculiarly capitalist phenomenon concerned with both individual and social reproduction. The crucial feature of the capital relation in this regard is the commodification of labour-power: for social reproduction is primarily mediated through and/or orientated to the wage-relation. The latter requires workers to exchange their labour-power for a wage and use this to buy the means to reproduce their labour-power. It also provides the starting point for welfare policy and welfare law. For welfare systems in capitalist societies usually assume that able-bodied adults can and must support themselves (typically through employment or self-employment) and/or will be supported, along with any children or other dependants, by other members of their family or household (cf. Zacher, 1985). None the less the capital relation has at least two features which militate against a harmonious, market-mediated solution to problems of social reproduction. Firstly, employees and their families are free to spend their wages without regard to the needs of capital and will often face contingencies which make it impossible to do so even if they were so inclined; and, secondly, competition stops individual capitals from undertaking activities necessary for social reproduction which do not

82

also generate private profit and it may also lead them into activities which actually undermine the general conditions for social reproduction. That neither employees nor individual capitals can solve these dilemmas unaided does not mean that the state can solve them - let alone that only the state can solve them. Nonetheless, although these dilemmas are handled on various economic levels above the firm and on various non-economic sites, the state has not only been a major addressee of demands in these areas but has also gained a major role in managing these dilemmas through its labour market and social policies.

The Nature of the Welfare State

A welfare state is a state in which organised power is deliberately used (through politics and administration) in an effort to modify the play of market forces in at least three directions - first, by guaranteeing individuals and families a minimum income irrespective of the market value of their property; second, by narrowing the extent of insecurity by enabling individuals and families to meet certain social contingencies (for example, sickness, old age and unemployment) which lead otherwise to individual and family crises; and third by ensuring that all citizens without distinction of status or class are offered the best standards available in relation to a certain agreed range of social services (Briggs, 1961, p. 228)[1].

This definition highlights three key problem areas in the welfare state but fails to note a fourth, equally crucial, aspect. Firstly, the relationship between market forces and welfare policies involves tensions, dilemmas and contradictions. Thus the balance between the market and the state must be seen as problematic, conflictual and unstable. Secondly, whilst market forces provide one axis of the welfare state and its development, another axis is set by the family as the core unit of social reproduction. Changes in the family form and its stability must also be included when explaining the changing forms of social reproduction. Thirdly, although some modern welfare states are indeed committed to the 'best standards available', defining these standards always involves a 'historical and moral dimension'. Moreover this commitment has not always existed nor is it found in all modern states. It is largely associated with the full development of welfare states in the Fordist epoch and its survival in a post-Fordist age must be questioned. Finally, in focusing on the types of social benefit which are provided through the welfare state, Briggs neglects the various forms in and through which these benefits are supplied. Yet, not only are the forms of provision closely related to the political conjunctures in which the welfare state developed, they also have a continuing impact on its functions in social reproduction and its role in shaping the balance of political forces.

Forms of Welfare State

Welfare provision can take different forms[2]. The typology developed by
Esping-Andersen (1986) is particularly useful in analysing these as it considers
not only structural features of the welfare state but also their genesis in, and
subsequent implications for, different balances of class forces. He
distinguishes: (a) the social democratic model based on universal welfare
rights attached to social citizenship, finance from general taxation rather than
an actuarially-based insurance system, and commitments to wide-ranging
egalitarian redistribution and high standards of public provision; (b) the
conservative model in which differential welfare rights are linked to
occupation and status, welfare benefits are financed on an actuarial basis and
linked to corporatist organizations, and social welfare has no egalitarian aims
even if it can sometimes involve extensive state provision; and (c) the liberal
model in which limited welfare rights and/or means-tested benefits are
provided for individuals, finance is based on individualistic actuarial insurance
or, when means-tested, on general taxation, and there is a basic commitment
to private, market-mediated provision for social reproduction with only social
security providing only a minimal safety net and involving only limited state
expenditure. The social democratic model is associated with a firm,
politically-concerted, and institutionally-supported policy commitment to full
employment requiring high levels of power mobilization by the organized
working class and its allies among the farming and/or new middle classes.
Liberal welfare states, in contrast, despite any formal policy commitment to
secure full employment, lack the long-term political base and/or adequate
institutional mechanisms to realize this goal and also prioritize other economic
and political objectives. Welfare states with a conservative historical tradition
cannot be firmly located as a group in terms of full employment
commitments. Much here depends on the nature of the barriers to left-wing
political mobilization and on the strength of social Christian mass parties with
economic and social welfare policies which challenge liberal market principles
(Esping-Andersen, 1986, pp. 226-34, 243-44).

The balance of class forces has a continuing relevance. Historically, the
conservative model is pre-eminent in nations where the church played a
powerful role in social reform and in nations where absolutism was strong and
slow to give way. Thus it is particularly evident in nations in which the
bourgeois revolution was weak, incomplete, or absent, such as Austria,
Germany, France, Italy, Japan and Belgium. Conversely liberal social-policy
regimes are associated with nations where the bourgeois impulse was
especially powerful. In addition to Britain we can cite such 'New World'
countries as the USA, Canada and Australia. Finally the social democratic

model is pre-eminent in countries where the working-class movement has been relatively unified and strongly mobilized for a long time, has formed durable alliances with other classes, and confronted a weak and/or divided bourgeoisie. Notable examples of this model are Sweden and Norway (Esping-Andersen, 1986; Flora, 1985). Moreover, once established, social policy regimes acquire their own institutional momentum: they establish the framework for subsequent social policy developments, transform the balance of forces, and engender vested interests among policy-taking as well as policy-making groups.

A second typology is equally helpful. Mishra has distinguished 'integrated' from 'differentiated' welfare states in terms of how the economic and social policy sides of state intervention are articulated. In the former type of welfare state, full employment and welfare policies are integrated by coordinating supply- and demand-side management, capitalist investment and labour supply, economic management and social policy. Mishra adds that this is also associated with a productivist justification for collective consumption in terms of human capital and is typically accompanied by centralized bargaining and trade-offs among organized social partners. He contrasts this pattern with the differentiated welfare state in which economic and social policy are separated. Full employment policy is largely pursued through macroeconomic demand management and public welfare policy tends to take economic developments as a given to which it must react or adapt. Welfare policy is also associated with its own policy communities in a context of interest group pluralism orientated to specific social rights, services and provisions (Mishra, 1985). These typologies overlap to some extent. Thus the liberal welfare state is typically a differentiated welfare state. But the integrated welfare state is not always social democratic. For, although the latter model does typically coordinate its economic and social policies in the interests of full employment, similar tendencies also exist in societies with historical roots in the conservative welfarism. Thus, whilst Mishra cites Austria as an archetypal integrated welfare state, Esping-Andersen treats it as conservative. Specific institutional structures and changes in the balance of political forces have clearly had a major role in determining current economic and social policy orientations in societies with a conservative welfare tradition. For they can be pulled towards a social democratic, integrated welfare state or a liberal, differentiated welfare state. In both cases this occurred in a context where global Fordism shaped developments in postwar welfare states and the current transition to post-Fordism will exert quite different influences. Indeed post-Fordism seems to point towards an integrated liberal welfare state. This would still coordinate flexible supply-side policies and social security policy but would do so in the interests of capital rather than labour. It would also need a balance of class forces quite different from that supporting the integrated social democratic welfare state.

The Political Context

The nature and limits of the welfare state must also be related to the political system in capitalist societies. Welfare states operate in a nation-state system and are a major site for struggles over national-popular hegemony. In general welfare policies are not directly concerned with how capitalist production is organized but with the social preconditions and consequences of such production. They are also typically mediated through law and money. This is particularly clear in the earliest welfare policies in the late nineteenth century: these were concerned with social insurance for industrial accidents, sickness, old age and, later, unemployment and typically involved the formal, rational-legal bureaucratic administration of cash payments. The subsequent development of the welfare state has often involved a growing discretionary element in social law and the provision of services which are difficult to control according to formal principles of financial accounting. The problems this involves for the welfare state are considered in more detail below. But it should be noted that the great majority of welfare spending is still accounted for by cash transfers which are subject to formal rules of legal and financial accountability.

Regimes of Accumulation

The state form and social policy are among the most important aspects of the modes of regulation governing an accumulation regime. Here we are concerned with Fordism and post-Fordism. The former can be encapsulated in the phrase: mass production and mass consumption. I discuss four different levels of Fordism in my chapter on Thatcherism and will focus here on two of its features which are relevant to welfare states.

Firstly, Fordism involves an enhanced role for the state in securing the conditions for capital accumulation and the reproduction of wage-labour by adapting markets to the rigidities of Fordist mass production. In managing the wage relation, labour market policies, and demand management, the Keynesian state reinforced the rather limited forms of microeconomic flexibility found in Fordism. By promising to smoothe out economic fluctuations and secure stable, calculable growth, it enabled Fordist firms to secure increasing returns to scale and encouraged them to invest (Galbraith, 1967; Kundig, 1984; Boyer and Coriat, 1986). And, secondly, Fordism needs the welfare state to establish a minimum social wage, generalize mass consumption norms, and coordinate the capital and consumer goods sectors. Indeed it was only with the transition to Fordism that the economic and social bases of the welfare state in its full sense (defined above) were secured. For Fordism enabled the state to link the interests of capital and labour in a programme of full employment and social welfare.

The crisis of Fordism can be seen in various areas and even its impact on the welfare state takes many forms. As the postwar boom slackened, wages grew faster than productivity and the welfare state continued to expand. State commitment to full employment also meant that 'reserve army' effects were limited to secondary markets and this delayed or halted the recovery of profits during downturns (Boyer and Coriat, 1986). This placed a double squeeze on profits and, in so far as welfare state expenditures were financed through taxes on wages and/or mass consumption or else paid for through inflation, it also subjected workers to economic pressures. When confronted with reduced returns to scale and lower productivity together with wages negotiated in terms of past profit and productivity performance, the Fordist system turned stagflationary. The growth of working class resistance to the Fordist accumulation regime due to alienation at work was also reinforced by growing disquiet with the Fordist state. The latter's attempts to restrict collective bargaining, limit wages, raise taxes and cut spending, its growing bureaucratic degeneration and mounting inability to cope with the social and environmental repercussions of Fordism in crisis also helped undermine support for the Keynesian welfare state.

The crisis of Fordism involves more than the forces of production or profitability in any simple sense. At stake is capital's inability to create a new regime of accumulation with appropriate institutional forms, social relations, and balance of social forces in the power bloc and among the people. Only if a new 'historic bloc' (to use Gramsci's phrase for a non-necessary fit between base and superstructure) can be constructed will capital accumulation (using both new and old technologies) experience a further long wave of expansion (Hirsch and Roth, 1986; Mazier et al., 1985, p. 295). Thus the qualitatively new character of post-Fordism must be sought not only in changes in how production is organized (most notably in new forms of flexibilization) but also in the emerging role of the state and the more general reorganization of social relations (*Vergesellschaftung*) (Boyer and Coriat, 1986; Hirsch, 1985b; Jessop, 1986; Mazier et al., 1985; Lipietz, 1985).

The details of the 'post-Fordist' system are still unclear and it will obviously share some features with Fordism. But two key differences concern the reorganization of production and the recomposition of the labour force. Firstly, post-Fordism sees an increasing emphasis on flexibility in organizing the labour process, internal and external labour markets, relations among firms, and so forth. This is not just a question of the enhanced flexibility due to the expanding role of electronics, the micro-processor, and information technology in producing goods and services but also of the flexibilization of social relations. Secondly, post-Fordism is accompanied by changes in occupational structures. Whereas Fordism was characterized by the key role of the affluent mass worker (or semi-skilled worker), post-Fordism is likely to see a growing polarization of the workforce into a full-time skilled core and an unskilled periphery often engaged only part-time and subject to new forms of Taylorization. This will extend beyond areas where flexible manufacturing is established and also occurs in the tertiary or service sector. Here the introduction of more flexible word- and data-processing machinery has been accompanied by more flexible work practices including work from home as well as flexible part-time and shift-work.

Whereas Fordism facilitated a policy of full employment and welfare rights to secure demand and thereby created the basis for a class compromise between capital and labour (cf. Przeworski, 1985), the new post-Fordist regime poses serious problems for full employment and its associated class alliances. This has major implications for the role of unions and the state as well as for new forms of class alliance. The polarization and segmentation of the workforce need not be inconsistent with a continued role for trade unions at plant and enterprise level. But factors associated with post-Fordism could weaken the role of the union movement as a social partner in a full employment alliance. In particular we should note lower levels of union density, the decentralization and fragmentation of national union organizations, and the emergence of a polarized labour force as compared with the rise of the mass worker under Fordism. In turn this will be tied to a reduced role for the state in securing full employment (although its role in managing the wage relation will be maintained). Indeed Mazier et al. suggest that the more important problem for the state will be mastering the ensemble of social expenditures (health, education, etc.) which increase the cost of the social wage. For them the risk is that introduction of new technologies enhances productivity without reducing unemployment or growing social costs (Mazier et al., 1985, p. 297). Clearly this makes some reorganization of the welfare state an essential element in the transition to post-Fordism.

Post-Fordism and the State

Much more is required for the onset of a new long wave than new forces of production and a reorganized labour process. Changes in the mode of regulation (or the social structure of accumulation) are also needed. The state system and the overall pattern of societalization must be re-ordered. In this context we must take care in periodizing the changing role of the state because its role in the present transition will certainly differ from its subsequent role in a consolidated post-Fordist system[3]. The present political conjuncture is one in which the state is simultaneously disengaging (from its supportive role in the dying phase of Fordism) and intervening (to facilitate the birth of the next long wave). This involves major contradictions in its policies, programmes, and legitimation.

Post-Fordism and the Welfare State

During the Fordist period the state in advanced capitalist economies has had a key role in integrating the capital and consumer goods industries[4] and managing the wage relation to this end. Full employment is often cited as a major policy objective during this period but its achievement was actually grounded much more in the basic dynamic of Fordist expansion than it was on fine-tuning through government employment policy. The real test of this policy commitment came only with the collapse of the postwar boom, the emerging crisis of Fordism, and such contingent events as the 'oil price shocks'. The apparent success of the welfare state during this period was also grounded in the nature of the postwar boom. For, firstly, the Fordist upswing generated the tax revenues to finance welfare expansion. Secondly, to the extent that full employment was achieved in a labour market which was relatively unified rather than segmented, it also reduced the volume of primary poverty among working families. In turn this created room for more generous income maintenance programmes for other groups (thereby generalizing mass consumption norms) and/or for welfare expansion into other areas (often tied to the changing social reproduction requirements involved in Fordism). And, thirdly, as the societalization pattern (*Vergesellschaftungsform*) associated with Fordism was consolidated, it created or intensified 'social problems' for which welfare state solutions could be sought[5]. But the expansion of the welfare state also came to undermine some of the conditions which sustained Fordist accumulation. For it altered the balance of class forces in favour of organized labour in the economic sphere - a shift which only became critical as the crisis of Fordism emerged and capital tried to restructure the labour process and restrain labour costs. It also institutionalized a social wage whose downward rigidity (if not its upward momentum) could act as a brake on accumulation. In addition the welfare state acquired its own expansionary drive with major structural as well as resource implications for the Fordist regime. Thus, alongside the self-evident increase in the social welfare budget (with its consequences for the restructuring of the tax and credit systems), the welfare state also underwent changes in its basic structural forms, associated social policy communities, and its political bases of support. These changes threatened the Fordist regime through their impact on both sides of the capital-labour relation (in terms of the balance of forces as well as the basic incentive to invest and/or work) and on the overall pattern of societalization (notably in terms of a relative decoupling of welfare policies from the circuit of capital). Thus one can see the crisis of the welfare state as an opportunity for capital forcibly to re-impose the unity of economic and social policy in the interests of renewed accumulation.

The Crisis of the Fordist Welfare State

The current crisis of the welfare state is a complex, many-sided, and overdetermined phenomenon. At issue here is its foundations in the interaction between the Fordist accumulation process and the *Eigendynamik* of the welfare state. These processes were mutually supportive during the boom years of Fordism but have interacted negatively during the crisis years. We deal first with the economic aspects of the crisis, then with its political aspects.

Economic Factors

The crisis of Fordism exerted a 'scissors' effect on welfare state finances. On the revenue side it reduced the tax-base for social security payments in so far as these were tied to wage-earner and/or pay-roll taxes. Capital's contribution to state revenues also fell because of the decline in gross profits and the redistribution of tax burdens to protect post-tax profit levels. At the same time the crisis increased demands for expenditure on income maintenance (e.g. unemployment, early retirement and family benefit payments) and, via the social repercussions of unemployment and recession, on other welfare services (such as housing, health and family policies). Moreover, in so far as the state increased its real and/or tax expenditures for technological innovation and structural reorganization and/or reduced taxes on capital in general, this further limited the resources available for social spending[6]. The resulting general fiscal crisis of the state was associated with conflicts not only over the level and incidence of state expenditures but also over the restructuring of the taxation and credit systems. This was reflected in growing hostility to the tax costs of the welfare state and/or to the inflationary consequences of financing welfare expenditures through government borrowing. Yet the chances of long-term retrenchment in social welfare spending (especially on the capital account) are limited: at most there could be a redistribution of their provision between the public and private sectors. At the same time there was growing hostility to the social and economic repercussions of welfare state retrenchment (especially in health, education and pensions) once cuts spread beyond more marginal state activities and/or affected core rather than marginal social groups.

If one only considered the fiscal and budgetary aspects of the welfare state, two key aspects of its economic crisis would fall from view. The crisis is not just financial and its underlying structural causes will not disappear with renewed expansion. The fact that the financial crisis of the state has been interpreted largely in terms of the excessive burden of social expenditures reflects a shift in the balance of economic and political forces rooted in the more general dynamic of Fordism. In turn this means that renewed capitalist expansion would not produce a simple return to the status quo ante. The economic crisis of the welfare state is, moreover, rooted in the growing discrepancy between its activities and the needs of capital accumulation. Tasks which benefited capital during the Fordist upswing acquired their own institutional inertia even though the needs of capital changed. Thus resolving the economic crisis required reorganization as well as retrenchment.

In addition to the continuing crisis of Fordism, the transition to post-Fordism also affects the welfare state. For, even were a new long wave of expansion to develop, the problems facing welfare state finance would have changed. Thus, assuming that something approaching 'full employment' is once again achieved, the weight of part-time, temporary and discontinuous employment patterns will be much greater than in the Fordist period. In turn this means that new patterns of taxation and welfare entitlements will need to be introduced (Gretschmann, 1986; Standing, 1986). Likewise, with increasing international capital mobility (especially in the service sector) and increasing competition among states to attract investment in sunrise sectors, the contribution of taxes on capital is likely to decline unless a concerted transnational policy can be developed. These shifts will also be reflected in the balance of political forces and the type of demands placed upon the welfare state. More generally, as we shall see below, the need for flexibilization will have major implications for the functions and organization of the welfare state. The crisis of Fordism and the transition to post-Fordism will thus affect not only the levels and methods of financing welfare expenditure but also the ways in which the post-Fordist welfare state will perform its functions in social reproduction.

In all these respects, of course, it is misleading to suggest that the fiscal, financial and budgetary dilemmas of the welfare state can be considered in isolation from the overall structure and finances of state expenditure. But the new right has managed to present these issues in isolation and to mobilize public opinion against the welfare state. This is associated with a withdrawal of the commitment to full employment - at first in the name of the battle against inflation and later in the name of international competition. This has undermined the compromise between capital and labour in which both stood to gain from full employment in a mass production, mass consumption system.

The Form of the Welfare State

Turning to the welfare state, it is clear that the welfare state has caused some of its own problems. The rational-legal form of welfare provision is associated with bureaucratism, the juridification of social relations, political empire-building, centralization, clientelism and the intensification of personal dependence. Moreover the professionalized and bureaucratized forms of help and support aggravate social problems and increase dependence. In addition the combination of the taxation, national insurance and means-tested benefits systems has created two problems: the poverty trap confronting the low wage employed (for whom increased earnings from employment are countered by loss of benefit) and the unemployment trap (which concerns the net real increase in income when an unemployed person takes a job). At the same time the forms in which welfare policies are administered has aggravated distributional and status conflicts in both the middle and working classes. It is often the middle classes who make greater use of welfare benefits and especially of the more expensive benefits (e.g. education, housing and health) whether these are provided through the public welfare system or through the so-called 'fiscal welfare state' rooted in tax reductions on certain classes of consumer spending. Indeed the relationships among public, fiscal and occupational provision serve both to disguise the extent to which the state supports the social reproduction of the middle classes and to provide new foci for distributional and status conflicts.

There is also some truth in criticisms that the welfare state has an inherent expansionary dynamic in so far as welfare needs are often defined by those who have a vested interest in their expansion[7]. This holds not only for politicians (spurred on by electoral competition) and welfare administrators and professionals (for whom welfare expansion implies jobs, career development and empire building) but also for client groups and the political lobbies which articulate their interests. This problem has become more acute as the social and environmental costs of Fordist expansion and the dynamic of welfare policy-making have created new issues and new interests around which social movements can organize.

Among these issues we can note the growing crisis of the nuclear family form which played a key role in Fordist societalization both as a locus of privatized consumption and as the site for social and emotional integration in an atomized society (Hirsch and Roth, 1986). The proportion of households which conform to the nuclear family pattern is falling. This is reflected in greater needs for state support (for education, sickness, single parent-families, old age, etc.) and attempts to impose the burdens of youth unemployment, sickness and care for the elderly on the family. Likewise inner city decline has concentrated social as well as economic problems in areas with a declining tax base and increasing needs for welfare expenditure and programmes. It is here above all that one finds the social problems of education, housing, health, single households and single parents, social isolation and mental illness and demographic imbalance.

Thus new forces have been active in lobbying for state support. They range from capital-labour cartels in declining industries and regions through ethnic minorities and single parents to alternative cultural and social collectives. The expansion of 'tax expenditures' to support the private provision of social reproduction goods and services (from pensions through housing and medical insurance to education) has also created a new set of policy-taking interests among tax-payers as well as creating vested interests among capitalist concerns (such as pension funds) which service them. During the boom years there were few financial or electoral checks on these processes - especially as the years of welfare expansion coincided with reduced military expenditures, rising productivity and full employment. These checks have recently become more important. The crisis of Fordism is linked to the fiscal crisis of the state and with growing electoral resistance to the taxation for welfare needs.

A further aspect is that the monetary and legal forms of social policy are less adequate to the problems the welfare state now handles. At first it dealt with simple economic contingencies (such as ill-health, cyclical unemployment, pregnancy, etc.) which disrupted the earnings stream of individuals and/or families; then it expanded into the provision of basic welfare services such as education, housing and health; more recently still it has become deeply involved in personal social services and the handling of socio-psychological problems ('people-processing'). In addition increasing attention has gone to the deeper, structural roots of individual economic contingencies (such as the operation of the labour market or health and safety at work) and, at least in integrated welfare states, economic and social policy in these areas has become more closely coordinated. Finally the state has moved into new fields of social policy (such as the crisis of the inner city, race relations and gender inequalities) which have complex roots in the overall mode of societalization rather than the operation of the capitalist economic system as such.

This movement is associated with a shift away from reliance on formal welfare state law, bureaucratic organization and cash transfers towards more discretionary intervention, professional organization and the provision of services. The latter trends make it more difficult to base welfare policy on justiciable welfare rights and/or formal methods of actuarial calculation and financial rationality (Zacher, 1985, pp. 26-29). In turn this shifts the initiative towards professional and/or client groups at the expense of central and local government and introduces criteria for success which are not only more orientated towards client needs and/or professional interests but are also correspondingly more opaque, personalized and financially uncertain (Vaccarini, 1984, pp. 124-25). In addition social issues such as racial discrimination or gender inequalities are not readily solved through the simple monetarization of social risks and welfare needs and/or through the implementation of a system of justiciable welfare rights. But the alternatives to formal, rational-legal solutions also involve their own dilemmas, contradictions and conflicts. Thus resort to social engineering or programming from above is often complicated by the multiplicity and indeterminacy of social objectives and the difficulties involved in anticipating all the repercussions of such interventions. Likewise attempts to encourage the participation of disadvantaged groups or communities in solving these problems often leads to escalating demands which go beyond the limits of market and bureaucratic rationality (Offe, 1984).

So-called Exogenous Factors

The interrelated crisis-generating dynamics of accumulation and the welfare state have been reinforced by important exogenous factors[8]. Chief among these is demographic change. This has affected both the scope and the finances of the welfare state. In particular the ratio of contributors to beneficiaries has changed dramatically in the last 25 years as retirement has increased (especially among the oldest cohorts with their greater need for long-term medical attention) and the numbers who are economically active has fallen. Costs in the welfare state have also tended to rise disproportionately - education lasts longer, medical progress has increased costs, one-parent families require more support and Fordist productivity raising techniques are less applicable to welfare activities. This has intensified the fiscal squeeze on welfare policies and made the search for solutions more urgent.

Political Repercussions

None of this implies that an unambiguous, unequivocal and inevitable logic of capital is somehow re-asserting itself. Even in the labour process itself, there is scope for significant variation in the 'politics of production' (cf.

Burawoy, 1985; Bowles and Edwards, 1985). Likewise different strategies can be adopted in the more general reorganization of social structures of accumulation. This can be seen not only in the contrasting patterns of the Japanese, American, German and Italian paths to post-Fordism but also in matters of more direct concern to us here. Thus we can expect different strategies to predominate in different societies.

It is how the economic and political crises in Fordist welfare states affect the balance of political forces and the struggle to develop competing solutions which is crucial for any reorganization of the welfare state. Thus one should pay particular attention to the different interpretations of the crisis in the welfare state, the changing balance of political forces mobilized for and against its present forms and functions and the articulation between political and economic strategies. Interpretations of the crisis are manifold. They include a romantic rejection of the welfare state (evident in the work of critics such as Illich); calls for an alternative, communitarian welfare state and/or one addressed to the problems of patriarchal as well as class domination; social democratic arguments for the reorganization and retrenchment of the Keynesian welfare state for a temporary period of economic austerity before it is resurrected in more or less the same form; and the new right's demands for the privatization of welfare services and/or the introduction of commercial criteria into the welfare state. Despite the variety of criticisms and solutions, however, only a limited range of solutions is compatible with a successful transition to post-Fordism. How they are combined and which of them predominates in particular societies will depend on the outcome of political and economic struggles on the terrain of different national regimes of accumulation and political regimes. Rather than making reckless general predictions, it is better to look at three basic alternatives around which specific solutions are likely to crystallize.

Beyond the Crisis of the Welfare State

Three main forms of political response to the crisis of Fordism can be distinguished: neo-liberal, neo-corporatist and neo-statist. However, while there are economic, political and intellectual forces which are closely identified with one or other response, they are best interpreted as the poles around which different national solutions will develop during an extended period of conflict and experimentation. They each have contrasting implications for welfare state policy.

The neo-liberal response emphasizes the recommodification of labour-power, the privatization of state enterprise and welfare services and the deregulation of the private sector. The flexibility crucial to post-Fordism is meant to come from the liberation of market forces which this three-pronged strategy is intended to accomplish. In particular the neo-liberal response involves wide-ranging legislative and administrative changes to shift the balance of power in the labour market towards capital and to transform the welfare state into a means of supporting and subsidizing low wages for crucial sectors of an economy which will be characterized by much greater income differentials. Examples of these changes include attempts to weaken unions' capacities for effective strike action, to dismantle corporatist structures and institutions, to reduce expectations about wage levels and working conditions, to facilitate labour market flexibility and mobility and to enhance the disciplinary force of social security measures and programmes. Thus the wage-relation is to be reinforced as a means of societal reproduction and the social wage is to be reduced and adapted to the requirements of a more flexible labour force. This implies cuts so that income maintenance and other welfare programmes assume a minimal, residual place in social reproduction and reorganization so that they are more closely tied through means-testing and differential targeting (e.g. poverty due to long-term unemployment, single-parent families, or old age) to the economic and social position of specific groups. This implies more means-testing over a greater proportion of welfare spending for income maintenance and other services. Likewise cuts in taxation to match reduced levels of public spending will be coupled with the reorganization of the tax system as a means of economic and societal steering. Thus the tax system will be used to encourage personal welfare provision through the market and/or occupational welfare systems negotiated with employers. It will also be used to influence industrial relations (e.g. through tax subsidies on profit sharing schemes), the labour market (e.g. through tax subsidies for employers to split jobs to encourage part-time work) and personal consumption (e.g. tax subsidies for private medical insurance).

Further, where socialized welfare services as opposed to income maintenance programmes are concerned, the neo-liberal welfare state will prompt a 'mixed welfare economy' in which direct public provision is reduced and private, profit-making services are encouraged. The state will also support joint state-business ventures, voluntary groups, charitable trusts, self-help and so forth. Fiscal, budgetary and administrative measures as well as straightforward privatization will encourage the commercialization of welfare services and/or their provision through non-state bodies. Moreover, whilst a residuary, 'last resort' role will fall to the state where these measures fail, it will attempt to off-load this burden as far as possible onto households, 'liable relatives' and the community at large. What this implies for the caring role of women needs no further comment.

The social basis of this regime can be found in key groups of workers in the leading economic sectors (high technology and services) together with the capitalist and professional interests which will service the neo-liberal welfare state. At the same time this implies: (a) the marginalization and economic and political weakening of some groups of workers in both the private and public sector and/or of those whose income derives largely or exclusively from state transfer payments; and (b) their resulting subordination to reinvigorated market forces and/or cash limits on state expenditure so that they can be made to bear the costs of economic change and reorganization. This fragmentation of the working and pauper classes will be accompanied by efforts to create a supporting class of small businessmen and other petty bourgeois strata and/or to transform privileged groups of workers into petty property- and/or capital-owners. This can be seen in the ideological and political importance attached to small business and to various measures intended to promote home ownership, profit-sharing schemes and share ownership (Jessop et al., 1984; Goldthorpe, 1985, pp. 336-337; Davis, 1986).

The neo-corporatist response relies on ex ante concertation of the economic decisions and activities of private economic agents orientated to their own economic interests. Thus economic and social affairs would be left neither to the market nor to the state: instead their governance would be delegated to various intermediary organizations. The liberal corporatist patterns associated with Fordism will be transformed owing to the increasing heterogeneity of the labour force and labour markets entailed in post-Fordism, the decomposition of the national economy as a feasible object of economic management and the need to re-orientate concertation toward the international race for modernization and continued expansion of the circle of functional interests beyond capital and organized labour. In the pursuit of economic flexibility corporatist arrangements could become more selective (e.g. excluding some previously entrenched industrial interests and more peripheral or marginal workers, integrating some 'sunrise' interests and giving more weight to core workers); and, reflecting the more flexible forms of the post-Fordist economy, the centre of corporatist gravity will shift to the micro-level away from macroeconomic concertation. In social welfare we can expect more 'regulated self-regulation' and private interest government among relevant policy communities, such as health, social work, education, pension, sickness insurance, housing and so on (Streeck and Schmitter, 1983). Functional interests, voluntary agencies and other 'third sector' forces will gain more autonomy and powers in welfare delivery.

The state is involved in neo-corporatist strategies as in the neo-liberal and neo-statist approaches. But its actions aim to back or support decisions reached through corporatist negotiation rather than pursue neo-liberal disengagement and/or resort to active state initiatives along neo-statist lines;

and compliance with state measures is either voluntary or depends on actions taken by self-regulating corporatist organizations endowed with public status. The social basis of such a welfare state would be closely tied to the pluralistic set of organizations involved in exercising these new or altered functions. They could be social democratic in so far as organized labour retains a prominent position but they could also be more pluralistic with a variety of professional, religious, 'alternative' and other third sector interests. Many vested professional interests will also be mobilized behind this state form.

In contrast the neo-statist response would involve further decommodification to compensate for deficiencies in the market, an active structural policy to improve market forces and regulation to limit the operation of market forces. Flexibility will be secured through an active, market-conforming structural policy in which the pursuit of flexibility goes beyond concern for the short-term allocative efficiency which comes with factor mobility and flexible prices (especially in relation to labour mobility and wage levels) to concern with medium-term dynamic efficiency grounded in the coordinated enhancement of skills, technologies, infrastructures, organizational capacities and so on. This implies an enhanced state role in promoting skill-flexibility in the workforce as well as more flexibility in the labour market. A further possible element in this model is the introduction of a basic income guarantee paid to all citizens regardless of contributions or work status. In one sense this would reinforce the decommodification of labour power and further consolidate trends towards universal social citizenship, egalitarian social relations and alternative household forms; but it could also facilitate labour market flexibility without the discriminatory and marginalizing effects associated with the neo-liberal model (see particularly Standing, 1986; cf. Jordan, 1985). The taxation system would obviously require a fundamental reorganization for such a basic income guarantee to be introduced but changes would be less socially divisive and less concerned to extend market forces into social reproduction. Likewise, whilst a 'mixed welfare economy' will also be promoted in the 'neo-statist' model, it will not be deliberately biased in favour of an expanding role for private capital. More emphasis will be placed instead on decentralization to self-help groups, voluntary organizations, occupational associations and non-profit making concerns.

The social basis of a neo-statist model will be a developed form of the social democratic or conservative-corporatist model. Thus its principal social basis could be found either in a cohesive, solidaristic citizenry (especially if there is a guaranteed minimum income) with organized labour at its core; or in a more fragmented ensemble of different economic, social and political interests which will benefit from the movement to a post-Fordist economy and a 'mixed economy of welfare' which are inflected in a neo-statist direction. In the latter case a selective corporatism could develop in which the skill-flexible workers at the core of the productive system are represented and workers who are predominantly time-flexible are excluded. A significant shift in the post-Fordist society will none the less be the enhanced role of organizations and groups rooted in the new social movements which developed in response to the social crisis of the Fordist social structure of accumulation. This holds not only for the 'neo-statist' model (which suggests that the term 'statist' is somewhat misleading) but also for the 'new voluntarism' much favoured in neo-liberal welfare states.

In all three cases the post-Fordist state will have different priorities from its Fordist predecessor. Priority must be given to promoting flexibility: the supply-side must take precedence over the demand side. Whereas the Fordist state tended to adapt to the rigidities of Fordist production by flexible demand management, the post-Fordist state must try to overcome such rigidities with a flexible supply-side strategy and a more rigid approach to the demand side to keep social expenditure (including the social wage) under control. This has significant implications for the future of the differentiated welfare state. When the economic policies of the state were primarily macro-level and demand-side orientated, it was not hard to treat social welfare (especially income maintenance) as a separate policy sphere. But once government economic policy shifts towards the micro-level and the supply-side, the connections between economic and social policy become crucial. In turn this implies the need for more radical changes (and thus less 'incremental' or 'decremental' change) in the differentiated (typically liberal) welfare state than in the integrated welfare systems more typical of social democratic and conservative welfare regimes. But even here changes in the form of the welfare state will be required.

In considering these changes we must take care to distinguish between the declared objectives of government policies and the actual politics of industrial relations and the welfare state. For there is often much greater continuity in these areas than government rhetoric, legislation, or action would suggest[9]. In part this stems from the functional necessities of certain general forms of intervention in the modern capitalist economy and in part from the institutionalization of a general balance of political forces in the very forms of the state and civil society themselves. Yet changes are occurring and they generally involve a recomposition rather than wholesale dismantlement of unions or welfare states. In the case of welfare states it is likely that the liberal model will be recomposed towards the neo-liberal welfare pole and the social democratic model towards the neo-statist pole with a strong policy commitment to economic democracy and a basic income guarantee; those societies with a conservative welfare state tradition are likely to combine elements of both models and to be based on selective corporatism, exclusionary dualism, or a 'two nations' social structure.

Post-Fordism in the Welfare State

So far we have considered the transition to post-Fordism in terms of its general implications for the welfare state. Now we should consider its introduction into the welfare state. This has three aspects: the flexibilization of welfare state services, the balance between the public and private sectors and the costs of welfare. The implications will be significant in all three areas.

Aglietta argued that Fordist techniques were difficult to apply to collective welfare services such as health care, education and public administration. Among the difficulties facing Fordism were the element of professional work involved and the need to combine service with social control. Professional workers resist both Taylorism and Fordism and the disciplinary aspects of the welfare state make privatization more difficult. This situation can be contrasted with other services where Fordism has been able to penetrate through the mass production of durable consumer goods which are then used by individual households and maintained by secondary service industries. Examples include transportation (the car), entertainment (television, videos) and domestic services (consumer durables). In contrast low growth in productivity and rising real wages mean that labour-intensive welfare services act as a brake on accumulation. Aglietta concluded that this problem could only be resolved by 'radically transforming the conditions of production of the means of collective consumption' so that accumulation would be renewed through 'a massive transformation of unproductive labour into labour productive of surplus value' (Aglietta, 1979a, p. 157).

Aglietta's analysis provides a useful starting point but must be refined by considering three interrelated issues. Firstly, can new labour processes be introduced into collective welfare services? Secondly, can new products be introduced into the welfare sector? And, thirdly, can the transition to post-Fordism alter the balance between public and private welfare provision? Each of these issues has a material and a disciplinary aspect.

In process terms it is information technology which offers the most significant opportunities to raise productivity in the welfare sector and to make it more flexible. This is most clear for those sectors involved in income maintenance through cash transfers as opposed to the provision of services in kind. But the linking of different information systems also provides the basis for a measure of privatization (e.g. in employment services). In product terms the profitable development of several new technologies and industries (such as bio-technology, pharmaceuticals and information technology) is closely bound to the further expansion of a reorganized welfare state. Moreover new products could radically change the mix of waged service labour, machinery and unpaid labour (as supplied through the voluntary sector, self-help groups, the extended family, the household, or welfare recipients themselves) in ways analogous to those which have already occurred in the private service sector. Finally, in so far as information technology and new products encourage flexibilization and decentralization, there are also opportunities for private sector firms to compete with the public sector. Here we can only provide some brief illustrations to support these general arguments.

Gershuny and Miles (1983) have identified several areas where post-Fordist techniques could radically change the service sector. In health care, for example, process innovations in existing services will include: computerization of records and office automation; more efficient catering; electronic diagnostic and monitoring equipment; computer-aided diagnostics using 'expert' systems; remote monitoring using established telecommunications channels; and the use of lasers and similar surgical techniques which are more cost-effective. Organizational innovations will include new drugs and biological diagnostic methods for various medical conditions; new preventative and simple diagnostic services based on information technology; paramedical and advice services; and wide use of automatic diagnosis and screening in health services. At the same time there is a growing trend towards introducing professional managers in place of medical professions to run health services (Blackburn et al., 1985, p. 183). In education there will be process innovations through distance learning systems backed up by telecommunications, video and computer equipment; and through the use of computers in secondary and tertiary education. And, organizationally, there will be new educational packages for community education and the educationally disadvantaged; plus educational packages combined with entertainment for home use. Thirdly, in the general field of social welfare administration, there will be progress in computerizing records, automating advice services and in streamlining administration. Organizational innovations could also include the development of self-help groups producing community services and seeking improved services from the state; and the blurring of policing/community work/surveillance roles in state agencies (Gershuny and Miles, 1983, cited in Blackburn et al., 1985, p. 152).

Secondly, in terms of the mix of unpaid self-service labour and private and public sector paid labour, new consumption norms are already developing which support the commodification and/or the self-servicing of welfare functions, especially when restructured around information technology. Thus preventative health care (jogging, sports centres, high fibre diets, etc.) is increasingly commodified and also provides a focus for sportswear and sports goods industries, alternative medicines and publications. Indeed,

> over the next twenty years ... there could be expanding markets for high technology health care products to be sold, not just to or through the formal health services - though this will be a large market - but also on a mass-consumption scale to individual consumers directly (Blackburn et al., 1985, p. 188).

In short, through the enhanced capital intensity of the welfare state and the shift to self-service welfare provision, the costs of welfare services could be cut and productivity raised. In turn this could permit an improvement in the quality of welfare services without additional cost and/or provide the means to control costs without reductions in services. This is especially likely where an integrated welfare state exists with a coalition of political forces which is still committed to public welfare provision. Conversely, where a political coalition has emerged favouring privatization and retrenchment, these innovations can be exploited to expand private sector provision alongside a residual welfare state.

The extent to which new techniques and organizational forms can facilitate flexibilization can be illustrated through the development of Health Maintenance Organizations (HMOs) in California and elsewhere in the USA. These are commercial enterprises which contract to provide medical care over a given period for a flat rate fee; they have an interest in preventative care, in medical innovation and in controlling costs and, in so far as they compete for clients, engage in normal forms of capitalist competition (for more details, see MacRae, 1984). One can imagine similar organizations developing in other areas that have previously been dominated by the Fordist welfare state and they could be run either for profit as capitalist enterprises or as elements in an alternative economy. Education, housing and health are the three most obvious fields for such developments but cases such as the privatization of American prisons suggest that many other areas of state intervention could be reorganized along similar lines. What is important in these examples is that they suggest that the welfare state can be made more flexible not only organizationally (through less rigid bureaucratic forms and more competition) but also in terms of the mix between labour-power, capital equipment and self-service.

Nonetheless recent British experience suggests that such flexibilization is unlikely to eliminate the need for residual state services and may not lead to an overall improvement in the quality of services. The rapid and profitable expansion of private medical insurance schemes in Britain has been threatened by the fact that new clients must be sought among higher risk groups in the working class and older age cohorts and some companies have made losses through expanding beyond low risk middle-class groups. Likewise the experience of privatization of ancillary services in the health service, education and local government suggests that not only are costs reduced but also the level of service (cf. Labour Research Bulletin, seriatim). These and other examples suggest that the dilemma between commodity and non-commodity provision will not disappear with the introduction of post-Fordism and/or privatization but will simply appear in new forms.

Conclusions

Recent developments in the welfare state are related to the crisis of Fordism. The latter cannot be understood purely as the crisis of a specific accumulation regime; it must also be related to the crises in its associated modes of regulation and societalization. Seen in these terms the growth potential of Fordism is relatively exhausted and the search is continuing for a new regime of accumulation. It is this crisis of Fordism which frames how the crisis of the welfare state will be resolved. For, in so far as the Keynesian welfare state had a central role in Fordism, it must be reorganized to fit into a new mode of regulation.

This does not mean that the crisis of the welfare state is reducible to the crisis of Fordism. There have always been problems concerning the levels and incidence of public spending in the welfare state and this has been reflected in recurrent bouts of expansion and retrenchment and/or shifting emphases on the current or capital account in welfare budgets. Likewise these have always been overdetermined by economic and political pressures: sometimes more weight is given to accumulation, sometimes to legitimation. None of this would itself have produced a crisis of the welfare state. The first real postwar crisis of the welfare state emerged from its *Eigendynamik* and unfolded through a gradual change in its organizational form, means of intervention and its links with the economy. The initial reaction to this crisis involved calls for *Verrechtlichung* (juridification) and disengagement and/or for moves towards decentralization and debureaucratization. This crisis was later overdetermined by problems rooted in the welfare state's role during the crisis of Fordism and the transition to post-Fordism. In turn this has major implications for possible solutions to the initial crisis. For any feasible reorganization of the welfare state must resolve not only the problems rooted in its own dynamic but also those rooted in its regulatory role in relation to accumulation. Further influences emerge, of course, from cross-national variation in welfare and modes of regulation.

Since we are still living through a phase of transition, experimentation and strategic intervention, caution is called for in dealing with the future of the welfare state. The final form of any post-Fordist welfare state will only become apparent later and vary from society to society. As Skocpol has recently argued:

> Especially in a period of global economic difficulties, the specific features of each national state and party system, and its distinctive array of social policy legacies inherited from the past, become crucial for explaining whether a 'crisis of the welfare state' occurs at all, exactly how the crisis is defined, and what ideas, movements, and leadership manoeuvres will define alternatives for the future (Skocpol, 1985, p. 311).

One general conclusion is justified, perhaps even banale. If our claims about social reproduction and the wage form are correct, then it will not be possible simply to dismantle the welfare state. 'Capitalism', as Claus Offe has noted, 'cannot coexist with, neither can it exist without, the welfare state' (Offe, 1984, p. 153). Thus the crucial question is how the welfare state will be restructured and within what limits its role can be reduced (from a neo-liberal perspective) or expanded (from neo-statist or neo-corporatist perspective) without seriously restraining the transition to post-Fordism.

The quantitative limits to retrenchment are clear in all advanced capitalist societies, whose expenditure on social welfare has not been drastically reduced even in relative terms since the onset of the first oil crisis (OECD, 1984). Whether this reflects the temporary costs of managing the current transition or implies that the state welfare budget will always remain at these levels is less clear. The OECD was even optimistic enough to maintain that 'it should be possible to maintain the gains in security and services which were reached in the 1960s and 1970s and to improve them in line with the rate of economic growth, but not faster' (OECD, 1984). But this view rests largely on an exclusive concern with financial resources and a fundamental neglect of the structural imperatives and changes in the balance of economic and political forces which are bound up with the transition to post-Fordism. This involves a qualitative shift in the economic and social priorities of the welfare state and is accompanied by the collapse of political coalitions which supported welfare state policies in the postwar period. Reorganizing the welfare state involves shifts in the quantity of resources and services typical in the 1960s and 1970s and the assumption of new economic functions and disciplinary tasks in social reproduction.

Social democratic welfare regimes could realize the optimistic scenario of the OECD in the coming decades but it is unlikely that liberal welfare state regimes would do this. The latter are more likely to turn in a neo-liberal direction which is characterized by an integrated social security system in which supply-side flexibility is combined with a minimal level of welfare state security. Many of the dilemmas and contradictions of the Fordist welfare state will be reproduced in the post-Fordist system. The search for alternative solutions for the central problems of social reproduction in a capitalist society, in which the wage relation is a fundamental fact of life for so many producers, will continue.

Notes

1. Cf. Wilenksy, 1975, p. 1; Donati, 1983, p. 57.

2. Vaccarini has reviewed recent German and Anglo-American approaches: 1983.

3. For more detailed analysis of changing state roles see Jacobi et al., 1985.

4. The relative weight of the two sectors obviously varies across national economies and this is reflected in different patterns of export- and import-dependence for these sectors: thus the state's role in integrating them also extends to exchange rate and foreign economic policies.

5. Labelling something as a 'social problem' always involves political and ideological assumptions about social order, the feasibility of different solutions, the proper scope of state action, and so forth. Social problems are socially constructed and this demands a sophisticated analysis of how problems emerge for which welfare state solutions are considered appropriate.

6. This squeeze has also been aggravated to the extent that the Second Cold War, which is not simply a reflex of the crisis of Fordism, has led to increased military expenditures.

7. But this argument should not be restricted to collective consumption: Fordism as a whole is based on the stimulation of new wants and products and private consumerism threatens valorization through wage claims and consumer credit expansion just as much as welfare consumerism does through taxation and public credit.

8. Considered from the viewpoint of the Fordist dynamic as a whole it could be argued that even factors such as demographic change are actually integral elements or inevitable consequences of a Fordist social structure. But this argument can be put to one side for present purposes.

9. On this discrepancy for industrial relations in West Germany and Great Britain, see Kastendiek, 1985.

6. The Eighties: The Search for Alternatives to Fordism

Robert Boyer

The Eighties, as a New Challenge to the Regulation Approach

During a long period the structural character of the present crisis has been neglected or down-played. In the early 1980s, the crisis might be seen as a European disease, while US was booming and Japan expanding its external surplus. But now many observers and scholars have adopted a more balanced view about the current state of international relations, and the strengths and weaknesses of various OECD economies.

Implicitly or not, most analysts realize that the present economic and financial system is not able to promote a long-term recovery which would simultaneously solve the mass unemployment in Europe, reduce the public and external deficits in the US, while finding a solution to Third World debt. This is precisely the diagnosis stated, almost a decade ago, by the regulation approach (RA). This might give some interest in presenting the most recent analyses of this current. The present paper is specially devoted to the following central question: out of the very complex processes going on, what are the potential accumulation regimes which could replace the Fordist one, now in crisis?

But paradoxically enough, this question is a challenge to the regulation approach itself. Traditionally its analyses have been retrospective and comparative, not that much prospective or normative.

The Concept of Accumulation Regime: The Need for Clarification

The (very modest) spreading of RA concepts has often been reduced to the concept of Fordism, i.e. the simultaneous evolution of production and consumption norms after World War II. Of course, this pattern of development was shown to be different from the previous ones: intensive accumulation without mass consumption in the interwar period, extensive accumulation during the previous century. But the concept of accumulation regime, in general, was sometimes perceived as rather unprecise and was left in the background, since most of the discussion took place around the notion of Fordism.

When the analyses turn from retrospective to prospective, the features and rationale of any accumulation regime have to be quite well defined, since it is far more difficult to prognose than to analyse and describe past evolutions. Therefore it might be useful to propose a definition which summarizes the core of the regulationists' vision.

A regime of accumulation (AR) explicits the whole set of regularities which allow a general and more or less consistent evolution for capital formation, i.e. which dampen and spread over time the imbalances which permanently arise from the process itself. Analytically, five features characterize such a regime:

- A pattern for production organization within firms, defining the way wage earners work upon production means.
- A time horizon for capital formation decisions, according to which managers can use a given set of rules and criteria.
- Income shares between wage, profit and taxes, in order to reproduce the various social classes or groups.
- A volume and composition for effective demand, which validates the trends in the capacities of production.
- Precise of relationships between capitalist and non capitalist modes of production.

The previous researches do suggest that these five components are not redundant since all of them are necessary. Let us stress four major results already obtained.

Firstly, it would be false to reduce any AR to the sole labour process, since the whole wage labour relationship is a central part in accumulation dynamics. Just recall that according to that definition, Fordism is not only a principle of economy of time via the assembly-line and specialized equipment, proposed by the pioneer work of Coriat (1979), but a specific articulation of a two sectional dynamics of production and consumer goods: this was first stated in the seminal book by Aglietta (1979a). Many misunderstandings have derived from such a confusion, pitifully enough since the regulation approach (RA) precisely aims at building macro models starting from the labour process.

Secondly, the wage labour relation is not the only component of AR: the other institutional forms such as the forms of competition, the type of linkages with the world markets or even structural State interventions do play a role in the regularity of accumulation. This has a major importance, when assessing the likelihood of alternative AR. Too often, the debate about flexibility have quite exclusively concentrated their focus upon labour and sometimes technology, without clear reference to forms of competition, financial mobility and so on (Boyer, 1988a; 1988b). Consequently, some of the reasons for the difficulties in industrial reorganization are severely underestimated, probably leading to rather misleading prognoses.

Thirdly, the prevailing AR sets the regularities and trends at the macro level, but does not suppose a complete homogeneity of the basic institutional form. For example, a frequent criticism against the concept of Fordism is probably misdirected: even if the assembly-line represents a limited fraction of the various labour processes operating in the whole economy, Fordism as an AR is still imposing its logic even to industries in which the labour process is at odds with traditional Scientific Management. The building and public works industry (Campinos-Dubernet, 1983) or the service sector (Petit, 1986) provide good examples of a functional complementarity between atypical labour processes and the core of the Fordist industries.

Fourthly, and this statement is related to the previous one, the same general Fordist AR may exhibit contrasted national variants. This is the common conclusion of many RA researchers (Aglietta and Bertrand in Boyer, 1986a; Baron and Keizer, 1984; Grando, Margirier and Ruffieux, 1980). The accurate configuration of basic institutional forms, particularly capital labour relationship, seems to explain significant discrepancy in macroeconomic performances, even during the roaring 1960s. A previous work has for example coined an illustrative, even if a little bit preliminary typology: hampered Fordism for UK, flex-Fordism for West-Germany, Statist Fordism for France, lagging and then excessive institutionalization of Fordism in Italy (Boyer, 1988). This feature has a paramount importance in searching national alternative models to Fordism: any close copy of a worshipped model seems out of reach, the general principles can only be translated and transformed according to national traditions and 'structural preferences'.

These hypotheses about the late Fordism may give some interesting starting points for investigating the characteristics of emerging AR. But the difficulties are not only theoretical, but empirical too.

A New Challenge: To Assess the Likelihood of Various Alternatives to Fordism

The core of RA has been to make explicit the ex post logic of past or existing modes of development, as elaborated by long run historical dynamics of capitalism. In the 1980s the question is far more ambitious: how to sort out from very contradictory processes and the succession of contrasting periods, the basic features of possible new AR? The difficulties are manifold indeed.

Firstly, the RA has the specificity to discard the existence of purely deterministic laws during structural crises, but this has some costs, as far as scientific explanation is concerned. The economist has to ask to other social scientists some basic hypotheses about the reasons of national different strategies and trajectories. A form of integration between economic, social and political factors must be searched for, not as an epistemological luxury requisite, but as the direct consequence of the very RA framework, facing the analysis of a period of structural changes.

Secondly, the previous structural crises suggest that the emergence of new AR and regulation modes is not at all a monotonous process, clearly perceived and perfectly expected by economic and social actors. On the contrary, this is a rather blind process, largely unintentional, even if some clear conceptions might play some role in enlightening and challenging collective and individual behaviours (remember the role of the Keynesian reformist programme, Boyer, 1985a). Therefore the analysis is far more difficult than for a stabilized AR. For instance, the functional coherence of institutional forms has to be analysed ex ante, and not ex post, which calls for an exercise of macroeconomic fiction: would a given set of partial regulations generate a steady state, with admissible evolution for employment and the rate of profit? The difficulties of such a programme are twofold: sorting out the relevant changes in institutional forms (CGP-CEPREMAP, 1987) and then building simple small macro models deriving their consequences upon AR (Boyer and Coriat, 1987) are not easy tasks.

Thirdly, this process is uneven and different among countries, roughly similar and inserted in the same world system. The national differences, already mentioned for the Fordist regime, are sharpened within the unstable and rather unpredictable evolutions observed since more than one decade. Consequently, social scientists have to think about the factors explaining such differences, via intensive international comparative studies. Recent works in RA emphasize such differences (Boyer, 1986a; 1988a; Jessop, 1989c for European countries; Ominami, 1986 for Third World).

Instead of presenting a more detailed account of all these researches this paper will propose a more general survey about the features, determinants and possible outcomes of the restructurations occurring within the advanced capitalist countries. The argument will be developed in five steps.

First, the debate about production reorganization, programmable automation and the search for flexibility at odds with the old rigidity of Fordist organizations can be enlightened by a short retrospect about the roots of the present crisis. Then is presented a characterization of various potential socio-technical systems which could replace the present one. The internal consistency of the corresponding accumulation regimes has therefore to be assessed according to different emphasis upon the main factors of the crisis. Furthermore, it is suggested that the future for capital/labour relationship and forms of competition will probably combine parts of these different features. A short conclusion call for a new research agenda including international comparisons along these general hypotheses.

The Specific Problems to be Solved: Back to the Roots of the Fordist Crisis

Even if now the structural character of the present crisis is rather widely recognized, there is seemingly no such consensus about its origins. Nevertheless the matter is important as far as prospective views have to be proposed; their likeliness, advantages and weaknesses are closely related to the precise factors explaining the present unstability and the slowing down of growth. Just to be simple, four arguments can be sorted out.

The Exhaustion of the Previous Technical Regime: A1

Basically the argument runs as follows: the Fordist method initially fairly efficient has become counterproductive due to the cost of gigantism, the decline in the output/capital ratio, the slowing down in labour productivity. Symmetrically, the impetus of mass consumption centred upon cars, home appliances and modern housing declines. Consequently, advanced economies have entered into a period of slower growth, with high unemployment. Such an evolution is largely common to any technical system, and copes with the neo-Schumpeterian views of long run capitalism growth, even if the analysis is a little bit more precise, and somehow close to RA.

The Social and Economic Contradiction about Fordist Methods: A2

In a sense, this is a peculiar variant of the previous general interpretation of the crisis, but the emphasis is now upon economic and social determinants. A closer investigation exhibits at least two arguments:

A2a - The limits are internal to the corporate firm: Scientific management has led to a huge division of labour, which calls for supervisory employees in order to monitor blue collars' work intensity. Up to a threshold the gains in productive labour vanish into unproductive labour, in such a way that average productivity rates may be declining.

A2b - The shift from a national to an international logic: as far as the minimal capital for running a given industry is climbing up, the search for increasing returns to scale calls for a worldwide strategy of large corporate firms. Therefore, most of the national institutions and methods of private and public management become obsolete, while adequate international institutions are not developed to deal with conflicts between national industries about trade shares.

The Conflict Between Rigid Techniques and Uncertain Macroeconomic Prospects: A3

Since the mid 1980s, the debate about flexibility has stressed such an interpretation. Old Fordist methods could not cope with the stop and go observed during a decade in macroeconomic dynamics, for they used to rely upon fastly growing and easily predictable demand. The argument is not only quantitative (rise in the variance of industrial output) but qualitative too: now consumers demand more differentiated goods and shift from one product to another; similarly a high rate in product renewal and a rapid obsolescence are at the core of the new forms in oligopolistic competition.

The Break-down of the International Order: A4

In an extreme conception, the tendencies towards stagnation and instability are related quite exclusively to the loss of international cooperation, as regards economic policies, exchange rate dynamics, monetary controls. Therefore, the technical system itself has little responsibility in the crisis, its so-called rigidity being the only consequence of international disorder. According to another vision, the analysis is two-sided: the present crisis derives from the conflict between regulation modes, still at the national level, and an emerging accumulation regime operating at the world level. This interpretation is coherent with previous interpretation A2b.

Given the evolutions observed during the last decade, the strength and likelihood of each interpretation has to be assessed. But it would be a task too large to be fulfilled in such a short space. Let us just take this taxonomy for granted, and investigate various ways out of the present situation.

What are the Potential and Alternative Accumulation Regimes?

In a sense each of the actual strategies overemphasizes one or the other of these interpretations.

The Schumpeterian Vision: A New Balance between Product and Process Innovations: R1

Each phase of capitalist growth has been launched by a set of structural innovations, combining in adequate proportion productivity advances and new mass production. During the downturn (the so-called phase B of a Kondratieff), process innovation outweighted product innovation, in such a way that employment is declining. A longrun boom can only occur when a new set of innovations promotes again a balanced process between investment, productivity and demand. The textile industry, the railways and the car industries have respectively been at the origin of the three Kondratieffs observed since two centuries. Many neo-Schumpeterians expect a new long run boom based upon the information revolution to take place at the end of this century.

This vision has been proposed particularly by the specialists devoted to the analysis of technical change, among them, Freeman and his colleagues in SPRU and authors like Mensch. One can diagnose significant differences in the precise interpretation: are the periods of stagnation related to too few or too many radical innovations? Another variant, as proposed by Perez stresses the incompatibility of the trends in technological change and the existing set of institutions and socio-political organizations in the phase B of the Kondratieff.

Two remarks about this scenario. First, it is assuming that the roots of the crisis are mainly technical, therefore referring to argument A1. Nevertheless very few analyses do explain precisely why technological exhaustion implies capital deepening and declining profit rate, as stated by such an interpretation. Second, every technical system seems to be equivalent from a purely economic point of view: the problems about automation, economies of scale, quantitative and qualitative productive flexibility are hardly considered. The implicit diagnosis is probably that these factors are of secondary importance.

Democracy in the Workplace: An Emerging Proposal for Reconciling Larger Autonomy and Better Efficiency: R2

According to this strategy, the roots of the crisis are mainly social and not exclusively technical, opposite to the previous one. For control purposes, bosses and managers have pushed labour division too far, rising workers' dissatisfaction and discarding personal know-how and involvement in quality and productivity. A way out of the crisis then supposes brand new industrial relations, at odds with Scientific Management as conceived by Taylor and his followers.

This point of view can derive from different analytical frameworks and various socio-political visions. In the US, authors like Schor, Bowles, Gordon and Weisskopf (1983) have stressed how the rise of the cost of control in corporate capitalism could be curbed down by a democratization of the workplace, and by extension of other basic institutions. As far as Japan is concerned Aoki has shown how the macroeconomic achievements of this country can be related to a high degree of decentralization of informational flows and decisions in the industrial system. Finally in the nordic countries, the social democratic traditions have promoted early tentatives for job enrichment, which in some case turned out to be more efficient than the traditional Taylorist or Fordist methods.

Implicitly at least, this proposal supposes that the present crisis derives from the social limits of the previous organization of work, in accordance with analysis A2. Contrary to the previous one, which emphasizes a set of invariant factors generating Kondratieff waves, the novelty and specificity of productive organization play a crucial role. Furthermore, the improvement of technologies stricto sensu is not considered as the unique determinant for a new economic upswing: innovations about division of labour, firms management and social organization (especially general education and professional retraining) might be necessary conditions in searching a way out of the crisis. Thus one might oppose the Saturn project, which initially was mainly based upon high automation, to the Japanese strategy of worker involvement with fewer but adequately selected, high-tech devices.

A New Industrial Divide: Flexible Specialization as an Alternative to Traditional Scientific Management: R3

In some respect, this scenario is an extension of the previous one but it emphasizes the elements of discontinuity, by comparisons with secular trends in industrial organization. At the end of the last century, the strategy of extreme labour division, large indivisible investment and mass production of standardized goods had overcome another configuration deriving from the deepening of craftmanship, small or medium sized plans and customized products. Nowadays, the very limits of this Fordist strategy and the characteristics of the crisis (uncertainty about the composition and volume of demand, sharpening of competition, stop and go in economic policies, ups and downs of exchange rate) would spur the emergence of a new pattern of flexible specialization, i.e. a modernization of the Proudhonian vision of labour organization benefiting from the advances in the technologies of information processing.

This vision seems to originate from the Italian experience about the productive decentralization taking place in Emilia Romana and has been documented by many researches of Italian social scientists. But it was extended and made more general by historical and international comparisons which led to the expectation of a 'second industrial divide', as proposed by Piore and Sabel (1984). This conception is now shared by a wide range of persons, from the specialists of prospective to theoreticians, not to forget firm managers themselves. According to this view, small is not only beautiful, but also versatile and flexible, and therefore usually more efficient. Consequently, small or medium sized innovative firms would overcome large, belated and clumsy corporations.

The superiority of such an industrial configuration is supposed to derive from two series of factors. The core hypothesis is clear: the mass production is now over because after a century of standardized goods, the consumers are asking for significant differentiation. The rapid decline in the cost of information processing and the upgrading of workers' skills via general education would allow, if not impose, this new pattern. From an economic point of view, economies of scope would replace economies of scale, thus promoting a new industrial structure and even an original macroeconomic management, far away from the Keynesian principles which basically were linked to mass production. In the short and medium run, this system would spread and overcome Fordist methods, since the corresponding firms can react far faster and more efficiently to an uncertain demand for new products and unstable macroeconomic environment. Basically such a strategy assumes that the present crisis originates from the contradictions between the rigidity of techniques and the large variability of demand (A3).

Keynesian Coordination and a New International Regime: A Partial Substitute for Innovations in National Institutional Forms?: R4

This intuition about the roots of the present crisis is precisely quite the opposite: it is the disorder and incoherence of the international system which sharpen competition and bring national macroeconomic instability via the unpredictability of exchange rate, the difficulties in assessing the real rate of returns in the long run (i.e. A4). The reasons are probably to be found deeper: the productive system and the accumulation process are now operating at the transnational level, while regulation modes and economic policies are restricted to the nation, even if with severe international constraint. Therefore, a joint reflation or the negotiation of new rules of adjustment when an economy is facing an external imbalance would promote a far better achievement for quite all national economies.

Two variants of this strategy have to be distinguished. On one side, most Keynesians seem to think that international cooperation is a necessary and sufficient condition for recovery: industrial restructuration, if needed, would automatically follow economic stimulation. Some, such as Holland (1982), would propose a joint and coordinated reflation. If impossible for lack of political consensus, others call for a national reflation with the protective barriers of sophisticated methods for controlling external trade. This was advocated a few years ago by the late Cambridge Economic Policy group and especially Kaldor. On the other side, any coordination at the international level has to be completed by other measures promoting the emergence and diffusion of new configurations in industrial organization. Contrary to the previous one, this strategy does not conceive a way out of the crisis simply by deepening the old Fordist methods. Under this heading one could find the researches made by CEPII and especially Aglietta (1986) and a significant part of the RA.

Contrary to all the previous scenaria, this one emphasizes the key-role of macroeconomic determinants promoting a transition from one industrial system to another. Consequently, it fills a gap of most analysis undertaken from a pure technological or industrial point of view. At one extreme, the corresponding structural changes are considered to have very few links with what happens to growth and unemployment: this seems to be the dominant point of view of most macroeconomists such as Malinvaud in France, but probably many other examples could be found elsewhere. At another extreme, the policies directed towards industrial restructuring and general macroeconomic policies have to be coordinated, both of them being necessary for overcoming of the crisis. My own work with Petit leads to this kind of conclusion.

It is now necessary to assess the internal consistency of these four regimes and examine their likelihood.

An Assessment of these Various Regimes

It would be fairly long to propose a detailed analysis. Only major features will be discussed here and symmarized by Table 1.

An Overemphasis about Secular Trends, Few Concerns about the Novelty of Information Technologies: R1

Of course, such a neo-Schumpeterian view is now rather widely admitted, for it presents many strong intuitions and interpretations. Firstly, it derives from one of the few theorizings for which innovations and structural changes play a dominant role in economic dynamics. Secondly, many detailed studies have tried to substantiate this hypothesis, especially concerning the present third industrial revolution led by information techniques. Thirdly, this analysis is part of a grand vision about the long run trends of capitalist economies: one would have to expect a new upward Kondratieff, in line with the regularities observed over the last two centuries or more. The Kondratieff framework, revised by the neo-Schumpeterians, is one of the few to present such a long run interpretation, contrary to most economic theory limited to the short run adjustment.

Nevertheless it is far from providing a completely satisfactory answer. The evidence about the regularities of long waves is not clear, specially when the post-World War II period is considered. Can one rely upon such a weak determinism, when almost no theoretical framework has been proposed to explain this cyclical pattern? This is probably not the simple consequence of technology and balance between product and process innovations: the social mechanisms according to which productivity gains are distributed are to be investigated for any theorizing of growth and crisis (Boyer, 1987). But then it is difficult to find any automaticity in the recovery and the beginning of a new long run boom. Historical studies suggest that it is a partially open process, which derives crucially from the invention of new organizational forms at the firm, the national and the international level.

A second series of criticisms can be raised against the neo-Schumpeterian vision. It provides no clear explanation about the bunching of radical innovations and the emergence of strong complementarities between new investment in various industries, a key, but puzzling, component in the Theory of Evolution by Joseph Schumpeter himself. Furthermore it underestimates the real impact of innovations which seem to play the same role in each Kondratieff, whatever the precise technological social and institutional content of these innovations. Rather intuitively, the present information technologies are not at all repetition of the previous revolution centred upon the steam engine or the internal combustion engine. For example it is not at all clear that the consumption norm will include more and more information and telecommunication goods, in order to compensate the labour saving bias associated with the new equipment goods in manufacturing and services.

Finally, the notion of innovation has to be taken seriously. It is not simply the repetition each half century of a bunching of innovations in general: their specific content matters greatly for industrial organization, social stratification and macroeconomic dynamics.

Democratization of Work is a Central Issue,
but Technological Change and Macroeconomic Regulation Mode
also Matter: R2

Such a strategy seems appealing to a large variety of observers, from managers to academics and specialists of industrial relations. Is it not now a commonly held view that Taylorism has become efficient, at the expense of the motivation and dignity of modern workers? Enrichment of work, decentralization of production, maintenance and control, group stimulation, firm's ethic and cultura are now at the forefront of the agenda. Such a conception is strengthened by a series of converging observations. Within the same industry, the less Taylorist or Fordist firms seem to be the more successful in increasing their market shares. Similarly, the various national economies are far better, the faster they transform themselves away from the typical principles of scientific management. This seems a salient result of any comparison of Japan with the USA, West Germany with France, Italy with United Kingdom (for some evidence about the two last comparisons see Boyer, 1988).

But of course, democratization of the workplace is not a panacea. Firstly, the few econometric studies available suggest that the excess of control has a negative and significant, but not overwhelming, influence upon productivity. Other more traditional factors such as the rate of investment, capacity utilization increasing returns of scale have to be taken into account (Weisskopf, Bowles and Gordon, 1983). That is to say industrial relations are one of the components to be taken into account, alongside with the mastering of new technology, an adequate investment in volume and composition, not forgetting the macro conditions of a minimum stability in the general environment. At any moment, divergences in labour motivation can explain large discrepances in productivity achievements. Therefore, a reform in work organization might promote significant increases in productivity and quality. But in the long run cumulative growth of productivity derives from a subtle mix of labour management, adequate investment, good specialization in fastly growing markets and wise technological choices. For example, the sources of learning by doing, using or organizing play a prominent role in the long run dynamics of any industry.

This second strategy too then appears as a piece of a wider and more difficult puzzle which consists in finding the structural compatibility of various

Table 1 : From diagnosis of the crisis to accumulation regimes: a brief summary

TYPE OF STRATEGY COMPONENTS	THE SCHUMPETERIAN REGIME R1	DEMOCRATIZATION OF WORK R2	FLEXIBLE SPECIALIZATION R3	INTERNATIONAL GROWTH REGIME R4
DIAGNOSIS OF THE CRISIS	Dominance of process innovations over new products Mismatch between new technologies and institutions	Excess of corporate control over blue-collar workers Social limits to Taylorism	Mismatch between rigid Fordist techniques and fluctuating and uncertain demand in volume and composition	Breaking-down of the Bretton-Woods system Incompatibility between national regulations and production trends at the world level
ADVANTAGES	Continuity with previous historical trends (the long waves) Emphasis upon information revolution, as an engine of investment and growth	Rather strong consensus from radicals to business men A key factor in national divergences in macroeconomic achievements	Numerous success stories of small innovation and fast growing firms Actual changes in firm internal organization and relations with sub-contracting	Higher and higher dependency of national industries with respect to world trends in trade and finance Therefore international stabilization is crucial
WEAK POINTS	Extreme economic determinism by technological exogeneous trends	A significant but limited influence along with economic and technological factors	Relative unlikeliness of a reversal historical trends in labour division	Underestimates the productive and internal side of the crisis in Fordism

WEAK POINTS (CONTINUED)		Lack of macroeconomic analysis of the origin and diffusion of productivity	What are the macro conditions for such a programm?	Static efficiency is not a substitute for cumulative productivity increases	Uneven national modernization rythms prevent cooperation and joint reflation
CONSEQUENCES INDUSTRIAL	Trade off flexibility/ increasing returns	No direct connexion in the genuine analysis	No consideration of this factor	Microelectronis brings a flatening of returns to scale and more versatility	Pressure towards fast adjustment to external shocks The search for increasing returns via internationalization still prevails
ERS IAUL PROOR	Skills and retraining	A new composition of the work force is needed The process is generational and takes around 25 years	The upgrading of skills might be the consequence of workers' motivation via democratization Learning in the labour process itself	Multiskilled workers are welcome Towards a modernization of the Proudhonian craftsman via microelectronics	Likeliness of a new division of labour; the medium and high-tech industries can spread towards Periphery Towards a polarzation of skills
ORGANIZATION	Firms' structure and size	Towards the constitution of new oligopolistic rents Opposite evolutions of average size in mature and new industries	Less layers of controllers Possible reduction of plants' size	Splitting up of the giant corporation Reduction of firms' size but quasi-integration	Possible productive decentralization but greater financial integration Size: smaller for plants, lager for firms

production methods with different social organization and "economic regulation". This regulation is defined as the methods making compatible sources of productivity increases with their distribution between consumption, investment and public spending.

Short Run Flexibility is Convenient
but Cumulative Long Run Productivity Increases are Crucial: R3

In some respect, the strategy of flexible stabilization is a cousin of that of work democratization. But here the emphasis is put upon the impact of programmable equipments over the relative profitability of piece, batch and mass productions. The drastic decline in the cost of shifting from one model to another would now make efficient small or medium sized firms, specialized in a specific type of product mobilizing the same know-how. The originality of the information revolution is taken into account, contrary to the two strategies previously analysed. This is not the unique advantage of this third scenario.

Firstly, many success stories seem to confirm the birth and very fast development of this new firm and more generally the complete reorganization of most large corporations as suggested by many economists (Williamson, 1975; Piore, 1986; Adler, 1986a). Secondly, and this is a consequence of the previous transformations, in most OECD countries the industrial employment for small and intermediate firms rises, whereas the giant plants are reducing their employment. Since this reversal of previous trends has persisted over more than fifteen years, it is tempting to expect such a structural recomposition of productive systems (Piore, 1985). Finally, the long run history of industrialization can be reinterpreted as the struggle of two alternative configurations. Either the production is significantly differentiated and adapted to the consumer's needs, via a moderate mechanization and adequate skills of workers who can shift from one job to another within the same firm. Or the goods are highly standardized in order to be produced over a large scale by highly specialized mechanical equipments, operated by blue-collar workers with low skills. At the end of the previous century, the second strategy had defeated the first one, imposing its own Taylorist and the Fordist methods to the whole industry (Piore and Sabel, 1984; Scranton, 1983) and by extension to social life (Giedion, 1948; Nobel, 1977). The limits of Fordist methods now clearly experienced after almost one century, the productivity potentials allowed by microelectronics and the rise of educational levels would now make flexible specialization more efficient than mass production.

Even if very stimulating, this vision may overemphasize the impact of this new industrial organization. In fact, various counter-tendencies do appear which inhibit the generality of this model. Far from implying a return to pure and perfect competition, these new firms are coordinated via implicit or explicit networks; according to some authors (such as Leborgne and Lipietz, 1988), the former vertical integration is replaced by quasi integration, via joint ventures, stabilization of sub-contracting over several years in order to foster joint modernization of the large firm and sub-contractors. In fact, financial centralization might continue to increase, even if technical concentration is declining. Furthermore, the control of a significant share of the market is still the dominant objective of most competitive struggles. If this analysis is correct, the surge of small firms would not necessarily point out a total breakdown of the previous historical trends in industrial organization.

Two other arguments help in relativizing this new industrial divide. Firstly, the flexibility observed at the level of industrial plants and firms may hide opposite trends towards more rigidities at the macro level. For example, the marriage of informatics and telecoms calls for massive investment in software, networks and training of manpower, as well as a minimum of standardization. Even the Italian productive decentralization of Emilia Romana is rich in such collective and social environments: adequate and efficient institutional forms are therefore needed as well as infrastructural investment. Adding up this contradictory changes might lead to a more balanced view, the new emerging system combining some of the tendencies of the previous system towards rising fixed costs and increasing returns to scale. Secondly, and this argument is perhaps the more important, a static gain in efficiency via flexibility has not to be confused with a cumulative improvement of global productivity. If the first factor is determinant for industrial structure, the second plays a major role as far as the model of growth is concerned. In that respect, flexible specialization - defined as production of customized goods at small or medium scale - is not necessarily the new engine of growth, contrary to flexible automatization, i.e. a new combination of mass production with more product differentiation. This is the preliminary conclusion of a previous research (Boyer and Coriat, 1987), which of course should be discussed.

A Hidden Dialectic Between Industrial Reorganization and International Cooperation: R4

A similarly balanced view can be proposed concerning the fourth strategy which in fact should be combined with the previous one, taking into account the fact that the present crisis derives from interrelated factors (Figure 1).

On one side, the influence of internationalization over industrial organization is overwhelming, even if contradictory. During the last two decades, the share of national production exported has steadily increased in most OECD

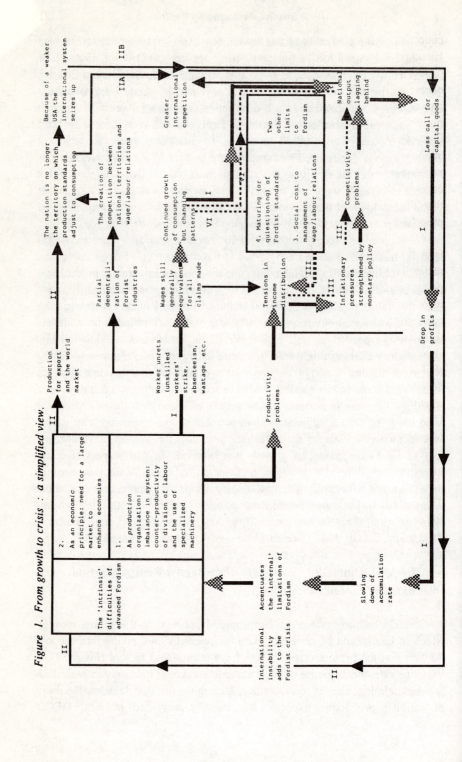

Figure 1. From growth to crisis : a simplified view.

countries, while large foreign investment and international credit have launched emerging industrial zones, i.e. new competitors. Therefore, productive reorganization in the North has to take into account what is occurring in New Industrializing Countries. Conversely one of the rules of the game for international trade and credit has broken down; a creeping protectionism and the surge of speculation might not only hurt modernization in the Centre, but in the Periphery as well. No doubt any cooperative strategy about exchange rates, national economic policies and the solution of the debt problem would improve prospective growth at the world level. Since it is easier to incorporate new technologies in a context of fast and steady growth than during a period of quasi stagnation and large unstabilities, the Keynesian proposals are welcome. But even if necessary, they are not sufficient.

In fact, on the other side, the benign neglect for productive reorganization is not to be accepted: if the 1929s crisis had derived from an inadequate national demand management and international system, the present one clearly points out the productive limits of Fordism and not only of demand management. Various evidences can be called for in order to substantiate this conception. Firstly, a detailed comparison of the origins and unfolding of these two crises (Boyer and Mistral, 1983; Basle, Mazier and Vidal, 1984) shows an unprecedented boom of productivity in the first case and the slowing-down in the second case. Therefore, sources of productivity matter. Secondly, as was pointed out earlier, the destabilization of international relations is somehow linked to the slowing-down of the modernization in the USA and symmetrically the surge of Japanese and European competitors (circuit II.A and II.B in Figure 1).

Similarly the previous joint international reflation (remember the 1978s experience) and the recent counter-oil shock have produced very unequal national growth and no clear acceleration of investment and modernization. This suggests that the building of a new international system is not a substitute for productive modernization in each country. Moreover, the polarization of external deficit (United States) and surplus (Japan and West Germany) clearly shows the unequal speed of adaptation to the new technological deal. Conversely, this feature plays a crucial role in any redefinition of the world financial system. In other words, industrial restructuring and the search for in new international system are to be analysed and undertaken jointly.

Therefore, the general conclusion is somehow trivial: the complexity and structural nature of the present crisis call for an eclectic strategy combining various components of regimes R1 to R4. Let us now present this interpretation and draw some of its consequences.

Some Consequences about Future Regulation Modes

Let us now summarize the previous analysis around the following question: what are the likely consequences of the present technological changes upon regulation modes? It is necessary to recall this notion as different from that of accumulation regime: basically, it incorporates much more precise determinations about individual behaviours, day after day, and not only in the medium long run. More exactly, a regulation mode is composed of any set of rules and behaviours which have the three following properties first, to bring into compatibility possibly conflicting decentralized decisions, without the necessity for individuals or even institutions to bear in mind the logic of the whole system; second, to control and conduct the prevailing AR; third, to reproduce the basic social relationships through a system of institutional forms, historically determined.

Attention will focus upon three major hypotheses.

The Present Trends are Not Straightforward but Rather Contradictory

Basically, the pressure towards flexibility at the firm level might be offset by opposite factors at the intermediate and macro level, which derive from the indivisibilities and the increasing returns associated with the emerging division of labour.

At the firm level, the modern information techniques no doubt allow more product differentiation and a shorter lag in reacting to market variations, since the present electronic equipments have reduced the costs of such changes. Just two evidences about this shift in the paradigm about the industrial organization. Firstly, one observes a sharp decline in the average run for traditional mass consumption goods. This feature seems outstanding for the manufacturing industry which is at the forefront of new industrial organization, i.e. the Japanese. Aoki (1987) gives impressive examples including such a mature industry as the car industry: the average production of a specific model is around a dozen to be contrasted with the millions of Ford T! Secondly, the relative performance of a firm within an industry, or a national industry within the world competition, seems rather closely related to product differentiation and quality, allowed by the new electronic equipment and software. Everybody knows such success stories.

But is it correct to transpose at the macro level these individual successes? The evidence is much more mixed than usually thought. Contrary to a widely shared intuition about the death of the giant corporation and the progressive domination of small and innovative firms the macro is not a simple transposition of a representative firm or household.

At the intermediate level, other factors mitigate the overwhelming advantages of micro flexibility and introduce old or new types of indivisibility.

Firstly, the large variety of the goods as use values ought not to hide that as value for exchange, they are submitted to a significant inertia. For example in highly automated plants, the amortization of equipments may represent the major part of unit costs: by definition these fixed costs cannot be varied with the fluctuations of demand. In other words, the possibility of differentiation of basic characteristics - i.e. product flexibility - is paid at the cost of economic rigidity.

Secondly, design flexibility is not necessarily equivalent to volume flexibility. A larger spectrum for product characteristics is for sure an advantage if the shift in demand occurs from one product to another of the same industry: the flexibility in the production organization allows a better capital utilization of electronized equipment goods. But the substitutability is always limited to a set of closely related products. Therefore if the demand shifts away from the corresponding industry, the internal substitutability is not at all a solution to this structural problem. Thus in the car industry, if the major shifts are among variants of the same product, technical flexibility induces economic flexibility. On the contrary, if one observes a saturation or a decline in total demand for cars, highly automated and modern plants might be an obstacle to adaptation, as far as they do not induce any competitive edge (at least if other firms adopt the same strategy), but imply large fixed costs. Similarly for the computer industry, technical flexibility is the adequate answer to unpredictable evolution in the precise composition of demand, but not necessarily to a general slump affecting the whole industry.

Thirdly, a large differentiation of final products can be reached by combining a series of highly standardized components. Again the car or the computer industries are good examples of such a combination: after all the customization of consumer goods is obtained at the end of the assembly line, by putting together items which are generally produced by thousands and even millions. In that respect, the opposition between mass production and product differentiation may be misleading: has not Hounshell (1984) shown that the rigidity crisis of the Fordist assembly line was overcome by the new figure of industrial organization invented by the staff of General Motors during the 1920s? Mutatis mutandis are not contemporary industries undergoing a new phase of such a process? From a more theoretical point of view, contrary to a common intuition, a careful investigation in the sources of economies of variety would show that economies of scale and economies of scope can be reaped simultaneously via a better utilization of skilled workers and general equipment tools or the share of the same basic knowledge between various lines of production and so on.

In order to push the analysis further on, it would be interesting to characterize the new information techniques with respect to previous trends in industrial organization. Measures for average size of series and numbers of different products processed by the same equipment could deal with various components of technical flexibility. But symmetrically, indexes about the share of fixed costs in total costs, the relative importance of capital depreciation and direct labour, the duration of depreciation, the time of return of new investments and the capital/output ratios could assess possible sources of economic rigidity. The future pattern for firm size and industrial structure would be conditioned by the relative balance of these two contradictory factors. A stimulating research programme could aim at elaborating or synthetizing such an information, if available.

The First Phase of the Present Crisis is not Necessarily Representative of the Way out of it

A comparison with the interwar period might help in understanding the present crisis, since some similarities are to be pointed out. At that time too, the severe crisis of corporate giants and the need for downward adjustment appeared for most contemporaneous observers as the premises of a new industrial organization based on smaller firms. Not to speak of the rigidity crisis of the typical Fordist assembly line, and the shift from the quasi integrated and continuous flow of totally standardized production to an assembly line recombining more differentiated products coming from a large set of subcontractors. Now we clearly realize that the relative rise of smaller firm was only a transitory adjustment, at odds with what followed a way out of the crisis after World War II.

Mutatis mutantis, we have to be conscious about a possible repetition of such a myopia, i.e. the extention to the long run of evolutions, which are specific to the first step of the crisis. At least four similarities should be discussed.

First of all, the competition via product differentiation was found compatible with a recomposition of mass production, not with its abandonment. It is for example significant that a historian of manufacturing technology, Hounshell (1984), characterizes the 1920s as 'the limits of Fordism and the coming of flexible mass production'. Symmetrically, some international comparisons suggest that nowadays the strength of the Japanese industry is not that much based upon flexible specialization in stagnating sectors, but flexible automation in new soaring markets (Cardif, 1985). It is likely that we are living a new era in the flexibilization of mass production.

Furthermore, a lower degree of concentration of production among industrial plants can be associated with a surge of financial centralization. Such a discrepancy has already been observed during the interwar period. Now again a complete revision of industrial organization of large corporations takes place: via productive decentralization, generalization of sub-contracting, incentives to competition between different departments of the same firm. This might correspond to a strengthening in the control of markets and a high degree of centralization of strategic decisions about innovation, investment, marketing and so on. In the present crisis, and for a decade, one has observed again a higher financial concentration with a larger productive decentralization. Fewer small and medium sized firms remain independent.

A third argument substantiates the same conclusions. Of course, a specific form for increasing return to scale apparently entered into crisis in typical Fordist industries. That explains the breakdown of the traditional Kaldor-Verdoorn relations (Boyer and Ralle, 1986). Nevertheless, new industries still exhibit a close and significant relationship between division of labour and market size and therefore between productivity and growth (Boyer and Coriat, 1987). At a more microeconomic level, the new electronic goods are characterized by higher learning by doing effects than the traditional mechanical or chemical industries, as clearly shown by the data collected by Ayres and Miller (1981). In a sense it is not really a surprise. Since these industries are evolving quite rapidly, they are reaping massive productivity increases, due to better knowledge of new techniques and an improvement in the management methods. Furthermore, these industries usually need massive investment in research and development, in the skilling and retraining of employees. There are possible roots for significant increasing returns to scale (Adler, 1986b).

Finally, a new technological evolution can be stopped by a lack of compatibility with the existing set of socio-political institutions. This is the explanation of structural crisis, as consequences of a mismatch between the technological paradigm and the prevailing social organization and economic regulation. In a sense the interpretation by some specialists of technical change (Perez, 1983; Dosi, 1987) is very similar to the analysis of the regulation approach. Let us just recall that in the 1930s some of the most innovative Fordist entrepreneurs in the car industry (Citroën in France) went into bankruptcy, because the competitive regulation mode was not allowing an adequate distribution of productivity gains (Boyer, 1983, 1987) and therefore was not validating new, even promising, methods of production. Now we might observe quite similar evolutions with significant bankruptcies or restructurations in the information industry (the Silicon Valley a few years ago). At this very moment the new productive system might need more and more computers, software and know-how of the same type which is in oversupply due to macroeconomic imbalance.

Taking into account these analyses, a final hypothesis can now be proposed.

A Composite Model is Likely: Towards a New Stage in Flexible Mass Production?

The debate about the consequence of information revolution upon technical flexibility is usually obscured by confusing two different issues.

First, the need for flexibility is seen as a reaction towards uncertain and therefore unpredictable macroeconomic evolutions. If these features go on during the next decades, the productive system will have to be reorganized in order to cope with this challenge. In other words the short run uncertainties call for a long-term recomposition of industries. This is no more than the extrapolation of the last decade. But the previous section has shown that it is not so evident. For example, would a return to macro stability imply a reswitching towards Fordist rigid organization? The doubt about a positive answer leads to a second vision.

The roots and reasons for the information revolution are far deeper, for it would be related to the emergence of a new paradigm in industrial organization. It would promote not only a better cyclical adjustment but a new principle of cumulative growth in productivity, via a brand new organization of productive flows in the manufacturing industries as well as in the various services. The longrun improvement in economic efficiency would then be the key question. The problem of product differentiation and volume flexibility could be solved by the same methods which are saving raw materials, investment, labour and processing time. Then would emerge a new economy of time via the generalization of computers to all industries, along the model of continuous production in process industries.

In the light of the previous observations, the second alternative is more likely, but with a caveat: this new ideal-type will transform unevenly the various industries and has to be combined with former configurations for productive organization. After all, this is coherent with the teachings of industrial history. For example, Fordist and Taylorist methods have had a dominant role but with unequal diffusion and even totally opposite models have existed in other sectors such as the services. It might be wise to expect such a superposition of various industrial configurations in the next industrial organization. Let us make a short list of them.

Flexible mass production might define the leading transformations in modern high-tech industries, as well as in mature medium-tech industries. A larger variability of product and design is made compatible with cumulative growth in productivity. The effective, if not registered, average size of the firm could remain fairly important in such industries since subcontracting might express a form of quasi-vertical integration.

Flexible specialization is also possible in declining sectors, characterized by frequent changes of models, such as the textile industry. This can be satisfied either by a return to older productive organization (including sweatshops) or by the implementation of informatics with totally new techniques (computerized laser). By contrast with previous configuration, productivity gains might be small in the first case, more significant in the second case. This could be the land of small or intermediate firms.

Old Fordist methods can be exported to less industrialized countries, with few significant changes to the configuration reached in the early 1970s in industrialized countries. This could be the case of heavy chemical or steel industry. The consequence would be a decline in the size of firms in the Centre, a rise in the Periphery.

The implementation of Scientific Management in traditional services might be a consequence of the diffusion of microelectronics. The rationalization of intermediate white-collar labour seems to have begun in the banks, the insurance companies and could be extended later on to the public sector (health, education, tax administration). The effect upon concentration and firms' size are not clear-cut.

New networks and collective services are simultaneously needed in order to conduct the so-called information revolution. For example, the communication sector now plays a dominant role and supposes significant indivisibilities. In other words, the private flexibility of individual firms call for infrastructural investment as a necessary condition. Similarly general education and professional training have to be redesigned in order to cope with this major change. In the Fordist system too, large public investments were needed for providing cheap energy and easy transportation. Nowadays, an open question concerns the type of public control and norms which would make compatible a series of private networks. If one adds the large amount of capital needed in order to step into high-tech research and development, it is wise to expect a high degree of concentration in these industries.

Concluding Remarks and Agenda for Future Research

The basic issues about new accumulation regimes and 'regulation' modes have probably been oversimplified in the previous developments. It is time now to list some qualifications and caveats.

The Need for Pluridisciplinary Approaches

Periods of structural crises usually emphasize the large interdependency between areas of analysis which would conveniently be considered in isolation within the previous stabilized development mode. Economic contradictions and imbalances put pressures upon existing institutional forms and are pushing for a reassessment of the relative position of various social groups. Conversely, the results of political struggles, compromises or alliances might imply alternative socio-technical restructurations. In other words, a joint research combining the competence of a large spectrum of scolars in social sciences is needed. One could for example imagine a fruitful confrontation with the corporatist approach (Berger, 1982; Schmitter, 1982; Katzenstein, 1984, 1985), the aims of which are quite similar, but the concepts and the tools rather different and probably complementary. This could be an answer to the frequent criticisms (Noel, 1987; Drache, 1983) about the lack of any clear political understanding of institutional forms in the RA. Similarly, new jointventures could be launched with interested sociologists who use to deliver careful and detailed case studies about industrial restructuring and capital labour relationships. A micro-macro, sociological-economic bridge would be welcome since it could deliver some insights about the determinants of the transition from one regime to another.

More Elaboration of the Basic Concepts

Maybe this new question calls for reworking the basic concepts and methods of RA. A first tentative clarification has been proposed (Boyer, 1986b), in order to promote a series of discussions and critical assessments. Two domains could be investigated. According to a first direction, it would be interesting to get a less economist definition of institutional forms. At the very beginning, the economists involved in this programme of research have been importing some hints and results from social and economic history, from sociology, law or even anthropology. In a second phase, according to the 'natural' propensity proper to any discipline, the regulationists have focused upon the economic consequences of institutional forms, somehow keeping their origins in the dark. Some noticiable exceptions have, of course, to be underlined (Aglietta, 1979a; Aglietta and Orlean, 1982). But new and more fruitful developments could derive from a more interdisciplinary approach, for example about the concept of the capital/labour relation, and more particularly about its possible post-Fordist configurations. Along a second line, the specialists studying the capital/labour relationships outside the advanced capitalist countries could probably propose new insights and maybe notions which could by contrast sort out some of the hidden characteristics of Fordism and post-Fordism. This could be an extension of the research programme proposed by Ominami (1986).

Analyses of the Transition from one Regime to Another

Until now, most of the prospectives proposed along the RA have only analysed the compatibility of a new set of institutional forms, fully diffused among the whole society (for example Aglietta and Brender, 1984; CGP-CEPREMAP, 1987). It is clear that this programme is far from being achieved. Nevertheless, it should be completed by another one, investigating the reasons for the success or the failure of innovations in institutional forms, and the determinants of their diffusion and speed, once successful. Various methods should be tried alternatly or simultaneously. On one side, comparative studies of firms belonging to the same industry and nation should deliver some hints about the micro-determinants of such a complex process. But the key message of the AR is to stress the lack of automaticity in passing from individual innovations to social norms. Therefore, on the other side, comparative studies of the present crisis with the previous ones (the so-called depression of the end of the last century and in the 1930s) might be enlighting about the major features of these transitional periods. Instead of simply compiling existing research in social and economic history (as was tentatively tried for Taylorism in France by Boyer, 1983), one could contemplate the feasibility of brand new investigations, testing the previous RA hypothesis for a given set of firms, industries or national economies.

International Comparative Studies

This is possibly one of the more promising areas for future research. Why do various nation states follow different trajectories, during growth periods as well as within structural crises? This is the old question raised by most of the scholars devoted to growth analysis. The question of the 1960s 'Why do growth rates differ?' (Denisson and Poullier, 1967) has now been turned into new but equivalent one 'Why do unemployment rates and patterns differ?' (Therborn, 1986). The economists do feel that historical and institutional arguments have to be advocated in order to explain the major divergences observed during the last two decades. Very different brands of analyses seem now to agree upon the importance of such a question: from Olson (1982) to Rowthorn and Glyn (1989), from OECD macroeconomists to labour economists and sociologists passing by the corporatist school. The regulation approach makes no exception and is part of this movement.

Part 2. Great Britain: State-Driven Liberalism

7. Thatcherism and Flexibility: The White Heat of a Post-Fordist Revolution

Bob Jessop

In 1964 the Labour Party entered office committed to a cross-class strategy of economic and social modernization. Sold under the slogan of 'the white heat of the technological revolution', it signified Labour's embrace of Fordism[1]. Labour aimed to boost productivity through indicative planning, sponsorship of large firms to increase economies of scale, an active science and technology policy, regional policy to boost manufacturing employment and reverse industrial decline, and state-sponsored industrial training. The resulting growth would finance political modernization through an expanding welfare state with strong commitments to education and health. It could not realize its programme and soon retreated to short-term economic crisis-management. The new Conservative Government under Ted Heath first tried a liberal market approach to economic and social modernization but then 'U-turned' towards more corporatist and/or dirigiste solutions. A third postwar Labour administration led first by Wilson and subsequently by Callaghan tried a social contract approach based on bilateral agreements with the trade union movement. This approach was dead on its feet in two years and was finally buried during 1979s 'Winter of Discontent'. This helped to precipitate a general election which was won by Mrs Thatcher's Conservative Party.

Her government initially pursued a monetarist strategy but gradually abandoned this from 1982 onwards. Indeed, whilst still committed to reducing inflation, the Thatcher regime embarked on a wide-ranging set of policies intended to create an 'entrepreneurial society' and 'popular capitalism'. It is committed to the white heat of a post-Fordist revolution and is seeking to flexibilize the British economy and reorganize British institutions and social relations to suit.

In short Thatcherism seems to involve a major break with key features of postwar politics. This does not exclude continuities between pre-Thatcherite and Thatcherite politics: clearly there are many. As other changes occur, however, even elements of continuity acquired new meaning as they are coupled with new policies and strategies. To explain this break I link the rise of Thatcherism to two interrelated shifts: the growth and crisis of Britain's flawed Fordism and an emergent crisis of the state.

Global Fordism and British Decline

The story of Britain since the war is often treated in terms of the rise and fall of the postwar settlement between capital and labour and its institutional embodiment in Keynesian economic management and the welfare state. But it is also important to see how wealth came to be produced during this period of the global rise and fall of Fordism. The United States pioneered Fordism (from its technological and economic base in mass production through its New Deal social and political base in mass consumption to its distinctive military Keynesian mode of demand management). After 1945, defeated or occupied nations also remade their economic, political and social institutions along lines favourable to integration into the global Fordist dynamic (most notably Japan and Germany, both under US influence).

The Nature of Fordism

Fordism itself can be analysed on four levels. As a distinctive type of labour process, it involves mass production based on moving assembly-line techniques operated with the semi-skilled labour of the mass worker. Not all branches nor workers will be directly involved in mass production in a Fordist economy, of course: the important point is that mass production is the main source of its dynamism. As a stable mode of macroeconomic growth, Fordism involves a virtuous circle of growth based on mass production, rising productivity based on economies of scale, rising incomes linked to productivity, increased mass demand due to rising wages, increased profits based on full utilisation of capacity, and increased investment in improved mass production equipment and techniques. As a mode of social and economic regulation, Fordism involves the separation of ownership and control in large corporations with a distinctive multi-divisional, decentralized organization subject to central controls; monopoly pricing; union recognition and collective bargaining; wages indexed to productivity growth and retail price inflation; and monetary emission and credit policies orientated to securing effective aggregate demand. In this context the key wage bargains will be struck in the mass production industries: the going rate will then spread through comparability claims among the employed and through the indexation of welfare benefits financed through progressive taxation for those not economically active. This pattern need not mean the demise of dual labour markets or non-unionized firms or sectors as long as mass demand rises in line with productivity. And, fourthly, Fordism can be seen as a general pattern of social organization ('societalization'). In this context it involves the consumption of standardized, mass commodities in nuclear family households and provision of standardized, collective goods and services by the bureaucratic state. The latter also has a key role in managing the conflicts between capital and labour over both the individual and the social wage. These latter features are clearly linked to the rise of Keynesian economic management and the universalist welfare state but neither element is essential for the growth of Fordism.

In broad terms the dynamic of global expansion after 1945 was based on the spread of Fordism with its mass production and mass consumption dynamic to other advanced capitalist economies. But we should not overlook the fact that small, open economies (such as Denmark, Sweden, Austria, or Canada) could also move toward a mass consumption Fordist society by filling expanding non-Fordist niches in the emerging supra-national productive systems. Under global Fordism, then, not all economies had to be Fordist in all respects. Rather, in an international division of labour whose dynamic was mainly determined by the leading Fordist sectors in the leading economies, economic success could be secured in at least two ways. First, national economies could themselves assume a mainly Fordist dynamic, with growth being primarily based on an expanding home market; or, second, they could occupy one or more key niches which permitted them to enjoy rising standards of mass consumption based on growing export demand and profits in non-Fordist sectors (small batch capital goods, luxury consumer goods, agricultural goods, and/or raw materials). If an economy is not itself predominantly Fordist, however, its mode of growth must complement the dominant Fordist logic. In this way it can still be involved in the Fordist growth dynamic rather than being (increasingly) excluded from it.

Britain's Flawed Fordism

In this respect the British economy was a double failure. For it neither moved successfully onto a Fordist trajectory nor did it find an expansive non-Fordist niche position within an expanding global Fordism.

First, although mass production industries, their suppliers and their distributors grew at the expense of traditional staple industries in the 1950s, they did not fully secure the fruits of the Fordist revolution. British-owned industry based at home rarely had the same returns from the new techniques of mass production as its overseas competitors or, indeed, as foreign-owned multinationals in Britain did. Among the factors which engendered this productivity gap were the slow rate of growth in Britain, the impact of Britain's distinctive form of union organization, and the inadequate managerial skills of British entrepreneurs. Among its consequences, given the government's commitment to maintaining full employment levels of demand

and to an expanding social wage, was the increasing satisfaction of mass consumption demand through imported goods rather than domestic output.

Second, to the extent that the British economy was non-Fordist, the manner of its insertion into the emerging global economy generated a logic of eviction, i.e. movement down the international hierarchy. This contrasts with the relative stability of an economy such as Denmark's or the upward movement of a Japan. Among the factors contributing to this negative dynamic were the City's position within the global economic order and industry's continuing commitment to (former) imperial markets rather than to the dynamic Fordist economies of Europe and North America.

Thus Britain's mode of growth could well be termed 'flawed Fordist'. It involved a limited expansion of mass production, relatively poor productivity growth, union strength producing wage increases from 1960s onwards not justified by productivity growth, a precocious commitment to social welfare and jobs for all, growing import penetration from the 1960s to satisfy the mass consumer market and, from the mid-1970s, to meet demand for capital goods. Despite these institutional problems, Britain did share in the prosperity of the postwar boom in the 1950s. As the conditions for Fordist growth weakened, however, British decline was much sharper. Indeed, not only has British industry long been in a structural disequilibrium (i.e. unable to secure sufficient net exports to pay for national import requirements at output, employment, and exchange rate levels which would be socially acceptable); its position has actually worsened over the postwar period (Singh, 1978). Moreover, this has been due to genuine competitive weakness across most markets and not just to slower growth in those markets where British industry was stronger.

These problems took a distinctive form in the 1960s and 1970s but some of their root causes date back to the industrial profile and related mode of growth inherited from Britain's brief period as 'workshop of the world' (1850-75) and to the mode of regulation which developed on this basis. Among these we can list schematically: (a) an industrial profile rooted in the first industrial revolution and dependent on small capital, coal, and cheap, unskilled labour - resulting in slow growth, low productivity increase, and stagnant or vulnerable markets; (b) weak vocational and technical training and a weak science and technology base for new industries tied to the second and third industrial revolutions - reinforcing static comparative advantage in first industrial revolution sectors and restricting any expansion in emerging sectors to domestic rather than world markets; (c) a host of atomistic family-owned firms and/or confederal monopolies without proper integration or professional management - which, coupled with inefficient capital markets and takeover mechanisms, meant the survival of capitalistically incompetent management;

(d) reliance on flexible craft workers rather than on the alternative 'American system' of mass production - with lack of standardization in product markets reinforcing the importance of craft skills; (f) captive markets in both formal and informal empires - making the staple industries (textiles, coal, iron and steel) vulnerable to import substitution strategies as world wars, protectionism and formal independence reduced British access; (g) a liberal state at home with weak capacities for engaging in economic guidance or management; and (h) commitment to sterling and the City's commercial and financial role to the detriment of industrial modernization. Many of these problems still remain to be addressed.

The British economy performed well during the period of postwar reconstruction because it faced a sellers' market until other economies (re-)established their manufacturing base. Thereafter it benefited from the general global economic expansion and the increase in trade during the 1950s and 1960s but began to suffer relative economic decline. Nonetheless it continued to import goods at rates tied to the rising incomes of workers. Although productivity growth did not match that of Britain's competitors, workers enjoyed rising real incomes in a sellers' labour market. The latter was underwritten by Keynesian demand management, the shortage of skilled labour, the social wage, increasingly favourable terms of trade in the early 1950s, and direct industrial investment by American multinationals. Behind the facade of relative prosperity, however, structural problems set in again and slow growth further discouraged effective investments.

How State Capacities Reinforced Decline

That these problems have continued is partly due to weaknesses in the British state. These involve far more than specific policy mistakes and are essentially underpinned by its limited strategic capacities. From the late 1950s there has been a rapid, seemingly schizophrenic succession of various policies to reverse national decline. These certainly conveyed a sense of purpose. Sometimes the government stressed liberal market solutions, sometimes it opted for corporatist strategies, and sometimes (often in despair at market failures and the weakness of its supposed social partners) it turned to dirigisme. But in each case it was thwarted by the lack of adequate capacities to pursue its preferred strategy. For the British economy was distinguished by market forces prone to market failures rather than spontaneous self-expansion, corporatist strategies without the corporatist structures and commitments needed to sustain them, and state intervention without an interventionist state able to steer an open economy dominated by monopoly capital.

In short the state's failure to facilitate, support, or direct economic, political, or social modernization is related to its chronic lack of strategic capacities. Elsewhere Fordist modernization has been variously linked with the predominance of liberal, corporatist, or dirigiste strategies. There is no fixed institutional pattern uniquely favourable to economic expansion under global Fordism. In all successful cases, however, the state had the capacities to pursue its preferred strategy effectively. The British state was ill-placed to pursue any such strategy consistently. In particular, when attempts were made to go beyond the liberal approach, the strategies were often crisis-driven, ad hoc, and temporary.

1. Liberal strategies were pursued within a Keynesian framework based on simple demand management. This involved neglecting the adverse supply-side repercussions of maintaining full employment levels of demand and implicitly relied on market forces to avoid the stagflationary tendencies inherent in Keynesian policies. But the operation of market forces was weakened by various market imperfections[2] and, even when market forces might have worked effectively, by a stream of politically motivated state interventions.

2. Corporatist solutions largely failed because their organizational preconditions were missing. Corporatist arrangements have typically been advantageous in economies with strong, unified peak organizations representing capital and labour and able to internalize both the costs and benefits of social partnership and with social democratic (or, sometimes, consociational) regimes strongly committed to supply-side policies and able to set the political agenda for other parties. In Britain there were clear divisions of interest between industrial and financial capital; industry lacked a strong peak organization and was fragmented; and the City preferred a liberal strategy based on an open economy, minimal intervention, and overseas investment and enjoyed a measure of economic dominance even when its views were not accepted. Organized labour was also weak, fragmented, and decentralized. On the political front, two parties with different programmatic commitments alternated in office and significant economic policy U-turns often occurred in the lifetime of any given government. The result was a cycle of failed corporatist strategies and, without a background of successful operation in easy times, they were subject to even greater strain when the going got tough.

3. Dirigiste solutions also seemed doomed to failure. For the state lacked the capacities to influence the micro-level of the economy and was obliged to rely on the relatively blunt instruments of money, law and moral suasion. In addition its efforts at dirigisme tended to be ill-informed, ad hoc, poorly coordinated (if not downright contradictory), and politically motivated. Commitment to dirigisme was weak because the dominant economic state apparatus comprised the Treasury-Bank axis, whose primary concerns were

the restraint of public spending, defence of sterling and short-term economic crisis management. Whatever their long-term benefits to the economy might have been, active structural policies proved inconsistent with these goals in the short-term. Other departments acted as sponsors of individual industries (or even of single firms) rather than as active planners with powers to ensure compliance down to enterprise or plant level. Where the state did intervene, it typically did so through legal restraints (e.g. prices and incomes policies) and money (e.g. subsidies). Both are blunt instruments for economic steering - especially where the state cannot control the allocation of credit. The use of law encourages the search for legal loopholes and can also provoke direct confrontation with the state. Relying on monetary channels often merely prompts economic activity orientated to the tax- or subsidy-efficiency of investments without regard to overall growth dynamics. In addition vast sums were spent on uncommercial prestige projects (e.g. Concorde), costly but unproductive defence and defence-related projects (e.g. nuclear power plants able to produce plutonium), and maintaining rather than restructuring inefficient industries (e.g. coal, cars, railways, docks). In short the state lacked the capacities to direct the economy.

The Crisis of Flawed Fordism

The resulting economic and political problems fused in the 1970s. The downturn of global Fordism exposed the UK economy more than most to structural economic crisis. State incapacities produced inconsistent strategies and U-turns within single governments and led to a growing sense of ungovernability and an emergent crisis of political legitimacy. The slow but steady economic and social changes consequent upon private affluence and public squalor had combined with the dynamic of party competition to produce class and partisan dealignment in the electorate and increasing popular dissatisfaction with the overall party system. Together with the failure of economic management these factors also prompted serious disputes about economic and political strategy in both major parties.

Especially important in preparing the way for Thatcherism were three aspects of the unfolding economic and political crisis. First, skilled workers were alienated by Labour and Conservative attempts to restrain wages as they suffered from the impact of rising prices and taxes. Thus they were attracted by Thatcher's promises to restore free collective bargaining, control inflation, and cut taxes. Second, as trade unionists tried to resist the crisis-induced restructuring of the economy, wage restraint and industrial relations reform, electors (prompted by the media and politicians) became unhappy about union power. The so-called 'Winter of Discontent' fuelled this disquiet because it seemed that the Labour Party no longer had a special relationship with the unions. And, third, whilst there had long been petty bourgeois discontent with the impact of the postwar settlement and the social disorder apparently accompanying its demise, this was now voiced by the leader of a major party. In these circumstances the Conservative Party under Mrs Thatcher was able to mobilize a new cross-class alliance against those identified with the postwar settlement and its self-evident failures.

The Significance of Thatcherism

The British economy was too rigid for fully exploiting the Fordist mode of growth and hence lacked the flexibility needed for a post-Fordist economy. Where an economy is too inflexible to move smoothly toward post-Fordism or find a niche in a post-Fordist world economy, this could still occur if the state can reorganize economy and society alike to make them more flexible. Where economic rigidities combine with state incapacity, however, the crisis will be sharper longer and require a more radical solution. This is the British case. Thus a two-step process is needed: state capacities must be reorganized and the enhanced state capacities used to remove institutional rigidities through direct state action and/or through action in support of other attempts. Thatcherism could be seen as just such an attempt to prepare a path to post-Fordism. Such an interpretation does not imply that Thatcherism will succeed in this ground-clearing operation nor that post-Fordism in one or another form will take root and flourish on this Thatcherite terrain.

One reason for caution here is the uncertainty surrounding two key issues. First, how far have post-Fordist labour processes and suitably flexible wage relations actually been established in Britain? And, second, to what extent might a stable mode of post-Fordist macroeconomic growth emerge to suit the changing position of British economic space in a changing global economy? Key issues regarding the labour process include: how far does any growth in flexibility reflect a sectoral shift in favour of services (as often low-tech as high-tech, Taylorized as emancipatory) rather than a fundamental reorganization of manufacturing, to what extent is any such increase cyclical rather than structural, and to what extent are its current forms primarily short-term, defensive responses by individual firms rather than part of long-term, offensive managerial strategies. Likewise, regarding the mode of growth, we must ask how far de-industrialization is reversible, the extent to which manufacturing exports can be replaced by service exports, and how long the City can retain its novel niche position as the international supplier of the financial and commercial needs of international capital. Favourable answers to these problems are clearly crucial for the longer run success of

Thatcherism's neo-liberal accumulation strategy but they cannot be guaranteed through state action alone even were this primarily concerned with getting the supply-side right. But let us first review the government's strategic objectives, its 'flexi-rhetoric' and support for an entrepreneurial society and popular capitalism, and its apparent efforts to create the political preconditions for a post-Fordist economy.

Enter Thatcherism

Thatcherism has contributed to reorganizing the state and preparing the ground for post-Fordism in two key areas. First, it is rolling back the frontiers of Fordist state intervention. This not only involves ending the crisis-induced interventions of the 1970s but also cutting back the 'normal' forms of intervention at national and local level which emerged during the 1950s and 1960s. And, second, it is trying to roll forward new forms of state intervention favouring the emergence of a post-Fordist economy in Britain. Some of its efforts here are purely transitional, concerned with installing the preconditions of a post-Fordist 'take-off'. Others may be precursors of the 'normal' forms associated with a new mode of growth which will emerge in the 1990s as the British economy (itself transformed) is integrated in new ways into a hanging global division of labour. Obviously these policies have a distinctively Thatcherite cast and are influenced by factors only indirectly related to the transition to post-Fordism. In this sense we must take care not to treat these policies as simple products of generic post-Fordist tendencies.

Indeed, as already noted for the British state's role in the Fordist era, the specific dynamic of the political system can introduce markedly dysfunctional factors into government policies for and on behalf of capital. Given the remarkably enhanced autonomy of the Conservative regime and Mrs Thatcher's commitment to conviction politics, it is not surprising that considerations of party advantage or partisan ideology are also at work. Indeed the economic failure of Thatcherism in its third term is partly related to the increasing primacy of party politics and 'two nations' redistributive measures.

This is not the place to describe the stages of Thatcherism. I will simply note that it has passed through four main periods: (1) its rise as a social movement, 1968-79; (2) its initial period in office, when Mrs Thatcher's main concern was to consolidate political power, 1979-82; (3) a consolidated phase, when the first real steps were taken to pursue a coherent post-Fordist course, 1982-1986; and (4) radical Thatcherism, attempting a general reorganization of social relations going well beyond the economic sphere, 1986 to the present.

In the first period Thatcherism was one of several responses to the crisis of the postwar order and Britain's flawed Fordism. In the second period, it was torn between its concerns with economic crisis-management and political consolidation. This was a deeply unsatisfactory time both from a governmental viewpoint and from the perspective of the transition to post-Fordism. Only in the third period did a new economic strategy crystallize: a combination of macroeconomic policies directed against inflation and microeconomic policies to stimulate economic growth and job creation. Finally, following the Conservative Party conference in October 1986, a radical, neo-liberal strategy for reorganizing British society was gradually defined and attempts were made to implement it (for more details on these stages, see Jessop et al., 1988). In the light of the 1989 Conference, the poll tax debacle, and the growing disarray in the Conservative Party, however, the future of the neo-liberal strategy must be in some doubt.

The Transition to Post-Fordism

So far I have left the nature of post-Fordism deliberately vague even its broad features are still uncertain. This is partly due to continuing struggle for dominance among its American, Japanese and German versions and the impact this will have on the international division of labour. Nonetheless, in crude terms, we can say that post-Fordism will be based on flexible production and differentiated, non-standardized consumption.

As a labour process post-Fordism will involve a flexible production process based on flexible machines or systems. It is organized to secure economies of scope and is operated through the combined labour of both multi-skilled and unskilled workers. It is not confined to areas previously dominated by mass production but can be applied to small-batch production and, indeed, going beyond the manufacturing field, to the production of many types of services in the private, public and so-called 'third' sectors. Thus the scope for the post-Fordist labour process to shape the dynamic of the emerging economic system is much greater than that of the Fordist labour process. As a stable mode of macroeconomic growth, the virtuous circle of post-Fordism would be based on flexible production, growing productivity based on economies of scope, rising incomes for polyvalent skilled workers and the service class, growing demand for differentiated goods and services favoured by the growing discretionary element in these incomes, increased profits based on technological rents and the full utilization of flexible capacity, and reinvestment in more flexible production equipment and techniques and/or new sets of products. Since the Fordist mode of growth was based on an expanding domestic market and the post-Fordist mode is more orientated to global demand, competition could limit the scope for generalized prosperity and encourage a market-led polarization of incomes.

As a mode of social and economic regulation, post-Fordism involves commitment to supply-side innovation and flexibility. Thus there should be a shift from the predominance of the bureaucratic 'Sloanist' form of corporate structure towards flatter, leaner, more flexible forms which enhance the strategic management of interdependencies. Competition will be based on improved quality and performance for individual products together with economies of scope (rather than the economies of scale typical of Fordism) and the search for technological rents based on continuous innovation. Engineering innovation and improved productivity in setting up manufacturing systems rather than manufacturing productivity within any given system will be crucial within industry; systems innovation will also be vital in the financial and commercial sectors. Industrial relations will focus on integrating core workers into the enterprise. And new forms of wage relation will be based on changing market conditions (flexi-wage and hire-and-fire or responsibility wages and regular reskilling) and a new role for the social wage.

As yet there is no obvious predominant post-Fordist mode of 'societalization' because of the competing Japanese, West German and American models. A plausible scenario for a Thatcherite Britain would be growing polarization of the provision for social reproduction: privileged members of the working and service classes would operate in an information-rich environment through the hypermarket and boutique, self-servicing, and popular capitalism to realize particular lifestyles and identities and those with incomes too small for this would be forced to depend on the small supermarket or corner store and a minimal, safety net system of collective consumption for routine survival. A system based on guaranteed minimum incomes could lead in quite other directions, especially if coupled with strong state support for cooperative, subsidiary and voluntary forms of collective consumption.

We should also recognize that the post-Fordist economy is inherently open. If the stability of Fordist economies was greatest when growth was primarily autocentric (within national or regional productive systems), post-Fordist growth will be irreversibly international. This has the paradoxical effect of reinforcing the state's role in promoting competition - not merely of individual firms or national champions but of productive systems and their various socio-political supports. In many cases this will require an enhanced role for continental or regional states (such as the European Community) since even individual nation states lack the means to organize competition. The post-Fordist world will be structured politically through national or regional rivalries in a race for societal modernization as well as economically through a global production system. If this marginalizes the state's role in national-level demand management, it magnifies its role in managing the supply-side.

There are already quite different patterns of transition to post-Fordism but they are all aimed at securing greater social and economic flexibility. Among the areas targeted for change are technology, production, industrial relations, labour markets, forms of competition and cooperation, financial and business services, taxation regimes, social security and welfare delivery systems, and education and vocational training. Governments must also manage the economic and social costs of transition as well as the political repercussions of the crisis of Fordism. How successful states are here will influence how far their associated national economies will maintain their general position in the international division of labour (which is itself changing under the impact of the transition) or will move up or down the global hierarchy. Nothing guarantees that strategies successful in the Fordist past will succeed in the post-Fordist future.

States are adopting various strategies in the current transition and we should not treat these as coherent or unchanging. Even during periods of relative economic and social stability, the state's relative unity is always problematic; and there are also many well-known limits to the state's capacities to steer economic and social change. Improvisation and trial-and-error experimentation are rife and policies must be adjusted to the changing balance of forces and new structural and/or conjunctural problems. None the less three basic strategic lines can be distinguished: neo-liberal, neo-corporatist and neo-statist (these are defined in my chapter on welfare states). One or other line tends to be dominant in specific countries and other strategic elements are aligned to it. In Britain this position is occupied by neo-liberalism.

Implementing the Thatcherite Strategy

I am not arguing that 'there is no alternative' to neo-liberalism in Britain nor even that it is the only path to post-Fordism for a Conservative Party. Instead I just want to explore its various dimensions, dilemmas, contradictions, and effects. First let me spell out its main features.

The Neo-Liberal Approach

The six most crucial elements in the Thatcherite strategy for securing flexibility are neo-liberal in character. They are: (a) liberalization, promoting free market (as opposed to monopolistic or state monopolistic) forms of competition as the most efficient basis for market forces; (b) deregulation, giving economic agents greater freedom from state control; (c) privatization, reducing the public sector's share in the direct or indirect provision of goods and services to business and community alike; (d) (re-)commodification of the residual public sector, to promote the role of market forces, either directly or through market proxies; (e) internationalization, encouraging the mobility of capital and labour, stimulating global market forces, and importing more advanced processes and products into Britain; and (f) tax cuts to provide incentives and demand for the private sector. These elements form the microeconomic basis of the Thatcherite supply-side strategy and complement the earlier and continuing commitment to a counter-inflation strategy based on some form of monetary and financial policy. Thus Thatcherism should not be reduced to a narrow or technical monetarism nor to a limited attack on trade unionism or the welfare state. It also involves attacks on the entrenched privileges of specific fractions of capital and private sector members of the service class. Not only has the government tackled union powers, for example, it has also begun disprivileging farmers, stockbrokers, lawyers and doctors.

In pursuing its neo-liberal programme the Thatcherite regime has been obliged to adopt complex and even contradictory strategies. In pursuing liberalization and internationalization in the City, for example, it further weakened the already crumbling patterns of informal self-regulation; in turn this has prompted new forms of state-sponsored, formally organized, corporatist regulation (see Burgi and Jessop in this book). Likewise, in privatizing natural or de facto monopolies, it has been obliged to set up regulatory bodies such as Oftel or Ofgas and, where strategic considerations are at stake, to keep a golden share or other powers to prevent foreign takeover. Again, in abandoning incomes policies and leaving training to market forces, its deregulation drive frees unions to exploit skill shortages and drive wages above productivity growth in the private sector. Thus we must treat the different planks of the neo-liberal strategy as elements in tension which are open to trade-off and may also demand flanking or supporting policies.

This is even more necessary because the process of neo-liberal modernization is most uneven in its incidence geographically, sectorally and socially. Its impact has generated tensions, conflicts and outright resistance which have in turn prompted additional forms of intervention intended to underpin the main policy measures. The further we move from the immediate sphere of production, the more varied these measures become. The neo-liberal strategy as the core accumulation strategy of Thatcherism rather than a general paradigm valid for its emergent state project or its hegemonic project.

The state project must also deal with the specific problems stemming from the crisis of the Fordist state system and is shaped by the specific political ambitions of the Thatcherite faction. Likewise the hegemonic project must also address the organic crisis of the postwar order. To develop these points further, we now review the broader political changes which have occurred during the Thatcher years.

The Changing British State

Many trends visible in the British state in the last decade were already there in the 1970s or earlier. Even in the areas most immediately subject to central government control, many changes continue trends already evident in previous regimes; and others are more linked to general economic and social restructuring associated with the continuing crisis in Britain's flawed Fordist economy than to its specifically Thatcherite features. But, just as diverse elements of the Thatcherite economic strategy have been articulated into a relatively coherent whole for the first time, so there is now a distinctive pattern to shifts in the state system. I will try to show this by reviewing six different dimensions of the political system centred on the state. These are the representational regime, the state's internal organization, patterns of intervention, the social basis of the state, the state project purporting to give the state system some cohesion and unity, and the hegemonic project defining the interests of the 'illusory community' allegedly represented by the government.

The representational regime has been restructured along three dimensions:
1. Tripartite corporatism has been largely displaced from the core institutions of the central state but other forms and sites of functional representation are still strong. Tripartite organs and social partnership ideologies have been undermined by the downgrading of 'Neddy' (the National Economic Development Council) and the abolition of many of its sector working parties; by the replacement of two-thirds of the tripartite statutory industrial training boards through weaker, voluntary boards under the auspices of trade associations (often excluding trade union representation); by the abolition of 'sponsorship' divisions within the Department of Trade and Industry in favour of 'market divisions'; by the deliberate exclusion or marginalization of union representation and the more fortuitous decline of the Confederation of British Industry as manufacturing collapsed and more right-wing bodies challenged it. But other forms of functional or economic representation remain strong. The government continues to back national champions. Essentially private, bipartite corporatist arrangements still flourish (Harden, 1989) and direct links between the government and the government-relations divisions of large firms

have mushroomed (Grant, 1989, p. 14). Public functions have been delegated to new self-regulatory organizations and private interest government has been established for favoured interests; new forms of 'partnership' linking community and market organization are also sponsored (securing legitimacy from community involvement and efficiency from market forces) (Harden, 1989, pp. 9, 44). Other shifts involve links with policy communities organized around common economic or social objectives as well as active encouragement to business representation in all areas of social and political life (e.g. schools, universities, health authorities, local authorities). Finally, corporatism has been shifted down to local government level (with social partnership still vital in many Labour-led local authorities in pursuing their alternative economic strategies and/or local 'anti-poverty strategies') and plant level (with closed shops and consultation stronger under Thatcherism than before).

2. There has been a continuing shift of political parties away from electoral catch-all parties towards more populist governing parties. The catch-all party emerged during the Fordist period when there was broad consensus around Keynesian welfare state goals and mass production and mass consumption were supposedly weakening class antagonisms and sharp social cleavages. The new party form no longer functions mainly as a relay for relatively stable interests or clear-cut programmes from below but as a means of mobilizing popular votes for the government. This approach was pioneered by the Tory Party under Mrs Thatcher and has since been copied by the new model Labour Party with its apparent support for 'market research socialism'. Such quasi-presidential, plebiscitary politics revolves around elite competition for office and is organized in and through the mass media (notably television) rather than the party organization. Linked to this is the personalization of party political competition - evident above all in the equation of the Conservative Party with Thatcherism and the increasingly presidential style of Kinnock's leadership of the Labour Party. Only the Green Party seems determined to resist this trend.

3. In place of broad-based corporatism or party mobilization from below, a mixture of populism and raison d'état has emerged. The Thatcher regime appeals directly to the people over the heads of intermediary organizations (parties, unions, etc.) and often resorts to the national interest as defined by its own good self in pursuing its 'conviction politics'. The growing failure to consult affected interests (including other state bodies), refusal to appoint Royal Commissions, reluctance to modify (or even publish) the recommendations of review bodies, and failure to provide reasoned justifications for many radical policies, are all clear signs of this. Courts have also proved willing to extend the area in which arguments about national

security are admissible (Shell, 1988). This means that the decline of corporatism has not so much seen a resurgence of parties and parliament as a shift towards plebiscitary populism and a strong state.

The internal structures of the state have witnessed several complex, sometimes reactive, sometimes strategic, but generally uncoordinated and constitutionally unreflective movements. Yet their overall thrust is clear - towards 'undemocratic centralism' (Graham and Prosser, 1989; Harden, 1989): (1) Power has been concentrated in Whitehall at the expense of the postwar, elected local government system whose functions were linked to the Keynesian welfare state. Thus the Greater London Council and six metropolitan counties were abolished and many of their functions transferred to non-elected bodies controlled from Whitehall. Even the surviving local authorities have seen their powers and responsibilities removed or reduced through privatization, obligatory tendering, tax and spending controls, delegation of local authority powers to other bodies (such as schools), promotion of 'partnerships' between local authorities and other public or private bodies, central diktat, and so forth. Moreover the government twice legislated to prevent them engaging in party political propaganda (sic) financed from local taxes at a time when central government's own advertising budget has grown remarkably. At stake here is the rolling back of the local Fordist welfare state and the rolling forward of local authorities as regulatory bodies which award contracts or franchises, set standards, monitor compliance, sanction poor performance and are overseen in these residual welfare activities by a centrist, executive power. (2) This is linked to the decentralization of new supply-side powers to the local or regional level through the creation of single-function non-elected government agencies; they are subject to closer control by central government, given specific resources for specific purposes, and obliged to encourage more involvement of local business interests and mixed forms of management. The London Docklands Development Corporation and similar urban development agencies are the best example of this trend towards various forms of market led planning to induce or guide economic and social investment (Brindley et al., 1989). (3) Although the Thatcherites promised mass 'quangocide', they have not significantly reduced non-departmental public bodies. Instead, 'what has occurred is a distinct tightening of central control over NDPBs, exercised through the largely uncontrolled discretionary power of appointment, financial controls and the power simply to abolish inconvenient bodies and create more compliant ones. The courts apart, central government now regards itself as having exclusive legitimacy within the state apparatus. This re-assertion of the authority of central government over NDPBs is an attempt to rationalise and control the 'public' sphere in pursuance of governmental objectives' (Harden,

1989, p. 34). In addition, whilst some NDPBs were abolished, others have been established. (4) There has also been an upward shift of some powers and responsibilities to the EC level and other multinational blocs. Some of these moves have been welcomed, if somewhat halfheartedly: examples include various European high-tech policies, regional aid and support for transport and communications infrastructure. Other powers are contested, sometimes vehemently: notably membership of the Exchange Rate Mechanism or proposals for worker democracy. This emergence of a Euro-state involves not only central but also local government. Thus we see new forms of linkage between the local authorities in Britain and their counterparts in Europe as well as liaison with central EC institutions concerned with technology transfer or innovation centres in areas of regional decline (Dyson, 1988, pp. 1-10). (5) Welfare delivery has been restructured so that Britain no longer has a 'differentiated' welfare state and is acquiring an integrated social security state. Welfare was defined in terms of the 'one nation' objective of providing a high and rising standard of benefit (in cash or kind) for all citizens as of right; and the economic welfare (full employment and growth) goals of the postwar settlement were managed separately from its more social (income support, health, housing, education) tasks. Now polarization is accepted and welfare policies are subordinated to economic objectives. Overall, 'two nations' effects will be marked not only in the polarization of income but also in the provision of services (further discussed in my chapter on welfare states). (6) In line with neo-liberalism, financial controls play a greater role in the state control; this reinforces the role of the Treasury and its role in policing public expenditure. Value-for-money, global manpower targets, good management practice have all been emphasized; and market proxies have come to play a key role too - albeit focused on input rather than output measures. Even where the regime emphasizes 'community' or 'partnership' in developing new forms of political organization and mobilization, it forces them to work within the limits of market rationality (Harden, 1989, p. 11). In line with the more general supply-side orientation, some state functions are transferred to departments with a stronger economic orientation. Thus urban policy has been moved away from the Home Office and the Department of the Environment to the Department of Industry, the Training Services Commission, and non-elected task forces and corporations. Steps are also being taken to decentralize the work of the civil service by hiving off service-delivery functions and operational tasks to executive agencies run on commercial lines (perhaps with a view to their eventual privatization) and retaining only a core group of ministerial policy advisers and their support staff within a career service in Whitehall. This would be coupled with relocation of the agencies out of London, regional variations in pay rather than a national pay scale, and increased reliance on part-time and temporary staff contracts to enhance flexibility and reduce wage costs (Threakston, 1989). (7) Although its output has increased, the power of Parliament and Cabinet have declined further. Parliament passes more legislation with less effective control over it and the Cabinet has been downgraded in favour of Prime Ministerial powers. The Cabinet Office has increased in importance as the focal point for the Whitehall network and the PM relies on a widened circle of personal advisers rather than a Prime Minister's Department. A further aspect of increased executive power is greater resort to legislation to reverse judicial decisions unfavourable to government and the novel use of clauses to exclude judicial review (Graham and Prosser, 1989, p. 337). 8. The state's repressive powers have been strengthened and reorganized on two fronts: first, the police have acquired more powers and more autonomy from local police authorities, have resorted to armed action more often, and have been given crucial ideological roles (e.g. in schools and ethnic communities), and central government itself has increased its powers over its employees; and, second, there has been increased political control over the mass media (especially television), increased coordination between the Conservative Party and the tabloid press (its 'long ideological arm'), and an attack on the autonomy of various ideological and cultural institutions (from from schools and universities through the churches to the Royal Family). Ideologically Thatcherism has been assisted by the rightward drift of the popular press and the relative growth in the readership of 'Thatcherite' papers and also takes matters into its own hands through its increasingly sophisticated use of public relations, the lobby and leaks to manipulate the political agenda (for a recent survey of the 'rights' record, see Labour Research Department, 1989a).

Consequent upon the developing neo-liberal economic strategy, there have been marked shifts in the forms and purposes of intervention in line with the transition to post-Fordism. In particular the boundaries of the state have been redrawn through growing privatization, (re)commodification, deregulation (and reregulation) and liberalization.

1. In part the state has simply ceased to support traditional industries (resulting in their accelerated decline) and turned to supporting emergent, high-tech industries (such as information technology, robotics, bio-tech, aero-space, microelectronics, and, notwithstanding market sentiment, nuclear power) and producer services. But it is also active in reorganizing some older sectors (re-industrialization) in line with post-Fordist needs - especially when they have a crucial infrastructural role or are still deemed potentially competitive (my chapter with Noelle Burgi illustrates the case with coal; steel and cars are two further examples). Moreover, despite the rhetoric of disengagement, many of the older forms of intervention have been retained,

such as interference in nationalized industry pricing policies (as hidden taxation and/or fattening for privatization). The continued commitment to nuclear power and the 'green dowry' for the water industry after their respective privatizations also exemplify such 'neo-liberal' interventionism.

2. From a primary concern in the 1950s and 1960s with the task of demand-management and promoting economies of scale, productivity and planning, there has been growing concern in the mid-1970s and throughout the 1980s with the supply-side and, above all, with promoting economies of scope, flexibility and entrepreneurialism. Thus we see new supply-side agencies (such as the Training Services Commission), the acquisition of new supply-side capacities by existing apparatuses (e.g. Department of 'Enterprise'), and, linked to privatization, new regulatory bodies to supervise private sector monopolies (e.g. Ofgas, Oftel). As the state has cut back on massive subsidies for lame ducks given without regard to economic restructuring, it has promoted new forms of subsidy (often linked to the tax system) to encourage supply-side innovation in areas as diverse as product design, technology transfer, quality control, marketing, financial and information systems, business planning, research and development. If dirigiste methods are less often used, the scope of substantive facilitation and support has been much increased to reinforce the impact of the more formal and general macroeconomic measures to restrain inflation and secure a favourable legislative and regulatory framework. Moreover, behind the rhetoric of laissez-faire liberalism, bodies such as the Welsh Development Agency, Scottish Enterprise and urban development corporations have been given major interventionist and dirigiste powers.

3. Local authorities have become key agencies for supply-side intervention. As they are closer to the local economic action than the central state, they can act more flexibly and effectively to encourage wealth and job creation. But, in the government's view, this depends on their becoming less accountable to local electors, their own employees, or traditional clients. Instead they should involve local business and its technical and/or ideological spokesmen (such as chambers of commerce) and form links with other relevant policy communities (universities, higher education, etc.).

4. Nor should we ignore the many and varied ways in which government has increased its resort to authoritarian powers and restrictions on civil liberties (cf. Norman Lewis's chapter). Indeed the Thatcher government has the worst record on human rights appeals to the European Court and has often been found guilty in British courts in its dealings with local authorities.

Turning now to less formal aspects of the state, we consider first its changing social bases. Broadly speaking there are two key sites of support: popular forces and 'establishment' forces. Whilst the former are mobilized and represented primarily through political parties and their several flanking or auxiliary organizations (such as unions or churches), the latter have more direct personal and organizational links to the state system itself.

The social democratic Keynesian welfare state in Britain had a 'one-nation' popular base. As it was orientated to securing 'jobs for all' and 'social welfare', everyone could in principle share in its purported benefits - whether by participating in the labour force and/or getting index-linked and expanding welfare benefits. Its chief beneficiaries were the organized working class (especially its skilled and semi-skilled male core in growth industries) and floating voters whose votes mattered to the 'pensioneering' parties committed to the postwar consensus. This base became less secure from the late 1960s, however, as three shifts occurred: the manual working class shrank and became more diverse, dispersed and disorganized; social movements developed around non-class cleavages and issues; and postwar growth began to falter. As the KWS seemed to turn against its beneficiaries, Thatcherism tried to mobilize a different set of forces.

With its consolidation after 1982, Thatcherism had a new social basis in the gainers from its commitment to the entrepreneurial society and popular capitalism. This implies a 'two nations' social basis of the state. The really rich are the most pampered (Rentoul, 1985) but the largest groups of winners are the new service class and the skilled and semi-skilled private sector manual workers in core parts of growth industries. These also have a strong (but not exclusive) regional base in the South, notably London and the growth triangle bounded by Cambridge, Bristol and Southampton. In contrast, even when the economy was performing well, a growing (if disparate and fragmented) number of people were excluded from Thatcher's boom - often due to policies designed to push down wage rates or to cut and/or restrict access to welfare benefits. They included the long-term unemployed, the new poor primarily dependent on state doles (notably low income pensioners and single-parent families), and a growing army of peripheral workers involved in the more part-time and/or temporary, flexi-wage, hire-and-fire economic sectors.

Thatcherism has also presided over a reorganization of the 'power bloc' at the cost of the traditional British Establishment. It has clearly rejected key parts of the old Establishment (notably the Church of England, the BBC, Oxbridge, the mandarin class of top civil servants, gentleman farmers, the 'wetter' elements in the royal Family); but the (newly internationalized) City remains strong. More weight is given to commercial values and multinationals have acquired an even more dominant position. These shifts reflect both the crisis in corporatist bias as well as major changes in the mode of growth and industrial profile of the British economy.

The Thatcherite state project is also distinctive: the emerging official state project combines conviction politics ('Is he one of us?'), a 'strong state' ideology, and an emphasis on resolute political leadership. This is quite consistent with pragmatism: there has been permanent improvisation, continuing trial-and-error experimentation, and a policy of institutional Darwinism (the survival of the fittest governmental institutions often deliberately pitched against each other). Whilst government powers have been redistributed at the local level, the executive typically reserves the right to redistribute resources across and among these bodies and to do so without meaningful prior consultation with affected interests. It can also pick and choose among different, often competing, experimental models promote those which seem to be advancing its objectives and to modify or close those which are not - because they are costly and ineffective agencies and/or serve as sites of resistance to the restructuring of society. Thereby the central state tries to penetrate into local niches and microeconomic sites to reinforce capital's ability to exploit even the smallest areas of surplus production and consumption and/or to influence the reorganization of civil society at the micro-social level.

Such experimentation is also evident at central level in the continuing war of manoeuvre conducted by Thatcherism within Whitehall. The centralization of power does not mean that it has been subject to any effective concentration and coordination through increased control over different parts of the central state and their associated policy networks. Whether this lack of concentration is rational cannot be assessed purely in administrative terms. It has clearly inhibited stable, long-term policy making in many institutions (e.g. local government, education, training, health, nationalized industries) and specific policy areas (e.g. exchange rate policy, industrial relations). But it also enables the regime continually to reallocate resources (selectively cutting or expanding financial and manpower budgets), redirect policy (closing, modifying or expanding specific initiatives and programmes), and to promote competition among agencies for further support contingent on their advancing its (often changing) objectives. This is all the more necessary because Thatcherism has encountered many institutional obstacles and much political resistance in its attempts to modernize Britain.

Finally, a new hegemonic project is discernible under Thatcherism. This has passed through three stages: (a) an oppositional phase when it criticized 'jobs for all' and 'social democracy' and stressed 'counter-inflation' and 'authoritarian populism'; (b) a consolidating phase, based on the 'social market economy', which justified rolling back the Keynesian welfare state, and the 'strong state', which was needed to deal with the repercussions of the crisis; and (c) a more positive, consolidated phase, based on commitments to 'the entrepreneurial society' and 'popular capitalism'. The 'decisive economic nucleus' of this new project would be the transition to a post-Fordist society - if only Thatcherism could get us there.

The Prospects for Success

Thatcherism is a high risk strategy with no guarantee of success. It faces problems due to structural constraints, policy dilemmas, and institutional obstacles and cannot rely for ever on such fortuitous events as a divided opposition or a Falklands War to keep it in power. Since long-term success depends on the success of neo-liberalism, we will deal with this first.

Economic Risks and Contradictions

In post-Fordist terms, Thatcherism has recorded some clear successes. It has rescued the City and encouraged its emergence as the international centre for international financial capital; it has promoted re-industrialization and neo-industrialization; it has attracted inward investment in the hope of revitalizing the economy; and the UK economy is finding new niche positions in a new global economy centred around financial services, business-to-business or producer services, pharmaceuticals, speciality chemicals, aerospace, defence production, food processing and the heritage industry. Each of these successes has a downside, however, and there are several clearly identifiable risks in the overall government strategy.

First, pushing the City as an international financial centre for international financial capital at a time when the international monetary system is prone to extreme short-term volatility and medium-term structural instability is risky. It involves high costs in exchange rate and interest rate management and there is also a danger of financial collapse. Moreover, as 24-hour trading, the information revolution, and the further expansion of an integrated, and lightly regulated, European financial system after 1992 become more important, London could lose its privileged position and Frankfurt become the main international financial centre in Europe.

Second, the policy of internationalization deprives the UK of a coherent industrial core around which secondary and tertiary economic activities could develop in a stable manner (Porter, 1990). This could make long-term growth depend on the decisions of multinational firms orientated more to their global strategy than to the impact such decisions may have on the UK economy. Thus it could deprive the government of effective control over the economy unless it can maintain a regulatory and financial climate sufficiently kind to business long enough for the synergetic effect of international investment to create its own incentives to remain. Somewhat worrying in this regard is the clear preference for some multinationals (e.g. those from Japan) to locate their assembly plants in Britain but their European R&D facilities in Germany. This reflects the weakness of Britain's education and training record and poor civilian R&D record. In turn this suggests that the quality of inward investment may be insufficient to turn the British economy round.

Third, the current strategy on flexibilization rests on a palaeo-liberal conception of a hire-and-fire, flexi-wage labour market and so shows insufficient official concern for educational and vocational training to produce multi-skilled workers. The training activities of private firms or the Training Services Commission do not seem to make up for past market or government failures. Fourth, the government's neo-liberal refusal to fund, support, or direct civilian research to the same extent as our main competitors means that many high-tech, R&D intensive industries will lose out in international competition, pushing the UK economy down the technological hierarchy. Import penetration is already greatest in high-tech sectors and the technological balance of payments is deteriorating fast. Finally, in adopting a market-led approach, the government has exacerbated the sort of regional imbalances typified in 'North-South' divide. This has recreated the conditions associated with the old 'stop-go' cycle with the result that overheating in the South prompts measures which damage a lagged recovery in the North.

Much of the apparent success of the neo-liberal strategy actually depends on trends in the South-East, where the dominance of City and rentier interests and the central role of various low-profile forms of government aid (e.g. airports, research establishments, defence industries and motorways) have long favoured strong growth. It is overheating in the South-East which has prompted the recent deflationary attempt to engineer a 'soft-landing' for the economy as a whole. Future investment in general and growth in more depressed regions in particular are likely to suffer from this. That manufacturing might recover to the same extent in the North is uncertain - especially as the 'internal market' and Channel Tunnel may further pull growth southwards. Whether the continued decline of manufacturing really matters is certainly controversial but so is the extent to which UK producer services and financial services can replace manufacturing in sustaining Britain's trade.

Political Risks and Contradictions

There are also problems rooted in the internal contradictions of its policies as the Thatcher government tries to secure political as well as economic benefit from neo-liberalism. There are real tensions in the commitments to popular capitalism and capital accumulation. In rolling back the social democratic state, the government has regularly sought political advantage at the expense of economic rationality. It has pursued short-term asset stripping of the public sector for the sake of a share-owning democracy, cosmetic reductions in the PSBR, and tax-cuts - all detrimental to long-term improvements in competition and industrial performance. It has sought to maximize revenue through the sale of monopolies rather than promote competition through dissolving them. It has sought to promote popular capitalism by deep discounting of shares rather than securing the best price for their underlying assets. And there is little evidence as yet that privatizing firms improves their subsequent performance once allowance is made for the more general growth in profits after the 1979-81 recession (Bishop and Kay, 1989).

More generally the government's political strategy has been less concerned with redirecting public spending towards modernization and welfare than with tax cuts and fiscal privileges for the middle class. This has encouraged a consumer boom and import penetration which have undermined the sort of domestic economic recovery which would sustain tax cuts in the longer term. The current state of disrepair in the nation's infrastructure (from public transport through education and housing to water and sewage) confirms this problem. It has also privileged middle-class consumption and tax havens rather than giving real incentives to the low paid and industry. Its housing policy, in particular, is fraught with contradiction. By privileging owner occupation in the hope of electoral benefit, it has promoted a consumer boom on the basis of housing equity, aggravated the crowding out effects of mortgage credit on productive investment, and discouraged regional labour mobility from areas of job scarcity to areas of labour shortage. Moreover, in promoting owner occupation, it has created a vested interest which proved fickle when faced with downturn in the housing market.

In addition, public support for core sectors of the welfare state (notably the NHS) and the retention of certain industries in the public sector (notably water) remains strong. This means that the government will encounter increasing difficulties in its attempts to roll back the Keynesian welfare state. At the same time there is considerable opposition to eliminating or reducing tax concessions on mortgage interest, life assurance, pensions and fringe benefits such as the company car. Both factors will tend to restrict the room for tax concessions if the need for infrastructural investment is to be met from the public purse. In short the government's concern to reward supporters is interfering with the pursuit of a rational accumulation strategy.

Conclusions

Forces favourable to the emerging strategy have clearly been consolidated - notably through the continued expansion of the City, the increased dominance of multinational capital in the growth sectors of the UK economy, the expansion of the military-industrial complex, and the rise of post-Fordist service and manufacturing sectors. Likewise the continued decline of manufacturing industry in less competitive sectors and the restructuring of the public sector has reduced the weight of industries, occupational groups and trade unions which opposed the strategy. But this is not wholly advantageous to the current Thatcherite strategy. For the City is increasingly servicing the international market and engaging in foreign and eurocurrency lending so that it is becoming less dependent on the British economy as such; multinational capital is footloose and orientated to global strategies rather than to UK policies and interests; the military-industrial complex is threatened by pressures on the defence budget, by the Defence Ministry's adoption of a less nationalistic procurement policy, and the limited spin-off from military R&D to civilian technological applications; and, as the House of Lords report in 1985 emphasized, it is unclear how far the low-wage, low-tech service sector can survive without a strong manufacturing base.

In this sense there is growing disquiet about Thatcherism's long-run impact on the competitiveness of the British economy. The latter is fast losing the last vestiges of an independent and coherent manufacturing base which could provide the basis for a national economic strategy. In contrast, despite their growing involvement in the international economy, Britain's three main competitors have industrial cores from which they can dominate the world and which are carefully fostered by their respective states through different types of industrial policy. Japan has a leading role in electronics, robotics and high-tech consumer goods, Germany in chemicals and high-tech capital goods and the US in military hardware, aero-space and information technology. Britain's role in these areas is increasingly that of a base for branch-plants of foreign multinationals and it has a leading position only in pharmaceuticals, speciality chemicals, aero-space and business services. Whether this can sustain an upward movement in the international hierarchy or merely serves to slow the British economy's long-term decline remains to be seen.

The obstacles to success are mounting. But, even another government would have to face the problems involved in moving beyond Fordism. Fordism implied that workers' interests in full employment and high wages were consistent with capital's interests in expanding mass production and mass consumption. This provided the basis for Keynesian welfare state policies and also enabled at least some social democratic parties to become the natural governing parties for postwar capitalism. Conversely 'post-Fordism in one country' does not seem to need full employment and even encourages the division of workers into high- and low-wage sectors. This makes it more difficult for social democratic parties to manage the transition and poses new political dilemmas.

But these same problems also make it more likely that the forward march of Thatcherism will be blocked. Its preferred economic path towards post-Fordism is undermining its own room for manoeuvre. Its policies have favoured footloose international financial capital, the military-industrial complex, and low-wage service industries. This means that the state has no real control over capitalist growth. Its Gladstonian concern with financial economies in public expenditure and with promoting flexibility in the market place has obstructed public investment and supply-side policies which would encourage a more concerted approach to the use of resources in organizing production within and among enterprises. Popular capitalism has a key role in Thatcherite strategy but it threatens to create a permanet underclass with destabilizing effects. Moreover, even the privileged participants in this popular capitalist bonanza have felt the pinch as the housing market has collapsed dramatically. Nor is Whitehall yet organized for real strategic thinking and Chequers meetings and prime ministerial seminars are not an ineffective substitute. Instead the neo-liberal strategy has become increasingly concerned with (regressive) redistribution and partisan advantage and has failed to grasp the nature of flexibility required in a post-Fordist era. Thus we can already discern emerging tensions between a Thatcherite politicians' settlement concerned with party advantage and a more productivist Thatcherite settlement concerned with Britain's international competitiveness in a very different world order from that of the postwar boom. Whether or not the politicians will once again win out over the producers - as occurred during the implementation of the postwar settlement - remains to be seen. The tea-leaves suggest that the increasingly blocked neo-liberal road pioneered by Mrs Thatcher could be bypassed by the sort of neo-statist approach favoured by Heseltine and the 'left Heseltinism' of Kinnock's new model Labour Party. Whether the new goverment led by John Major can move in this direction or we must await a Labour goverment remains to be seen.

Notes

1. The Fordist aspects of Labour policies are discussed in Jessop (1991).

2. These included atomism in markets where concentration was required to secure economies of scale, monopolistic restrictive practices in cartellized sectors, collusion in cases such as defence or farming, and poor management generally.

8. The Fetishism of Flexibility: The Case of British Rail

Richard Hyman

This paper is organized in three sections. The first considers briefly the experience in Western Europe during the 1980s of 'deregulation' and 'flexibilization' as features of employer strategy and state policy, referring in particular to Britain under Thatcher. The second part examines the case of British Rail. Where management in the past decades has embraced commercial priorities in anticipation of eventual privatization. Finally it is argued that governments, employers and academics alike have tended to fetishize the notion of flexibility.

Flexibility and Deregulation in Europe

The 1980s saw a major shift across much of Western Europe - particularly, but not exclusively, associated with governments of the right - in the relationship between the state, capital and labour. Whether this marks a decisive break with earlier patterns (which many have termed corporatist) is not the concern of this paper. Rather, I wish to focus on the issue of deregulation of labour relations.

In the past decade there have been widespread initiatives to restrict, dilute or eliminate statutory protections for workers against arbitrary employer practices and against the vicissitudes of the labour market. Such protections - whether the product of working-class strength, consensual paternalism or the populist programmes of the successors of Mediterranean dictatorships - have been increasingly denounced as obstacles to enterprise. Among the OECD countries, concerted pressure by employers' organnizations has achieved broad support for the principle of deregulation (OECD, 1983b; Barkin, 1987). Of particular importance has been the issue of the employer's right to hire and fire; legal restrictions have been depicted as an obstacle to employment creation. In a range of countries - France, Italy, Spain, Portugal and Britain are obvious examples - there have been sustained efforts to 'liberate' the commodity status of labour power from external constraint and regulation, allowing the (im)balance of market power between employer and employee to operate unconstrained. At a different level, curbs on publicly funded payments to workers who suffer redundancy or are otherwise unemployed have also been widespread. Here, the sin of economizing on state expenditure in the face of sharp increases in umemployment levels meshes neatly with the rhetoric of the 'disincentive' effect of such payments on the jobless.

How is deregulation to be interpreted? Is it an essentially conjunctural response to intensified competitive pressures in the world economy, facilitated by a shift in the balance of class forces? Or does it mark a structural shift in the political apparatuses of production relations? We may note that deregulation has not been a significant feature in certain European countries which have survived the global economic crisis better than others: conservative Germany no less than social-democratic Sweden, for example. We may also note that increasing the market autonomy of individual capitals is not necessarily a recipe for the vitality of capital-in-general. 'Market failure' is the normal characteristic of market economies. Hence, in Bruno's terms, 'micro-flexibility' leads naturally to 'macro-rigidity'.

The British case is an exemplary illustration. 'Building Businesses Not Barriers' has been the self-proclaimed goal of the Thatcher regime. Not only has most of 'positive' labour legislation of the 1974-79 Labour government been dismantled, but far longer-standing protections (notably those intended to set more floor to the wages of the lowest-paid groups of workers) have been substantially weakened. Other statutory protections (for example in the field of health and safety at work) have been renders largely ineffectual by cutbacks in the enforcement machinery. How successful has this been in strengthening the competitiveness of British capital? In the view of MacInnes (1987, p. 168), 'It may have been the signal achievement of Thatcherism to give a further powerful twist to the process of the decline of the British economy and society in the name of doing precisely the opposite.' Redundancies and bankruptcies have characterized a process which, to apply a term coined by Evans and Lewis (1989), may be regarded as 'destructuring' rather that restructuring. The 'upswing' of the late 1980s - fuelled by North Sea oil revenues and the proceeds of denationalization - has clearly revealed one consequence of deregulated labour markets: a serious shortage of key skills. This in turn is the predictable outcome of the dismantling of most of the modest state-sponsored initiatives in industrial training which had occurred since the 1960s.

Is deregulation therefore a dogma rather than a strategy? An obvious feature of Thatcherism is the selective natura of the retreat from state interference. Trade unions, for example, have become subject to the most extensive and oppressive regulation since the Combination Acts. New and comprehensive rigidities circumscribe any attempt to initiate industrial action. Within the state sector itself, direct government controls have been introduced to an umprecedented degree. Economizing has been imposed by the intensification of the 'cash limits' system, originally introduced in less draconian form by the previous Labour government. (Here, though, we may note paradoxically that the electricity supply industry has been encouraged to press ahead with its nuclear programme regardless of cost; a consequence of the determination to cripple the mineworkers.) Health Service managers have been required to band over areas of their activities to private contractors. So have local authorities, whose ability to raise and disburse their own funds has been drastically curbed by the mechanism of 'rate-capping'; their traditional autonomy will be more severely circumscribed still with the enactment of the current Local Government Bill. Teachers have had new, and rigid, conditions of employment imposed upon them in 1987; education as a whole will become subject to an unprecedented degree of centralized state direction under legislation currently before parliament. Is this less than even-handed commitment to flexibility a sign of confusion, selective vision or bad faith?

Let us turn briefly to the changing policies (strategies?) of employers in their management of labour. It has become common in Britain in recent years to speak of the 'flexible firm' (e.g. Atkinson, 1984) in which the twin principles of 'numerical' and 'functional' flexibility are applied. According to this model, a core of multi-skilled and adaptable workers enjoy relatively stable employment contracts, while a (large and expending?) periphery are hired and fired according to fluctuations in the product market. Such analyses often refer to Japanization, in two senses. Firstly, attempts to restructure production on 'kanban' lines, eliminating perosity within the work organization in order to maximize productive intensity. Secondly, efforts to win core workers' loyalty and commitment through assigning staff status and through management-controlled communication mechanisms (sometimes designed to displace or marginalize trade union representation).

The problem is to determine how this model matches reality. As recent critics have argued (MacInnes, 1987 pp. 113-124; Pollert, 1987), on any rigorous definition the 'flexible firm' is a fiction. Likewise, the whole notion of Japanization tends to reflect a mythologized view of Japanese labour relations and the changes which these have aspired in Britain (Graham, 1986; Turnbull, 1988). Yet if a looser and weaker definition of Japanization or the flexible firm is adopted, then it is far from clear what is new. Labour market segmentation, efforts to cultivate the 'trust' of key employees, attacks or 'restrictive practices', all are familiar features of British industrial relations. The evidence suggests that most employers in Britain have sought only cautious and piecemeal alterations to traditional employment practices and forms of work organization. One significant feature is the lack of any widespread attack on trade union organization as such, along American lines (even through efforts to restrict union influence have been more common).

Nor, interestingly, have there been widespread moves to introduce flexibility in working time, an important development in countries of Western Europe.

Do we perceive here an inherent conservation among British employers - or a rational fear that new rigidities may result from an overenthusiastic pursuit of flexibility? Streeck's recent discussion of management strategy is relevant here. Certain industrial relations systems, he suggests, sustain the status of employers, underwriting a stable structure of rights and obligations; others reinforce contract, the relationship of market exchange based on the pursuit of short-term advantage. The latter system facilitates numerical flexibility, and in some labour market situations may boost direct management control within production; but it provides no basis for employee loyalty, commitment and initiative. A status-based relationship is more likely to achieve the latter, but at the cost of other inflexibilities in the handling of the labour force. 'Being caught is a structural arrangement that is shaped by a complex interaction of contract and status,' he concludes (Streeck, 1987a, p. 295),

> and having come to appreciate the functions and dysfunctions of both,
> employers cannot but find it hard to formulate a consistent strategic approach to building
> a more flexible system of labour relations.

In Britain, where the historical interaction of contract and status has been complex to an almost unique degree (cf. Fox, 1985), the obstacles to coherent strategy are correspondingly great.

Flexibility and Rigidity: The Case of British Rail

The dynamics of state and employer policy formulations coincide in the context of nationalized industries. Significantly it is here that many of the most notable exceptions to the above generalization have occurred. It might be thought that this is because a government dedicated to the enforcement of commercial principles within public sector management has proved unusually ready to disregard commercial logic in pursuit of ideological ends. What private employer could have borne the costs of the 1984-85 dispute in the mining industry? On the railways likewise, recent management initiatives in pursuit of enhanced flexibility have typically seemed to owe as much to a political as a commercial rationale. In consequence, most such initiatives have been profoundly contradictory in their implications.

One broad element in the transformations of the past decade has been explicitly politically determined: privatization. The dismantling and disposal (often on give-away terms) of what are denounced as 'public sector monopolies' have been a major feature of Thatcherite commitment to market discipline. In the case of British Rail (BR) this has entailed selling off most of its ancillary activities, including shipping, road haulage and bus operation, hotels, and a number of engineer workshops. BR has now been required to place station catering out to competitive tendering, and is on the point of contracting out more central elements of its operations such as permanent maintenance. Within the railway system itself, meanwhile, there has been a radical restructuring designed to install greater commercialism (and, many would add, to facilitate eventual privatization of the core of BR). In place of the highly centralized organization established after nationalization four decades ago has been created a system based on five 'business sectors'. The five regions, largely matching the former private companies, which previously enjoyed a measure of decision-making autonomy, have been virtually dismembered, with lower-level management acquiring substantial operational discretion within specified budgets. Such localized initiative now extends to a range of personnel and industrial relations managerial functions.

While the implications of this set of organizational transformations have not (as far as I am aware) been systematically analysed, certain contradictory effects are apparent. Most centrally these concern the importation of market dynamics into what were hitherto organizationally integrated production relations. Where privatization or competitive tendering has occurred, bargains must be struck and performance monitored between BR and autonomous private companies; while within BR itself, sector management involves a large measure of 'contracting' between quasi-autonomous business concerns. Designed to overcome the problems of 'organizational failure', these changes open the possibility of 'market failure'. How do market relations ensure the standards of safety and punctuality essential in a railway system? What are the transaction costs involved in assessing the relative responsibility for (say) track maintenance and signalling on a line which serves several different business sectors? If a derailment occurs, must operating management negotiate a one-off salvage contract with workshop management? Such problems, only now emergent, exemplify the interactional rigidities which result from the 'flexibility' of market-based relations. Nor is this a novel insight; for example Trist et al. (1963), in a classic exercise in managerial sociology, described in detail how the attempt to control mineworkers' labour through an internal subcontract relationship generated pervasive inefficiencies and inflexibilities. This lesson must almost certainly be relevant in organizations which, in the 1980s, seek to manage complex interrelationships through the mechanisms of economic exchange.

In a variety of forms, BR in the 1980s has sought to introduce greater flexibility into the organization of labour within production. The most prominent instance was the 'flexible rostering' issue, which precipitated a national strike by engine drivers in 1982. BR's insistence on terminating the

1919 agreement which limited drivers' hours on a daily basis, in favour of day-to-day variability within each week, owed much to pressure from government and such public agencies as the Monopolies and Mergers Commission (Ferner, 1985, 1987). While simple commercial considerations doubtless also inspires management, the cost of the 1982 dispute and the terms on which the change was implemented entailed that 'flexible rostering' was economically disastrous in the short term and of questionable value in the longer run. Paradoxically, as Pendleton has commented (1986, pp. 241-242), 'the greater complexity of work arrangements has reduced flexibility and strengthened the reliance of managers and supervisors on footplate staff'.

Symbolism was undoubtedly an important factor behind the flexible rostering dispute. In modern circumstances, footplate staff comprise a small proportion of employment and costs in BR; yet they represent a proud and cohesive craft-based sector of the workforce which enshrines, far more than contemporary management (now increasingly, and deliberately, recruited from outside the industry), the traditional ethos of the railway system. Challenging its status would seem to hold intrinsic importance; hence the high significance attributed to the issue of 'driver-only operation' (even though safety constraints limit the practical applicability of this principle); and also the enthusiasm to eradicate the traditional 'line of promotion' for footplate staff by merging drivers and guards within an integrated 'traincrew concept'. The importance which BR management attributes to these initiatives is scarcely explicable by their cost-saving and productivity advantages. Undoubtedly, however, they are comprehensible as an assertion of managerial prerogative in the face of rival bases of employee collective identity - and this calculated to win the goodwill of the current government in its role as 'banker of last resort'.

It is possible to interpret in similar terms BR's recent challenges to establish mechanisms of collective representation. Management has increasingly sought to marginalize the National Union of Railwaymen (whose loyalty to the railway industry was traditionally of great value to management in its rationalization initiatives (Hyman and Elger, 1981); has made strenuous efforts (see below) to eliminate much of the local consultative machinery originally created by the private railway companies; while as a substitute, there have been attempts to foster supervisor-employee relations through 'team briefings'. It might be argued that the established mechanisms of collective representation and consultation have provided a lowcost and largely consensual means of processing and defusing the grievances inevitably generated in a large and complex communications industry highly dependent on employee commitment and goodwill. Whether a more assertive managerial stance can achieve these outcomes as economically and effectively is questionable. The new managerialism however possesses its own inbuilt justification, particularly in an industry being groomed for privatization.

There are nevertheless serious contradictions in such management policies, particularly since quality of service and 'customer care' have been explicitly identified as major priorities. Where flexibility is pursued through the use of part-time and temporary labour - one of the current BR initiatives - such objectives are likely to suffer. Much more generally, BR managerialism in the 1980s represents in new guise the change from 'status' to 'contract' in employment relations. Traditional railway employment involved extensive formal rules governing recruitment, transfer, promotion, duties and payments. This highly inflexible (and employer-created) system helped sustain a workforce imbued with an ideology of railway 'service'. Dismantling these mechanisms and transforming railway employment overtly into a simple market transaction will enhance managerial discretion, but at the potential cost of the disaffection and alienation of a workforce whose ability to disrupt and sabotage the system is immense (as they will often confide to the sympathetic listener).

After a decade of Thatcherism, these contradictions have had explosive consequences. In industrial relations, BR suffered a humiliating defeat in 1989. In the previous year management announced that it wished to obtain major alterations to the existing machinery of national negotiation and local representation, and in November 1988 gave the necessary twelve months' notice that it would withdraw from the machinery if no agreement was reached within this period. Underlying this initiative was the aim to move from standard national conditions to variation between regions and 'business sectors', and to undercut the status of those trade unionists who acted as officials of local and regional consultative committees. No doubt it was assumed that the unions would find it hard to mobilize resistance on such an issue; but when negotiations for the annual pay increase broke down in April 1989, they were able to ballot successfully for industrial action over both matters. The method adopted was a series of 24-hour strikes, on six separate occasions during June and July. BR attempted unsuccessfully to have the action declared illegal - the first major case in the 1980s when the judges backed unions rather than the employer. Their resort to the law probably strenthened the resolve of rail workers and the unions, while publicizing the opportunism and internal divisions of BR management.

Eventually a settlement was reached providing a minimum pay increase of 8.8 per cent, with larger rises for some groups of worker, as against the pre-strike 'final offer' of 7 per cent. BR also agreed to maintain existing machinery of negotiation and consultation until changes were mutually agreed, without any time limit on negotiations. This was almost universally viewed as a severe defeat for BR; as *The Guardian* commented (18 July 1989),

> step by step, BR management has been forces to capitulate in the face of a united work-
> force backed by a travelling public - particularly in London and the south east - which for
> too long has had to suffer an inadequate service, overcrowding and poor investment ...
> There are those on the board who last night thought that the episode has seriously dented
> the chances of privatization.

As a direct consequence, the hard-line personnel director of BR lost his job three months later.

The second crucial blow for BR's single-minded pursuit of commercialism stemmed from the impact on operational safety. Investment curbs, staffing cutbacks and worker disaffection all increase risks in what has always been an accident-prone industry. Injuries to railway workers, some fatal, have increased during the 1980s. Far more dramatic, however, was the devastating fire in November 1987 at Kings Cross underground station, when 31 people died and many others were injured; an incident widely attributed to staff cuts and other cost-saving measures. While the London Underground is not part of the BR system, the incident raised doubts about its own safety levels. Such doubts proved all too well founded when in December 1988 a crash at Clapham Junction claimed 35 lives, with nearly 300 passengers injured. The subsequent public inquiry found staff shortages, excessive working hours and inadequate training among the contributory causes. As yet it is unclear how far BR management is willing - or able - to reverse its economizing policies in the interests of safety. But unless it is seen publicly to do so, the whole rhetoric of 'customer care' on which its marketing efforts rest will appear hollow.

In BR today, flexibility is not a coherent and integrated managerial strategy. Rather, it seems to comprise a piecemeal set of initiatives, linked by a politically driven rhetoric which perhaps misleads managers themselves even as it alarms the workforce. The partial and uncertain nature of the pursuit of flexibility is understandable: a railway, more than most other forms of flexibility activity, requires a large area of regularity, routine and predictability. Yet there is also a more general conclusion to be drawn: 'flexibilization' is one more instance of the attempt to strengthen management's ability to direct and manipulate labour, an attempt however constrained by management's dependence on workers' unforced initiative. Ultimately, it is an effort to reconcile the incompatible imperatives of accumulation and legitimation.

In Conclusion: Some General Propositions

Flexibility has been identified as a key and perhaps overriding imperative, by employers and governments of the right, for roughly the past decade. While the theoretical rationale for this commitment stemmed initially from unreconstructed believers in the virtues of 'free' markets, support has also come from analysts who identify institutional rigidities as the central explanation of faltering economic performance (e.g. Williamson, 1975; Olson, 1982). Within the labour movements of Western Europe, the need for greater flexibility is now virtually unquestioned, despite differences over the nature and extent of the rigidities to be overcome. In academic analysis likewise, the diagnosis of a problem of rigidity and the identification of flexibilization as the decisive trend of the 1980s have become something of a new orthodoxy.

This consensus however masks substantial differences in levels of analysis and empirical focus. As Bruno has insisted (1987, p. 139),

> although everybody talks now of flexibility, and even trade-unionists are ready to agree that the system 'requires more flexibility', the first thing to notice is that flexibility has never been precisely defined as a conceptual category, and is therefore fundamentally ambiguous.

At least three distinct conceptions may be distinguished within the recent literature. The first is a new, systemic imperative and/or dynamic within contemporary (post-1970?) capitalism. The second is a novel and distinctive strategy pursued by employers and/or governments. The third is a rhetoric or ideological legitimation used to support anti-labour policies. These various meanings need to be clearly differentiated. They also require critical scrutiny.

Systemic analyses of capitalist dynamics can assume a number of forms. For 'regulation' theorists, the Fordist organization of production which became dominant by the mid twentieth century generated increasing problems of employer coordination, psycho-physical fatigue and collective employee resistance. 'Neo-Fordism' is identified as a recomposition of the detail division of labour, accompanied by more automatic systems of technology, which allow the orientation of production to more diversified product markets on the basis of 'a new flexibility' (Aglietta, 1979a, p. 125). From a very different analytical approach - centred primarily around transformations in the sphere of consumption rather than production - Piore and Sabel (1984) have also posited a crisis of Fordism. For them, however, the resolution is post- rather than neo-Fordist, involving a technologically based enhancement of worker skill and initiative within a system of 'flexible specialization'. Other, more eclectic interpretations are also available: for example, analyses founded on the global restructuring of capital, or proposing some form of technological determinism.

The high level of abstraction involved in analyses of trends within capitalism-in-general creates problems of application when the focus is on specific national economies or even Western Europe as a whole. Whether, and how, broad theorizations can be established empirically is of course a familiar conundrum. An equal problem is the tendency to identify regimes or social structures of accumulation as essentially homogeneous and unilinear. As I have argued elsewhere (Hyman, 1987, 1988), it is essential to emphasize the contradictory dynamics of capitalist production and the consequent inevitability that any mode of restructuring will generate new problems for capital even as it relieves the old. 'Flexibility', in other words, may remove certain obstacles to accumulation but can be expected to create others.

Analyses in terms of strategy adopt a more voluntarist and particularistic approach to recent trends: the force and cunning deployed by agents of capital and the state are here identified as the main determinants of flexibilization. Yet what is meant by strategy? Many writers use the term as little more than an equation for decision-making. This is indeed the vacuous manner in which the label 'business strategy' is commonly applied today; strategy and tactics are confounded. But there is a stronger definition of strategy, which reflects the derivation of the term as the overall planning and direction of a military campaign. This implies the existence of a grand design, encompassing long run objectives and the sequential means to their attainment, with a rational evaluation of alternatives at every stage. This conception, however, gives rise to two problems. Firstly, it is often unclear who (in a context of collective decision-making) is doomed to perform the role of strategic calculator; much of the literature is curiously evasive on this question. Secondly, much of the (unfortunately limited) empirical evidence suggests that in both cabinets and boardrooms, decisions are commonly ad hoc, idiosyncratic and ill-informed. An actor-centric analysis which posits a coherent flexibility strategy is thus somewhat difficult to ground empirically.

A different order of issues arises when flexibility is addressed primarily as an ideological discourse. It is certainly important to expose the ideological character of 'flexi-talk'. A totally flexible system is empirically (and probably logically) impossible. Any form of social organization requires certain relatively stable structural regularities - in other words, rigidities - for purposive action and interaction to occur. 'Any type of organization', as Daniel aptly puts it (1970, p. 6), 'is a set of restrictive practices in so far as it allocates certain defined tasks and responsibilities to certain individuals and groups of individuals and not to others'. Dore (1986) chose the seemingly paradoxical title 'Flexible Rigidities' to encapsulate his argument that the capacity of Japanese industry for flexible adaptation rests on trust relationships which are founded in turn on long-established distinctive, and rigid social institutions.

In most industrial situations, then, the issue is not rigidity-versus-flexiblity but: what kinds of rigidity? And in terms of policy, what institutional rules and arrangements should be sustained, which altered or abandoned, and which new rigidities established? And here the ideological dimension is of crucial importance: for a key influence on the discourse of flexibility is who gains or loses from a particular set of institutional arrangements, and whose interests would benefit or suffer from their alteration. As Bruno puts it (1987, p. 147), 'the bulk of flexibility strategies ... amount to a redistribution of existing rigidities rather than to a net gain of overall flexibility'. Moreover: 'every rule or regulation which has been introduced into industry to provoke workers with some protection restricts management's freedom of action' (Flanders, 1964, p. 32). Is it then surprising that 'the notion of flexibility in the United Kingdom context has been virtually synonymous with the idea of labour being flexible in the interests of capital?' (Atkinson, 1987, p. 98)

The notion of flexibility, then, has become something of an ideological fetish. Its whole discourse is a one-sided, and often intentionally misleading, means of characterising what might better be described as a specific constellation of choices, advantageous to employers, among different types and patterns of rigidity. If one of the objectives of social science is to demystify, social scientists should take care to avoid embracing, within their own conceptual apparatus, the fetishism of flexibility.

9. Flexibilization and State Strategies: Coal and the City

Noelle Burgi and Bob Jessop

Comparing the coal industry and the City since 1945 illuminates the state's changing economic and political policies as well as the longrun development of Britain's political economy. We will relate coal and the City to the postwar settlement, describing the forms and timing of their respective structural crises and looking at the various strategies followed to make them more profitable and/or more flexible. We will also discuss the state's involvement and try to explain why coal and the City have so often been treated differently.

Coal mining played a key role in Britain's early industrialization, soon became a leading domestic staple industry, and helped underpin Britain's overseas expansion through its export earnings[1] coal-miners themselves became the lance de fer of working class economic and political organization owing to their strategic position in British industry, their dense web of occupational and community ties, and their political role in Liberal, and then Labour, politics. Total coal production began to fall after 1913, however, as export markets declined; and several interwar inquiries reported a growing structural crisis. A different type of crisis emerged in the 1950s. Demand for coal was first weakened by the rise of an international oil regime promoted under US hegemony and then by the turn to nuclear power. Moreover, within this global decline for coal, British output failed to compete with overseas competition from state-subsidized and/or opencast mines.

The City played an equally crucial role in Britain's rise to economic predominance and acted as the clearing house of the world economy in the nineteenth century. Its role became more restricted after World War I with the crisis in the gold-sterling standard and a gradual retreat first into empire and then into the overseas sterling area. The City's international orientation was still significant after 1945 but it proved more and more difficult to retain market shares in financial services. Moreover, just as miners were a leading force in working-class political life, the City is often credited with a dominant, even hegemonic, role in bourgeois politics.

Here we examine only the last 40 or so years: from the nationalization of the Bank of England (1946) and coal mining (1947) to the recent deregulation of the City and the efforts to make the coal industry more flexible and cost-efficient. This comparison should prove interesting. For the coal industry and financial capital: (a) involve contrasting types of activity - hewing raw

173

materials from the bowels of the earth and making money by triggering electronic impulses in the heart of a computer; (b) represent opposite poles in the changing balance of economic forces since 1945 - with output and jobs falling in coal while turnover and employment have expanded in financial services; (c) are tied to opposite poles in the changing balance of political forces - with the collapse of union power in coal and the rise of unregulated entrepreneurs in the City; and (d) have been differently affected by the contradictory dynamic of Britain's postwar settlements. In addition both sectors have reinforced, as well as suffered from, the growing crisis of Britain's 'flawed Fordist' economy. Indeed, against the conventional wisdom, we argue that British financial institutions as well as coal were in decline in the 1970s. Likewise both sectors have been subject to state sponsored restructuring as well as the discipline of market forces (but to different degrees and in different ways). And, most recently, both have undergone reorganization and flexibilization - promoted in both cases through the neo-liberal strategies of the state.

The Postwar Settlements

After World War II ended, the Labour Government began to reorganize the economic boundaries and activities of the state. Among other steps in this regard it nationalized the Bank of England and key sectors in energy, industry and transport.

These measures were more a reflection of political pressures in the trade union movement and Labour Party rather than technical desiderata, the demands of economic planning or efficiency, or a means to promote social justice by redistributing income or wealth (Cairncross, 1985, pp. 464-467). Indeed the subsequent evolution of Labour and Conservative government policies alike toward these sectors shows that nationalization does not in itself fully determine state policy toward specific sectors let alone the entire national economy. Instead such economic policies must be located in a much broader structural and conjunctural context.

For our purposes this can be studied through the two postwar settlements: an informal producers' settlement and a politicians' settlement. The former settlement emerged in a period when normal party politics were suspended, the state was near corporatist, the 'audit of war' focused attention on production, and financial constraints on government action were not significant. It was supported by the major economic interests and was mainly concerned with economic modernization through the reorganization of production and economic and social policy. The politicians' settlement came to the fore as normal party politics was resumed (with the Tories' 1947

Industrial Charter signifying a bipartisan consensus) and set the agenda for electoral competition and government action. Its primary concerns were securing full employment through demand management and effecting a more egalitarian distribution of income and wealth through social welfare policies (see Jessop, 1989c).

Postwar history until the rise of Thatcherism can be told in terms of the complex and changing relations between the two settlements and the forces mobilized behind them. During the immediate postwar years the politicians' settlement came to dominate the producers' settlement as the basis of party politics and economic governance. The failure to pursue the productivist project aggravated the 'flawed Fordist' character of the British economy. It was revived occasionally, however, in the guise of corporatist and/or dirigiste strategies for modernizing the economy, state and civil society. Attempts to pursue both settlements foundered as their internal contradictions and mutual incoherence became clearer and the crisis-tendencies of the international economy intensified in the 1960s and 1970s.

The dominant politicians' settlement embodied two contradictions affecting coal and the City. Full employment was challenged by commitments to the pound sterling; and welfare spending by the overseas military and imperial role of the state. These contradictions were associated with two contrasting economic and political strategies pursued by the state: (a) state intervention based on a changing mixture of corporatist and dirigiste arrangements within the context of an overall commitment to demand management and social welfare - reflecting the employment and welfare commitments; and (b) reliance on market forces and laissez-faire - reflecting the commitment to sound finance, a limited public sector and support for Britain's interests overseas. The coal industry figures prominently in the first strategic ensemble: taken into public ownership, subject to short-term and ad hoc interventions to promote exports, import substitution, full employment and stable prices, used for regional and social policy purposes, and involved in tripartite patterns of consultation. The history of such efforts clearly reveals the limits of the strategic capacities of the British state in exercising dirigiste powers and in encouraging and underwriting corporatist agreements reached by producer groups. The City's postwar development belongs to the other strategic ensemble: commitment to the reserve and transaction roles of sterling, a neo-liberal state, and self-regulating institutions.

The history of these commitments clearly reveals the weakness of the market and laissez-faire in securing economic expansion: for the City also shared in the relative decline of the British economy and attempts to reverse the latter led to ad hoc interventions which restricted its pursuit of market rationality. The contrasting strategic orientations were reflected successively in the stop-go cycle of the 1950s, oscillation between planning and laissez-faire in the 1960s, conflicts between advocates of corporatism and supply-side liberalism in the 1970s, and, after the gradual, intermittent, discontinuous shift in dominance from one pole to another, the eventual defeat of postwar Keynesian welfare state commitments at the hands of Thatcherism with its emerging project for a supply-side social security state. We now relate coal and the City to these changing economic and political strategies.

The Coal Industry after Nationalization

The Coal Industry Nationalization Act, 1946, established a National Coal Board (NCB) with its members appointed by the appropriate minister. The Board was responsible for the routine operation of the industry and the development of policies in an arms-length relation to government; it was expected to cover its operating and investment costs taking one year with another. But the Act also stipulated that the Minister, after consultation with the Board, could give the Board general directives on how to exercise and perform its functions in the light of the national interest and that, in drawing programmes of reorganization or development involving substantial capital outlay, the Board should follow guidelines approved by the Minister.

From 1947 to 1956-57 (when output reached its postwar peak), the NCB's operations were subject to increasing state intervention. This was mainly concerned with the macroeconomic implications of NCB policy rather than specific output and performance targets. As with other nationalized industries there was constant interference in pricing and commercial judgements. The NCB was told to hold prices below world market levels at the same time as it was requested to maximize output (despite high marginal costs of production in peripheral pits) and legally obliged to break even (although this was not achieved). This produced low investment and inefficiency and contributed to the lack of competitiveness in later years. The NUM had only limited direct contact with government and negotiated instead with the NCB. The NCB and NUM were left to reach agreement on industrial relations and social issues concerning the industry. Both groups opposed government cuts but they also accepted the need for retrenchment. The cosy corporatist compromise concluded between management and union officials did not benefit the miners themselves since officials failed to press for higher wages lest jobs be lost and this in turn reduced the pressure on management to reorganize production. Strikes were mostly concerned with local issues, were rooted in the difficulties of working specific pits or faces, and turned on local wages and conditions[2].

After 1956-57 governments increasingly attempted to reorganize coal mining as such and as part of attempts at overall economic planning. Until 1971-72 the emphasis was on pit closures but without significant reductions in production capacities. In line with the growing interest in corporatist programming (and further prompted by the oil shock and the miners' strikes), government concern then turned to a corporatist plan for coal. The oil shock encouraged greater union militancy since the tide seemed to be turning back to coal. Under the Thatcher governments since 1979 there have been growing efforts to reduce capacity. At first this reflected an austerity programme (prompted by excess capacity and falling home demand) as well as Mrs Thatcher's preference for nuclear power; later it expressed the government's neo-liberal strategy for economic modernization and political transformation. Even so the NCB's inability to cut costs rapidly enough at a time of falling demand and rising interest rates required growing state support for the industry in the first few years of the Thatcher regime.

During the period of the postwar settlement, there were three main methods of intervention. Firstly, the state tried to manage the disequilibria provoked by national and international competition in the energy sector through post hoc revisions to corporate plans. Despite occasional criticism from parliament and self-criticism in white papers, state strategy did not change significantly until 1970. Secondly, from 1970 onwards, the Public Expenditure Survey Committee was supposed to produce integrated quinquennial plans for the state sector and this led to a more uniform policy towards nationalized industries. The NCB was included in this process. And, thirdly, from 1974-79 there was an open dialogue between the Labour Government, mining unions, and NCB as part of the attempt to implement and then to 'save' the social contract.

With the open attack on the postwar settlement launched by the Thatcher government, radical cutbacks have been occurring in pits and capacity since 1981. The government required self-financing within 3 years with a view to privatization: the NCB was to be more commercial, to eliminate unprofitable pits, to cut production in peripheral regions, and to insist that management was the sole judge of the general interests and profitability of the industry. Ian McGregor was nominated chairman of the NCB in September 1983 to pursue this strategy for the government.

Flexibilizing the Coal Industry

Coal mining enjoyed a brief revival after the first oil shock. Under the Labour government the tripartite Plan for Coal (1974) envisaged an annual growth in output of 15 million tons and a global production target between 130-200 million around 2000. This soon proved too ambitious owing partly to competition from other energy sources and coal producers elsewhere and partly to declining home demand. The NCB accumulated a chronic deficit but, thanks to the NUM's close ties to Labour, it was not obliged to review the plan annually - which would have accelerated closures, redundancies and capacity cuts.

The incoming Thatcher government's response was quite different. The Ridley plan called for closures in declining public industries such as steel, railways and coal mining and for privatization in expanding sectors. Conflicts were expected and contingency plans made for strengthening the law, police and the courts in handling these. Indeed coal was regarded as the most likely battlefield: coal stocks were increased, imports encouraged from 1981, non-unionized lorry drivers recruited, mixed coal/oil burning introduced in key power stations, nuclear power encouraged and a hard-line boss (MacGregor) appointed. This was coupled on the NUM's side by demobilization and a loss of combativity in a context of rising unemployment (13 per cent in 1981) and the defeat of the steel unions in 1980 and health and rail workers in 1982. There were also serious internal divisions within the TUC over the 'new realism' and the NUM leadership opposed the emerging TUC line on this issue. Moreover, in the NUM itself, despite agreement on combatting government policies and pit closures, there was little agreement on the most appropriate and effective methods. These divisions reflected both particular regional differences and general strategic differences. Under the leadership of Arthur Scargill, however, 'pit politics' came to dominate national as well as local responses to the joint squeeze exerted by market and government pressures for cuts in both output and costs.

The strike began in March 1984 over pit closures. It lasted for twelve bitter months and ended in an unconditional return to work. Three major themes dominated talks during the strike: renegotiation of the Plan for Coal, criteria for pit closures and review procedures on the performance and future of individual pits (with a view to possible closure). These themes were linked and MacGregor's strategy was to make concessions on one or another but never on all three at once: thus no agreement was possible. Behind this lay the desire of government and management to impose a new industrial relations system that would decisively weaken the NUM.

Thus the confrontation between NUM and NCB after the strike moved gradually from the problem of jobs and closures towards reformulating the rules for conciliation and consultation. The two key axes of conflict were: first, management's desire to adapt the bargaining system to a new type of production planning and to link this directly to market forces; and, second, its efforts to impose substantial changes in work organization, bigger wage differentials, and reduced bargaining power on the unions.

For the first time since nationalization, the NUM found itself opposed by another organization (the Union of Democratic Miners or UDM), officially registered on 6th December 1985 and claiming 30,000 members (around 21 per cent of all miners at that time).

The NCB recognized the UDM without consulting the NUM (let alone securing its consent) and insisted on its general right under normal industrial relations law to recognize unions whatever the 1947 Act might imply for the rights of the NUM in the coal industry. Later it unilaterally suspended the conciliation scheme in order to secure the UDM's right to take part in conciliation procedures as well as in wage bargaining on the national as well as regional and pit level. Indeed MacGregor insisted that, where no joint UDM/NUM agreement could be reached, at regional level the union with a majority would decide for all.

Meanwhile the NCB had negotiated a local wage agreement directly with the UDM, granting an increase denied to the NUM. Thus continuing talks about talks and its recognition of the UDM gave the NCB more room for manoeuvre in negotiations on wages and other issues after the strike. Without legal or regulatory restraint, the NCB could favour the working miners (mostly UDM members) and extend the role of productivity criteria in setting wages.

More generally MacGregor's plans for negotiation and consultation aimed to reduce union power and restrict access to information: less information would be available to consultative committees, fewer committees would exist and they would have more restricted powers, fewer meetings would be held, and decisions would be taken on a more decentralized basis. Individual members of minority unions could by-pass traditional disputes procedures; a direct channel of communication would develop between management and workers; and there would be no union involvement in combatting redundancy - individuals would make a direct appeal to tribunals. Subsequent proposals for conciliation and disciplinary schemes aimed to give management significant powers against activists and to enhance their abilities to recompose union membership. The NUM has found it hard to develop a joint front with the UDM against these proposals because of its initial rejection of joint negotiations.

Management strategy has clear implications for wage negotiations and pay flexibility, numerical flexibility, functional flexibility, the use of subcontracting and other forms of 'distant' labour, and technological change.

1. The traditional annual cycle of wage negotiations was orientated to an annual percentage rise which then formed the basis for local incentive payments based on the productivity and profitability of individual pits. During and since the strike the NCB (first under MacGregor and then under Haslam) has successfully imposed several new features on the wage relation. These

include breaking the NUM's national bargaining power and encouraging a shift to decentralized bargaining; imposing differential wage awards on the basis of the union (NUM or UDM) to which miners belonged; encouraging other unions not just the UDM but also the electricians' union and the TGWU) to represent miners instead of the NUM; and transferring workers deemed by management to be guilty of industrial misconduct - a very broadly defined category indeed.

2. In relation to pay flexibility, there has been a further marked shift to decentralized pay bargaining. A shift towards pit and face bargaining had already been initiated by the incentive scheme introduced in 1978 but the broad outlines of this scheme were still negotiated at the national level. The greater stress on market forces prompted NCB managers to revise the incentive scheme and devise new schemes more closely tied to output and profit than to 'effort' (as measured by the difficulty of mining coal on a particular face). The dismantling of national level negotiations has eased this development. For example, the 'Doncaster option' establishes two pay systems: a 'task achieved bonus' for installation workers and a 'pit tonnage bonus' for outbye and surface workers calculated on different bases and tied to different percentages of individual pit breakeven points. This is said to divide workers and transfer money to the 'core' installation workers at the expense of other miners. A similar agreement was concluded in June 1987 in the Nottinghamshire area.

3. The recent history of pay bargaining confirms the principle of pay differentials based on union membership; the Board's move towards no-strike agreements; its use of the UDM to break the NUM's bargaining power; and its introduction of much more market-orientated criteria for pay bargaining. Similar tendencies are present in the Board's proposals for conciliation.

4. Planning has also become more flexible. MacGregor's New Strategy for Coal in October 1985 moved from the previous indicative planning system orientated to medium-term production targets revised periodically towards a more flexible, rolling annual response to market imperatives. It had three principles: to close uneconomic pits, to maximize production in the most profitable pits, and only to invest where reserves are potentially profitable (i.e. production costs of less than £23.50 per ton). This has reinforced the tendency to centralize decisions, reducing regional directors' scope to cross-subsidize production for social reasons. The cost of production is now the only criterion for pit closures and this will lead to a few superpits in the central coalfields.

5. Other aspects of the ongoing reorganization of work include: (a) a shift in pit deputies' role away from safety issues towards promoting competition among work teams; (b) a likely diminution in the special status of pit deputies

as their tasks are shifted up to management or down to chargehands and/or as safety functions are integrated into machinery and computer-based surveillance; (c) replacement of tight statutory regulations on health and safety with looser, non-statutory codes of practice which will leave managers free to decide on how to discharge their health and safety duties and assist them in intensifying the labour process; (d) reforms in working time in order to reduce overtime payments - notably through the effort to introduce six-day working and longer shifts with fewer hours worked each year; (e) efforts to reorganize tasks to secure greater flexibility, higher productivity and tighter control over wage effort bargains through such measures as the introduction of incentive schemes offering contracts to small teams of men, subcontracting surface craftsmen's jobs to local tradesmen; (f) a radical plan for teams of self-employed miners to work blocks of coal under contract to British Coal (the new name for the NCB from April 1986) and moves have also begun to re-introduce the 'butty' system, i.e. a pattern of team work for a lump sum payment; (g) attempts to economize on craft and skilled labour through increased use of heavy duty, high technology machinery, automation of various processes, automatic monitoring, and more flexible technologies such as free-steered vehicles; (h) plans to replace craftsmen by workers who have received special training in electro-mechanics and/or by sub-contracted local tradesmen able to undertake maintenance work; and (i) the setting up of a new Information Technology unit and increasing emphasis on the use of computer-aided design in planning, surveying, assessing geological problems and diagnosing faults with expert systems.

The overall results of these changes, which have been accelerated since the strike in 1984-85, is the development of a more flexible system of coal mining in which labour is intensified and costs of production drastically reduced. Indeed the emerging system marks a historic turning point in the postwar coal industry. The old system involved consultation and conciliation and was based upon the free agreement of both sides, systematically protected by a tradition of respect for mutually agreed decisions and by the relative non-involvement of the state. The emerging system involves much reduced bargaining power for the NUM, recognition of a new moderate union which is based in the most profitable pits, and challenges to the representative monopolies of the NUM and NACODS. New channels of communication are being introduced and attempts are being made to win local union branches to a new, more market-orientated, local corporatism.

For a time the financial, legislative, coercive and judicial powers of the state played a key role in preparing the conditions for this new system. Increasingly tight financial controls reinforced by the imminent privatization of the electricity supply industry (which takes about four-fifths of British

Coal's output) have combined with increasing exposure to world energy markets to impose market disciplines on the coal industry. At the same time state subsidies have been committed to win support for redundancies and to permit the restructuring of the coal industry. Most recently we have seen the write-off of around £5 billion in accumulated debt (a typical prelude to privatization) and government pressure on the electricity supply industry to enter contracts with British Coal which will hold for the first three years of ESI privatization. Legislative changes have been crucial in industrial relations and health and safety and the police and courts played a crucial role in breaking the miners' strike in 1984-85.

With the strike broken, however, the coercive role of the state has diminished. Today the emphasis is on financial and managerial controls together with attempts to secure local union support.

The relative success of this strategy is not in doubt. Since 1982-83, daily output per coalface has risen by 94 per cent and output per man/shift by more than 85 per cent. This has been associated with a 25 per cent cut in operating costs as measured in pounds per gigajoule (a measure of thermal value); a 59 per cent cut in the number of coalfaces; a 51 per cent cut in the number of pits; and a 58 per cent cut in manning levels (from 207,600 men on pit books in 1982-83 to an estimated 70,000 in 1989-90)[3]. A more recent estimate puts the number of miners at 64,000[4]. Moreover, although plans for what one minister described as the 'ultimate privatization' have been postponed into the indefinite mid-1990s, there has been a certain amount of privatization by stealth through increased resort to open-cast mining undertaken by wholly independent or NCB-subcontracted private firms as well as increased use of subcontracted labour for pit-top and non-extractive deep-mine work (Beynon et al., 1990; Gibbon and Bromley, 1990, pp. 62-63). Conversely there are some clear limits to the overall strategy which can be seen in the limited extent of weekend working, the reluctance to undertake a 9-hour shift system and thereby sacrifice opportunities for overtime, a failure to introduce new categories of worker such as 'electro-mechanic', and limited displacement of directly employed surface workers with subcontracted labour. But these signs of relative failure in BC's strategy may be due to the fact that informal labour flexibility has risen substantially (Gibbon and Bromley, 1990, pp. 71-72). Further reflections on the implications of these changes follow the presentation of our second case study.

The City after the War

The Bank of England was nationalized on 1 March 1946. Its Court was directly responsible for managing the Bank subject to such directions as the Treasury, after consultation with the Governor, might deem necessary in the public interest. The Bank of England Act also gave the Bank qualified powers to 'direct' the commercial banks. Both types of direction were often given as part of the overall monetary and financial policy of the authorities. There were five broad groups of regulations governing banking activities: rules on the balance sheet ratios (cash and liquid assets) observed by clearing banks, official advice on the composition and amount of sterling lending to the private sector, controls on hire purchase terms for consumer durable goods, a state-sponsored interest rate cartel linking the clearing banks, and exchange controls. In addition a Capital Issues Committee controlled foreign access to the London capital market and also regulated new issues by UK companies. Thus, although banking and financial services were competitive, competition included simple monopoly (e.g. cartels) and state monopoly (e.g. lending ceilings) as well as liberal, free market forms[5]. It is the impact of the organization of financial services and its modes of competition that concern us below.

The Bank served as spokesman for many different City interests but, in so doing, tried to restrict its activities to contact with the Treasury. City institutions[6] were granted self-policing powers rather than being subject to legal and administrative oversight by government. This meant that issues vital to the interests of financial markets - the extent of competition, the definition of honesty and prudence, the distribution of ownership - became 'non-decisions' beyond the reach of Whitehall or party politics (Moran, 1982, pp. 53-54). At the same time self-regulation helped City institutions to maintain restrictive practices which inhibited real competition and provided monopoly profits - threatened loss of which helped in turn to maintain self-regulation. This situation lasted into the 1960s. But from then on it was subject to increasing pressure from the combined impact of competition from new financial intermediaries at home and abroad and the growing interest of Whitehall, the parties and the press in City activities which had previously passed unquestioned. Some of the problems this created are discussed later.

The development of City institutions after 1945 is complex and involves several developmental tendencies and shifts. In the three decades after immediate postwar reconstruction, however, an emerging (but incomplete) division between two 'Cities' can be discerned (cf. Plender and Wallace, 1985, pp. 15-16). At one pole, an 'international City' developed which not only specialized in ever more complex and novel forms of international business but also came to be dominated by foreign finance houses. The expansion of this role depended as much on various restrictions which prevented New York from developing as an international financial centre as it did on any intrinsic merits of City institutions themselves. Indeed British institutions which had once dominated international capital (government and business loans) and commercial (sterling bills of exchange) markets suffered a declining market share in these areas. And, with global deregulation, the advantage London once enjoyed as the least regulated of the major financial centres has disappeared and New York and Tokyo have become real threats to London's position (Coggan, 1988, pp. 19-21). At the other pole, a new 'domestic City' developed, continuing trends already evident in the 1930s: this was orientated to the financial and commercial needs of domestic industry, trade, and household consumption as well as to an expanding central and local government financial market. It was still dominated by home-grown financial intermediaries which had became more concerned with the British economy as it entered the Fordist phase; but even here an increasing role was also played by foreign-owned transnational intermediaries with a British base.

With the decline of sterling as an international currency and the gradual loss of world market share by the British economy, British financial institutions faced growing problems in doing business abroad. For their sterling-denominated capital base shrank and thus limited the scope of their operations; and, in addition, the state restricted their business activities outside the sterling area in order to safeguard the reserves and protect the value of sterling. The main impact of these twin problems was on the mobilization of capital rather than overseas commercial and trading activities (such as trade finance in sterling or insurance). Institutions concerned less with capital flows than these other activities managed to grow in absolute terms because of the rapid expansion in international trade and commerce after postwar reconstruction - despite losing world market share. The postwar boom also brought relative prosperity to financial and/or commercial intermediaries which had been traditionally concerned with the home market or redirected their activities to it as mass production and mass consumption expanded and autocentric growth became relatively more important.

This process of recomposition was reinforced as the City acquired a new international role in the late 1950s and 1960s which extended well beyond the sterling area. This was most obvious in three areas: the rapid growth in Eurodeposit banking business and the Eurobond market, the increase in foreign exchange dealing which followed the collapse of fixed exchange rates in 1972-73, and the need to recycle petro-dollars after the first oil crisis. It was precisely these markets, however, which were soon dominated by foreign financial houses. For they acted outside the exchange controls and restrictive practices which limited British institutions' chances to participate fully in the new markets. The same web of restrictive practices and entry barriers surrounding old-established British institutions also meant, however, that they were protected from foreign competition in such core areas as domestic securities, the marketing of state debt, or Lloyd's insurance market. But this did not protect them in new or newly important markets from competition from domestic and/or foreign institutions which were more innovative and flexible.

This set of circumstances produced three startling paradoxes. First, although traditional City institutions were dominant in the circuit of capital owing to their key roles in the exchange and credit markets and were also effectively insulated from Whitehall control in many of their core activities, their concern with short-term gain and their trade association consciousness actually led them to neglect their own long-term economic and political interests. Second, the commitment to the reserve and transactions roles of sterling encouraged traditional City institutions to focus on markets (in the overseas sterling area) which not only grew less rapidly but also required policies to support these markets which harmed the domestic manufacturing base on which City strength depended. Third, the cosy protection afforded by self-policing, cartels and restrictive practices made traditional City institutions vulnerable to more flexible and innovative secondary or 'fringe' institutions and/or to more aggressive foreign financial intermediaries. The growth of the non-clearing banks was particularly rapid in the 1960s in both domestic and, even more obviously, foreign business. Thus many of the so-called successes of the City, whether ascribed to its alleged political hegemony or its economic drive, were counterproductive in the long term (such as defence of sterling) and/or really due to outsider institutions (such as the expansion of the Euro-markets).

Indeed the corporatist order of the City's traditional core institutions entailed rigidities which made it difficult to adjust to growth and innovation in both global and domestic markets. This can be illustrated for many of the traditional City institutions: the London Stock Exchange, merchant banks, clearing banks, and Lloyd's (see Jessop and Stones, 1991). In short the traditional City suffered relative decline and institutional sclerosis at the same time as there was rapid expansion and financial innovation among secondary and/or foreign institutions. This produced a double crisis in the City: a crisis of market share for traditional institutions (due to new, more flexible players) in particular and a general crisis of regulation (due to the entry of new market players and the development of new financial instruments). Thus, although both the coal industry and the City faced crises in the late 1970s, the forms these assumed were different. This reflects a key difference between the coal and financial markets: whereas the coal industry produces a limited range of products (even allowing for new processes such as liquefaction or gasification and new products such as carbon fibres or chemicals) in an energy market where coal's market share has been declining, the financial services industry is more open, competitive and complex and offers a rapidly growing range of instruments and products in an expanding market. Thus the forms of flexibility and rigidity and the crises with which coal and finance are associated are different and, even though the dominant strategy in the 1980s in Britain has been neo-liberal, it has still involved different types of response in each case.

We now turn to the measures taken in the City's case to make it more flexible in the face of these crises.

Making the City More Flexible

Worries about the dominance of City interests over those of industry were already voiced in the late 1950s and early 1960s; they were reflected in the abortive move to planning and a continuing concern with industrial policy. Doubts about the performance of traditional City institutions themselves became more evident later in the 1960s and, under Heath's neo-liberal government 1970-74, were reflected in an attempt to make the British banking system more competitive. This occurred with the 'Competition and Credit Control' policy introduced in 1971: this was concerned both to promote competition and to secure a more flexible but still effective control over the banks. The policy failed to control inflation and precipitated rapid growth in bank advances, many of which went into property and commodity speculation and personal consumption rather than into investment. Among other effects, the 'secondary banking crisis' was particularly severe.

The policy on credit control was reversed when supplementary special deposits (the 'corset') were introduced in December 1973, eventually terminated in 1980 as growing disintermediation and the 1979 abolition of exchange controls made the 'corset' unworkable. Competition and Credit Control itself was abandoned in August 1981.

The next major attempt at reform was initiated under the neo-liberal, supply-side Conservative government of Mrs Thatcher. The liberation and regeneration of the City is meant to be one of her government's most notable successes and is often presented as a triumph of the entrepreneurial culture and laissez-faire. I have my doubts about the long term stability of the City in its emerging role as the international centre for international capital but we are quite clear that much more was involved in securing this role than unfettered market forces. For some of these forces had first to be unfettered through state intervention going well beyond deregulation or liberalization and/or through their takeover by foreign finance houses as part of the internationalization process.

The Thatcher government's measures have been concerned with promoting competition and reorganizing the regulatory framework in the financial services sector. In both cases state intervention has occurred with the support of progressive reformers in the City. Some of the state's measures were meant to be facilitative, such as the 1979 abolition of exchange controls[7] or the abolition of the 'corset' on bank lending in 1980[8]. But others seemed to be aimed directly at smashing the City's restrictive practices and injecting greater competition. Among these measures we can include the deregulation and liberalization of building societies' activities[9] and the reorganization of the securities industry.

Crucial in the latter case was the 1979 reference by the Office of Fair Trading (OFT) of the Stock Exchange rule book to the Restrictive Practices Court: a reference which led to the 1983 'Goodison-Parkinson' agreement that produced three 'little bangs' and one 'Big Bang'. The smaller changes involved: an end to the single capacity arrangement whereby member firms specialized either in jobbing or broking, a two-stage relaxation of the rules on outside ownership so that eventually outsiders could wholly own member firms and inject capital into them, and new rules on membership of the Stock Exchange to widen participation. 'Big Bang' itself occurred in 1986 with the end of fixed commissions. In addition to the OFT, key roles were also played by the Bank of England and the Department of Trade and Industry (DTI). The Bank pushed for mergers between banks and stockbrokers to create giant British investment banks and also pressed for reforms so that these could compete effectively with foreign investment houses. It also reformed the gilt-edged market by creating a US-style primary dealing system. And it promoted the private Securities and Investment Board as the umbrella Self-Regulating Organisation (SRO) for all the financial services industries. Whatever the government and OFT intended, however, the chairman of the Stock Exchange claims that the delay in reform due to legal action gave American firms the chance to dominate the securities and investment markets after exchange controls were ended (quoted in *Financial Times*, 27 October 1987).

The City has also become more flexible in other respects ranging from the introduction of new 'back-office' technology as well as using new technology to extend the range of client services[10] through more flexible working practices in individual firms and the frenetic competition to introduce new financial products and services to the overall development of a flexible system based on giant one-stop financial conglomerates plus 'niche' or 'boutique' financial houses which specialize in high value-added financial services. These changes parallel those in industrial production and the labour force as the transition to more flexible, post-Fordist practices continues.

In addition to the continuing flow of innovations in existing markets in financial assets, new markets have been created both for equity capital (e.g. the unlisted securities market from 1980, the 'over-the-counter' market, the third market, and London Securities Exchange for smaller firms) and other financial markets (traded options, financial futures, etc.). The government has also been active in promoting more flexible provision of finance through the tax system (e.g. Business Enterprise Schemes) and boosting investment through privatization, personal equity plans, changes in stamp duty, capital gains taxation, and so on. Indeed the success of the City in recent years can be attributed in large part to continuation of favourable tax status for institutional investment (pensions, insurance) and certain forms of saving (building society funds, home ownership), new measures intended to encourage stock exchange turnover (such as reductions in stamp duty on transactions), and to the typically neo-liberal preference for fiscal expenditure (tax subsidies and tax shelters) over direct revenue spending in support of industrial investment. Deregulation and liberalization have reinforced these measures.

Accompanying deregulation and liberalization has been re-regulation. In part this has involved strengthening the hidden 'prudential controls' exercised by the Bank of England. But a formal regulatory framework has also been established through the Financial Services Act 1986. The new Securities and Investment Board represents, according to Moran (1987), a new type of negotiated corporatist franchise along American lines. It is still too soon to evaluate this claim but it is clear that the state retains oversight of the system and that self-regulation has certain corporatist features which mean that financial markets are not yet run according to the laissez-faire principle of caveat emptor.

Re-regulation is needed to control the effects of flexibility. Financial services in an age of accelerating financial innovation, electronic money, global telecommunications, and computer driven trading and arbitrage have in certain respects become too flexible; complete deregulation would render the whole system unstable. In this respect the need to examine flexibilities in the context of rigidities receives further support from the experience of Black Monday and the growing scandals of insider trading, share support operations, Lloyd's insurance frauds, and so forth. Whether the new regulatory framework will be effective remains to be seen.

Concluding Remarks

We have argued that both the coal industry and the City experienced a gradual decline which turned into structural crises in the 1960s. That in the coal industry stemmed from a global decline in demand for coal (due to the growing importance of oil, natural gas and nuclear power) as reinforced by deindustrialization in Britain (which particularly affected heavy industry - in turn a heavy user of coal) and by continued competition from other producing countries. The crisis required decisive intervention to reorganize the coal industry and make it competitive once again: this is not to argue that the neo-liberal strategy pursued by the NCB under MacGregor and prompted by the Conservative government was the only solution. The structural crisis in the City was the product of the long-term decline of sterling as an international reserve and transactions currency and the rigidities in financial adaptation induced by the traditional cartel agreements and restrictive practices in different financial markets. Thus new opportunities were often seized by foreign financial institutions (e.g. the Eurodollar market) or by domestic institutions operating outside the traditional cartels and controls (e.g. secondary banks). The position continued to deteriorate in the 1980s and required decisive action by the Bank and Stock Exchange - prompted by the government - to bring about the deregulation and liberalization of financial services which has helped to turn the City into the international centre for international financial capital. Even this apparent triumph of the neo-liberal strategy is double-edged, however, since the City has survived only at the cost of its growing domination by foreign financial institutions. It can also be asked whether the increased flexibility of financial institutions has not occurred at the cost of the real economy.

The general strategy adopted by the Conservative government in resolving these crises has been similar. This is the neo-liberal strategy based on six main elements: liberalizing competition, privatizing the state sector, deregulating the private sector, introducing commercial criteria into the residual state sector, internationalization as a source of competitive pressure and of learning experiences, and tax cuts to create the space for private market expansion.

In the coal industry this strategy has been pursued mainly through an emphasis on commercial criteria and increased flexibility in all areas. Key elements in its commercialization have been reduced subsidies and external finance limits, the shift in the planning system from output targets to target rates of return, growing emphasis on productivity and profitability in pay settlements, internal competition among individual coalfields, pits and even work teams. This has prompted growing flexibility in many areas. This primary strategy has been supplemented by deregulation (in industrial relations in general and through legislative changes bearing directly on the coal industry, e.g. health and safety in the pits), by the pressures stemming from privatization elsewhere in the state sector (most notably in the electricity supply industry), and, last and so far least, through internationalization (both in the form of MacGregor with his experience in the American coal industry and through the growing reality of coal imports - not merely during the strike but also since). This has occurred against the background of careful government planning to confront and break the NUM through the miners' strike (whether or not the government itself can be said to have directly triggered the strike). After the active intervention of industrial relations law, the police, and the courts during the strike, the law now has a more passive, unspoken but still present, role in legitimating managerial power, maintaining divisions among the mining unions, and promoting the unilateral imposition of flexibility where the latter is not voluntarily conceded. This is part of a long-term strategy for the coal industry aimed at producing a small, profitable, high-tech, largely automated industry; this will be based on the most productive central coalfields where the 'new realist' UDM is predominant; it will be orientated not only to coal production but also to high-tech coal products and processes; and it could be privatized either wholesale, by competing coalfields, or through management buy-out. This is considered to be the 'ultimate privatization' and, should the strategy succeed, a flexible, post-Fordist coal industry organized along the lines of the 'flexible firm' will emerge.

The City has also been transformed through the neo-liberal strategy - notably through internationalization and deregulation. Deregulation clearly involves the state. But, even if internationalization depends more on relatively autonomous market forces driven by the rise of multinational industry (with banks and insurance companies following industry) and the more general global integration of financial markets, it also depends on state action and has driven in turn the move to deregulation and other facilitative measures. For, whilst the authorities could take a national financial system for granted in the 1950s and 1960s and impose various constraints on financial intermediaries to influence the availability and/or the cost of finance, internationalization of finance in the 1970s and 1980s has spurred competition for business among financial centres. In this context state action to attract international financial capital and business-to-business services comes to play a key role in international competition. The Thatcher government has been especially active in this regard. In this context liberalization and deregulation have a broad significance. Since success in this competition depends on things such as good telecommunications facilities, the availability of skilled labour, the tax regime, reserve requirements imposed on banks, the time zone in which a centre finds itself, and many others, governments must consider many factors when embarking on policies to sustain a financial centre. Two examples of recent action by the British state will suffice. Firstly, the liberalization and deregulation of telecommunications has harmed British equipment manufacturers but has produced a revolution in the supply of equipment and a significant reduction in prices to financial users as British Telecom, Mercury and suppliers of value-added network services have competed in the lucrative City market. In turn this has boosted the attraction of London as an international finance centre. Secondly, since the office requirements of modern financial centres are radically different from those of traditional finance, the government has promoted the redevelopment of the London docklands as a site for high-tech financial services buildings - this has involved a combination of compulsory purchase, state-sponsored infrastructure (rail link, airport, roads), a quango (London Docklands Development Corporation) with major powers over development and limited accountability to local residents, and enterprise zone status which enables major construction firms to offset investments against tax. In short, whilst the expansion of the City may owe something to the entrepreneurial drive of new City institutions and/or foreign intermediaries, the favourable circumstances for this expansion also depend on state intervention. This can be seen most recently in government promotion of the EC's 'internal market' - which particularly affects financial and business services - and its demands that other EC member states open these sectors to international competition.

Privatization has necessarily been limited in financial services and banking because nationalization had not existed outside the post office: a partial exception was the privatization of the Trustee Savings Bank but, since this was not state-owned, proceeds went straight back to the TSB. Yet financial institutions have gained indirectly from the state's privatization programme and commitments to wider share ownership, home ownership and pension ownership: this has generated fee income from flotation and increased demand. Additional favourable factors have been the emphasis on commercial criteria in the state sector (associated with reductions in public sector borrowing and restraint in the growth of public spending) and favourable tax treatment of financial institutions and investment. Commercialization (or, in banking jargon, 'marketization') has also been advanced through the ending of administrative control over interest rates (via the Bank Rate and the clearing bank interest rate cartel) through the increased importance of the active short-term money markets[11] in setting interest rates competitively. These markets are international and have become an integral part of the financial system; extensive business is premised on their continued existence.

The effects of this strategy for financial services are double-edged. Deregulation began with the abolition of exchange controls in 1979, passed through the deregulation of building society activities, and culminated in 'Big Bang' and the shift towards self-regulatory organizations. But the effect of deregulation has been the dominance of international financial institutions in City activities - including the takeover of many British institutions by Japanese, American and other investment banks. In addition deregulation in the City has been accompanied by re-regulation. Deregulating the securities industry not only involved state intervention in the shortterm, however, it has also left more statist forms of regulation. For, alongside the corporatist SROs, the Department of Trade and industry has acquired major supervisory and investigative powers. Paradoxically this is 'intended to ensure that the industry's corporatist institutions do not once again use their power to preserve established interests in the face of market change' (Moran, 1987, p. 22). Likewise the 1979 Banking Act brought all banking activities (whether of recognized banks or licensed deposit takers) under Bank supervision to prevent a recurrence of the 1973-74 secondary banking crisis. Further efforts at re-regulation were prompted by 'Black Monday' (1987), the instabilities produced by excessive flexibility in the financial markets, and a series of scandals involving fund managers and investment advisers. How much further state intervention proceeds will depend on the evolution of market practices and the state of public opinion. For another paradox of Thatcherism has been further politicization of the City as the drive for popular capitalism exposes the wider public to the general adverse impact of a flexible, volatile market system as well as to specific abuses by insiders.

The City's long-term strategy must be continuation of the dual process of internationalization: the growing penetration of the City by international financial capital and its increasing concern with servicing international capital. This specialized role for the City (which distinguishes it from the New York and Tokyo markets with their primarily domestic orientation) is likely to be reinforced with the move to the internal market in financial services in the European Community by 1992: indeed a key element in the Conservatives' economic strategy is to promote the City's dominance in this context.

Thatcherite economic strategy cannot, therefore, be treated as monolithic. For, although it has a certain coherence as a neo-liberal strategy which has been pursued fairly consistently for some twelve years, it has also been continuously adapted to changing circumstances and modified from case to case. The contrasts between coal and the City are especially instructive here since both have been subject to neo-liberal interventionism by the Thatcher regime but with quite different objectives, techniques and consequences. This lesson will hold for other sectors too and cautions against over-ready generalization about the nature and impact of Thatcherism. None the less the fact that such vastly different sectors have been subject to different versions of the same overall neo-liberal strategy suggests that there is probably more coherence to the Thatcherite project qua project than was true of earlier periods of state intervention.

Whether this is necessarily good for the sectors in question or the national economy as a whole remains to be seen. Current indications do not augur well[12].

Notes

1. Especially as Britain enjoyed a virtual monopoly in coal exports and could set prices above British domestic rates until new sources of world supply emerged in the late nineteenth century: see Debier et al., 1986, pp. 176-179.

2. Such strikes are characteristic of 'pit politics' as opposed to the corporatist tradition of 'mineworkers' politics' at national level; the rise to power of Arthur Scargill signified the dominance of 'pit politics' at national as well as local level.

3. *Financial Times*, 14 February 1989.

4. *Financial Times*, 23 May 1990.

5. On this classification, see Jessop, 1982.

6. In this paper institutions refer both to specific markets, such as the London Stock Exchange or Lloyd's, and to ensembles of intermediaries, such as the clearing banks, subject to common rules and procedures and with their own trade associations; intermediaries will refer to individual organizations or firms in these markets.

7. Although in the shortterm this encouraged even more foreign investment banks to move to London.

8. A move by the Bank which followed soon after the introduction of the Medium Term Financial Strategy and immediately threw money supply targets off course.

9. They have been allowed to engage in commercial lending, second mortgages, unsecured loans, mortgage credit elsewhere in the EEC, residential development, money transmission, foreign exchange business, estate agency, insurance broking and property management. The larger societies want to become all-purpose financial intermediaries and the Abbey National is already seeking a stock market quotation.

10. For example, automatic teller machines to extend effective banking hours, simple 'home banking' and complex 'office banking' through the installation of terminals in clients' homes or offices, electronic funds transfer at the point of sale.

11. These include markets for short-term bank deposits, discount house deposits, certificates of deposit, short-term time deposits from non-bank sources, other deposits of various kinds, such as local authorities, finance houses, ECUs, and SDRs.

12. For an analysis of the economic consequences of Thatcherism and their impact on the crisis of Thatcherism, see Jessop et al., 1988.

10. Changes in Socio-Legal Structures: The British Case

Norman Lewis

Introduction

There has been much debate lately about 'flexibilization strategies'. Not only have scholars detected changes in methods of production to overcome production rigidities, including a move to flexible working practices, but forms of state regulation and intervention are also seen to be undergoing important changes. These include deregulation, the 'regulated autonomy' of particular private groupings overseeing major areas of public concern, and the restocking of the armoury of styles of intervention by the state at large. Even old-fashioned territorial politics have been weakened in favour of experiments involving community and voluntary groups, new disciplinary regimes and the like. Privatization of state assets has also been stressed, representing in part a belief in the greater flexibility of markets. In other words, the settled ways of operating the economy and conducting the business of governing evident for almost fifty years have given way to greater experimentation in forms and structures (see, for example, Boyer and Coriat, 1987, pp. 509-586).

This essay joins that debate by looking at the constitutional flexibilization of British government and charting recent changes in modes and styles of intervention. It then argues for a balance to be struck between flexible styles of governing and larger civic and political expectations of the sort which characterize the 'real', the enduring British Constitution.

We live in a rapidly changing world with major shifts in communications, general technology, industrial formations and the like. It is often remarked that many of these changes have created rationality and learning crises which have caused severe planning and goal-achievement problems both for governmental and other social sub-systems (see, for example, Harden and Lewis, 1986, especially ch. 10). The lack of a complete constitutional monitoring machine to check the drift of the body politic and to rework national and regional priorities is a particular disadvantage at such times. In Britain and elsewhere the inability to see clearly has produced some disturbing side-effects. One is that the planning of social priorities, being necessarily harder to achieve in such turbulent times, has begun to appear almost impossible. Another is that the 'moral universe' might be falling into decay and considerations of social virtue may be luxuries which are ill-affordable. Electorates are looking more than ever for the managerial expertise to hold the ship of state afloat while it is being buffeted by unforeseen elements.

If such a perspective is adopted, it is tempting to scorn alternative world-views, especially those which smack of commitment to expectations rooted in earlier accords. They will seem romantic at best, weak and reactionary at worst. Rather than responding to major changes through openly addressing all the significant issues through institutions which offer multiple points of access so that the learning and adjustment process can be eased, we are urged to rely on the invisible hand of market forces to compensate for our new-found ignorance. Under the Thatcher government, instead of underlining and guaranteeing the enduring human insights and decencies, human freedom is being reaffirmed through the gradual diminution of collective provision and the lifting of the state 'incubus' from each individual who is thereby better placed to make choices in a competitive market.

This situation raises vital questions about the institutions for constitutional legitimation. For these developments are leading to a more closed society. Instead of building new institutions for collective learning while reinforcing guarantees about personal freedoms and liberties, Britain is gnawing away at pluralism as a social philosophy, both atomistically and through our political institutions. I shall argue that exactly the opposite course of action is needed to face these new problems.

Change and Rationality

It is difficult to separate pure ideology from a more objective 'economism' or managerialism but it certainly seems that many on the new right were opposed to Keynesian demand-management techniques and indicative planning on the grounds of informational shortfall and accelerating trends towards industrial and economic contingency. The economic world was no longer knowable; we had not, after all, mastered the dismal science. Hayek has made this point in arguing that the dynamics of the market are too complex and variable to be grasped by the policy-maker who, continually erring in his appreciations of market malfunctions, enacts corrective legislation which soon leads to visibly inefficient results and the need for further correction (Hayek, 1960, p. 154).

This does not exclude macroeconomic priorities but it does rule out the idea of bending the economic world as a whole to our will. In particular we should forsake the idea of socializing it. We should certainly ensure that the market will not falter for lack of adequate supplies of various sorts; finance capital, manpower, infrastructure, etc.. There is also good reason for concentrating political/national energies on sectoral capital. Here we may combine a belief in markets with an expectation of at least being able to understand the major problems associated with a particular sector, whether it be electronics, telecommunications or finance capital. Such decisions involve several changes of approach.

One such change is the dismantling of corporatist structures for the tripartite planning of the economy on the grounds that it is elitist and anti-democratic. The relative demise of the National Economic Development Office is the clearest example. The belief has arisen that, since corporate structures operate beyond Parliamentary scrutiny, dismembering them would simultaneously advance Parliamentary democracy. Corporatism was said to involve the progressive deterioration of the democratic form but this is massively wide of the mark (Birkinshaw, Harden and Lewis, 1990). In reality Parliamentary control over the executive is probably now at its lowest ebb since the Glorious Revolution of 1688 (Lewis, 1988a).

Linked to this is the undermining of the British trade union movement in key respects. First, where trade union cooperation is required, some kind of partnership is clearly an advantage; where it is not required, however, its resource base is less valuable to the state (Lewis and Wiles, 1984). Secondly, if supply-side economics requires an adequate supply of competitively-priced skilled labour, then the trade union movement may be positively obstructive. Thirdly, to anticipate another theme, if it is judged important to marginalize potential sites of intellectual opposition (to change as such or to its ideological justifications), then the trade unions historically pose a considerable threat. A recent illustration of the government's mixed motives is the Dock Work Act 1989 which removed the job tenure guaranteed to British dockworkers since 1946. This clearly secures much greater flexibility in working practices for the port employers, but there is little doubt that the government has also greatly enjoyed bloodying the noses of some of its sternest opponents.

Alongside these developments, unforeseeability and alteration rapidly render detailed regulation outmoded and positively obstructive (see, for example, Gower, 1984; Harden and Lewis, 1986). The City of London is the clearest example, following in the wake of Wall Street several years earlier. If regulation makes no sense in a dense and fast-changing world, it follows that one should deregulate or at least make the regulation more flexible. Other financial institutions are increasingly being regarded in the same way and subject to the same imperatives (see, for example, Treasury, 1984). Moreover, the symbiotic nature of finance and industrial capital, in harness with advances in information technology in particular, has suggested that a number of other sectors should be treated in the same or similar fashion. A light touch on the tiller is what is required in such fields as the world's airlines, land-based passenger transport, or broadcasting (see, for example,

Hunt, 1982). The form taken by privatization of former state assets, and to some extent even the impetus for privatization, is part of the same logic. Indeed, deregulation can take and has taken a number of different forms. Thus the British government is committed to lowering bureaucratic burdens from business in various ways, many of them similar to the American 'paperwork reduction' initiative which requires that paperwork demands made by government on business should be justified or abolished. Likewise the Enterprise and Deregulation Unit of the Department of Trade and Industry is responsible for coordinating the process of reform across Whitehall and examines all new proposals for requirements on business to see if they can be justified (HMSO, 1988a, 2.35). The new approach to major sectors of the economy is one of 'regulated autonomy', a matter about which I shall have more to say in due course.

Managerialism vs Social Choice: Getting Government off People's Backs

I hope to have indicated a number of different strains have converged to alter the way in which Britain is being governed, some of them distinctly ideological and others less obviously so motivated. The attempts to reduce public spending or its planned rate of growth is a case in point. In the initial years of the first Thatcher government, a reduction in public spending was seen as an integral part of the Treasury's commitment to the tenets of monetarism. As the years have elapsed, this justification has mostly disappeared while others have taken its place. Various factors now seem to combine to ensure it centre stage in government thinking. Its association with reductions in personal taxation most obviously, its links with public patterns of spending associated with the old commitments to planning and socialism, its squeezing out of private spending, its distortion of markets and its consequential diminution of personal freedom.

We are becoming familiar with some very sophisticated arguments in favour of the movement towards placing confidence in professionals or managers at the expense of politics. It is claimed that complexity requires expertise, and that experts must be substantially trusted to make whatever technical adjustments are needed to ongoing socio-economic systems without interference from those who would inhabit a different kind of world. This is the beginning of the slippery slope to substituting managerialism for politics (Poggi, 1978; Habermas, 1979). This neo-modern philosophy might well be misplaced, as indeed has recently been argued in Britain concerning the Office of Fair Trading: it is now seen that the autonomy of the expert was a delusion and that policy-making is, in fact, politics (Ramsay, 1987, p. 198). Be that as it may, the philosophy is being embraced with increasing conviction as part of the reborn fascination with the power of the market. These trends were observable at least a decade ago, at the same time as a general disenchantment with economic demand-management was setting in. Those on the left of British politics will recall that it was a Labour government which was loudly accused of failure to defend the Keynesian faith. In any event, circumstances since that time, the nature of which have already been touched upon, have tended to reinforce the conviction that the state should tend the machine rather than seek to reprogramme it. Mrs Thatcher used to be referred to as 'Tina', since she was prone to attack all opponents by declaring that 'there is no alternative'. This was a more loaded proposition than appears at first sight, for not only was she declaring that her policies were correct but also that she was moving with the grain of economic forces rather than contesting them. Thus not only would it be foolish to seek to inject social choice antibodies into the world of market economics but even to canvass such ideas was extremely irresponsible. Two things seem to follow from this position. Firstly, rather than governments making social choices for people en masse, individuals should make their own choices. They will, will they not, be more flexible? Happily this confirms the superiority of markets while championing a particular version of civic freedoms. Secondly, and not without a real sense of contradiction, it becomes near seditious to preach other world-views about the nature and tasks of government and citizenship. This marks, I believe, the onset of state censorship. I develop this argument later but a few comments may be appropriate even here.

If only one world-view is appropriate - or 'realistic' - in new right language, then the certainties have to be reinforced and their guardians protected, whether they be the born-again political elite, or those private sectors or groups which merit the official seal of approval. It is worth recalling here that even industrialists could not be sure of entry into the inner sanctum until they had passed their initiation tests into the new world of realistic expectations (Lewis and Wiles, 1984). Once they had met this test, they would be expected to become partners of the new nightwatchman state even though operating under the flag a private enterprise culture of renewal and regeneration. This new version of public/private associative conduct is a new style of policy intervention with major implications for the mechanics of constitutionality and accountability.

Yet another anomaly appears at this point: the fate of the National Consumer Council. This was established in 1975 as a 'counterweight to the TUC and CBI in the policy process' (Ramsay, 1987, p. 183). It was a liberal/social democratic attempt to widen the constituencies consulted in the policy-making process. Among its intended functions was probably an attempt to broaden the base of grand corporatism from tripartism to something with a greater claim to legitimacy. Viewed thus it was naturally functus officio with the advent of Thatcherism but it could also buttress the meso-corporatism developing under her stewardship. For example, it worked assiduously on codes of practice for self-regulatory bodies, thereby lending them greater legitimacy (Birkinshaw, Harden and Lewis, 1990). It might also have been seen as the representative body for all the players in the market (i.e. the consumers) and hence as corporately 'kosher' in new-right terms. However, not only has it been staffed over the years by political 'pluralists' but it also tends to ask uncomfortable questions of government. There is a real tension here. On the one hand it represents the consumer sovereignty much trumpeted by Thatcher in other contexts, such as the body of ratepayers. On the other hand, it stands for difference, differentiation and criticism. The immediate government response was to appoint as Chair of the Council a former Tory cabinet minister with no trace of 'wetness'. The ideal role for the Council to have played in the Thatcher drama would be that of representing 'populist' consumers with the correct world-view. Life, happily, is not that simple and the intervening years have shown no real sign that the NCC has become a Thatcher poodle. 'Liberal flexibility' to that extent is challenging new-right flexibility.

Finally, in this section, it must be said that reinforcing the certainties and protecting their ideological guardians from public criticism requires a further turning of the screw of the secret state apparatus and the effective removal of sites of potential opposition. The present government's obsession with secrecy is now well-remarked - with the prosecution of the - Spycatcher case and the Official Secrets Act 1989 paying eloquent testimony to a control of the state apparatus far tighter than anything we have previously seen in peacetime. Attempts to remove sites of opposition have already been noted above but crucial to this stratagem is the policy adopted towards local government.

Local Government as an Impediment to the New Realism

The power of elected local authorities in Britain has been slowly seeping towards the centre for some decades, under governments of both right and left. However, the process has changed in both tempo and degree during the years of the Thatcher administrations. This movement has been well documented in the literature, not least that of the non-socialist variety (see, for example, Coopers and Lybrand, 1984; and HMSO, 1984). Despite the centripetal tendencies of the postwar years, local government has traditionally retained a considerable relative autonomy. Crudely speaking, Conservative local authorities have pursued laissez-faire policies and adopted relatively low levels of spending and taxation, while Labour councils have generally been interventionist and pursued high-spending and taxation strategies. The latter have offended Thatcherite philosophy on almost every count. High public spending is bad per se, as are subsidies of collective social goods, such as public transport and housing. Furthermore, some left-wing labour authorities seem to have committed themselves to 'experiments in living', which embrace not only local socialist communities (formerly described as municipal socialism) but also espousal of alternative world-views and life-styles, in stark contrast to those associated with the new rights neo-Victorian values. These authorities have not sufficiently valued the market and have reverted to failed techniques of socio-economic planning widely shown to be ignorant and reactionary. Their fate was thus inevitable.

Local government has been relentlessly enervated by a series of legislative and administrative measures. Particularly important in recent times have been the Education Reform and Housing Acts of 1988 and the introduction of a new system of local government finance, the 'community charge', introduced in England and Wales in 1990. Through provisions in the Education Reform Act the Secretary of State for Education has gained the power to establish a 'common core' curriculum for schools and to allow schools to opt out of local authority control on the election of the current generation of parents. However, equally significant has been the abortive attempt to introduce City Technology Colleges (sponsored by private industry and outside local authority control) and to remove the tertiary-sector Polytechnics from local authority control. In the same vein the Universities are to be held more responsive to the needs of industry by the removal of 'liberal rigidities'.

Some of these developments will create greater flexibilty of manoeuvre and some will not. But they are all directed to reinforcing the single correct world-view. In removing certain bureaucratic rigidities, the ability to take advantage of new opportunities as they arise may well be enhanced. On the other hand, these movements are accompanied by a rigid centralized view on a number of strategic issues which limits opportunities for debate and is therefore on the politico-philosophical level anything but flexible. We are being driven to educational market in a number of ways (buying courses, buying students, then buying schools) but the choice of pigs to buy is becoming severely restricted.

Again, the Housing Act includes provision for local authority tenants to switch their landlord from the public sector to an 'approved' landlord (read here: approved by the Secretary of State). Moreover, the provision rigs the election process in favour of the Secretary of State's preferences even though most tenants clearly wish to remain with the local authority. Added to this, the Act will almost certainly lead to higher rents for the poorer sections of the community and a higher profile for private investment schemes outside the public sector. In fact, such developments further blur the divide between the public and private sectors in circumstances where subsidies for 'private' housing are not matched by institutional guarantees of public accountability. This is a classic illustration of how the 'flexible' nature of the British constitution allows the most radical developments to occur in spite of widespread opposition and without adequate debate and consultation. Only deep-seated constitutional reform can alter this state of affairs. Two features of the progressive diminution of local government need to be stressed. One is that it is coterminous with a diminution of political and intellectual pluralism, i.e. tolerance. The other is that elective local government is in the process of being replaced by personnel and institutions not elected, and largely unaccountable. The political market is thereby being replaced by a political compact of right-thinking centre and right-thinking localized groups sharing the same or similar world-views. The reason for making the latter statement is that no modern government can operate social sub-systems unaided, and no 'perfect' market exists to relieve the need for central government to govern in a quite positive sense, regardless of the diminution of the public sphere, at least in the economic sense. In fact a variety of partnerships between the distinctly public (i.e. central) sphere and those of the private are being installed to replace the elected member. Various forms of associative conduct, whether termed corporatism or not, are occurring whereby private individuals and associations who have received the central government's certificate of approval (they must, of course, share the faith) combine to fulfil a significant number of essentially governmental functions.

Regardless, then, of the information which markets are capable of signalling to governments, it is clear that the rationality crises occasioned by novelty require structures for responding to and handling contingency, and for re-ordering priorities where necessary. Lower-level tiers of government are used in most developed countries for these, among other, reasons. Indeed a recent study has stressed the case for a heightened local government presence in the enforcement of trading standards. Local government argues strongly that it has more information and greater expertise than central government (as one might expect from a political 'market'), allowing it to move more swiftly and expertly to eradicate instances of unfair trading (Ramsay, 1987, p. 196). However, given that the present government has set its face against local government, regional government, or other major constitutional reforms, then it is likely that any substitute will tend to operate in the constitutional shadows.

The New Constitution

One can encapsulate the methods of governing adopted in contemporary Britain by referring to undemocratic centralism, neo-corporatism and regulated autonomy (Lewis, N., 1988a). Such arrangements are made possible by the extreme flexibility (or manipulability) of the constitution. Not only has the power of Parliament been diminishing for most of this century, it can now safely be stated that even the British cabinet is presently shorn of its former pre-eminence. It has been largely overtaken by cabinet committees and, especially, by informal Prime Ministerial initiatives, whether in the form of 'seminars' (as with the future of broadcasting in 1987) or through committees of advisers, increasingly of unwavering political persuasions (see Wass, 1984). Recent legislation has also given ministers enormous powers of direction, thereby giving centripetal forces a massive impetus. It is also interesting to note that Mrs Thatcher has effectively put Royal Commissions into cold storage. There is no room for differences of opinion being given institutional status, especially when backed by state resources for empirical research. Her advisers are mostly committed, undeviating and will simply furnish her with information on how to effect policies, rather than spending time on feasibility studies and alternative ways of doing. It is interesting here that the rules and regulations adopted under the Financial Services Act 1986 are exempted from the normal competition policy laws, and in particular from effective court scrutiny. Once again the application of a major area of economic policy is to be firmly subject to political rather than judicial control. Yet the City Capital Markets Committee had argued that the criteria to be taken into account by the Secretary of State should be spelled out in the legislation, thus rendering his decisions amenable to judicial review (Page, 1987, p. 315)

There is a link here between centralism and neo-corporatism in the sense that Thatcherism operates with and through those who are like-minded or at least tolerant of government strategies. Whereas in most of the postwar years, corporatist policy styles were conducted in cooperation with most significant groupings which had resources to offer the current government, present government policies are being increasingly targeted through sympathisers. There is little room for trade union representatives, local government or radical-left groupings in general (see Birkinshaw, Harden and Lewis, 1990). For present purposes corporatism can be defined as a style of policy intervention whereby tasks traditionally reserved for government are shared or bargained through a combination of public and private actors. The articulation between public and private actors for the purposes of creating and/or implementing public policies is a necessary response to the problems of information shortfall involved in supplementing market signals. Those closer to the problems of choice and action undertake some of the business of governing on the government's behalf, or in conjunction with it. Such strategies also increase the resources available to government, or substitute 'private' for public monies in varying proportions. Naturally this appeals to a government which objects to public expenditure and high taxes and is looking for help in resolving fiscal crisis and reinforcing its political ideology. We may be speaking of industrial policy, the world of finance, social welfare or some combination of these.

First, let us consider the process often known as 'offloading'. Although this is normally illustrated from the voluntary or welfare sector, research conducted for the ESRC has uncovered numerous instances of government soliciting the private sector to undertake both industrial and general economic functions which have traditionally been within the public domain, in return for advantages conferred upon the private parties by government. Before dealing with some of these examples, we can briefly refer to 'social welfare corporatism'. As Winkler, in particular, has argued, recent governments, and not merely the British, have been developing institutions for involving the community in providing welfare services (Winkler, 1981). This amounts to the off-loading of traditional welfare functions back on to groups of citizens; such groups include voluntary associations, user cooperatives, mutual aid societies and various non-profit organizations (Birkinshaw, Harden and Lewis, 1990). To some extent these voluntary bodies are seen as the institutional embodiment of the market.

Turning to neo-corporatism in the economic field, let us now consider employment and vocational training. The government's unified training programme, announced in February 1988 is to operate within a framework of mixed input from government, quasi-government (in the form of the Training Agency), private industry and its associative bodies (e.g. Chambers of Commerce) and voluntary organizations.

The government are very concerned that voluntary organizations and others which have an established role in the Community Programme should have the opportunity to make a major contribution to the new programme. The Community Programme continues to serve a very useful purpose in enabling people who would otherwise be unemployed to undertake work which is of benefit to society, notably in the fields of crime prevention, energy conservation and environmental improvement (HMSO, 1988b, para 5.13).

Plans for training during the 1990s are even more radical, being a combination of neo-corporatism and privatization. The chosen instruments are to be TECS (Training and Enterprise Councils) which will restructure Britain's approach to training and enterprise development. Employers, in partnership with the broader community will be charged with reskilling the workforce and stimulating business growth. Each TEC will be an independent company operating under a performance contract with the government. Two-thirds of its board of directors will be private sector employers, with the balance drawn from the fields of education, trade unions, voluntary organizations and the public sector.

Another example concerns third-force or voluntary housing. The relations between the Department of the Environment (DOE), the Housing Corporation, the housing associations and the National Federation of Housing Associations are extremely complex, even without reference to the role of local authorities and the building societies. The deep-layered corporatist forces previously at work in this area have recently been steered in new directions. The Housing Act 1988 aims to replace local authority housing departments as landlords with either private landlords, housing associations or housing trusts. Indeed, a few local authorities have sold their stock to housing associations, though links between the local authority, the associations and private interests will be retained. As to the housing trusts, elected councillors will be replaced by government appointed officials in circumstances where it becomes difficult to identify the beginning of the public sector and the end of the private, or vice versa. The government sees the role of local government as essentially strategic; identifying housing needs and demands, encouraging methods of provision by other bodies to meet such needs, maximizing the use of private finance, and encouraging interest in the revival of the independent rented sector. Market solutions buttressed by public support.

A third example of economic neo-corporatism is inner-city regeneration. Recently, the government has become committed to private sector led cooperation in the inner cities with Business in the Community (as private industry broker linking up employers, their staff, their resources and their funds with voluntary organizations and training projects) playing a leading role. Even so, many local authority or housing association partnership projects have become established in recent years with prime movers in the industrial development field, and bodies such as the Northern Development Company have attracted government grants to supplement other cooperative arrangements. Some genuine corporate bargaining, in the sense of the trading of mutual advantages, remains in this area, as witness governmental attitudes towards regional policy. The encouragement of business development is aimed largely at achieving improvements in the managerial skills and strategies of business which are seen to be essential 'but which would generally not have been achieved through reliance on open markets' (HMSO, 1988a, 7.6). Increasing reliance has also been placed upon Urban Development Corporations, quasi-government bodies which can purchase and distribute parcels of land within derelict urban communities for the purposes of regenerative development. There is little doubt that their ability to sidestep a deal of bureacratic regulation makes them extremely flexible in pursuing their goals single-mindedly. They also, by the same token, avoid over-dependence on local government and raise certain questionmarks about their overall social accountability.

The English Industrial Estates Corporation provides another interesting example. Its task is to provide and facilitate the provision of industrial and commercial premises in the 'assisted' areas and inner cities of England where shortage of private sector provision is a constraint on development. Its role appears more vital than ever. Thus the Department of Trade and Industry (DTI) has remarked:

> Despite recent improvements in market conditions, the private sector is still reluctant to invest in certain types of property in parts of the Assisted Areas and in some non-Assisted Area inner city locations. English Estates will continue to provide industrial and commercial premises in the Assisted Areas where there is no prospect of private sector provision. It has also been asked to give particular priority in future to a new programme of managed workspace primarily in inner city locations and with considerable private sector involvement (HMSO, 1988a, 7.112).

The DTI is also responsble for coordinating the work of the City Action Teams in major cities and running a series of Inner City Task Forces. These two initiatives seek to pull together the combined efforts of a number of government departments, and works with the private sector and local government.

Many of these developments will take time to bed down but it is clear that terrritorial politics will play a diminishing role in the near future. More decisions will be taken by a combination of private industrialists, government appointees and community organizations, with local authorities possessing more responsibilities than powers. Reference should also be made here to the growing requirement that local authorities contract out many of their services to the private sector. Given the absence of a specifically 'public' law of contract this again poses important questions of accountability. The absence of a public law tradition in Britain, and the new right's antagonism towards new forms of constitutional accountability ought to be the cause for considerable civic concern.

The final point to be made here is that, with government and its partners operating under a large measure of agreement, voluntary or forced, the regular choices made by the private partners will be largely 'managerial'. They will not be accompanied by open debate about objectives or even their variation. This further undermines the realm of politics in the grand sense, especially since such partners will be replacing elected representatives. In the government's own words, market forces and the commitment to privatization help 'to prevent the economic distortions of the past which subjected particular parts of the economy to political rather than economic decisions'. The extension of this philosophy is a clear indication that the open society retreating and that accountability and constitutionality are at a depressingly low ebb. Ironically perhaps, the European free market planned for 1991 may yet provide more mechanisms for constitutional accountability than the British would otherwise choose. In a small way the change is signalled by Directive 88/295 which seeks to remind governments that Public Sector Supply Contracts are not the same as contracts for buying a dozen eggs at the corner shop.

Markets, Learning and Regulated Autonomy

The third, related, strain of current British politics concerns what can best be termed 'regulated autonomy'. As we have seen, recent British administrations have been very committed to markets as a way of providing maximum output, and as a way of satisfying requirements. In part this is because governments have inadequate information upon which to base its interventions and because markets represent the most flexible response to changing circumstances. The market itself is an academy; it is a place where lessons can be learned and digested. It is sometimes claimed that it is also intrinsically democratic since anyone can participate. Yet of course we understand that markets are frequently imperfect and that governments have overarching concerns which some markets tend to overlook. A clear example of this is the British government's Pauline conversation to ozone friendly politics. The dilemma for governments then becomes how best to respond. The traditional dispute between left and right over this issue has been blunted even if their heated disputes remain over the shape and size of the public sector. Detailed regulation has become unfashionable in several areas with 'regulated autonomy' becoming the preferred solution. In Britain, this trend can be seen as far back as 1972 in the field of health and safety (Robens, 1972) where Codes of Practice were held preferable to detailed regulation in several areas. The notion of regulated autonomy has also been given a certain intellectual chic through socio-legal writings on 'soft' or 'reflexive' styles of law (see, for example, Teubner, 1983). This has also been favoured in relation to 'deregulation' of the City of London and the delegation of generally-expressed supervisory functions to professional and disciplinary associations (Birkinshaw, Harden and Lewis, 1990). It was strongly argued that the City would be improved by practitioner involvement in drawing up rules and enforcing standards since they would not only be more practical but more flexible than Parliamentary supervision. Ironically by late 1989 the intendedly flexible City regime was under attack for being too cumbersome and unwieldy so that within three years of the new arrangements being in place, they were likely to be removed in favour of a more 'flexible' three-tier system of supervision. Whatever the final outcome, the arguments for a looser regime coincide with the government's emphasis on less government while seeking to ensure that neither innovation nor international competitiveness are inhibited. There is little doubt that an independent regulatory authority such as the American SEC could have produced similar results with a higher level of public visibility and accountability but, although sufficiently flexible, such an arrangement might not be thought to be sufficiently market-orientated.

The notion of regulated autonomy is that control over general criteria is retained by government while these criteria are specified as necessary by the oversight body. This is as valid in the field of investor protection as in competition policy, broadcasting standards, and other areas. Unfortunately no general philosophy underpinning the need for or nature of regulation seems to have been developed (Graham and Prosser, 1987). The most prominent government statement concerning this issue states that open markets are free markets, which are informed and fair markets. To this end regulation must be kept at the minimum level necessary.

> Regulation can be a positive force to promote competition but, as a general rule, neither the efficiency of open markets nor competition is improved by prescribing detailed requirements which impose costs on consumers and business and limit the scope for freedom of choice, enterprise and innovation... Some regulation is needed to prevent anti-competitive behaviour and to provide a framework which achieves a fair level of protection for the individual consumer and investor. The bland conclusion was that a balance must therefore be struck between regulation needed to promote competition and give confidence in the working of markets, and the risk that regulation will divert economic activity and promote unnecessary costs (HMSO, 1988a, p. 10).

One thing is clear. Our constitutional law has not been updated to secure maximum debate and participation concerning the regulative process (Harden and Lewis, 1986). The British law of judicial review, whereby the administration broadly conceived is supervised against canons of general legality is nothing like as developed as it needs to be given the developments outlined here.

The phenomenon of privatization presents the same difficulties. Leaving aside the desirability of this strategy either in general or particular terms (again our constitutional machinery for debating these issues is quite lamentable - Graham and Prosser, 1987), no coherent philosophy has accompanied the setting up the agencies to oversee the newly privatized concerns (see Lewis, N., 1988b). The 1988 DTI White Paper does not analyse the minimum conditions for general accountability within the industries. Interestingly, one of the justifications for privatization has been that, unlike the nationalized industries, private firms have access to the money markets, thereby affording much greater managerial flexibility. It is unclear why public industries cannot have the same freedom.

In the case of gas privatization, not even a White Paper or consultative document was published, and this was apparently one of the reasons for the decision of the Energy Select Committee to produce a legislative report to the House. Regarding telecommunications, a brief White Paper was produced, but this merely repeated a ministerial statement about the future of the industry with less than a paragraph concerning the proposed regulatory arrangements. Somewhat fuller coverage was given in the White Papers on airports policy and the privatization of the water authorities. However, even here, little was said about the rationale of regulation beyond stating that a system of economic regulation would be designed to ensure that the benefits of greater efficiency are systematically passed on to the customers in the form of lower prices and better service than would otherwise have been the case (Prosser, 1988). Clearly the nature of regulatory arrangements is unlikely to be properly discussed without at the same time discussing the rationale of regulation itself. This would involve a more sophisticated root and branch assessment of pure markets, the nature of the state and other fundamental issues. That it is not occurring is indicated by the failure of analysis accompanying arguments for competitive bidding for broadcasting franchises (Briggs and Spicer, 1986; Peacock, 1986).

Space forbids developing the arguments over privatization further but a few points are worth making. Leaving aside the institutional arrangements for debate over policy, there are considerable shortfalls in relation to the regulatory styles adopted which pay inconsistent regard to expectations concerning the rule of law. It is widely accepted that privatization has not led to better service nor cheaper prices for consumers. There has, in fact, been some difference in the way public industries have been privatized, but Telecom, for instance, despite having a Director-General committed to maximal openness, has been shown to be defective in various respects. Most obviously, complaints have flooded in about the corporation's apparently declining standards of service as witness, e.g. the National Consumer Council survey conducted in July 1987. Furthermore, where competition has been encouraged, as with Mercury Communications, the response has been to stop publication of the quality of service measurements on the grounds that they are commercially sensitive (*Observer*, 25th October 1987).

The arrangements for both privatized and self-regulatory bodies appear haphazard and uninformed by any doctrinal considerations of due process and participative politics, in spite of the occasional public victory by a regulatory agency, such as the Director-General of OFGAS securing information on pricing policies which the industry was reluctant to divulge (see, for example, *Guardian*, 28th August 1987). Grievance mechanisms and consultation devices are scattered around the scene but hardly in a way that would satisfy either Continental or North American requirements (Lewis, 1989).

Markets, FOI and Human Rights

Although a basic minimum set of functions is necessary even for the neo-liberal state, in the form of infrastructure, removing blips which impede free markets and the like, it seems to be no part of modern new right thinking in Britain to encourage a free market in information, in spite of the technological possibilites now being globally presented. This statement might need some qualification. Encouraging a free market in information is clearly understood to be necessary as regards financial markets; otherwise the City would not be able to function efficiently and competititvely. In fact, the government has recently paid lip service to the notion of available information to oil the wheels of the market, but the claims carry little conviction (HMSO, 1988a, 2.31). The Treasury remains as impenetrable as ever.

It has also to be said that certain maverick figures on the new right, such as Sir John Hoskins, generally favour FOI on the American model, but this view is not widely shared. There are genuine dilemmas to be faced here, though Thatcherism seems prepared to resolve them in favour of a closed political society. One strand of new right thinking is that if 'consensualism' is to be broken, if we are to think the unthinkable and break every mould in sight, then traditional widsoms need to be challenged. That requires as much information as one can muster, so that the siren sounds of impossibilism can be silenced. FOI would represent a potent weapon in such a battle. However, this conflicts with the need to reinforce the certainties and to protect the guardians of the new faith from energy-sapping attack by those who would reassert the claims of socialism and the nanny state. Since this would be in nobody's real interests, then the informed centre must be strengthened, and government energies not dissipated by engaging in fruitless exchanges with those who would undermine the new vision. We have already seen how this has resulted in reinforcing the centre of politics at the expense of the periphery, a move which in some ironic respects is likely to be strengthened by proposed changes in the structure of the civil service intended to increase flexibility and local autonomy. In 1988 it was announced that new executive agencies were to be set up to run the purely administrative activities of much of the civil service, leaving policy-making and general guidance with a core elite, essentially sympathetic to governmental aims (HMSO, 1988c). Some estimates suggest that 60 per cent or more of the civil service will be hived off in this way. How autonomous they will be is currently being decided but they will be tied to the centre by Framework Documents which limit their constitutional independence while increasing their managerial flexibility. Agencies which were previously constrained from functioning in commercial markets may soon be allowed to operate, at least in part, as trading companies. Needless to say, privatization may still be the preferred option, in which case no question of accountability arises by definition. The fiction of ministerial responsibility is being retained for the executive agencies though clear accountability dilemmas are being posed which current research indicates are unlikely to be resolved in favour of new methods of legal control.

FOI is unfashionable except, of course, for local government (Birkinshaw, 1988). Civil servants, per contra, owe a life-long Trappist loyalty to the political machine which they serve. The Official Secrets Act 1989 is merely the most recent manifestation of this belief. Human rights, in the sense of an irreducible private sphere of autonomy immune from state intervention, is protected by the market and by a government committed to making it prosper. Human rights protected by law infringe that autonomy, which makes the European experience and that of our Commonwealth cousins simply, but profoundly, mistaken.

What this all adds up to is a political society which frowns on pluralistic debate. Almost every move over recent years has been aimed suppressing opposition from whatever quarter. The great ontological certainties of humanistic philosophy will be played out in the market or else shown to be of dubious validity through the self-same mechanism. The law has little or no part to play in these matters. One reference to church and state may be a suitable place to close this section. The moral world has become the world of neo-liberal conservatism, with all its contradictions and inconsistencies. Those who fail to uphold these insights are falling down in their public duty. The Church, in particular, has recently been berated by the Home Secretary for failing to uphold these tenets: public order, respect for authority, the sanctitity of family life, the enterprise culture, the sanctity of private property and so on. Instead, it has been engaged in politics, i.e. debating and disputing the stewardship of the nation by the present incumbents. It goes without saying that this is to err and to misplace notions of duty.

Conclusions

Recent years have seen remarkable changes in how Britain is governed - albeit that some developments have simply built upon trends which have been discernible for some time. The nature of British constitutional arrangements is such that few formal impediments stand in the way of a government which has a clear philosophy and a burning commitment to change. This is, to a substantial extent, what occurred in the Thatcher years.

I have deliberately conflated the 'social' and the 'legal' for present purposes on the grounds that every society, indeed every group, must perform certain basic functions in order to survive. Karl Llewelyn termed these functions 'the law jobs' and he was clearly correct, even though this involves a more expansive concept of law than is traditional in Anglo-Saxon thinking. Broadly speaking, these jobs include the resolution of disputes, the establishment of legitimate criteria for 'public' action, establishing the parameters of legitimate authority, and providing machinery for planning the overall direction of the society concerned (Llewellyn, 1940; Lewis, 1981). This need not be the subject of formal or 'legal' direction but of equivalent ways of performing law jobs. The crucial issue is legitimation. What is legitimate to do and what not? Is there a moral underpinning for a nation which has great expectations and great traditions but no Great Tablets of Stone? I have argued elsewhere that this moral touchstone is embodied in the notion of the 'rule of law'. This is not an issue with which the British have really come to terms or adequately debated. The recent campaigns for FOI and Bills of Rights and the Charter '88 movement express some unease; opposition parties in the House of Commons are now addressing issues of constitutional and administrative law reform; and a new think tank, the Institute for Public Policy Research, may help to launch national debate. But the national malaise goes much deeper and Thatcherism has certainly used the flexibility of British constitutional arrangements to work major changes in both structures and habits of mind.

In particular there has been a serious failure of intellect and integrity in blurring the distinction between the public and the private spheres. Formally the distinction is hard to draw, given that the British Parliament is supposedly omnicompetent: there is no reserved business into which it cannot intrude. Thus, strictly speaking, in spite of its international obligations, it can intrude upon human rights. However, the rhetoric (much stronger under Thatcher than for some time past) does proclaim the sanctity of the private realm, though like most rhetoric it is long on passion but short on analysis. Thatcher proclaims the virtues of the market as the ultimate forum for pursuing private interests and increasing the material choice of those it favours.

Neither Mrs Thatcher nor previous administrations have been prepared to enshrine state guarantees about the rights and expectations of each individual; there has been no commitment to offer guarantees about each human being accorded equal concern and respect. Instead, they should mind their own business; they should earn their own respect. Perhaps, most fundamentally of all, freedom of speech, and the associated freedom of information and right to privacy as the ultimate hallmark of humanness, are not for the state directly to guarantee. Indeed, pluralistic debate about possible worlds is something the modern British state is actively discouraging (on the moral constitutional duty of the state, see Gewirth, 1978; Beyleveld and Brownsword, 1986). As to the contemporary separation of the public and the private, the rhetoric is again deceiving, quite apart from well understood problems concerning how the state is to determine the nature and character of markets which are to be free but protected and directed.

Market ideology obfuscates the complex, networked interrelation between government and the private world. Many recent studies show clearly that corporatist networks are operating in Britain at both the micro and meso level in broad areas of policy-making and implementation. Thus public policies are being formed and effected to varying extents by private bodies, resourced in major or minor degrees by public authority, with issues of public accountability being largely glossed over. The requisite sleight of hand necessitates declaring these configurations essentially private, declaring that the state must not intrude into the private sphere, and then hiding these activities from the public gaze as far as possible. This allows government 'friends' considerable freedom of action even as they exploit access to public resources. It also allows a strong central government to have its way through informal means, again without public debate. One isolated example may serve the general theme. Business in the Community has swung firmly into the government orbit in relation to inner city regeneration. Not only do working parties within the organization report directly to 10 Downing Street but BIC helped to write the inner city and employment policy sections of the Prime Minister's speech to the 1987 Conservative Party Conference (*Guardian*, 6th January 1988). It is also sells its services to the governmental Training Agency in training workers in private industry.

'Neo-neo corporatism' is flourishing and is central to understanding how Britain is governed. The balance of influence in such bargaining may have tilted in the government's favour but it is being used to reduce public funding on desirable projects in favour of employing private capital. Even the road building programme is being examined with a view to increasing private sector involvement. The government is trying to create a lightly-regulated, 'reconstructed' market which reflects Thatcherite priorities. Territorial politics is declining with a consequent diminution of public accountability mechanisms. At least on the official side, there is no affection for constitutional change or institutional innovation to offset these developments. The Thatcher government is even opposed to reform of the House of Lords lest it limits the influence of the elected House of Commons and its Thatcher-dominated majority party. There is no move towards 'sunshine' legislation, FOI, a Standing Administrative Conference or towards constraining the power of patronage in the hands of the Prime, or other, Ministers (Lewis, 1989). Evidence of principled thinking about the constitution is hard to find.

Deregulation is internationally modish for a mixed bag of motives ranging from the ideological and selfish to the realistic and prudent. Among the latter the pace of change in several strategic sectors makes detailed regulation irrational to the point of being counter-productive. This should neither surprise nor worry us, anymore than we should be afraid to extol the virtues of the market. After all the bureaucratic/administrative constitutes only one of many legal forms. Gesellschaft and Gemeinschaft may well be older and more significant in the long run (Kamenka and Tay, 1975). Thus self-regulation or, indeed, reflexive structures, have significant 'gemeinschaftlich' elements and can offer considerable advantages in some situations. The crucial thing is that the self-regulatory or reflexive bodies conform to overall social goals, and that the legal order in the larger sense is institutionally equipped to monitor overall performance. After all, especially in British constitutional theory, this degree of autonomy is a gift from the state: it is, if you will, a delegation of power to be exercised according to general group norms. This is the test against which deregulation and regulated autonomy must be judged. But, if these processes are to be efficient, they must also be made accountable (Birkinshaw, Harden and Lewis, 1990, especially chapter 7).

Not only should self-regulation be as open as possible but, like other activities 'tainted' with governmental duty, the law jobs it involves should be performed with as much regard for the canons of social accountability as possible. Reviewing the regulatory regime for the City of London and the general arrangements for regulated autonomy associated with the newly privatized industries and other regulatory regimes, we see a patchwork quilt. Those for the receipt and handling of grievances are mixed and unpatterned; rule-making procedures are sporadic and not adequately supervisable by the courts; corporate planning and monitoring occur almost totally outside the formal legal system. The courts are hardly ever invited to consider whether the agencies concerned have maximized rational discourse, have shown that they have taken a hard look at policy alternatives and objections made to current practices. In short, we have nothing resembling the American Administrative Procedure Act which sets ground-rules for institutional accountability for Federal Agencies.

The form of corporatist bargaining is just as unsatisfactory and central government has largely sidestepped its obligations to the rule of law. Devices to put modern developments back in touch with the obligations of a society committed to democracy and accountability do exist: a range of experiments across the world exists to be assessed and adopted. Change is in the air and some experimentation is inevitable. Constitutional arrangements must be adapted to ensure that we know where we are going and that we approve of the choices being made in our name. All this needs to be done while guaranteeing the maximum opportunity for all to participate in the life of the nation, which in turn must protect each person's right to express their humanness.

The British constitution has been too flexible for its own good. It offers opportunities for narrow sectarianism to remake our world in an image which cannot be challenged. Britain is becoming an increasingly closed and intolerant society, with the shadow of censorship lurking around every corner. In a changing world, options need to be kept open; we need to think long, to experiment with styles of living, and to respect all views expressed in good faith. We are moving in the opposite direction. The art of government needs strong intellectual commitment allied to a belief in elevating 'high politics' above power politics. I am happy to associate myself with the view that

> imperfect central government regulation must be compared with imperfect markets and private law regimes, and imperfect local authority enforcement. Ultimately "in the real world a choice among institutional arrangements for dealing with social problems is a choice among highly imperfect alternatives". There is no first-best solution (Ramsay, 1987, p. 200).

Interestingly, the quote within a quote is from Richard Posner, usually regarded as very much the high priest of marketism. Striking a balance requires open institutions that think long and think reflectively. In Harden and Lewis (1986) I argued for several pieces of new constitutional machinery, including a new Administrative Procedure Act. This now seems to me to be more desirable than ever, though I would add to that the requirement for an entrenched Bill of Rights to stem the tide of anti-humanistic illiberalism which has gathered pace in the meantime. Flexibility within modernity is all to the good. However, for it to operate intelligently and acceptably it must work in a context of intellectually-grounded institutions. Above all, the enduring truths about human rights must be assured. I can see no ultimate guarantee of their survival which does not involve constitutional entrenchment and their vindication through the autonomy of the legal order. Perhaps the supreme irony is that the greatest modern market of all may be in the process of becoming the newest and most modern state. If this is to be the future of the

European Community, it is extremely doubtful if it will be dominated by Westminster-style politics. The best traditions of the Civil and the Common Law may yet come together in a union to which all democrats can give their blessing.

Part 3. Germany: The Neo-Corporatist Road Beyond Flexi-Fordism

11. Neo-Conservatism and Modernization Policy in West Germany

Hans-Joachim Schabedoth

Modern conservatism tries to present its traditional concern with preserving authority and the social status quo in a way which enables it to go on the political offensive by propagating positive values and themes. A policy restricted purely to beating back threats to the structures of social power - the typical approach of classical conservatism - could be dismissed as merely static or reactionary. Thus enlightened conservatism (or 'neo-conservatism' as it will be called here) tries to offer an interpretative framework for daily life and to define values that appeal to the lived experience of ordinary people. Outlining this approach, Heiner Geissler, a protagonist of neo-conservative modernization policy in West Germany and a former general secretary of the Christian Democrats, claimed:

> Nowadays, political developments and revolutions are no longer initiated by occupying railway stations and telegraph offices but by occupying concepts (...). Today, one dominates people when one succeeds in determining their ideas and thoughts (*Die Zeit*, 3 June, 1988).

However, in the midst of social change and a growing pluralization of life styles, it is hard to organize majorities as a durable social basis for a given regime simply by offering a comprehensive, closed ideology. If there is a need for some sort of programme, then it is for one which lists general principles and policy orientations which are easy to justify. The programmatic statement, *Politik auf der Grundlage des christlichen Menschenbildes* (Policy Objectives based on a Christian View of Man), adopted by the 36th Party Conference in June 1988, pursues just such an approach with its catalogue of policy measures and political objectives.

Much the same purpose was served by the concepts of 'democratization' and 'detente' in the heyday of the social-liberal governments (1969-82). For they effectively symbolized the policy and established the identity of the social-liberal coalition. Likewise, just as their counterparts in other countries have done, the West German neo-conservatives and their supporters in business organizations and the media, have developed a new set of values and principles. These include 'individualism', 'flexibility', 'differentiation', 'deregulation', 'technological progress' and 'competitiveness'. These themes can be traced back to a book published in 1985 by Lothar Späth, the minister-president of Baden-Wuerttemburg (a Land or local state in West

Germany). With its programmatic title, *'Wende in die Zukunft'* (Turn to the Future), it opened a debate on the *'Industriestandort Bundesrepublik'*, i.e. on the current role and future prospects of West Germany as an industrial power. This debate has been furthered by advocates of the neo-conservative modernization project in their attempt to shape a public discourse. Key themes in this debate have been eagerly seized on in discussions as the European single market approaches in 1992.

The modernization policy recommended by Späth is premised on the need to maintain the international competitiveness of West German industry in order to secure its position on the world market. From this follows his question: 'what has to be changed in our country so that the future does not happen without us?' (Späth, 1985, p. 26). By 'us' Späth means those German firms and businesses trying hard to improve their starting position for the intensified competition likely to accompany the completion of the single market. From the viewpoint of capital accumulation, modernization means timely adaptation to the increasing internationalization of commodity and financial markets. In both manufacturing and service industries there is a clear need for higher productivity and further rationalization. Since preserving and improving profitability is at the centre of this policy, people must either adapt to the imperatives of modernization or risk being marginalized.

Neo-conservative modernization policy and its rhetoric of social progress asserts that private property owners, in orientating their economic activities quite properly to their own profit interests, thereby also ensure the highest possible flow of benefits to society. In this context the state must support market competition for the highest rate of profit by means of infrastructural policies; in doing so, however, it must be careful not to create a dense web of political interventions and regulations which would narrow the scope for entrepreneurial decision-making. In line with this general argument, the programmatic statement of the Christian Democrats mentioned above announced a commitment to introduce 'an extensive reform of business taxation' after the next election. 'Business taxation, the level of wages and additional labour costs of precautionary measures to protect the environment and deregulation, i.e. debureaucratization and increased competition' are all mentioned as being crucial factors in decisions about whether and where to invest. Consequently, it is argued that the state must withdraw from an overall responsibility for the social security system: instead social security should become a matter of private provisions to be agreed upon by those who participate in the economic process. Likewise governments are no longer seen to be responsible for the state of the labour market. On the one hand, people must be made to understand that the high level of unemployment is a structural problem. On the other hand, the argument runs as follows:

Apart from other costs like capital resources the burden of taxation and other charges as well as the costs of bureaucracy, it is also the development of labour costs, including the supplementary or indirect costs of employing labour, which is decisive in the preservation of existing, and the creation of new, jobs. In times of unemployment, additional jobs can only be created if productivity increases more than labour costs. The two sides of industry are requested to consider this aspect in their wage agreements (Schmid and Tiemann, 1988, p. 4).

This means that the parties to collective bargaining and especially union representatives are made responsible for the struggle against unemployment. Any co-responsibility of the government is denied. Even dealing with problems arising from the deployment of new technologies, it is assumed, has to be left to companies because they alone can ensure that the decisions are taken in the interest of an optimal valorization of capital. Only this criterion will best guarantee an outcome which serves the common benefit. Regarding the framework of economic activities to be secured by the goverment, only one obligation is mentioned: the state must compensate for 'supply deficits in the production factor of information and communication' (Späth, 1985, p. 185). As Späth understands it:

It conforms much more to the principles of market economy to instal an information system which is accessible for everybody and can be utilized by those economic agents who take the initiative than to create a system to which access is restricted and prejudged by the state.

Accordingly, governments promoting new technologies should provide the initial finance and then maintain an informational infrastructure with as few restrictions on access as possible and they should also take responsibilty for securing its acceptance and covering for any risks which might occur. Although it sounds different in their 'Sunday speeches', neo-conservative, politicians leave the employment risks and social consequences of technological innovations to the working population. The promotion of new technology in the context of neo-conservative modernization policy serves company strategies for rationalization which exclusively aim at securing the maximal return to capital. Humanization of work, supposedly the main aim of technological innovation, remains a decorative cover or merely relates to some side-effects (Schabedoth and Weckenmann, 1988, p. 84.).

Demonstratively, neo-conservative policy wants to abandon a pre-emptive or pro-active structural policy which may help avoid economic crises. Confronted with structural change which has led entire industries into a slump, the scope of state activities is reduced to a crisis management of a reactive and 'aftercaring' kind. A policy which defines the framework of economic activity this way cannot, however, eliminate unemployment and social inequality, and does not pretend to aim at such targets. As a result, there is no policy for regional development. How far regional structures move into opposite directions, leading to a concentration of a new poverty and environmental problems in some parts of the country and to an increased quality of life and to relatively safe economic prospects in others, is left entirely to market forces. It is no longer assumed to be a concern for the coordinated efforts of governmental and private initiatives so characteristic for traditional social democratic models of social order.

Problems of the Neo-conservative Modernization Project

Neo-conservative politicians are confronted with a persistent dilemma: in order to retain political hegemony for themselves against competing right-wing currents they must safeguard the political and economic priviliges of their clientele, especially those in command of business and industry without putting at risk, however, the equally essential loyalty and support of the masses. The coalition of Christian Democrats and Liberals has been able to walk this tightrope since 1982 even if there have been signs on several occasions that the government might have become exhausted. To date it seems that falling approval ratings in the opinion polls indicate discontent with the government's performance in political management more than with the overall objectives of the neo-conservative approach (Schabedoth and Scherer, 1990). None the less the neo-conservative project will probably generate new conflicts and contradictions as long as critical public debate continues and its own protagonists seem motivated more by the lust for power than genuine concern with economic and social problems. In this context it is likely that fresh efforts will be needed to justify the politics of restructuring and to maintain the credibility of its main actors.

Within the coalition, all parliamentary groups agree on the overall direction of the modernization policy. But it is becoming harder to translate the common objectives into actual policies and then to sell the outcome of these policies to the voters. The more the Christian Democrats subscribe to a 'project of modernity' the more threatening the risk becomes that they lose support of voters on the conservative right and beyond. Therefore, the strategies for securing the hegemony for the neo-conservative modernization project also include verbal attacks on persons seeking asylum, on the young unemployed, who are denounced as work-shy, etc., in order to mobilize voters who traditionally are more receptive to law and order slogans than to signals from the high-tech and high-culture world. This was well demonstrated by Lothar Späth in his reactions to a loss of voters in regional and local elections to the benefit of NPD and Republican parties.

The Christian Democrats, intent on securing their hegemony, have never hesitated to promote possible successors to their current leaders as soon as the latter seem to lose their integrative appeal. Lothar Späth had proved his flexibility and agility when he supported the politics of change symbolized by Chancellor Kohl without being identified with the difficulties Kohl's turn implied for maintaining mass loyalty. Thus, Späth has been regarded as capable of continuing the neo-conservative modernization project in the 1990s not only by his own party supporters but also in circles beyond the CDU. We should be well advised, therefore, to have regard for the theoretical and practical implications of his approach to capitalist modernization.

Lothar Späth's Mission for Progress

Lothar Späth's reputation of being able to add a fresh impetus to the modernization project of the Kohl era followed from his performance as minister-president in Baden Wuerttemberg. His skilful management of politics and especially his emphasis on a regional policy for promoting technology and industry have contributed much to Baden-Wuerttemberg's image as a 'model' state' within the Federal Republic. Although this Land has benefited from favourable economic structures it was Späth's policy which was singled out for praise in explaining its outstanding success. Compared with other Länder it has achieved the highest income per capita, the strongest financial capacity, the highest export rate and the lowest level of unemployment. As a politician Späth virtually regards it as his personal mission to convince people of the need to promote new technologies without imposing regulations and restrictions on the shape they may take. Thus it is his mission to secure consent and create a general mood favouring a new departure towards technical progress and economic upswing. The role of politics is to organize events and occasions which at least give an outline of the global character of the race for a technical lead, e.g. public congresses, round tables, exhibitions and information meetings Späth, 1985, p. 41). In this context also the foundation of new 'venture centres' and technology factories as well as the appointment of expert commissions are mentioned - as is the need to stage these activities perfectly in order to secure broad media coverage.

Späth pursues his policy of infrastructural promotion for business and industry by expanding the telecommunication network and directing this technology policies towards growth-orientated research sections. A spectacular example of this is the advancement of the University of Ulm which is designed to become a 'Science Town of 2000' *(Wissenschaftsstadt 2000)*. As a joint venture between the state of Baden-Wuerttemberg and its industry, with Daimler-Benz playing a leading role, this project will integrate 'big science' departments of industrial firms into university institutes. In close cooperation with research foundations, these institutes will then be able to secure real-world applications of research and training. Currently, Baden-Wuerttemberg already has a network of technology transfer centres, i.e. 'technology parks' and 'innovation centres' at several of its polytechnics. As 'chairman of the board of Baden-Wuerttemberg Inc.' - to use his own phrase - Späth regards it as his specific task to stimulate (for example) Daimler-Benz's merger policy and its approach to site location in order to assist its ongoing transformation from a car producer to a technology group. In his numerous trips abroad, he is also very active in representing Baden-Wuerttemberg's business firms and industries to establish commercial links and to facilitate exports.

Even the further development of the cultural infrastructure became a matter of his jurisdiction. In Baden-Wuerttemberg, cultural affairs are now seen as another field for the promotion trade and industry. Späth is still far ahead of social democratic politicians in his understanding that the manifold cultural opportunities offered by a region increasingly rank high in the contest to attract manufacturing and service industries. An arts editor of one of the leading national newspapers called this a 'functional interaction of the arts' (Peter Iden in *Frankfurter Rundschau*, 27 July 1988). This cultural policy not only reflects Späth's attempts to give himself a distinctive political profile but also indicates, according to Iden, Späth's recognition of the impact of the sphere of industrial production on societal change. Späth, Iden continues, has recognized two aspects of modern society: on the one hand the additional leisure time resulting from increased automation; on the other industry's increasing dependence on 'creative potential'. This explains why Späth has been almost inevitably attracted by cultural affairs. Identifying 'desire and talent for creativity' as the main driving force of culture, Späth concludes that policies designed to promote this reservoir of fantasy and creativity may help the individual to take advantage of the additional leisure now available; and, at the same time, these policies should be productive in economic terms as well (Späth, 1989).

For Späth, new technologies will not only improve the competitiveness of the West German economy but also help tackle other problems of industrial society such as environmental pollution and unemployment (Späth, 1985, pp. 14, 85, 122, 132). In his argument, the idea of 'technical progress' is not problematized as he treats this progress as an autonomous factor which is positive in itself. Almost inevitably, therefore, he assumes that the continuing process of structural change will take us beyond the industrial society and already points to the prospects of an information society. It is the task of politics to assist a development which will bring positive options for new technologies to fruition. However, these options can only be seized if a new view of society gains ground which is no longer defined in terms of conflict but of coalition. Consequently, state activities have to contribute and to conform to such a reorientation.

One way of achieving this task is to reduce the social demands which burden the state. To strengthen the principle of individual responsibility and to encourage the expansion of subsidiary networks would also extend the state's financial capacities to pursue its economic policies. For Späth, this does not mean an abolition but a restructuring of the welfare state. A restructured welfare state could help to make people more ready to accept work in sectors which are less attractive. This could be achieved by deregulation policies whose intention is to make human labour more competitive. As not all the knowledge and skills of employees are equally important in the labour process, and as the trade unions neglect this in their bargaining policy which aims at generally stated and therefore inflexible agreements, there is a danger that workers cannot compete with machines or that their jobs are lost to the informal economy. To prevent the shedding of jobs by a more flexible technology, working-time should be flexibilized so that an optimal utilization of machinery can be achieved (Späth, 1985, p. 218). Generally, Späth favours a 'flexibilization of individual and collective labour law' on the grounds that realizing the full potential of new technologies is incompatible with uniform regulation of labour relations and with a general commitment to codetermination. This would also enhance a necessary self-determination of employees as well as of employers.

For Späth there is not a 'crisis of labour' but rather a 'crisis of labour regulation'. The reduction of protective rights, the flexibilization of labour law, and the legal support given to the systematic advancement of individualization within the labour process are understood as an attack on the positive effects of trade union activities and social welfare achievements. However, Späth plays down his objectives for the trade unions when he talks of a necessary 'correction of faulty developments' in this area (Späth, 1985, p. 117). The reduction of protective rights, the flexibilization of labour law, and the legal support given to the systematic advancement of individualization within the labour process are understood as an attack on the positive effects of trade union activities and social welfare achievement.

Towards an Overall Adaption to the Actual Need of Capital Valorization

The demand for deregulation and flexibilization comes with the expectation that the trade unions must act as middlemen in securing the interests of capital in encouraging their own members to adapt as necessary to the changing needs of valorization. What people are asked for is to reduce their demands and expectations concerning work and leisure and thus to conform with the working conditions offered to them. There seems to be the notion that human labour has to be at the disposal of management just like the geni emerging out of Aladdin's bottle. Leisure requirements as well as wage demands are of minor importance when it comes to the changing of design of labour. Those who adapt and sacrifice, i.e. accept a smaller share in the rewards of progress, are either awarded the seal or rewarded with the seal of approval which allows them to remain as fellow players in the Germany's winning team on the world market; whereas those who consider non-compliance must face losing their jobs to others who may, if necessary accept, lower paid jobs and are more willing to accept any working conditions. In this constellation, women are doubly affected. Like men they have to suffer from the inhumane consequences which follows from the application of new technologies. But in addition to that, as they are still expected to take the primary responsibility for the family and for private reproduction, they are threatened by an even more perfect dual exploitation resulting from the combination of flexible and shorter though more labour-intensive work.

No politician is as good as Späth in idealizing the new positive image of life for those who are on the winning side of social change. For him, it is self-evident that industrial policy is more than just a policy which benefits industry. Industrial policy à la Späth must include the production of discourses, symbols, and a vision of the future. His vision of a 'reconciliation society', however, is a bill of exchange which rewards the acceptance of present needs for adaptation with the promise that this will pay off in the future through increased welfare flowing from technical progress. Any argument that this progress might not be identical with the social advance of society is deliberately ignored, minimized or suppressed. This clearly contrasts with the fact that some developments which the neo-conservatives mistake for progress have already proved to put further strain onto entire regions, affecting social conditions and the environment alike. Sectoral crises such as those currently affecting the coal and steel industries, shipbuilding, and in consumer electronics and, probably in the future, in the car industry as well, are obviously regarded as unavoidable risks to be accepted on the road of progress. In this respect they are similar to the nuclear catastrophe of Chernobyl or the creeping poisoning of the environment as a result of massive chemical production. This attitude was nicely demonstrated by the Federal Minister of Science and Research when he addressed a congress of the Association of German Engineers (VDI) in 1985: 'In our push for progress we have to accept that occasionally we may fall flat on our faces'.

The view of the employers has been stated as follows:

> Those who demand more than a solution of problems which are actually detectable, who want conditions which do not bear any risks, and who argue that the responsibility for a reasonable pattern to individuals' lifecourse also falls into the realm of politics, all those obstruct the view of what is politically feasible. It is exactly by overloading politics in this way that we could fail to recognize the educational tasks of political leadership. We and our children have to live with the inevitable residual risks of life, and we must not despair at this fact (Krüger, 1988, p. 416).

Also for Späth there is no alternative. He asks 'whether, precisely by failing to utilize our full potential we would not make ourselves partly responsible for the continued poverty of others, the ability to do something positive does not also entail the moral duty to do so' (Späth, 1985, p. 151).

Of course, neo-conservative politicians do not deny that employees have to face certain dangers regarding their interests in the sphere of work and in general life. But these dangers, they argue, have to be accepted as 'a price which has to be paid for progress', and they do so because, for a time, it has become the actual though uncleared aim of their policy to increase the return on capital. By invoking the alleged pressures resulting from the requirements of the world market they hope that employees and trade unions will more easily accept losing some of their former gains in social and financial security. Being ready to live with so-called residual risks seems inevitable, and this readiness is then mystified as an expression of a pioneer spirit and a progressive mind.

Trade Unions as the Grit in the Machine

The protagonists and supporters of the neo-conservative modernization project were aware that they would encounter forces which put up resistance to a policy favouring property owners' monopolization of the gains of rationalization and productivity improvements. Anticipating this challenge they have concentrated on the argument that any modernization depends on a change of those structures which have become ossified and form the main obstacles to progress. Rights to collective bargaining, working conditions secured by collective agreements, collective safeguards against risks in one's private life and a state genuinely committed to the further improvement of living conditions: all these have resulted in structures which set limits to the rightful claim of capital owners that they should be allowed to exercise their power without restriction. Hence, under the pretence of modernization, neo-conservatives try to tackle 'ossified structures' in order to shift the limits of action against labour's interest and in favour of managerial prerogative in the factories and in society. Since rights protected by collective agreements as well as collective safeguards against individual risks are discredited as 'obstacles to progress', it is only logical to pursue a policy of deregulating labour relations and curbing provisions for social security. Social divisions do not endanger their own political dominance as long as they are not only tolerated by the neo-conservatives but even expected and actively promoted. In this context they do not fear resistance which can be dealt with through political exclusions and will therefore have no effect; nor are they afraid of mental reservations, e.g. on the part of those who regularly vote for the present opposition parties. But they certainly fear the real or assumed capacity of organized labour to defend their achievements by putting forward their demands via trade unions actions. German conservatives are realistic enough not to question the legitimacy of the trade unions' very right to exist, at least not in as many words. On the contrary: the unions are accorded a legitimate role in the process of organized interest representation. In this, the neo-conservative modernization project in Germany differs most clearly from that in Thatcherland (for an attempt at an explanation of this difference cf. Hans and Hella Kastendiek, PVS, 1985). Only in so far as the unions do not conform to the assigned role of being a factor for the maintenance of order and as they do not limit themselves to acting as just one petitioner among others, are they regarded as real threats to the neo-conservatives (Schabedoth, 1985).

The unions proved that they have to be taken seriously as a disruptive force especially in 1983-84 when they took action for a reduction of the working week in order to fight mass unemployment by means of collective bargaining. This was preceded by protest rallies against the cuts in social policy expenditures and also by many activities against the plans of NATO and the West German Government to station a new generation of missiles. One of these activities was a five minutes standstill of work, successfully organized on 5 October 1983, which made clear that the West German unions, often smiled at, still have the strength to stop all machines if they want to do so. In 1981 and the following years this was also demonstrated in the bargaining rounds in the metal industry. By organizing token warning strikes, a policy which was called 'a new flexibility' (*'neue Beweglichkeit'*), the unions succeeded to some extent in exerting actual economic and not just some moral pressure on the employers. This explains why the employers have tried for many years to have this type of industrial action outlawed by labour courts. In the confrontation about the 35-hourweek the employers were forced to give in, however, even though they were supported by the government. The employers had tried to uphold their view that a reduction of weekly working-time without a corresponding reduction in wages was unacceptable. But their intransigence revealed the intention to weaken the unions as an oppositional force in society. The employers' association did not want to fight unemployment but to fight the employees and unions. There is no need to speculate for long about the motive for such a challenge: obviously, the employers wanted to exploit the disciplinary effects of mass unemployment on those with jobs, i.e. they wanted to profit from a situation in which rivalry for jobs and de-solidarization gain ground and render it more difficult for the unions to do their job. Mass unemployment offers entrepreneurs and capital owners an excellent opportunity to impose their interests on the workforces and on society without making concessions to labour. Moreover, it is against the capitalist logic of profitmaking to share the gains of advanced productivity and successful rationalization with the actual producers of social wealtlh, e.g. by creating better working conditions, by reducing working-time or by offering higher wages.

Consequently, the unions had to organize lengthy strikes (seven weeks in the metal and thirteen weeks in the printing industry) in order to overcome the resistance of the employers who had put under a taboo any agreement of a workingweek below 40 hours. As never before the right to strike was counteracted through the resort to lockouts. Nevertheless the unions involved in the conflict were able to achieve a reduction of the weekly working-time by ninety minutes and to defend their capacity for action. Furthermore, as a result of the 1984 struggles the unions altogether were strengthened. Therefore the attempt to weaken the trade unions in their role of an actual and potential oppositional force has been kept on the policy agenda of the federal government. Just two years after the events of 1984 § 116 of the Labour Promotion Act was modified: In the case of 'cold lockouts', i.e. of industrial actions taken by employers who are not directly involved but only indirectly affected by a strike, the national labour office was allowed to cancel provisions which hitherto had entitled employers to receive unemployment benefits. For trade unions and many others 'cold lockouts' have clearly to be regarded as a misuse of economic power. Federal government was forced to learn that it had underestimated the extent to which large sections of the public disapproved of its intentions to curb the unions' position in industrial disputes. But this did not prevent it from forcing through the measure against much opposition.

However, as the conflict about this piece of legislation had proved to be unexpectedly fierce, the government concluded that its fight against the unions would have to be conducted through less spectacular measures. With some success, it had already started a further initiative. The Employment Promotion Act, which came into effect on 1 May 1985, was not just intended to facilitate a policy of 'hire and fire' as a superficial reading might suggest. More important, it created two categories of employees: those with safe and permanent jobs and a standard employment relationship on the one hand, and an increasing number of employees with short-term contracts on the other. Within a few years, one out of two new appointments were contracted in this way, and only one-third of those with short-term jobs were kept and offered permanent employment. As a result, the number of fixed-term jobs has grown much more than the total employment figures (Adamy, 1988). It is obvious that in a situation of high unemployment those who only have short-term contracts are less willing to struggle for improved working conditions and to support the initiative of works councils and the unions aimed at this target.

A second measure for restricting the unions' oppositional power in the companies and factories was secured through an amendment to the Works Constitution Act. Its alleged purpose was to introduce special representational bodies for senior staff members together with new provisions for the so-called protection of minorities. The real purpose, of course, was to favour those groups which actually and potentially compete with the unions affiliated to the German Federation of Trade Unions (DGB), especially in the elections for the works councils. To achieve this, the election procedures and the legal provisions for the composition of certain works committees were changed. There were also new guidelines for the release from work to be granted to members of works councils. All the experience made so far indicate that these changes will inevitably lead to works councils spending more time on international struggles than dealing with management policies. The fragmentation of interest representation in the factories and firms should make it harder to organize employees and their interest articulation along the true line of conflict between capital and labour. It was exactly along this cleavage that the social conditions of the workforces have deteriorated as a result of government policies. So far only those welfare provisions achieved by means of collective bargaining have been left untouched, and some of them have even been strengthened. Therefore it seems only logical that neo-conservative modernization policy is now concentrating on the attempt to undermine the legally binding character of collective agreements (so typical for German labour law). This can be illustrated by the campaign which argued that the minimum standards of pay, working conditions and working-time regulation established through legally binding collective agreements have hindered the competitiveness of West German industry. There have been several similar attempts at imputing partial responsibility to West German unions for the emergence of mass unemployment.

For the unions to submit to these campaigns would mean abandoning their claim to be an oppositional force and, as far as past achievements in conflicts over earnings, working-time and living conditions are concerned, to accept the sort of claims that employers and their representatives write into the speeches of the Minister for Economic Affairs. A self-imposed moderation of this kind would at the same time relieve government policy-makers of their responsibility for eliminating the unfair distribution of income and wealth, social inequalities, mass unemployment, and the discrimination against women in the sphere of work and in the social security system (Schmid and Tieman, 1988). If they agreed to act in the way proposed by the right, the unions would join in the neo-conservative modernization game without being able to contribute to defining its rules.

Lothar Späth even argues that the trade unions have deliberately to withdraw their claim to participate in determining further developments. For him, it is quite justified to request such a withdrawal. In his view, the close relationship among capital accumulation, the strength of productive investment and job security points directly to a constellation of 'highly identical interest of employers and employees'. Thus he asks:

> Is it really, in this situation, in the well-reflected interest of the unions to maintain the fiction that employment relations can be regulated in a uniform manner? Isn't it now time to attach more importance to the idea of selfdetermination at the workplace instead of clinging to generalized models of codetermination, especially as there are more and more types of companies to which these models cannot be applied, neither in practise nor with regard to the overall logic of economic activity? The unions must learn to grant the works councils more freedom of action and content themselves with becoming an umbrella organization which settles skeleton agreements with the employers and thereby sets guide lines for union representatives in the works councils. Wouldn't such an arrangement be better than clinging to the outmoded ideology that there still exists a collective entity of industry and of the labour force . They will increasingly direct their attention to those who want to be among the "winners" of technological change, and they have to show them how to reach this destination (Späth, 1985, p. 36).

Even if Lothar Späth got it right that the problem how to organize effectively the employed has considerably changed because of the new conditions in the work sphere there is no need for the unions to accept his conclusions in their own self-modernization which is already on its way (IG Metall, 1989a, b). The apparent contradiction of neo-conservative modernization policy which combines attacks on employees' social achievements and on the forcefulness of the unions with an invitation to cooperate in the reconciliation of technology and labour is resolved when one asks about the position the unions and the Social Democrats alike are offered in the modernization project as promoted by the neo-conservatives. Only as long as they do not ask to participate in decision-making about the direction of the modernization process are they accepted as fellow-runners. Their idea of solidarity and their collectivist values are declared to be incompatible with the requirements of the development and application of new technologies.

So far, in the actual politics of Baden-Wuerttemberg, the thrust of the process of technological innovation has been determined in a way which resolutely excluded opposition parties and the trade unions from any involvement. Only when it comes to the implementation of already settled policies are they asked to guarantee the smooth introduction of new technologies in every possible field of application. Although the offers for cooperation are pseudo offers they oblige the unions to respond. Rejection could be interpreted as an ideologically motivated strategy for refusing any participation and would not get much sympathy from the public. It is expected from the unions that they confine themselves to the job they have to do in the factories and companies and that they concentrate their representational claims on those who want to be among the winners from technological change.

To exceed this limited scope of cooperation means to go beyond the neo-conservative interpretation of the modernization project and thus to get into a situation in which the unions have to explain and justify their own objectives from a defensive position. But they cannot avoid this if they want, at least in a long-term perspective, to dissolve the hegemony of neo-conservative concepts. According to the unions' claim to be active participants in the formation of society, it is their task to identify alternatives to modernization which are also acceptable in social terms. Consequently they are interested in how the conditions can be improved for realizing such alternatives. A retreat from these claims and concerns merely to behave like an advisory service for the works councils would be the wrong response. In any case, solutions to problems at the level of companies and factories can only be found if the needs of entire industries and the requirements for regional developments are also taken into account. The claim to participate in the future design of the work sphere could hardly be maintained if trade union policy were nothing but a mechanical sum of syndicalist approaches and activities. If the unions really want to insist on their more ambitious claims they have to resist any attempts to atomize their potential for the direction of collective bargaining and for the coordination of policies forwarded at company and factory level. On the contrary: as company- and factory specific regulations are very important for the prospects of the sphere of work as a whole it is more than ever necessary to investigate the consequences of these regulations. In this way unions can create a framework for action which takes up the main concerns of employees as well as their individual demands for a course of work and life which is as self-determined as possible. Unions which seriously adhere to this self-image surely have to be considered as a persistent disruptive force in the pursuit of the neo-conservative modernization project (Schabedoth, 1989, pp. 85-90).

12. Departures from Taylorism and Fordism: New Forms of Work in the Automobile Industry

Ulrich Jürgens

Traditional System of Labour Regulation in the Automobile Industry

The focus of this paper is on the changing patterns of labour deployment and of management control over the labour process in mass production. I will present some findings of our research on these questions in the international auto industry.

In the 1920s, an innovation came in the area of management control which is connected with the names of F.W. Taylor and Henry Ford. The attempt was made to find an objective and neutral basis for the delicate labour policy questions dealing with rating work performance, guaranteeing an appropriate performance level, and preventing the withholding of performance. The aim was to limit the arbitrariness and high-handedness of the lower level supervisors as well as the self-regulation and job control of the 'shop floor' in the new production facilities of industrial mass production. The regulation of performance by scientificallly trained experts in questions of human work performance and through the pace of the machines and assembly lines was to take the place of the direct, personal forms of control by a continually growing corps of supervisory personnel and by even more autonomous forms of work regulation in jobs that still had the character of crafts. The new system of labour regulation had three supporting columns:
1. the pace of the assembly line and of the machines as 'backbone' and structuring element for the work rhythm and the task allocation,
2. the experts for time and motion, the industrial engineers, who give the production area standards for its time and personnel need and who control the keeping to these standards, who, however, do not deal with the everyday processes and conflicts over performance in production.
3. comparatively high wages as the main mode of integrating the employees to the system and compensating its negative aspects.

Although they are not necessarily connected, both elements of labour regulation grew together in Western factories to the extent that one can speak of a unified form and a specific mode of control over the labour process.

It did not take very long before the novelty of the new production concepts of the 1920s had worn off. The assembly line and the stop watch increasingly became hated symbols of the working conditions in the industrial mass production.

Goldthorpe thus determined in the middle of the 1960s that: 'The auto industry is the locus classicus of dissatisfying work; the assembly line its quintessential embodiment' (Goldthorpe, 1966, p. 235). Protest and criticism had already attained their classical form in Charlie Chaplin's film 'Modern Times'. This inspired countless scientific studies and socially critical discourses which dealt with the negative effects of automobile work on the workers: mindless work requirements which were bereft of content, self-estranged regulation of the work rhythm and work methods, forced pace and work pressure, stifling of initiative and responsibility at the level of the work performed, physical work strain and psychic stress (Friedman, 1974; Widick, 1976).

The advantages of the Tayloristic-Fordist control forms also became increasingly questionable for management. The degrees of utilization of available human and material resources which were thus achieved seemed to be much lower than that which should be possible. In this regard the concept of 'X-inefficiency' was coined by Leibenstein for describing the phenomenon of many strange, little understood causes for inefficiency in traditionally organized Western mass production factories (Leibenstein, 1987). For a while this was neglected. A poor quality of worklife and high control costs were treated as the inevitable disadvantages of Taylorism-Fordism. Attempts at reform which had referred to the positive connection between an increased quality of worklife and sinking control costs have a long tradition (see Lawler III, 1986 as representative for many others). The real burden of the 'X-inefficiency' became evident in the comparison with the Japanese companies, and this comparison was not motivated by theoretical or philanthropical interests, but rather by the pressure of competition.

The criticism of Taylorism-Fordism has grown since the beginning of the 1980s, and the demand for an increased priority for human resources and the self-regulation of work through the workers themselves is experiencing an enormous upswing in the public discussion in Western countries. One speaks of the 'new plant revolution' (Lawler, 1978). A mixture of ideas on questions of work motivation, social and technical system-designing of work, and industrial democracy which had been developed over decades now came to fruition and was translated into textbooks for personnel policy (representative for many: Milkovich and Glueck, 1985) and industrial engineering (Barnes, 1980). Titles like 'Improving Productivity and the Quality of Worklife' (Cummings and Molloy, 1977), 'Productivity Gains through Worklife

Improvements' (Glaser, 1976) and 'High Involvement Management' (Lawler III, 1986) hint at a new way of thinking in management.

It is no wonder that the interpretations of what these labour reforms comprise, and what their goals are, diverged widely in the discussion at the beginning of the 1980s. On the one side there is the assessment that one is only dealing with a symbolic policy of management to guarantee the acceptance for far-reaching technological and organizational restructuring, within the workforces as well as outside the company, and that the core of this restructuring is to be found in a secular process of automization and mechanization which has the fully automated factory as its final goal. On the other side, there is the assessment that the labour reforms are striving for a more comprehensive usage of human labour power and that the future of industrial labour will be characterized by exactly such new forms of usage.

In the following I would like to make a contribution toward examining these assessments. In this, I will be pursuing three principal questions:

1. What signs can be seen of a turning away from the traditional Tayloristic-Fordist paradigma for regulation of labour?

2. What are the differences in this regard between different countries, companies and factories? What conditions support or hinder the establishment of new forms for labour regulation?

3. Are there models for the establishment of a new non-Tayloristic and non-Fordist labour regulation?

But beforehand I will give some information on the research project which provides the basis for this paper. The research was concerned with the effects of the 1980s restructuring of the world automobile industry on its workers. The units studied were 17 assembly plants from three automobile companies in the three countries USA, Great Britain and the Federal Republic of Germany.

I shall present first the general results of the study and then analyse the national differences with special reference to the German data. 'The German model' of skilled worker orientated labour regulation seems to be one of two models for future development of labour relations within the automobile industry. The other is the Japanese model (or 'Toyotoism') of group oriented labour regulation. The final section of the article presents these future models and the problems of application in other countries.

Developmental Trends

I would like to summarize our findings about the trends in the forms of labour regulation in the factory in five points.

Change in the Forms of Control over Production Work

In the traditional Tayloristic-Fordist organized automobile factory, everything was geared to prescribing the course of work to the last detail from above and outside the 'shop floor'. Pace-binding of work through the assembly line, standardization of work performance by the experts of industrial engineering, and direct monitoring by the line supervisors - this control structure of Taylorism-Fordism did not tolerate a self-regulation by the workers themselves. This constellation, which was stifling for the initiative and sense of responsibility of the workers, is now beginning to loosen up because of developments which soften the deterministic character of the traditional control structure:
- An increasing number of workplaces are being freed from the strict pace-binding through alternative work design and mechanization.
- The task of setting production standards is being increasingly shifted into the phase of production planning, and thus avoids the direct confrontation of the experts with the 'shop floor' as was the case during the traditional work study.
- Increased demands of technical expertise requires a different type of supervisor, who has to be able to deal with problems of production control, material flow and the technical equipment of his area; routine matters of labour allocation, work organization and personnel mobility are given back to the shop floor, partially, for self-regulation.

The forms of management control - all of the developments point in this direction - are thus settled to a greater degree in the structures of the equipment and process lay out or in the planning phase. With this, scope is opened up for a certain amount of self-regulation of the operative tasks in the production process. The question of how much autonomy in which functional areas is now being debated in all the companies of our sample. External control functions can be carried out independently, in a more or less non-hierarchal cooperation of the workers on the spot. This means that the employees would have to accept the factory goals of quality and work efficiency to a certain extent as their own in order to carry them out independently: external control is 'internalized', so to speak.

Strategies

Job integration concerns management organization just as much as labour deployment. It is coming to a widening of areas of responsibility and the ranges of jobs, and to an erosion of the strict divisions between direct production and the indirectly productive production areas. A part of the indirect tasks of maintenance, quality control, or material supply is integrated into the production tasks again. Our empirical findings show that job integration did only very seldom involve a significant increase in the qualification or compensation of production work. Job integration reduced waiting times and cycle time losses and thus made an expanded usage of worker capabilities possible. In this respect it complies with the classic Tayloristic objective, which is being carried out with measures of 'de-Taylorization' under the conditions in the 1980s.

Automation and Skilled Labour

The job integration of direct and indirect tasks does not lead to a general increase of the qualification demands. The unqualified mass labourer still dominates in the labour-intensive areas of assembly line work. It is different in the high technology areas. On the one hand, new jobs of equipment monitoring with more demanding qualification requirements are emerging here, on the other hand there is the emergence of less qualified servicing jobs, like feeding and removing parts. Measured on the type of qualified semi-skilled labour which predominated before the mechanization (e.g. welding) we see a polarization of qualification requirements. But this left-over work, 'residual work', is losing its importance as it is filling into mechanization gaps, many of which will be eliminated by the next wave of new technology. Thus there is a tendency toward a relative increase in qualification in high technology areas as a result of the rationalization process. As to the allocation of the new task structure there are differing options for combining or separating maintenance, monitoring and the residual work.

From the point of view of management, wage costs would speak for segmentation of the few highly qualified from the many low qualified jobs (Babbage principle). But the increased importance of avoiding machine down times would demand, on the other hand, that all of the workers assigned to the installation could detect process irregularities as early as possible, intervene preventively and support the experts in the event of a disruption. That is why there is an interest in also retaining appropriate qualifications at the 'residual workplaces' and to reduce the demarcations between skilled and non-skilled workers. Although there are remarkable exceptions, the demarcations have become more impermeable for the non-skilled workers in recent years. Their opportunities for a substantial expansion of their work competencies and qualifications have become poorer in the course of the technological modernization of the 1980s. In the expanding high technology areas a new type of skilled production worker is emerging at the same time, to whom simple 'residual jobs' are being transferred in addition to their more demanding tasks of installation monitoring. Demarcations are becoming more permeable 'from the top down'. This development has been most characteristic in the West German automobile industry. It is made easier through a considerable expansion of apprentice training in German automobile companies which has led to an oversupply of qualified skilled workers. This oversupply forms an important potential for coping with the technological modernization.

Assembly Line Work and Pace-binding

The tying of work rhythm and task allocation to the pace of the machine and the speed of the assembly line, a central characteristic of the Tayloristic-Fordist production organization, is beginning to exhibit signs of breaking up. Fewer and fewer operations in the expanding high technology areas are determined by the production cycle. The new jobs are determined by irregular demands of machine servicing and equipment monitoring. The number of such workplaces which are uncoupled from the production cycle is increasing. The gradual abolition of the assembly line in favour of stationary workplaces and the establishment of work areas outside the main production line leads to the fact that job design can now be more orientated to meaningful division of production, and less dominated by the priorities of the running conveyor belt. By this, the share of extremely short-cycle, repetitive operations is being reduced. Nevertheless, the classical assembly line will still govern the majority of the jobs in assembly operations; the new module (preassembly areas) comprise only one-third of the jobs even in the most modern factories. An end of the assembly line in the auto industry is presently not in sight.

Moreover, uncoupling work from the flow of production and establishing stationary workplaces do not mark the end of time pressure or the beginning of time sovereignty in work. The job cycle at stationary workplaces can, of course, be varied corresponding to differing work contents of the respective workpieces. But nothing has changed with respect to the predetermination of time. The time requirements for each workpiece are contained in the computer assisted system for process control, and this system registers deviations from the standards more mercilessly than the lower level supervisors in the traditional course of work could ever hope to. Holding to the preplanned labour time in the flow of production is here just as necessary as on the assembly line. In the high technology areas, the time pressure and hectic increase with the growing costs of a standstill in the case of a break down. The reduction of the pace binding of work furthermore goes together with an increased pressure of responsibility of the personnel in the high-tech areas.

Quality of Worklife (QWL) Goals and the Development of 'Human Resources'

In the question of worker participation and the development of human resources one can see two directions of thrust in the management strategy:

The first aims at personal work behaviour and work motivation and at the labour relations between the workforce and management. In the process, management intends to reduce individual and collective resistance (absenteeism, strikes), and to create or improve the identification of the workforce with the company goals.

The second direction of thrust aims at an expanded usage of the potential for productivity and problem solving found in the capabilities and experience, as well as the informal social relationships, within the workforce. This potential should be mobilized for work related solutions to problems and for improvements in the operative work process.

The first direction of thrust, the improvement of work motivation and labour relations, is more characteristic in the American and British context than in the German context. The considerations of management in the German automobile industry revolve more strongly around technology related demands and problem-solving competencies. The potential of skilled workers in production who also have the flexibility for jobs which are below their qualification is considered to be the central human resource which management likes to tap in the German context. Technical qualification, and above all the original vocational training, is at the centre of this strategy. Whilst one cannot ignore the interdependencies between QWL related 'skills' and technology related skills, the QWL efforts in the American context are above all aimed at the formation of teams in the area of non-skilled work.

Let me summarize briefly: the general findings of our investigation send out a clear message. The work reforms of the 1980s cannot be interpreted as a purely symbolic policy or even cheap propaganda of management in order to ensure the 'acceptance' of the workers and the general public for personnel reduction, the introduction of new technologies, and the restructuring of the industry. But one can also not speak of a sweeping renunciation of the traditional Tayloristic-Fordist production model. We can rather observe an unfinished process of development in which differing configurations of the Tayloristic-Fordist regulation mode and its negation forms are visible.

The Influence of Company Strategies

What influence does the company affiliation of the factories have in explaining the differences in the ways that were taken, in the degree of acceptance and in the focuses of new forms of labour deployment The difference which is clearest and which has the most serious consequences can be brought to the point of whether human factors or technology factors are seen as the decisive productivity resource. It is true that the companies were in very different positions in regards to their financial strength at the beginning of the 1980s. But the respective technology or human strategies which were pursued were nevertheless the result of strategic choices of the companies in light of the demands for adaptation which they had diagnosed at the beginning of the 1980s.

In this question, Company A clearly emphasized the development of human resources. The focus of the measures in its factories was on the integration of management responsibility and on the integration of work tasks in production. The institutionalization of programmes for employee participation went along with this. A further characteristic of this strategy is the remarkable emphasis that Company A places on the increase in efficiency and the rationalization of labour deployment. The use of new technologies was secondary in the course of this strategic concept.

In contrast to this, Company C clearly emphasized mechanization in its measures at the beginning of the 1980s. Supplementary to this, Company C expanded its programmes for initial and further vocational training considerably and adapted them to the new technological requirements. A comparatively lesser importance was attached to questions of organizational structure and social organization.

The strategy of Company B can be characterized as maximization of options. Both developmental variants are being tested in pilot plants in the company. The long-term goal is to achieve a synthesis of the technology and the human factor strategy. To this end, the programmes of the company management regarding human factors and social organization aim both at vocational qualification and at the use of motivational human resources.

Just as important as the differences in the main emphases of the strategies are the differences in the way they are implemented. One can also observe profiles which are typical for the companies here. As far as Company A is concerned, the human resources strategy was pushed on in the factories - company-wide - with remarkable consistency and terrific speed. This was true for the goal of job integration as well as for that of employee participation. The speed and the breadth of this process of reorganization can be summed up in a paradoxical formula: The strengthening of the decentral management and the decentral employee participation was pushed through by means of a tightly centralized company organization. This paradox of a new combination of highly centralized company management and the strengthening of decentralized self-regulation at the lower levels is the key to understanding the organizational change in Company A. The highly centralized form of control is faced, admittedly, with the limits of the national industrial relations. The measures could be rapidly introduced by the American and German factories in the company with good initial successes, while they were defeated for the time being by union objections in the British factories.

Company B, with its strategy of the maximization of options, that is the testing of several development alternatives, increased the variance in forms of factory labour regulation within its system. In comparison with the far-reaching innovations in production technology or in work and social organization in some pilot plants, the bulk of the assembly plants remained limited to an onlooker role at the time of our empirical investigations. At the level of local management there existed a greater insecurity over the prospective goals of future development than we had observed in the local management of Company A. The process of diffusion of new organizational concepts into the factories of Company B proceeds less centralized and is more strongly orientated toward individual local initiatives. In view of this pattern of diffusion it is no wonder that the influence of the national affiliation of the factories showed through to a greater extent than in Company A.

In Company C there was, as in Company B, no campaign of fear and motivation to achieve the allegiance of the workforces and factory management for company strategy that could be compared with that of Company A. In contrast to Company B, the clear orientation to technology as the central productivity reserve for the future did not cause any orientation problems. Here, on the contrary, there appears to be a problem in the fact that decision makers primarily look at questions of work and social organization from the viewpoint of necessary adjustment to the mechanization. At Company C, questions of qualification for adjustment to technology are indeed at the forefront.

The differences in deciding on emphases and priorities - human factors or technology factors - do not have anything to do with the company strategies being closer or further away from the goal of a humanization of labour. Company A's strategy was chosen to take advantage of a potential for ratonalization which was obviously redeemable in the shorter run. Holding back with mechanization meant at the same time that the lay-out of production technology frequently remained unchanged, so that possibilities for improvement in working conditions which are tied to measures of technology and process design could not be realized. Company A thus still retained the traditional forms of assembly line organization in the factories we studied. on the other hand, the factories of the companies B and C have already transferred a considerable share of their assembly tasks to production structures without an assembly line. These structures, which are generally introduced in connection with new production technologies, provide significantly improved working conditions at least from an ergonomic point of view.

The Influence of the National Affiliation of the Factories

The influence of the national affiliation of the factory site modifies and overlaps the company affiliation in many aspects. The national labour policy institutions form an element of inertia in the general change in the automobile industry. They do not remain totally unaffected by this process of change, however. There are three notable differences in the forms of institutional change in the three countries we investigated. At the core of the question of inertia or change at the national level are the institutions and arrangements of industrial relations and the patterns of action and policy orientations that are characterized by them. In addition to these, the nationally specific vocational training is of great importance.

In the USA, the companies have made the transformation of industrial relations to a central element of their strategy of restructuring. Since the beginning of the 1980s, the purposeful change of industrial relations and measures has been formulated and carried jointly by the top representatives of the companies and the unions: A high-level agreement for the channelling of institutional change at the factory level. The policy of ensuring the rank and file acceptance by means of the carrot and stick is jointly supported because the future of the individual production sites is also tied to the demonstration of decentrally created institutional change.

The transformation strategy, introduced in the manner from above, had already grown roots at the factory level in the American automobile industry at the time of our investigation. The traditional model of conflicting labour relations had been suspended to a great degree on all of the factories. A return to the conflict model has already become improbable in some factories because of the dynamics of the development which have been introduced. The traditional structure for regulating labour deployment (seniority and demarcation rules) were still partially in force. They had already lost their unconditional validity, however.

The decisive importance of the cooperation of the union for such a strategy of institutional change can be seen in the case of the British companies. Here it was not possible to obtain a consensus at the top level of the companies and unions and to develop an appropriate integrated concept as in the USA. Because of the differences in the union structures, a strategy 'from the top down' would have hardly had chances of success even with an agreement at the highest level. The influence of the unions on the process of change in work has always been extremely strong. But it limited itself to the establishment and consolidation of a veto power. This led to a special selectivity which furthered traditional strategies for rationalization, because conventional measures (e.g. tightening up the performance screws) can be pushed through unimpeded by management. Measures of de-Taylorization and rationalization supported by QWL, on the other hand, were blocked by the unions.

The prerequisite for a greater autonomy and for the stabilization of their own way beyond the traditions of Taylorism-Fordism which are dominant in the British automobile industry would be, under the British conditions, a process of institutional change which would be jointly supported by the factory parties. This prerequisite does not yet exist, despite remarkable individual examples of a change in behaviour in the period of our investigation. Independent innovations of work and social organization for the regulation of labour could not emerge under these conditions. The British way is still characterized by the principles of decentralized negotiation and the direct representation of interests. These principles apparently do not form a particularly fertile soil for the development of independent non-Tayloristic forms for the regulation of labour, so far.

Characteristic for the German development is that the change in labour is being carried out in and through the existing institutions. The process of restructuring of the companies in the German automobile industry does not include a specific strategy for the transformation of institutions. The system of industrial relations remains, so to speak, outside the brackets of the restructuring. The dual system of interest representation and co-determination as the central institution of industrial relations has shown a relatively high receptivity for recent approaches for de-Taylorization. Along with this came a specific furthering of mechanization measures and forms of labour deployment centring on skilled workers.

The statutory rights of the works council to information and participation have led to a firm establishment of cooperative problem-solving patterns at the factory level. At the same time the works council members and union representatives were able to develop their own concepts and alternatives for designing the forms of labour deployment, not least because of the institutions of co-determination. We did not find such an independent profile of union policy at the level of job design in either of the other countries studied. It was possible on this basis to negotiate future orientated arrangements between management and works councils which form a 'strategic reserve' for future adaptation requirements. With this, the institutions for labour policy and vocational training have had the function of a societal productivity resource for the restructuring process of the 1980s.

Let us summarize: the national systems of industrial relations and labour policy institutions in the three countries show an independent selectivity in each case with regard to objectives and priorities of restructuring in the factories. According to the findings of our study, this leads to three different nationally specific types of rationalization. For the USA it is the type of participation-orientated rationalization (QWL-rationalization); for Great Britain the Tayloristic type of rationalization is still dominant; and for the Federal Republic one can speak of the skilled worker-orientated type of rationalization. These nationally typical patterns of selection mix themselves with the company profiles in which it comes to characteristic overlays and mixed forms. The institutional peculiarities in the German context seem to foster specific solutions concerning work organization and labour deployment patterns. One can find three indications supporting the thesis of a special German development:

1. The exceptional vocational training and labour market situation provides the factories with a skilled worker potential which is also deployable for semi-skilled tasks, and which can also be used for new forms of work organization and new job descriptions in direct production. The growing use of skilled workers in direct production increases the necessity and the possibility of creating intelligent work structures. Corresponding to this, a close connection has emerged between the surplus of skilled workers and the degree of innovation in the work organization in the German assembly plants.

2. Because of legal and contractual regulations, the absentee rates due to illness and the percentage of disabled workers in the German plants are significantly higher than in the British and American plants. In order to overcome the restrictions for labour deployment which are thus created, management is more dependent on job design and the use of technology here. In the American and British plants, restrictions lie more in the area of informal work practices and are tackled by management in the arena of industrial relations.

3. The particular profile of demands by the unions and the factory interest representations in the Federal Republic of Germany is clearly aimed at lengthening the work cycles for paced work. This has led to the fact that alternative solutions were considered in process design and work organization. In comparison, short work cycles were still considered by the production planners in the USA to be the ultimate in work layout for the 1980s.

The average work cycles in West German plants, which are far and away longer than in American plants, go along with qualification requirements even for assembly line work which are considerably higher than in the American plants. With this, the distance to the requirements at stationary workplaces with more comprehensive work tasks is clearly smaller, and that is why changing over to forms of labour without an assembly line with a given workforce faces less difficulties there than in the American context. On this basis a particular combination of mechanization and labour deployment has emerged, in which the first signs of a model for future forms of labour regulation are becoming visible.

Models for Future Developments

In the process of dissolution of Tayloristic-Fordist control system there are above all two lines of development which would be capable of fulfilling the function of a model: the 'German model' (or the 'Swedish-German model') of skilled worker-orientated labour regulation and the 'Japanese model' of group oriented labour regulation[1]. Both developmental models stand out through the degree of self-regulation of shop floor work. And both stand out through a worker type which, through its competence and willing to accept responsibility, is clearly different from the dequalified mass labourer. Despite these common features, there are important differences between the two models.

At the centre of the 'German model' is the skilled worker and a specific understanding of skilled work as a 'profession'. This understanding of profession includes the aspect of technical skill, but also the aspect of interest in the work, the willingness to accept comprehensive responsibility which also crosses over the borders of their own task area, and the aspect of a large degree of self-regulation in carrying out the work. This model presupposes a 'qualification offensive', also above and beyond the direct company needs for skilled workers, which on its part is dependent on institutions and strategies of vocational training. With this we are referring to the aspect of societal prerequisites for a specific form of labour regulation as they exist in the educational system in the Federal Republic. It is clear that the model of a skilled worker centred work regulation is especially important for modern technology management. Against the background of the strong position on the world market that the German automobile industry enjoys, this model is not without attractions for the foreign competitors. The ideal-typical goal of the German way is qualified labour, uncoupled from the production cycle and the rhythm of the machines. The uncoupling of work from the flow of production forms the prerequisite for a type of labour with increased possibilities for self-regulation and with increased responsibility. This skilled production labour though, in contrast to skilled labour outside of direct production, comes under the pressure of production and holding to time and amount goals. The skilled production workers can escape less and less the simple production tasks (setting dies, feeding parts, transporting material, etc.). With this, the classic professional understanding of skilled labour thus loses its foundation. In the long run, the German way requires the establishment of a 'new' type of skilled worker, also for German conditions.

The 'Japanese way' also gives a central role to qualified labour. This is not, however, in the sense of uncoupled skilled labour. The ideal for the Japanese model is rather the self-regulation under the pressure of the assembly line and the production pace. Characteristic is a personnel allocation which aims at the best possible performance and its permanent improvement, i.e. the permanent intensification of labour. This is in contrast to the industrial engineering practices in western companies which aim for 'normal' performance ('fair day's work principle') and are restricted in its possibilities of a continuous review of the established time standards. It has its basis in group solidarity, and in the formal and informal possibilities for balancing the work load and supporting within the group. In the Japanese model the group plays a central role. Societal and cultural prerequisites play an important role here, too. In the Japanese automobile industry, the work group is the starting point for an integrated job understanding, for the flexibilization and expansion of labour deployment, and for the qualification of the workers. Self-regulation is not just based on skilled worker training and a professional ethic.

The question of the transferability of group- or skilled worker-orientated organizational alternatives is also posed for the British and American companies in view of the future perspective of increasing technological requirements. The considerable increase in vocational training in British factories hints at the German way. Although such a development is presently not yet achievable in British labour policy, it could come to an expansion of the skilled worker potential beyond the needs of the skilled labour departments in the British factories with similar consequences to those one sees in the German automobile industry. Such a development is being furthered through centralization and the creation of European company networks and the corresponding standardization of production and rationalization concepts.

In contrast to this, the considerations in the American companies are obviously more influenced by Japanese concepts. The formation of production teams in the semi-skilled area and a flexibilization and expansion of the area of deployment is being sought after. Measures for further training with the goal of the formation of groups and the conveyance of group related problem-solving techniques also play a much more important role in policies for worker qualification than the training of skilled workers. The strategy of group related on-the-job qualification of semi-skilled workers supported by new wage systems like 'pay for knowledge' wages could, on the other hand, in the long run allow the necessary qualification potential to emerge from below.

A transfer of the German or the Japanese management concept faces problems in both cases. In the course of this the Japanese way appears more capable of being generalized and more transferable. Not least the high interest of many Western companies in Japanese management methods points in this direction. A point in favour of the transferability is that it is much less tied to conditions of the institutional framework than the German model. The strong anchoring in the structures of co-determination and an educational system which was governmentally drawn up means, on the other hand, a greater degree of institutional and legal limitation of the company headquarters' scope for action and decision-making.

Notes

1. See for the most recent development of work structuring in the Swedish auto industry: Berggren, 1988; for the role of the work group in Japanese car plants: Jürgens et al., 1985.

13. Debureaucratization and Flexibility

Otto Jacobi

One aspect in the present debate on flexibilization refers to the rearrangement of traditionally hierarchic management organization structures based on the Fordistic-Tayloristic production model. This involves tendencies towards debureaucratization through the downward transfer of responsibilities. It is hoped that the elimination of hierarchic controls and the setting-up of self-regulating work groups, project teams, quality control circles, etc. will affect productivity to the benefit of profits, since better use can be made of the production intelligence of the qualified regular workforce and the company can react in general more flexibly to changing market conditions and to specific customer wishes. It remains to be seen whether these development trends, amounting to the establishment of company-based micro-corporatism, herald a historic change of alliance, to the effect that the old coalition between top and middle management is replaced by a new alliance between management and the operator basis within the development, production and customer-related departments. This outcome remains uncertain, mainly because high trust forms of organization confront management with the risk of reduced control, whilst the trade unions face the risk of workforces and their internal representatives being incorporated through company loyalty.

Given that such processes of integral restructuring of management organization forms are still at an experimental pioneering stage, it is not possible to present wide-ranging empirically backed findings. For this reason, the contribution offers a brief overview of current research as well as initial information on cases of practical implementation, concluding with presentation of certain problems in research methods.

Mistrust Organization and Production Intelligence

The themes of debureaucratization and decentralization have become increasingly important for years now in business management literature. Reference is made to the weaknesses and rigidities of mistrust organization based on formalized system structures when faced with more and more rapid changes of markets and in technology. In view of the highly dynamic conditions of the present day with its structural ruptures and discontinuities, hierarchic management organization is claimed to be obsolete. Mistrust organization, with its commitment to security, is said to be effective only under stable background conditions - such as predictable market, social and technological developments. Under the prevailing circumstances of uncertainty, the needs of the moment would call for the rectification of all-powerful and proliferously bureaucratic organizational structures, thus creating scope for initiative and a willingness to take risk, as well as exploiting the creative potential of the company's human capital. It is asserted that the new organizational structure should ensure that the know-how and responsible autonomy of the regular workforce can be further developed within a constantly flexible organizational framework (Tunstall, 1983; Walton, 1985).

Criticism of the rigidity of formalized management systems is certainly nothing new in business management theory. The emphatic response with which it meets today is the outcome of the coincidence of pressure to flexibilize under stiffer market competition with greatly increased possibilities to achieve organizational flexibility, thanks to the development of modern information technology. The use of microelectronics in production and office communication technologies offers the opportunity to overcome the previous 'magic triangle' between productivity, flexibility and motivation. These objectives can now be reached simultaneously and no longer at the expense of each other. Organizational decentralization is also facilitated by the use of electronically based management information systems which, despite decentralization of responsibility, permit central management to retain detailed examination and control of results data and of internal operating, communication and decision processes. The centralization of strategic decisions by management is fostered, giving rise to the paradox situation of a 'centralized decentralization'. Particularly in view of the complexity and susceptibility to interference of increasingly capital-intensive production structures, but also in the light of demands for better quality in customer service, 'psychologization' strategies gain in significance over 'mechanization' aspects. A dilemma is thus to be noted between efficiency and controllability: a decentralized strategy based to a greater extent on the autonomy and individual responsibility of employees may promise greater efficiency, but its success depends on institutional and social background conditions, on functionally ordered and cooperatively evolved industrial relations over which management has only limited control.

It is at this point that sociological research on organization and industrial relations becomes involved. The question is raised in industrial sociology research as to whether signs of a 'paradigmatic change in labour policy' are to be detected in 'new production concepts' which aim to exploit to the full and make profitable use of the innovatory potential and productivity reserves hidden in human capital. The new production concepts, of which empirical evidence is to be found both in industry and in the service sector, imply that restrictive control of labour wastes important productivity potential, whereas the integral form of job profile can secure qualification and the specialist efficacy of the labour force to the benefit of company objectives. It is the aim of the new production concepts to gain from the production intelligence of skilled workers and white-collar employees, whereby these concepts are seen to represent a fundamental change in form and a historical break with considerable chances of spreading (Baethge and Oberbeck, 1986; Kern and Schumann, 1984a, b). The more new technologies are used, the more complex the production of goods and services becomes, the more industry is forced to react flexibly to fluctuating demand, the greater will be the need for employees capable of diagnosis and confident action, the more necessary it is to achieve a more concerned and enlightened treatment of living labour. The aim is said to be a comprehensive and flexible utilization of labour which would depend on a high level of qualification, employment security and cooperative labour relations (Streeck, 1987b; Streeck and Sorge, 1987).

Unlike business management research which thinks in organizational configurations, industrial sociology research has mainly concentrated up to now on the qualifications and employment effects of decentralization policies in individual departments or work processes. This generally referred to work in production, only seldom to the white-collar employee in administration. It has only gradually been realized that policies of organizational decentralization - often linked to the use of information technology systems - harbour processes of 'systemic' rationalization which result in far-reaching changes in the overall company organizational, qualification and employment structure, as well as influencing intra-company forms of cooperation. 'Exploding technological development or the increasingly difficult competitive world market cannot be met simply by restructuring the shop floor and maintaining the traditional hierarchy upwards' (Gustavsen and Hethy, 1986).

Agreement prevails in the most recent industrial sociology literature that decentralization as an organizational strategy aimed at increased productivity and improved profitability is not determined by the choice of certain technology, but that modern information technologies, in offering opportunities to decouple man and machine, are particularly inclined to broaden the scope of organizational arrangements. In this connection, industrial relations now acquire a new and changed significance. They become an 'independent variable' with active influence on organizational strategies. It is particularly emphasized in industrial relations research that in contrast to the phase of prosperity and full employment in the postwar period, there are now clear signs of a shift of emphasis in the objects of regulation and regulation competences on the microeconomic level of individual firms. If consideration is also given to the fact that the social make-up of the labour forces becomes further differentiated in the course of changes in employment structure and that increasingly heterogeneous working conditions and interests are more likely than unlikely, it is understandable that many observers assume that there will be a growth in the competency of internal company authorities, namely both management and the works council (*Betriebsrat*). These observers also speak of the emergence of works or company centred micro-corporatism which like previous macro-corporatism is characterized by compromise and exchange, in this case perhaps flexible use of labour in exchange for employment security and participation. Whether and to what extent a change in alliance does occur depends on the strategic decisions chosen by the protagonists involved. Both management and trade unions act within the context of their respective specific organizational aims and interests. Their options need by no means be compatible, so that the 'change of alliance' can misfire or may only be achieved in the course of possibly very conflictive processes of rapprochement and negotiation. The dilemma facing the top management responsible for choice of strategy is that retaining the old alliance with its 'control mechanism' is expensive, but less risky, whilst the implementation of a change in alliance is a risk in terms of internal control in the company, but could be more favourable for profitability and cost considerations. The key question for the trade unions in their choice of strategy is whether this change of alliance takes place over their heads or within the framework of established negotiating systems. International literature refers repeatedly to the wish of industry to replace collectively agreed industrial relations by individually settled employee relations and states that unions avoidance strategies are gaining ground (Crouch, 1986; Edwards et al., 1986); other authors speak of the possible refeudalization of labour relations (Baethge and Oberbeck, 1986).

It is not yet clear in what way labour relations can make a contribution to the solution of this problem, or whether they are more likely to aggravate rather than solve it. It could turn out that their effect will be to conserve structures rather than to favour organizational change.

Genuine and Fictitious Decentralization

Two types of change in configuration are conceivable for the alterations in overall company configurations of organization, personnel and internal labour markets as associated with policies to reduce bureaucracy.

• A 'genuine' decentralization in the sense of the 'coathanger model' described by Gustavsen (1986). This implies a 'net shift' of competencies, qualifications and personnel out of administration, in other words out of strategic management, middle line management or the teams, into the operative departments. Central staff and management departments will at best be extended below a proportional level. A model of this kind is reflected in efforts by a number of West German companies in mechanical engineering, the electro-technical industry and the car industry to reduce relatively the number of their salaried employees in administration in comparison to the directly productive and closely market-related parts of the labour force.

● A 'fictitious' decentralization which could also be described as the 'egg-timer model'. Although related to the 'coathanger model' through a reduction in hierarchy and the cutback of middle management personnel, this form not only implements a limited downward shift of competences, qualifications and personnel, but also includes a stronger move up to strategic management. The top-heavy effect of the management structure is virtually intensified in the process. According to Baethge and Oberbeck (1986), the beginnings of such developments are apparent in the West German banks.

In order to be able to demonstrate the influence of the system of internal and industry-wide labour relations on the cited change of configuration, the metal-working industry and the banking business are suitable comparative contrasting cases because of the clear divergence in their degree of unionization. The central hypothesis, although it can only be tentatively formulated at this stage, is that a high degree of unionization and the 'steadfastness' of the works councils (Betriebsrat) are more likely to promote the establishment of restructuring processes along the lines of the 'coathanger model', whereas weak trade union representation and a passive works council are inclined to favour restructuring according to the 'egg-timer model'. Several arguments can be offered in support of this hypothesis.

'Genuine' decentralization of organization depends on cooperation between production operators or the white-collar employees responsible for customer services and management. Management will only be able to achieve the intended improvement in efficiency if it is able to arrive at a motivated integration of the production intelligence of the qualified regular workforce and thus protect the fragile, since highly complex, process of goods and services production against possible industrial action disturbances. Another aspect is that the restricted opportunities facing employees with firm-specific skills when wanting to change jobs is only one side of the coin; the other is the company's dependence on the willingness of employees to make this qualification available in the best possible way in accordance with the company's aims. It is also true that the varied and diverging interests of the workforce must be represented in coordinated form. In other words: a bargaining situation arises which can be exploited by well-established works councils and encompassing unions in the interests of a 'genuine' and thus always participatory-democratic decentralization. The management which is faced with a 'steadfast' works council backed by an industry-level trade union is one which deals with competent discussion partners in its bargaining, partners with whom agreements can be reached and implemented.

The 'passive' works council which functions merely as a 'management organ' is far less capable of developing a bargaining situation, on the other hand, or of playing the part of an internal discussion partner. Management's debureaucratization policies then tend on their 'downward' path to be in danger of losing their way in the thicket of particular group interests. The internal trust base is then missing, without which the inevitable risk involved in hierarchy elimination through decentralization will be incalculable for top management. The outcome can be a consolidation rather than the dismantling of hierarchical structures. When competences and qualifications are shifted to the customer-contact levels in dosed and controlled form, this could prove to be associated with tougher personnel selection and the marginalization of low-qualification employee groups.

The employer associations and trade unions facing one another in the metal-working industry are in each case the strongest in the FRG. It is the only branch with a history of conflict involving strikes and lockouts throughout the postwar era. It has been characteristic here that, although not planned, the two battle-tried parties have de facto functionalized their labour disputes and that these have served as instruments for socially pioneering compromises, giving rise again and again to the stable form of 'antagonistic' cooperation. The counterpart within the companies of the metal-working industry has been a type of works council which can be described as 'respected as steadfast' or as orientated to 'cooperative hostile power'. These are conditions which are more favourable for an alliance constellation with 'genuine' decentralization. This is also particularly true because the metal-workers' union, the IG Metall, is an industry-wide trade union and has at its disposal regulating resources for intervention, commitment and loyalty internally in relation to its members and its associated works councils, while externally dealing with an employer association which is also an intermediary organization with which reliable agreements can be reached.

Due to the low level of trade union representation, the banking sector in the FRG offers conditions more favourable to a fictitious decentralization of the 'egg-timer model' variety. Sometimes in competition with one another, the trade unions are never able to make an independent mark in bargaining policy; they have followed with a time-lag agreement already struck on other sectors of the economy, primarily the metalworking industry. The predominant type of works councils is that of an 'organ of management'.

Precisely because the trade unions have at their disposal comparatively few strategic control variables and intervention potential either internally or externally, management could feel compelled to pursue entrepreneurship union-avoidance strategies on the basis of developed participation offers of employee involvement.

Both forms of decentralization give rise to their respective specific problems for the internal employee representation. A 'sympathetic ear' towards the interests of salaried employees can be expected from the passive works council, without it being in a position to focus effectively and represent these. But, in view of the importance of the salaries employees as a source of recruitment for the trade union, the 'steadfast' works council will not be able to afford a policy of total indifference either - as first investigation findings have shown. A similar problem arises from the fact that skilled workers as the most important clientèle of the 'steadfast' works council could ultimately benefit most from debureaucratization, whilst semi-skilled workers and white-collar workers in clearing sectors will mainly suffer a negative effect. It should be clarified as to what extent trade union concepts which aim to avoid marginalization of semi-skilled and unskilled on the internal labour market can be implemented in practice. The general question is therefore whether the works councils and trade unions traditionally orientated in the FRG to global representation of employee interests will be able to solve the dilemma inherent in debureaucratization policies in the form of a segmentation privileging the regular workforce and putting the peripheral workforce at a disadvantage.

The central questions and hypotheses which can be formulated for further research are:

• Will organizational decentralization by the company be paralleled by a 'decentralization' of industrial relations, in other words by the separation off of internal policy from the context of sectoral trade union organization and collective bargaining regulation, associated with an increasingly flexible handling of collective agreement norms?

• Does decentralization result in the creation of direct communication paths between the workforce and management, undermining the function of established employee representation? Here again, first empirical findings suggest that a development of this kind is more likely in plants and companies with a less solid representation than in those with historically rooted and firmly established internal and trade union employee representation. Strong works councils and trade unions can apparently benefit more than the weak from microcorporative tendencies and can profit from the fact that clear positions on internal fronts and lines of conflict between 'workforce' and 'management' are less likely than in the past.

Diversity of First Empirical Findings

It was a pleasant surprise in our empirical research to find a whole series of plants and enterprises with advanced decentralization programmes. While our investigation concentrated on medium-sized enterprises of between 500 and 4000 employees in the electro-technical and machine-tool industries, it covered banking enterprises of varying magnitude from small local banks to large banks operating on a world-wide scale.

Despite all the differences which can be established in the decentralization processes taking place among the companies in the metal industry and those involved in the financial service sector, they do share some common features:

• The driving force behind decentralization measures is usually top-management. It takes up these measures as a reaction to market turbulence faced by the concern, or in hopes of carrying out unavoidable adaptations in a timely fashion when structural changes in the market are anticipated.

• Furthermore, decentralization means that previously untapped potential for rationalization should be exploited by shifting decision-making jurisdictions and responsibilities downward. In a conscious departure from the Tayloristic method of asserting control by means of supervisors and orders, qualifications such as technical and communication skills are specifically promoted in order to increase the motivation and flexibility of the employees.

• As a rule, the decentralization of the concern's organization leads to the formation of profit centres which are managed as if they were independent companies. The task of this operational management is to achieve the best utilization of the existing potential for economic success (by means of decentralized units); the task of strategic leadership at enterprise headquarters is the timely building up of the concern's future potential. Formulated in another way: the relationship between strategic and operational management finds tension-filled expression in the relationship between present and future success. We are dealing with a newly balanced organizational structure whose goal it is to combine the synergistic advantages of centralization with the advantages in flexibility offered by micro-units.

The difference between the two sectors can be described as follows. In the electro-technical and machine-tool industries - traditionally the employers of highly-qualified skilled workforces and manufacturers of high-tech products, mainly for the world market - decentralization programmes (with the exception of enterprises which consider themselves social and organizational vanguards) are mostly answers to economic setbacks. These have frequently been caused by the mistakes of management and have led to the endangerment of the company's market position which is based on technological superiority. Decentralized reorganization programmes are aimed at promoting the motivation of the employees who are competent in diverse specialized fields, raising their awareness of cost and quality factors and increasing their capacity for flexible reactions to the ever changing and more demanding desires of their customers.

Decentralization in the high-tech companies of the metal industry is usually bound up with the establishment of profit centres. As a rule, project teams are also found which have been assembled from various tiers in the company hierarchy and from across departmental boundaries. The most current examples include project teams which have to develop programmes for business activities in the former German Democratic Republic and the virgin markets in eastern Europe.

Semi-autonomous work groups have been integrated into the recently decentralized production organizations. As an operating unit they are autonomously responsible for a particular phase of production. The goal is often for every group member to be in a position to carry out every job in the unit, thereby opening up a greater potential for flexibility through all-around qualified teams in which each member is capable of substituting for another. In the area of manufacturing, flexible production islands quickly spread out. They are considered the most advanced attempts to use technical knowledge in the most optimal way by means of decentralized autonomous units. In not a few enterprises the networking of production islands into complete and complex production systems can be observed. According to statements by trade union representatives, flexible production systems are 'mall factories autonomously directed by self-confident and universally qualified system teams'. Such positive evaluations are supported by empirical findings which show that the reversal of Tayloristic principles means work is organized more comprehensively, responsibility for independent execution of tasks is transferred to the groups and further training is significantly promoted. Comparisons between the assignments of workers to various qualification and wage/salary categories before and after the establishment of semi-autonomous groups and production islands allow recognition of a clear shift to the higher end of the classification spectrum. This is because specialized knowledge, social competence and, as a consequence, wages and salaries all go up. In addition, the traditional boundaries between white- and blue-collar workers becomes more blurred. These social and wage/salary aspects frequently make it possible for works councils to become advocates of decentralization measures.

A very characteristic and already largely completed pattern of decentralization among the banks can be seen. The enterprise's strategic leadership is separated off from operational management in such a way that two cornerstones of equal standing have taken shape in banking practice: one being centrally concentrated, the other being compartmentalized in a decentralized manner.

The growing necessity to have a presence near banking customers has led to a shifting of spheres of competence and jurisdiction. In this context a sharp division is developing between the work of highly qualified specialists and advisors, on the one hand, and personnel doing routine clerical work who are frequently even physically separated off from the others in the back office area. As a rule, a decoupling of work which can be standardized off from work of a more demanding character is taking place through the phasing out of personnel positions with both types of tasks and the creation of positions requiring either simple repetitive skills or higher qualifications. The banks thereby exploit two sources of rationalization: first, the Tayloristic potential for the rationalization of work which can be standardized and, secondly, a 'communicative' potential for all positions which require specialized personnel who serve their customers with communication skills and a knowledge of the market and customer needs.

While clear tendencies toward the melding together of status groups within the workforce of the high-tech companies of the metal industry (specifically between blue- and white-collar workers) can be distinguished, a two-class society seems to be emerging among the employees of banks. The reason for this development, according to bank management, is the fact that qualified bank employees are too expensive; something confirmed by a labour market which has been swept clean by exaggerated demand. In other words, economic profitability compels them to free employees from subordinate forms of routine work.

On the whole, the banks are operating under the assumption that the sector is experiencing a process of radical structural change and is heading in the direction of becoming an 'all-finance' banking industry. Given that an uncertain and complex environment combined with a high degree of organizational decentralization is considered to be an inefficient, even counterproductive constellation, the banks are betting on the decentralization of business dealings with competent personnel. There is much that speaks for the fact that the tension-filled relationship between control and autonomy is the central problem and inclines the banks to solve it with a gentle management style which remains, however, thoroughly neo-paternalistic. To a growing degree there are indications that the booming industry of corporate identity is aimed at the neutralization of the contradiction between autonomy and control and between the demands of individuals with regard to work and life-style and centrally set, authoritative corporate strategies. In the Tayloristic field, reliance on orders and a poverty of job variety should be kept to a bearable level; in the communicative field, leadership teams and the personnel directly serving customers should be held together by 'dialogue' structures and 'hierarchy-free communication' as it is called.

The representation of employee interests by the works councils has been so well established and proven in practice that management is consciously striving to integrate them into decentralization programmes. Almost without exception, empirical findings show that the works councils in both sectors do not reject the decentralization measures put forward by management, but rather support them as a rule. In some concerns, there has been a splitting up of the works council's representation of interests in such a way that representation on the operational level results which is decentralized and parallel to the organizational structure of the concern and representation of interests on the strategic level, with its long-term perspective and total-enterprise orientation, remain centrally concentrated.

With regard to the relationship between works councils and trade unions it can be said that the councils are sufficiently independent and competent to get along in the enterprise's internal affairs without the aid of unions. It does, in fact, make a difference whether a works council is heavily involved in a trade union's organizational functions and other activities, as is overwhelmingly the case in the metal industry; or whether the trade union landscape is characterized by weak and divided organizations as with the banks. In the first case, works councils add a certain independent flavour to the decentralization programme with regard to representation of employee interests. In the second case, they remain playing the role of reinforcements with little influence in the realm of social policy.

A momentous crossroads is suggested here for the development of industrial relations given that the increasing independence of the works councils can become the foundation of a new division of labour between themselves and the trade unions in representing employee interests. Conversely, labour relations almost entirely free of trade unions could be established and spread. It can easily be imagined that a new stage of industrial democracy will be reached in the metal industry, while in the 'all-finance' banking industry - the new core sector of a tertiary economy - industrial relations will be subordinated to a conservative paternalism.

International Aspects

From a business management point of view, the aspect in favour of debureaucratization and decentralization is the gain in profitability, from the industrial sociology perspective it is increased productivity and from the point of view of industrial relations research it is the gain in regulation. Since these factors are not peculiar to the Federal Republic of Germany, international comparison should be particularly useful in examining the thesis that relatively favourable conditions for the introduction of participatory-democratic decentralization prevail in the FRG, since institutionally ordered, functionally separated, cooperative labour relations have been developed and practised over decades. It is of interest to see how the process of 'systemic rationalization' with its associated discarding and transformation of internal alliance constellations and lines of conflict actually develops in systems of industrial relations of extremely different institutional structure. Three countries can be taken as contrasting cases with respective specific characteristic labour relations:

- Great Britain as a model case of fragmented relations,
- Italy as a model case of political orientation and
- Japan as a model case of company-orientated industrial relations.

Great Britain is characterized by strictly hierarchical, entrenched class-based management bureaucracies, which makes their elimination difficult (Pollert, 1987). The shop-floor centred multi-trade union system has a similar effect when it is a question of avoiding conflicts between the organizations of those who stand to gain from rationalization and those who will lose out. None the less, there are increasing signs of a fundamental change. Companies wanting to modernize their factories or move to less industrialized zones, often foreign investors, are now in search of new forms of labour relations; they want neither non-unionized nor multi-trade unionized workforces. In the form of a newly emerging type of trade union, associations are increasingly available to serve as competent negotiating partners with a spirit of company loyalty, and are willing to draw up strike-free agreements on condition they have sole right of representation (Bassett, 1986; Lewis, R. 1988).

In Italy on the other hand, with its traditionally authoritarian and patriarchal employers and highly conflictive industrial relations up to now, a remarkable and substantial change is apparent, quite clearly borrowing from the northern and central European model of institutionalized and legally normed employee representation. Three Italian peculiarities are responsible for the perceptible change of paradigms in industrial relations. The militant trade unions with their commitment to the class struggle and to levelling out have had to face the fact that they are less attractive to qualified blue- and white-collar employees, leading to a crisis in representation. Secondly, with cooperation offers to workforces and employers, the trade unions are trying to gain a foothold on the shadow economy, a sector strongly expanded as a result of external decentralization tendencies. Thirdly, the specific Italian form of political unionism has made it possible for pioneering settlements to be reached on the state-controlled sector of the economy. These have involved far-reaching information, consultation and negotiating rights for the trade unions in exchange for their support of the economic and organizational restructuring of state-owned firms (Del Turco et al., 1985).

Japan, on the other hand, is a country with flexible and less sharply defined forms of industrial organization in which there is none the less a further need for flexibilization - above all in the wake of an overstaffed and too old middle management caused by the system of 'life-long employment'. Decisive support of such measures by the trade unions representing the entire regular workforce is hardly likely, however, since this could affect the system of life-long employment as an institutional basis of the trade unions themselves. On the other hand, the collective bargaining system is characterized by a high degree of fragmentation and a marked economic dualism. From the point of view of management, external decentralization solutions could appear advantageous, if necessary over the heads of the trade union and reaching into 'union-free' sectors.

In all three countries - albeit for very different reasons - the situation is characterized by ambivalent initial conditions for debureaucratization policies. Comparative observation of the tendencies for change promise to be all the more interesting.

Part 4. Scandinavia: Negotiated Economy and Bargained Flexibility

14. Flexibilization and the Alternatives of the Nordic Welfare States

Pekka Kosonen

Introduction

In the strategies of flexibilization the welfare state is often seen as an obstacle to growth and flexibility. Does this hold true? Or could some kind of restructuring of the welfare state help to avoid rigidities? In this article, these issues are analysed in the light of a comparison of the Nordic countries.

My general point of departure is that the ups and downs of accumulation are not a strictly economic phenomenon, but rather a manifestation of the behaviour of the overall socio-economic and institutional system. Crisis forces a restructuring of the socio-institutional framework and the final form the structure takes will depend on the interests, actions, lucidity and relative strengths of the social forces at play. Thus, social struggles lead to social innovations that can either stimulate or check growth.

If we pursue this institutional explanation, we may argue that in the inter-war years a rapid transformation of the conditions of production came into conflict with the permanency of slow growth in workers' wage income, but the postwar years witnessed the return to a synchronization between the effects of scientifically-based methods of work organization on productivity and the participation of workers in mass consumption. However, in the 1970s these social innovations became destabilizing factors, and a recession ensued.

An important social innovation in the postwar period was the expansion of the welfare state, which is characterized by the vigorous growth of state activities, especially in the areas of social security and education. In the light of the new doctrine of economic policy, the welfare state came to be seen not so much as a burden imposed upon the economy, but as an inherent source of economic and political stability. This does not mean that all social reforms went unquestioned. On the contrary, there were clear political differences between various parties and countries. But all in all, the public expenditure/GDP ratio increased rapidly between 1960 and 1975 in the capitalist countries.

In the new situation after the mid 1970s the welfare state is often seen as an obstacle to growth or even as a source of crisis. Rigidities in the capitalist economies are explained by the social security commitments or the structures of the public sector; some kind of restructuring or flexibilization is necessary. However, the words flexibility and flexibilization are used in many contexts, and even if it is clear that alternatives to the postwar organizational forms have to be found not all strategies of flexibilization are very useful (Boyer, 1987). I shall make some distinctions between various forms of flexibilization below.

In the following, I shall outline the growth of the welfare state in the Nordic countries and its attendant difficulties. Because the public sector is unusually large in these countries, it is possible to evaluate what the public sector really has meant for economic and political problems and what need exists for restructuring the welfare state in the context of flexibilization strategies.

The Expansion of the Welfare State and the Nordic Models

The Nordic countries, especially Sweden and Denmark, are often seen as the welfare states with a high standard of social security and a high level of taxation. As background for the analysis of the present problems, it is useful to ponder how these peripheries developed into modern welfare states. This can be done with the help of the so-called Nordic models.

The Nordic models have been outlined in an internordic project on economic policies (Mjøset, 1986, 1987). These models trace the complex interplay between economic structure, economic policy routines and a political-institutional framework (dependent on class structure and the pattern of political mobilization). The postwar growth phase enabled policymakers to develop a series of economic policy routines that worked well. However, these economic policy routines, as well as class structures and political coalitions, were different in Sweden, Norway, Denmark and Finland respectively. It is in this context too that the various ways of increasing public expenditure become understandable (Kosonen, 1985, 1987).

The background to the Swedish model is a many-sided industrialization, a large workingclass but small petit bourgeoisie, an extensive unionization of blue-collar and white-collar workers, and one of the strongest social democratic movements in the world. According to the economic policy model, full employment can be maintained through a solidaristic wages policy, rationalization in the industrial sector, and active labour market policy.

The rapid growth of public expenditure was an inherent part of this Swedish model. The role of the state was to promote the export industry, but at the same time to secure the services and income of the labour force. This role is seen in the pension politics. In the reform of earnings-related supplementary pensions the aim of social democrats was to strengthen public steering of the credit market so as to establish greater collective assurance of investment behaviour (Esping-Andersen, 1985, pp. 159-165). Also, the strong commitment to full employment in Sweden as characterized by Therborn (1986), meant that when a real danger of mass unemployment arose in the 1960s and 1970s, the state was ready to implement large programmes to counteract unemployment and provide the unemployed with occupational training and jobs.

The expansion of the Swedish welfare state can be described by so-called social expenditure. According to the OECD definition, the social expenditure share increased in Sweden between 1960 and 1981 from 15 to 33 per cent, which was the same level as in Denmark. In Norway the change was from 12 per cent to 27 per cent and in Finland from 15 to 26 per cent (OECD, 1985, p. 21. The social expenditure is here defined as direct public expenditure on education, health services, pensions, unemployment compensation and other income maintenance programmes and welfare services).

In the Norwegian model, the state has directly regulated incomes and investments. The basis for this has been capital-intensive production and a high investment rate. Because of regional differences, the state has distributed subsidies and transfers in such a way as to maintain peripheral local communities and to save jobs. Altogether, income maintenance has made up the largest portion of public expenditure after the mid 1960s; in particular the share of pensions has increased. However, public services have not been as developed as in Sweden (Kuhnle, 1986, pp. 127-128). Thus, in the Nordic comparison the Norwegian model may be termed as a distributional welfare state.

Norway bears some political resemblance to Sweden. In both countries, the working class has been relatively large and the social democrats have governed for most of the postwar period. However, with a large agrarian population in Norway, the social democrats have not had as extensive economic and social programmes as in Sweden. For example, the reform of earnings-related supplementary pensions was not a fierce political question in Norway, and eventually it was fulfilled by the bourgeois government. Social expenditure has risen, but not as rapidly as in Sweden and Denmark.

The Finnish model is based on relatively one-sided exports (the forest industry), although the export sector diversified rather rapidly after the mid 1960s; on a large and politically powerful agricultural sector; and on unstable political coalitions between the left and the centre. The business cycle fluctuations have been quite dramatic in Finland due to the one-sided exports. According to the traditional point of view, economic policy has to concentrate on competitiveness more than on employment problems. Therefore, economic policies have often reinforced business cycle fluctuations by devaluations and fiscal policy measures, and unemployment has increased during recessions.

This kind of economic policy has restricted the expansion of the welfare state in Finland. Public expenditure is allowed to increase within the limits of economic growth, but this increase must not endanger the main political target, i.e. the competitiveness of the export sector. Secondly, state activities have been needed in large investment projects and in the maintenance of agricultural employment; a relatively large share of public expenditure in Finland has consisted of expenditure on investments and subsidies to agriculture. Also, state-owned enterprises have played a significant role, not only in energy supply but also in manufacturing. However, because of limitations in social reforms, the level of public expenditure has been lower than in Sweden, Norway and Denmark (OECD, 1987, table R8).

Finland is also one of the countries where Parliament's economic powers are subject to qualified majority rule (Lybeck, 1986, p. 192). According to the legislation governing parliamentary procedure, which in Finland has the status of a constitution, a qualified majority (two-thirds of the votes) is required for legislation on taxation. This requirement applies in the case of a new or increased tax which is proposed for a period exceeding one year.

The political coalitions in Finland became more stable after the mid 1960s and social democrats strengthened their positions. At the same time there occurred an unusually rapid structural change from agriculture to industry and services; thus the sectoral transformation took place with a simultaneous expansion of the secondary and tertiary sectors. Now, a more comprehensive social security net was required, and because of increasing economic resources it was possible to create it. Public consumption expenditure and transfers to households increased their share of public expenditure gradually (Alestalo and Uusitalo, 1986, pp. 205-209).

The Danish model may be described as a social-liberal welfare state. There have been few elements of economic management by the state, and liberalist tradition has been strong. Denmark is characterized by modest public subsidies to private and public firms. However, the public expenditure share of GDP rose very rapidly in Denmark in the 1960s and early 1970s. This was primarily due to the creation of a system of social transfers and public services. The level of social expenditure became one of the highest in the world.

To understand this, the basic features of the Danish model must be considered. Danish exports have mainly been dependent on agricultural products. Often the external restrictions have been felt in the economy, and economic policies have been orientated according to these restrictions. However, in the 1960s these restrictions eased up, and there was room for the use of public expenditure. Various classes and interest groups tried to realize their interests and objectives through the state. In Danish politics, coalitions have alternated. There has been a relatively large urban petit bourgeoisie in Denmark, and the coalitions have combined the interests of agriculture, petit bourgeoisie and working class. Thus, the result of reforms in the 1960s and 1970s was a heterogeneous net of transfers and services. In some areas, especially in pension policies, universal reforms were not put through (Esping-Andersen, 1985, pp.163-164), whereas in other respects the Danish social security became rather comprehensive.

Hence, in each Nordic country, the welfare state was related on the one hand to accumulation, on the other hand to the interests of various classes. There was broad political support for this development. At the same time, there were differences in the size and working of the welfare state based on the differences in the Nordic models.

The Crisis and Structural Rigidities

After this rapid expansion of the welfare state, what was the response to the international crisis in the Nordic countries? Did the Nordic models accommodate to the new situation?

Initially, from 1974 to 1977, all Nordic countries responded by maintaining or even strengthening the routines developed during the growth phase (Mjøset, 1987, pp. 420-433; Andersson, 1987, pp. 171-177). Sweden and Norway, and to some extent Denmark, mobilized countercyclical policies (traditional demand management) to bridge the gap created by the business cycle downturn of 1975-77. Finland implemented more restrictive policies in combination with devaluations; this economic policy was aimed at restoring the competitiveness of the export sector by reducing relative unit labour costs.

The slackness of the world economy gave rise to increasingly serious problems of imbalance and stagnation in Denmark and Sweden. In Denmark, unemployment and public debt increased rapidly. In Sweden, full employment was maintained despite industrial stagnation in the 1970s. Norway was able to displace some of the problems thanks to its new dominant export sector, oil from the North Sea continental shelf. This helped to secure full employment. In Finland, there was a period of stagnation in 1975-77, and unemployment jumped from 2 per cent to 8 per cent. However, Finland was successful in exploiting its trade with the Soviet Union as a factor that would stabilize the growth of Finnish exports. Because of bilateral trade, high oil prices automatically increased exports to the Soviet Union. After 1978 the GDP-growth was relatively high in Finland, but unemployment was there to remain.

Now, it became clear that the stagnation was not only a cyclical downturn;

it was a more profound phenomenon. The Nordic models were prepared to cope with shorter recessions - all in their own way - but not to deal with a longer phase of uncertain economic development. Some kind of reorientation was needed.

First in Denmark, and then in Norway and Sweden, counter-cyclical policies became the scapegoat: they had caused large wage increases, thereby harming the competitiveness of the export sectors. The Finnish model served as an example of policies which managed to maintain competitiveness with restrictive measures, although these policies had generated higher unemployment than expected. Thus, restrictive policies were proposed in all countries.

At the same time, discussion concerning structural rigidites in the Nordic models arose. The structural conditions in the world market had changed remarkably but there were not sufficient restructuring capabilities in the models, it was claimed. The export problems were not caused only - or even primarily - by loss of competitiveness. They were connected to the structural composition of exports, which is shown in calculations based on the method of constant market shares: in the 1970s the country/commodity-composition had a negative influence on the export growth in all the Nordic countries (Horwitz, 1984). Why then was this structural composition not changed? The answer was: institutional and political structures did not allow the change required.

According to a Nordic survey (IUI, DØR, ETLA and IØI, 1984) Finland and Denmark have chosen to keep their unemployment open and abstained from creating artificial jobs within industry or within the public sector. Danish and Finnish industries have a relatively fast output growth on record despite large reductions in employment. Secondly, Denmark has a long experience of high loan rates and practically no firm specific subsidies. This has efficiently prevented the financing and prolongation of bad investment projects and has also served to keep labour from being locked up in commercially impossible production. On the contrary, if bad plant investments are kept alive, then factor costs increase and labour is tied down in the wrong place, as has happened in Sweden.

These institutional problems or structural rigidities were blamed for the depth of the crisis. Among these institutions, the public sector and the welfare state were often mentioned. The argument went as follows. Because the public sector had expanded rapidly in the Nordic countries, especially in Sweden and Denmark, there was not any more room for private accumulation and creation of wealth. The market forces were restrained and the result was an ineffective economy where private initiative was killed. This was to a great extent due to high taxation that leads to a reduction in working time. Another problem is the crowding out of private investments because the state has to finance the public sector deficits (Lundberg, 1985).

All this was interpreted to show the crisis of the welfare state. The welfare state was not any more generally accepted; criticism mounted both from the right and the left.

Already in the late 1960s and early 1970s, a political and ideological debate on the welfare state was under way. It was argued that high taxation would lead to tax evasion and benefit cheating and the pursuit of illegal and tax-exempt trades and professions. This, again, is a reason why the authorities would strengthen their efforts against such activities. The development of a strong controlling state is pronounced, with increased reporting, inquiry and control over the lives of citizens.

In the 1973 elections in Denmark, the Progress Party suddenly became the second largest party in Parliament. Its founder, Mogens Glistrup, became famous during a short appearance on television, when he bragged about paying no tax on his income of more than a million kroner. The party programme was a demand for a massive reduction in the public sector and for a massive retraining of public employees for 'useful' productive work. Taxes could then be reduced, real wages would rise, and incentives to invest and work would again come into existence (Christiansen, 1984). This programme was supported by the petit bourgeoisie but also to some extent by the working class. An anti-tax party was formed also in Norway, and it achieved a victory in the 1973 elections, albeit more limited than in Denmark.

Quite a considerable amount of research has been devoted to examining the question whether the welfare state really has lost its popular support in the Nordic countries. Of course, these opinion surveys do not permit thorough analysis of the legitimation problems of the welfare state. Nevertheless, they can be used to describe the overall changes that have happened (see a summary in Pöntinen and Uusitalo, 1986, pp. 19-21).

In Denmark, in 1969-74 opinions changed to a more critical direction. After this the trend turned, but not until 1979 was the 1969 level reached. However, by the mid-1980s the support for the social reforms registered in the 1960s seems to have been re-established (Goul Andersen, 1986, p. 169). Norwegian public opinion polls show a status quo orientation: the majority wishes to maintain social security at its present level. This stability was broken down only in 1973, when anti-welfare state opinions were much more popular than before or after. In Sweden, public opinion tended to favour the welfare state in the 1960s, but this trend was gradually reversed in the 1970s.

Finally, Finnish public opinion has been rather stable from 1975 to 1985. Each year the majority has regarded the pace of development of social security as proper and this majority has increased during these ten years, strengthening the status quo orientation observed in Norway as well. In the late 1970s the trend was towards a more critical view, but this development did not continue into the 1980s (Pöntinen and Uusitalo, 1986, p. 28).

Thus, tax protests were experienced in the 1970s, which is reflected both in elections and in opinion polls. However, this 'welfare-backlash' was a rather short-lived phenomenon.

In the late 1970s and early 1980s, the limits of the welfare state and taxation were increasingly seen in economic inefficiencies (Lindbeck, 1986). According to this point of view, there are induced inefficiencies in the economic system due to various disincentives on the allocation of resources and on productive effort in general. These are caused by substitution effects in favour of leisure, lower intensity to work and against investment in human capital, labour mobility and saving.

Also, the term 'crowding out' was used in the Nordic countries to describe how private sector growth was hampered by tax-financed public expenditure growth. The arguments were based in particular on a suspicion that the financing of growing public deficits had reinforced the industrial crisis. Public deficits rose in 1982-83 to 8-10 per cent of GDP in Sweden and Denmark, while in Finland the level was lower, and Norway had a surplus (IMF, 1987).

By way of concluding this analysis then, a reorientation of the public sector was required as a part of the flexibilization strategies. The effectiveness and productivity of the public sector will have to improve if economies are to achieve the greatest possible gains in performance from more open and responsive product and factor markets. At least four measures have been proposed, of course in various terms in the Nordic countries. (These can be compared to the OECD programme, see Vinde, 1988).

First, deregulation is required. Regulations need to be relaxed or radically altered where they constrict needed economic flexibility. This is especially true in agricultural and industrial policies.

Second, when governments' basic responsibility for promoting health, safety and the environment must not be relinquished, a restructuring of the public sector is needed. This includes a shift to greater competition combined with better information and increased charges to the consumers of, for instance, health services which would provide more direct incentives for containing costs and improving the quality of service.

Third, these changes on the expenditure side should be accompanied by measures to reduce taxation - by broadening the tax base and cutting marginal taxes, shifting from personal income to consumption taxes, and exploiting all opportunities to reduce tax burdens overall.

Fourth, privatization has been a central topic on the political agenda especially in Denmark and Norway. Privatization implies that large parts of the public sector are transferred to the private sector.

What Has Been Done?

The political background to the Nordic models changed after the mid 1970s. The bourgeois bloc governed in Sweden since 1976, and in 1979 the Conservatives came to be the largest party inside this bloc. In Norway, the Conservatives took power in 1981, and in Denmark in 1982. In Finland the system of broad centre-to-left governments established in the late 1960s prevailed until 1987, when a new coalition between Conservatives and Social Democrats was initiated. What consequences did these changes have for the economic policies and the welfare state?

The debate on structural rigidities had significant implications for economic policies (Andersson, 1987; Mjøset, 1987). The Finnish case is discussed above. Restrictive economic policies were implemented in the mid 1970s; when competitiveness and exports had been secured there was also room for some expansionary measures, and severe austerity policies were no longer necessary in the 1980s.

In the late 1970s, attempts were made to tighten policies with devaluations and higher interest rates also in other Nordic countries, although in Sweden the bourgeois government tottered between tight and expansive measures until 1980. After this, public transfers were cut, labour market expenditure was reduced and further devaluations were conducted. The Social Democrats too continued these restrictive policies after 1982 - when they were returned into power - although not as eagerly as the previous bourgeois government.

In Norway, the Social Democrats had already restricted economic policies since 1977: monetary policies were tightened, exchange-rate policies were changed, and a full wage freeze was implemented. After 1981, the conservative government continued these austerity policies, exploiting the emerging tax resistance.

In Denmark too the Social Democrats tried to restrict fiscal policies, but not very successfully. From 1977 until 1982 private consumption was squeezed through strict incomes policies and gradual devaluations. In 1982, the government presented a total plan to reinforce austerity, but it did not win a majority, and the Social Democrats freely handed over government power to four bourgeois parties. The period since 1982 has been characterized by *'Schlüterism'*: cuts in public expenditure and tight monetary policies.

It has been argued that these changes led to a certain convergence between the Nordic models (Mjøset, 1987, p. 452). Indeed, this holds true in incomes policies and with respect to the business cycle aspect of fiscal policies; a slight counter-cyclical orientation has emerged in Finland, where earlier policies were pro-cyclical, whereas Denmark, Norway and Sweden have moderated their 'Keynesian' orientation. In particular the monetary policies have undergone a reorientation, and the other countries are approaching the Danish pattern: interest rate levels and credit regulations have been liberalized. In Finland, for instance, this can be interpreted as a massive deregulation of one important field of the economy.

However, this convergence thesis should not be exaggerated. The differences between the Nordic models are still clear. This is especially obvious with regard to full employment/unemployment.

As Göran Therborn has emphasized, a divergence can be seen in the unemployment rates of different countries, including the Nordic countries. According to Therborn, the existence or non-existence of an institutionalized commitment to full employment is the basic explanation for the differences. This means that there is an explicit commitment to maintaining full employment and that there are some - albeit diverse - methods to achieve this target even during economic difficulties. Thus, full employment was given the top priority in the postwar period in two Nordic countries, Norway and Sweden. Also under pressures and constraints after the mid 1970s governments have maintained low unemployment in these countries. In Denmark and Finland, a commitment to full employment was never really institutionalized, and during recession other targets have been more important than full employment (Therborn, 1986, pp. 101-148).

This explanation is in accordance with my own analysis above. The existence or non-existence of an institutional commitment to full employment can be seen as one of the basic characteristics of an economic-political model. This commitment has been stronger in the Swedish and Norwegian models than in the Danish and Finnish models which is clearly reflected in fiscal and monetary policies and employment policies during the recession. So, in this sense the differences between the Nordic models have persisted or even increased.

Is there, then, a convergence or divergence with regard to the welfare state in the Nordic counties? What has really been done?

One should be careful in analysing attempts to slow down the growth of public expenditure. A list of medium-term budgetary objectives from the early to mid 1980s reveals that there have been quite similar plans in every OECD country. The plans aim at reducing public sector deficit and at stabilizing or reducing tax level (Lybeck, 1986, p. 193). It is a completely different matter whether these plans have been realized or not.

The expansion of public expenditure continued in the first phase of recession (1974-78) in all Nordic countries. When economic growth was slow, the public expenditure/GDP ratio increased rapidly, especially in Sweden. At the same time, tax incomes rose much less. After the 1973 'tax revolt' in Denmark, governments had promised to reduce tax levels. Also in Norway and

Finland, governments claimed that taxation would not be increased. Therefore, also public expenditure should be stabilized.

However, these measures were implemented earlier in Finland and Norway than in Denmark and Sweden. In Finland, tax ceilings were promised in 1977: the gross tax burden should not rise above the 1976 level, that is about 40 per cent of GDP. In fact, tax level was reduced in the late 1970s. On the basis of restrictive fiscal policies, the public expenditure/GDP ratio also decreased. In the 1980s this ratio has increased somewhat, being still much lower than in other Nordic countries (OECD, 1986, 1987). In Norway, public debt was high because of oil investments, but after the mid 1970s oil revenue eased the government's financial situation. After 1978, when the Social Democrats governed, a reduction of the public expenditure/GDP ratio was realized and this was continued under bourgeois governments in the early 1980s.

In Denmark the Social Democratic government did not manage with its restrictive fiscal policies in the late 1970s. Thus, tax level increased again. This was the main reason for government change in 1982: a bourgeois government should take responsibility for restrictive measures. From 1983 to 1986 the public expenditure level decreased remarkably. Also in Sweden, the rapid expansion of public expenditure seems to have stopped. Bourgeois governments did not succeed in this aim, but under Social Democratic governments public expenditure level stabilized after 1982 and decreased in the late 1980s.

All in all, the public expenditure/GDP ratio still differs clearly in the Nordic countries in the late 1980s. In 1987, total outlays of government/GDP ratio was 60 per cent in Sweden and 58 per cent in Denmark, whereas in Norway it was about 52 per cent and in Finland only 42 per cent (OECD, 1989, table R 14). This does not confirm the hypothesis of the convergence of the Nordic models in a new situation.

Because of growing government debt in Denmark and Sweden the interest payments burden has also increased in relation to public expenditure. In 1982, this relation was about 10 per cent in Denmark and Sweden, 8 per cent in Norway and 3 per cent in Finland (Saunders and Klau, 1985, p. 72).

What kind of reductions have been realized? Have there really been essential cuts in social expenditure which would indicate a deviation from the welfare state ideology of the postwar era? Three kinds of measures can be analysed: i) cuts in benefits, ii) selectivity and changes in criteria of entitlements and iii) privatization (Johansen and Kolberg, 1985, pp. 167-170).

i) General attempts at reducing public sector deficits have implied plans to cut benefits. Such plans have been presented especially in Norway and Denmark. In Norway, indexation procedures regarding the base amount in the pension system have been changed. Direct cuts have been made in the field of social assistance in Denmark, where a benefit ceiling was introduced in the late 1970s; social assistance must not exceed the maximum of daily cash benefit in case of unemployment and sickness. In the 1980s, unemployment benefits have been frozen at the 1982 level, and given the high rate of inflation, the real value of unemployment benefits decreased dramatically by 15 per cent in only two years. In Finland, direct reductions of standard benefits have been rare (Alestalo and Uusitalo, 1986, p. 269). In Sweden, bourgeois government suggested some reductions in social programmes in 1981-82, but these were not enacted under the social democratic government (Olson, 1986, pp. 86-87).

How effective were these reductions? On the basis of the Nordic Statistics of social expenditure it is possible to insist that the social expenditure/GDP ratio has stabilized in the 1980s and clearly declined in Denmark. This ratio decreased in Denmark in 1982-87 from 30.7 per cent to 26.4 per cent and remained the same in Sweden and Norway; in Finland there was an increase in 1982-86 from 22.5 per cent to 25.5 per cent. One interesting detail is that Finland in the late 1980s has reached Norway where the social expenditure level now is lowest (Nordisk Råd, 1988, p. 318).

ii) Selectivity and changes in criteria of entitlements have also been accentuated in Denmark. Entitlement to child allowances has been made income-related; a new concept of 'social income' has been introduced in order to tighten the relationship between income and benefits; one waiting day in case of sickness benefits was re-introduced (and then again abandoned). Although these changes in social legislation do not destroy the whole system of social security in Denmark, they indicate a clear move away from universal entitlements towards a more selective policy. In the other Nordic countries changes in criteria of entitlements have been smaller.

iii) Privatization would indicate a sea-change in respect of the earlier tendency of welfare state expansion. Two essentially different meanings can be given to privatization: on the one hand it may refer to a transfer of functions from the public sector to capitalist markets ('marketization'), on the other hand it may refer to a transfer of functions from the public sector to the family, neighbourhoods, small communities, to the voluntary sector ('community responsibility') (Kosonen, 1987, pp. 284-285).

Community responsibility may assume many forms. Self-help and mutual aid are currently enjoying a revival in the informal sector of the economy. This is an actual issue also in the Nordic countries. For instance, in Denmark an initiative called 'B-team' tries to organize activities on a help to self-help basis dealing with both material and existential problems (Abrahamson, 1987).The members of this team are actually creating their own social structures as a sub-culture in Danish society, some kind of 'second reality' as Oskar Negt calls it.

Large-scale marketization of welfare services has not been applied in the Nordic countries. However, there are tendencies towards increased privatization in the form of fee-for-services and private pension schemes.

All in all, the essential institutional pillars of the Nordic welfare states are still intact. Some cuts, changes in criteria of entitlements and fee-for-services have been introduced, particularly in Denmark but also to some extent in Norway. In Denmark, Schlüter's government has emphasized the problem of effectiveness. The aim is to have a more cost-effective public sector by charging clients more for public services, by encouraging specialization, and by stepping up competition in the production of services (Gunst and Heinesen, 1985).

Drawing conclusions from responses in economic policies and social policies it is possible to maintain that in two cases, Sweden and Finland, continuity has prevailed, whereas in two other cases, Norway and Denmark, reorientation is more accentuated.

In Sweden there is a change in fiscal policies towards a more restrictive direction, but in main issues, full employment and social security, the targets of the Swedish model have been realized. Also the Finnish model has been maintained or even strengthened in the 1980s. There is a general agreement to keep the tax burden at a certain level of GDP, which sets limits to public expenditure, although due to relatively fast economic growth it has been possible to increase social expenditure somewhat.

Meanwhile, in Denmark the reorientation is profound. Full employment never was first priority, but after the mid 1970s unemployment was allowed to increase to huge amounts (and in the late 1980s it is still highest among the Nordic countries). A move towards greater selectivity and cuts indicate an explicit change in social policies. This change occurred also in Norway, where the social expenditure/GDP ratio is now the lowest of these countries. However, full employment is continuously a priority in the Norwegian model, although economic difficulties led to a rise in unemployment in the late 1980s.

The Welfare State as the Cause of Crisis?

In the analysis of the Nordic models a distinction between external and internal pressure has been made; external pressure originates outside the model, whereas internal pressures emerge from tensions within it. In the 1970s, external pressure implied destabilizing changes in the international institutional environment and a sudden drop in demand for most export commodities. In such a context too, internal pressures caused by the rapid processes of structural change are difficult to contain. There are two types of internal pressure. The first originates within established political structures and can be denoted 'ungovernability'. The second type consists of groups - social movements - mobilizing outside traditional parliamentary channels. The political colour of these protests may be red, green or blue (Mjøset, 1987, pp. 411-412).

This distinction may be useful in describing and classifying various contradictions in the economic-political models. However, if we try to tackle the problem of a crisis of the welfare state other distinctions are needed. The economic-political model may be said to be stable, if there are stable conditions for transformations and changes. The changes and challenges may, however, be too great so that accommodation is not successful. The crucial question is, then, to what extent is this due to the breakdown of the economic and political preconditions of the model and to what extent to the contradictions in the functioning of the model itself? One example of the second case is that state activities have generated problems in accumulation, divisions between various classes and social groups, or a decline in class mobilization on which the model is based. This kind of situation could be denoted as a crisis of the welfare state.

In the late 1970s, the stagnation of accumulation in the Nordic countries was often connected to the welfare state and institutional sclerosis, as noted above. However, it is possible that these problems were exacerbated by export structures.

Sweden's relatively diversified industrial structure proved favourable during the growth phase but in the late 1970s it proved very unfavourable. According to Lennart Erixon, large Swedish firms showed small price flexibility (Erixon, 1985). In the 1980s, these firms have shown greater flexibility and transformation, and exports have increased again. Also the Norwegian manufacturing industry has considerable problems and an unfavourable export structure, which is counteracted, however, by the expansion of oil production.

Denmark and Finland have had more dynamic manufacturing sectors, and the development of exports has been relatively good since the mid 1970s. In Denmark, short series production with high quality standards in small firms may give more flexibility. Finnish exports have clearly gained from Finnish trade with the Soviet Union, but also the structure of exports to western markets has remained favourable. One explanation for the Finnish growth rates is that relative manufacturing export unit values (in Dollars) jumped up in the mid 1970s and have since then remained at this level, while in other Nordic countries these values have decreased (OECD, 1987, Table 4.2.).

What, now, is the effect of public sector on these problems? Recently, many studies have been made on this topic without any definitive answer. Attempts to establish links between the size (or growth) of public sector and other economic performance indicators have largely proved unsuccessful. Why? The main reason, according to Peter Saunders, is that the cross-section method will not be appropriate if the relationships are in fact influenced by the social, political or institutional conditions in individual countries in ways that cannot be controlled for in statistical analysis (Saunders, 1986, p. 2).

Fortunately, these social, political and institutional conditions can be dealt with in the context of the Nordic models. The relationship between the growth of the public sector and economic performance can be analysed on the basis of disaggregated data, whilst keeping in mind other important changes in these models.

In the discussion on the relation between the welfare state and economic difficulties, income taxation, social security payments and public sector deficits have been main issues. What has their role been in the Nordic countries?

First, if it is true that income taxation weakens work incentives, the problem should be felt especially in Denmark and Sweden, where personal income taxes are high. However, participation in the labour force has increased in these countries despite taxation which means that there are no direct links between taxation and work incentives.

Second, are the economic problems then caused by high social security payments? The so-called indirect labour costs have increased most rapidly in Sweden and Finland, whereas in Denmark they play a minor role (SAF, 1986). Thus, Finnish growth rates seem not to be due to low indirect labour costs, nor are the Danish problems due to high indirect labour costs (Schwerin, 1984, pp. 241-245). Social security payments do not explain economic difficulties.

But, third, are public sector deficits 'crowding out' private investments? In the Nordic countries, only Denmark and Sweden have run up sufficiently large deficits over several years to give rise to crowding out as a problem. However, the private sector's net lending has increased when the public sector's net lending has decreased (Schwerin, 1984, pp. 245-253). The interest rate has increased, but this has been a general international tendency associated with the liberalization of credit markets (and happened also in Norway and Finland) so that it is difficult to isolate the role of public sector deficits in this development.

All in all, in the Nordic countries the economic crisis is not primarily caused by the welfare state, as analysis of taxation, labour costs and crowding out shows. Furthermore, subsidies to enterprises are scarcely a significant cause of the crisis, since they have been more a reaction to the crisis, especially in Sweden. However, if subsidies remain, they may create structural rigidities and slow down technical change.

Is it possible, then, to speak of a political crisis of the welfare state? The shifts in public opinion cited above seem not support this hypothesis, and strong tax protests have disappeared in Denmark too. The legitimacy of the welfare state is not lost (Ringen, 1987, pp. 47-69). For instance in Sweden, discontent has not generally increased despite the rapid expansion of the welfare state (Hadenius, 1986, p. 23). On the other hand, in the 1980s political conditions have changed and Social Democrats have lost ground at least in Denmark and Norway; cuts and reductions have been made.

Income taxation - in particular the rise in personal income taxes - clearly does affect the welfare state backlash. Sweden, Norway and Denmark are all countries where taxes are high, in 1985 about 50 per cent of GDP. In Sweden and Norway there is a balance between income taxes, social security payments and consumption taxes, but in Denmark taxation consists mainly of personal income taxes, whose share of GDP rose between 1965 and 1975 from 12 to 23 per cent (McKee, 1988, p. 33). This led to tax protests in the mid-1970s.

Another important variable in this context is employment (Therborn and Roebroek, 1986). First, if participation in the labour market is high, nearly all citizens are paying for transfers and services. In this respect, Norway (where participation is low) has had the greatest problems. Second, if full employment is maintained, there is no need for extensive transfers and selective social policies which create dissatisfaction towards the welfare state. This is seen clearly in the Danish case. Third, large public sector employment creates a political bulwark against reductions which would endanger the position of these employees (Goul Andersen, 1986). Employment policies and social policies are therefore closely connected. Because the Danish Social Democrats were unable to maintain full employment, the social and political basis of the welfare state eroded and bourgeois government could get through its restrictive measures. On the contrary, in Sweden nearly full employment has been maintained, participation in the labour market is high, and the social and political base of the welfare state is stable.

The New Accumulation Strategy, Flexibilization and the Alternatives of the Nordic Welfare States

I posed the problem for this article by relating the welfare state to the postwar accumulation strategy and the Nordic models. The welfare state can be seen as an important social innovation, as a precondition for the growth phase. However, in the phase of flexibilization the role of the welfare state seems to become questionable. According to an OECD report, it is necessary to improve the effectiveness of the welfare state. In the education and health programmes the task of improving effectiveness and efficiency resolves itself into a management issue. Efficiency can be improved also in redistribution, because in principle the same amount of redistribution could be achieved with vastly reduced gross flows. This all takes time, so that OECD sees reforming the welfare state as a long-term objective (OECD, 1985, pp. 54-63).

However, in practice a restructuring of the welfare state usually means cuts and more selective measures. Among the Nordic countries this is most pronounced in Denmark in the 1980s. If this continues, we can expect a dualization of society, pointing to a stratification of the population in one group of affluent, fairly securely employed, and another strata composed of various marginalized segments (redundant workers, long-term unemployed, immigrants, etc.) (Abrahamson, 1987). A more selective welfare state is likely to strengthen this division, reproducing the differences which originate from the labour market. In Denmark, there is an increased spatial segregation in the large cities which forms the basis for a 'network activity' as a new - and cheap - part of social policy. The problem seems to be that this selective strategy cannot work without control from above (Tonboe, 1988).

This kind of dualization is connected to an accumulation strategy, where resources are channelled to productive export firms which need only a qualified labour force and where a large part of the population is living on public support. As I reported above, this probably weakens the social and political base of the welfare state.

My point is, based on the Nordic experiences, that this kind of neo-liberal flexibilization is not the only alternative. There are also other strategies of flexibilization which may be more social and even more effective. Distinctions could be made at least between neo-liberal (market-orientated), neo-corporatist (state-orientated), and participatory (participation-orientated) flexibilization strategies. Sweden, Norway and Finland seem to follow some kind of neo-corporatist strategy, where social security arrangements and public services - in a modernized form - are seen as significant conditions to economic structuration.

The Nordic models do not appear to have been too inflexible in the 1980s. Industrial growth in Finland, Sweden and Norway has clearly been above that of most West-European countries, and their unemployment has remained at a relatively low level. This does not tell of dramatic rigidities.

A shift to flexible production systems is clearly going on in the Nordic countries. In the high-technology production and exports Sweden already has a long experience, but in the 1980s other Nordic countries have followed the example. In Finland, the electronic and electric product industry has grown quite rapidly. Medical-, industrial- and telecommunication electronics are the fastest growing sectors inside this industry. New flexible manufacturing systems are used as a part of new specialization strategies. A distinctive feature in this development is the role of national development programmes which are led by governmental organizations (Ranta, Koskinen and Ollus, 1988).

This structural change towards flexible specialization proves, as a matter of fact, the performance of Nordic industrial complexes in a new situation. Nationally controlled export sectors and coordinated economic and social policies, cornerstones of the Nordic models, have created a basis for further diversification and specialization. Of course, new solutions are needed especially inside the enterprises in order to answer to new challenges. The idea of developing new, democratic patterns in work organization as a part of flexibilization has been accentuated especially in Norway and Sweden (Gustavsen, 1986). In this respect rigidities are greater in Finland.

There are differences between the Swedish, Norwegian and Finnish models, as I described above, but in any case it can be argued that Finnish politics have evolved in a 'Nordic' direction. All great traditional sources of conflict in Finland (class conflict, language conflict, tensions between town and country) have gradually developed a more peaceful and less acute character, which is at least partly due to the fact that the political forces representing all sides in these traditional conflicts had a seat in the country's government during the 1980s (Allardt, 1989).

In a situation of economic growth there have not been strong pressures to cut down social expenditure in Sweden, Finland or Norway. There has also been a broad political basis for the welfare state. For example, the Norwegian parliamentary election of 1985 was a victory for the Social Democratic Party, which was able to direct the attention of the voters to the issues of the welfare state. According to Ola Listhaug and Bernt Aardal, the economic surplus, which was caused primarily by the high price of crude oil, made the voters receptive to arguments that the government should use more money on welfare and social programmes (Listhaug and Aardal, 1989). However, in the late 1980s the price of crude oil went down and in this situation a protest party - called the Progress Party - got support with a programme directed against the Scandinavian type of welfare state. The consequences of this shift cannot be seen yet.

So, it seems that the Nordic models have formed national modes of development which have worked also during a phase of uncertainty. This may be partly due to strong, nationally controlled export sectors, partly to national coordination of incomes and public expenditure between all interest groups. Thus, a large welfare state can be maintained in a coherent national strategy aiming at flexible conditions of industrial growth.

Actually a developed welfare state could form one part of an alternative strategy of flexibilization. Jan Otto Andersson and Lars Mjøset argue that there are important characteristics in the Nordic models which can be utilized in a 'red-green' strategy (Andersson and Mjøset, 1987, pp. 227-243). Concerning the welfare state they argue that the welfare state could be a possible comparative advantage in the development of new technologies. The idea is that economic linkages could crop up in the borderland between the public sector, the research institutions and enthusiastic entrepreneurs from the private sector. New private firms would specialize in innovations which are used by the state. For instance, the potential for rationalization in the health sector is great, and interesting solutions might give rise to production of hospital equipment and medicines which would prove strong also in export markets.

In conclusion, it must be emphasized that there are genuine differences between the various welfare states and that flexibilization strategies should be related to these differences. The neo-liberal flexibilization strategy is usually connected with a weak welfare state, which has lost its economic and political basis because of problems in employment and taxation. There are, however, also other possible flexibilization strategies that aim at specialized ways of production and tackle at the same time the unresolved issues of the welfare state. These strategies are connected with relatively strong welfare states where unemployment is low or moderate. In this perspective, employment problems and welfare state problems should be considered together in an effort to maintain the basic results of the postwar period, utilizing these in turn in the new strategies.

15. Learning to Manage the Supply-Side: Flexibility and Stability in Denmark

Klaus Nielsen

Darkness on the Edge of Scandinavia?

Denmark is one of those small, advanced countries in western Europe which achieved above average postwar growth rates until the mid 1970s. The successful development of these countries was, according to Katzenstein (1985), due to their mutually reinforcing combination of economic flexibility and political stability. Smooth and continuous adaptation of economic and industrial policies to the ever-changing world market conditions co-existed with an elaborate system of domestic compensation to prevent the costs of change from causing political eruptions. World-market flexibility not only occurred in spite of, but actually appeared to depend upon this political stability. This, in turn, arose from the corporatist involvement of all major political forces in processes of consensus formation which constantly reproduced the legitimacy of the system and at the same time preparedness for change.

Denmark is also part of Scandinavia - all of whose member countries had below OECD-average income per capita in 1950 but achieved levels significantly above the OECD-average in 1975. At the same time the 'Scandinavian model' has been singled out for its unique combination of growth, welfare, equality and democracy.

The general economic and political evaluation of Denmark has changed from positive to negative in recent years. The reasons are evident. For, with the exception of 1983-1986, Denmark has had relatively low growth rates since the first oil shock. It also seems stuck in a mess of macroeconomic imbalances. Deficits on the balance of payments every year since 1963 have caused an accumulated debt of almost Latin American magnitude (38.6 per cent of GDP in 1989) which has decisively limited the room of manoeuvre in Danish economic policies. In addition, Denmark has experienced high levels of unemployment for 15 years, in sharp contrast to the other Nordic countries.

The Danish postwar economic development model had already collapsed in the late 1970s (Mjøset, 1987). Denmark has appeared politically highly unstable, almost Italian in its 'ungovernability', ever since Glistrup's 'poujadist' movement blew the traditional party system to pieces in 1973. The

Danish capitalist class has always been comparatively weak and divided, while the farmers and the petty bourgeois have retained more economic power and political influence than in other industrialized countries. Social Democracy never became as dominant as in Sweden and Norway and, during the 1980s, the influence of Danish Social Democracy and the trade unions is seen to have diminished decisively; traditional labour movement values such as solidarity and equality have lost their attraction; and the belief in the compatibility of equality and efficiency seem to have faded away (Amoroso, 1990).

Sweden is often seen as much more successful than Denmark. Not only has Denmark been unable to maintain full employment and social democratic political and ideological dominance. The struggle for economic democracy apparently ended in nothing in Denmark while it led to the law on co-determination (*MedBestemmelsesLagen*) and the establishment of wage earner funds (*Löntagerfonde*) in Sweden. Nor has Denmark, contrary to Sweden, been able to sustain the fundamental universalist principle of the social democratic welfare state, either at the crucial point in the 1960s when supplementary pension schemes were introduced (Esping-Andersen, 1985), or in recent years (Kosonen, this volume). Until recently, Swedish economic policy was still seen as a particularly successful case (Bosworth and Rivlin, 1987). Others have seen Norway as a model to follow because of how it has used its oil and gas revenues to achieve general social objectives (Rowthorn and Glyn, 1989). And Finland is the one of the Nordic countries which has developed most favourably during the last decade; it has now surpassed Denmark in its per capita income (Andersson, 1989).

It might even be argued that Denmark is no longer part of Scandinavia on any important economic and political variable. Many observers do not include Denmark in the 'Nordic alternative' (see for example *The Economist Survey*: 'The Nordic Three', 21 November 1987) because of its membership of the EEC and the divergent development trends in relation to the other Nordic countries. Denmark is increasingly seen as a low growth area on the edge of Scandinavia where darkness is descending on the traditional values of the 'Scandinavian model'.

Some of the reasons for this negative evaluation have long existed but it is mainly the Danish development since the mid 1970s which has caused this change. Denmark seems to have been unable to cope with the crisis of Fordism and the challenges of the transition to post-Fordism. The Danish capacities for smooth adaptation, filling in niches in the international economy, and incremental process innovation based on diffusion of technology, are seen as insufficient in the new era of systemic technological change and major socio-institutional restructuring (Edquist and Lundvall, 1990; Mjøset, 1987).

In this article I shall not only give a more nuanced account of the Danish case but also present a strong case for a more positive judgement. I believe that some of the features which have been seen as backward might be turned into future advantages. I refer to the specific forms of pre-Fordist and post-Fordist forms of production, and to the flexible and highly developed Danish welfare state. Above all, I refer to the forms of representation, coordination and consensus formation ('the negotiated economy') which have been developed in a multi-centred political system where big capital and big labour never gained the strength to dominate society by means of big government in accordance with the prototype Fordist mode of regulation.

In my view Denmark is equipped with some of the basic preconditions for the development of 'flexible corporatism' (Soskice, 1988) or a reorganized version of 'democratic corporatism' (Katzenstein, 1985) with its mutually reinforcing combination of flexibility and stability. If corporatism is to survive in non-segmented forms it has to involve a certain measure of international coordination as well as more openness for corporatist variation at the sectoral and local level; and it has to rely less on strictly formal ways of coordinating decision-making among privileged groups and more on informal coordination of a multitude of organized actors. Whether it is appropriate to call this corporatism or something else will not be discussed here (Nielsen and Pedersen, 1991; Moore and Booth, 1989).

The above point could easily be overstated. The short- and medium-term economic perspectives are muddy, and short-sightedness, or even stalemate, seem to dominate the national political scene. I cannot point to obvious developmental trends that promise to lead Denmark into a glorious post-Fordist future. I can identify some of the basic preconditions as well as some institutions, structures and regularities of behaviour which act as blockages and may even lead in other directions.

This article concentrates on one of the areas where a break with the past appears necessary but also hard to accomplish as a result of various blockages. My primary focus is the adaptation of macroeconomic and industrial policies to the on-going changes and the future challenges. I believe that these changes and challenges have important consequences for the role of the state (Jessop, Nielsen and Pedersen, 1991). Among these consequences are the following: the primary concern within national economies with demand management and the generalization of mass consumption norms has to be replaced with a concern with the international competitiveness of the supply side and the subordination of welfare policy to the demands of flexibility; and the support for declining sectors has to be replaced with support for new sectors, promotion of new technologies and organization of technology transfer. In general we see a pressure for the adoption of appropriate forms of supply-side management to replace the established methods of demand management.

However, the redistributive aspects of such a change are detrimental to the immediate interests of powerful groups. Furthermore, the political and administrative system needs major reorganization in order to handle the new forms of economic and industrial policy. This is particularly so in Denmark where industrial policy was vitually absent until quite recently and macroeconomic policies were exclusively concerned with demand management and promotion of RUCL (relative unit costs of labour) competitiveness. The blockages to the adoption of supply-side policies are probably larger in Denmark than in most other countries.

The article is structured in two major parts. In the first part I present my conception of the Danish economic and political structure inspired by the regulation theory and the 'negotiated economy' approach (Nielsen and Pedersen, 1991). The second part of the article concerns the Danish response to the crisis of Fordism and, in particular, the troublesome process of learning how to manage the supply-side of the economy.

The Danish Mode of Development

The French regulation school use the term 'mode of development' to signify the combination in a national economy of an industrial paradigm, an accumulation regime and a mode of regulation. The Danish mode of development is the product of the Danish history of industrialization and the specific insertion of the Danish economy into the international economy. Compared with the ideal-type Fordism, the Danish mode of development had several peculiarities even in the heyday of Fordism. The industrial paradigm could hardly be characterized as Fordist because of the predominant craft organization of production. The accumulation regime did not involve any virtuous circle of mass production and mass consumption[1]. Fordist norms of consumption co-existed with extremely high import ratios for consumer durables and mass production was almost totally absent. Only the mode of regulation can partly be characterized as Fordist although the system of industrial relations had several pre-Fordist features.

In other words, Danish Fordism is best interpreted as 'demand-side Fordism'. On the supply-side of the economy - whence the concept originates - there is almost no evidence of Fordist structures. However, the demand side (mass private consumption of standardized consumer durables and mass collective consumption of welfare services), the institutional framework generalizing Fordist consumption norms (the welfare state, Keynesian demand management, 'productivity-linked' collective bargaining and a generous credit system) and the form of urbanization were Fordist as in few other countries.

Denmark is poorly equipped with industrial raw materials. Conversely it has much arable land and its agricultural sector has for at least a century been among the most advanced in the world. The structure of the Danish economy still reflects the radical transformation of its agriculture in the last two decades of the nineteenth century. The dramatic fall in world market grain prices was followed by a major reorientation of production from grain to pigs and cattle, and gradually to more processed products. At the same time the Danish peasants were mobilized towards self-reliance involving self-organized education as well as farmers' cooperatives which later developed into a coordinated national movement. These socio-institutional innovations created a highly efficient framework for the diffusion of new technology, upgrading of skills and quality of products as well as marketing of Danish agricultural products on the world market. The cooperative movement gained control of the manufacture of agricultural products which effectively excluded this strategic sector from private capital accumulation. This is the main reason for the limited power of big capital in Denmark.

As late as 1958, more than 60 per cent of total exports emanated from agriculture and the present export specialization still reflects the importance of agriculture. Butter, cheese, pork and bacon are still today dominating export products earning an important part of foreign currency (Edquist and Lundvall, 1990). The most important industries are part of the agro-industrial complex which evolved around manufacturing agricultural products and production of machinery for agriculture; two-thirds of the internationally competitive commodities (defined as SITC-groups with more than 1 per cent of world exports) are either agricultural or part of the agro-industrial complex (Møller and Pade, 1988). Another traditional stronghold of Danish exports is the shipping-shipyard complex. Even today, 40-50 per cent of total export earnings stem from the two traditionally dominant industrial complexes.

In Denmark, the postwar economic growth tide did not take off until after the liberalization of international trade in the late 1950s. In the 1960s Denmark experienced a relatively short but very hectic prosperity phase with high growth rates, comprehensive economic restructuring and reorganization of lifestyles. In this prosperity phase the demand side of Fordism was implemented at high speed. The supply-side, however, was not imported.

During the 1960s a number of manufacturing industries emerged and three new industrial complexes developed (Frøslev Christensen, 1980): the house-building and construction complex, the welfare-industrial complex (based on the interaction between industry and welfare state provision of social and health services and regulation of the environment), and the machinery-industrial complex. The first of these new industrial complexes arose from internal demand for products from sheltered industrial branches. It did significantly improve the international competitiveness of Danish industry. The development of the welfare-industrial complex was accompanied by important positions on export markets due to the international competitiveness of Danish firms producing specialized equipment, e.g. medical equipment and environmental technology. The most important new positions on international industrial markets, however, were achieved within production of traditional machinery and components to engineering products.

Others have identified a wider range of industrial complexes, or 'development blocks' (Dahmén, 1988), in the Danish economy (Forum for Industriel Udvikling, 1988a, b). Of course, not all parts of the Danish economy are integrated in such development blocks. For example, a number of technically advanced firms in electronics expanded in the 1960s. However, they are enclaves in the Danish economy with export and import ratios approaching or exceeding 90 per cent (Edquist and Lundvall, 1990, p. 17).

By international standards, Danish manufacturing industry comprises many SMEs (small and medium sized enterprises) and no large firms - by international standards. They produce specialized, often design-intensive, high quality, goods in short series for unstable niches in international markets or products for the internal market in equally short series. Mass production of standardized consumer products has never evolved (except for standardized agricultural products). The major 'sunrise' industries are poorly represented among Danish firms but so, too, are the 'sunset' industries.

The predominance of SMEs is one of the reasons for the modest R&D effort (for a description of the 'national system of innovation' in Denmark, see Edquist and Lundvall, 1990; OECD, 1988b). Denmark spends 1.3 per cent of GDP on R&D which is low even in relation to other small countries. Another reason is the sectoral mix of internationally competitive Danish industry. The strategic export sectors in Denmark have weak links to science and limited technical opportunities, e.g. in terms of prospects of developing radically new products. The Danish system of innovation is characterized by a one-sided focus of innovative activities and rapid diffusion on process technologies.

Even if Denmark is highly integrated in international trade (exports constituted 35.5 per cent of GDP in 1989) and has no ambitions of selective self-sufficiency, it is far less integrated in the international economy than the other small, rich countries in western Europe. Danish multinationals have modest weight in the economy. Danish FDIs are almost exclusively in sales divisions. Foreign ownership is not legally resticted but still remains rather modest (15 per cent). Nor do foreign aquisitions of Danish firms have much importance expect for Swedish acquisitions in recent years.

The growth of the competitive sector in the prosperity period in the 1960s and early 1970s was never sufficient to finance the imports and the competitive sector is still too small. The result has been uninterrupted current-account deficits for a quarter of a century. The specific delay and temporal concentration of the postwar 'second industrialization' of Denmark precluded significant market shares in big and fast rising markets which were dominated by large firms. Other effects were the high growth of the public sector and the house building and construction sector which accompanied the high-speed urbanization and the transformation of life patterns and took up high proportions of capital and labour.

In particular the growth of the public sector was remarkable. In 1960 public expenditure in relation to GDP was lower in Denmark than the OECD average. However, as a result of comprehensive reforms of education, health and social welfare the share of GDP rose from 25 per cent in 1960 to 40 per cent in 1970 and to 60 per cent in 1982 and is now far higher than the average OECD level.

The public expenditures reflect highly developed welfare services. Whilst other types of expenditures are relatively insignificant in Denmark, the shares of public expenditures on education, health and, in particular, social services, in relation to GDP are the highest in the EEC. The level of income transfers is generally high but transfers are by no means as dominant an instrument in welfare policies as in other EEC countries; nor are they typically financed through public insurance arrangements. Instead Denmark is, like the other Scandinavian countries, characterized by provision of free or highly subsidized services by public institutions financed (mainly) through income taxes.

The growth of the public sector was accompanied by an extraordinary growth in the labour force participation rate of women which has been the highest in Europe for the last 10-15 years. The majority of the new female workforce found jobs in the public sector. Many of them found part-time jobs which are much more frequent in Denmark than the EEC-average (Boje, 1991).

Female workers also got a high proportion of the unskilled jobs in the fishing industry and the few other industries with a Taylorist organization of the labour process. Such jobs never became prevalent in Denmark. Neither the techniques of the production process nor the organization of the labour process have ever been typically Fordist except in a few industries. Machine-paced, semi-skilled labour which is typical for Fordist mass production never became widespread. Indeed alternative craft-based industrial models successfully challenged the Fordist model even in the most prosperous Fordist period (Hull Kristensen, 1989, 1990).

... mass production in Denmark was left with what fell outside petty bourgeois economic complexes. The dynamics were for a long time determined by the farmers. Processes of mutual reinforcement between these and the artisans created in railway towns a smallholder republic linked to the economy at large by railways and craft educational institutions (Hull Kristensen, 1990, pp. 176-177).

An important reason for the dominance of craft principles is the early establishment and rapid diffusion of a system of local craft-based technical schools. Unions were established later and chose to organize workers according to their craft. The craft-based educational and union systems created a labour market of horizontally highly mobile workers.

The dominance of Fordism in Denmark was restricted to the ideological field. In the 1950s and 1960s, managers tried to modernize the labour process in accordance with the ideals of Fordism but the organization of work remained basically structured according to craft-principles. The Social Democrats pursued the ideal of Fordism, too, in their efforts to transform Danish society in the postwar period. As it did elsewhere, the labour movement accepted the prospects of degradation of the content of work in exchange for the prospects of rising levels of income but they also saw concentrated efforts within education and cultural stimulation as counteracting moves. This involved massive investments in basic education as well as schemes for re-education of skilled workers creating possibilities for individual upward social mobility to semi-engineer status or through self-employment. It also involved the creation of a national system for transforming unskilled into semi-skilled workers.

One effect was continuous upgrading of skills through the educational system rather than on-the-job training which is rather modest in Denmark because of the predominance of SMEs. Another effect was the high mobility between skilled work and self-employment. The general upgrading of skills contributed to the maintenance of the craft-based organization of production. Craft workers acted to capture the superior positions within factories by adapting their own educational institutions. On the other hand, the unskilled workers changed themselves into semi-skilled workers and, thus, spread the craft character of workers to groups with no formal apprenticeship (Hull Kristensen, 1990, pp. 180-181).

Important problems of vertical mobility remain. The system of industrial relations has pre-Fordist features as trade unions are organized along craft lines while semi-skilled male and unskilled female workers are organized in separate unions. There have been several aborted attempts to reorganize along industry lines or otherwise (cf. Amoroso, 1990, pp. 79-81). Even if the borderlines between craft and semi-skilled workers have become rather weak as semi-skilled workers are accepted by craft unions and join the craft educational complex (Hull Kristensen, 1990, p. 181), they are sufficiently strong to create important bottlenecks in the short run, as are the splits between various groups of craft workers. In 1990 it was decided to replace the many craft-based unions with five to six large industry-based unions. It remains to be seen whether this, in principle, radical reform of the union structure will be implemented.

Apart from these problems the functional flexibility of the labour force is generally high because of the quality of the educational system. The Danish labour market is also characterized by a rather high numerical flexibility when measured by the normal indicators. Not only the share of part-time workers but also the share of temporary workers in total employment is relatively high compared with the EEC-average. Moreover, the level of mobility among the employees is considerable; more than half of the labour force changes position in the labour market in a year (Boje, 1991); and as high as about one-quarter of the labour force experiences a spell of unemployment in any given year.

These labour market features are effects of the high female participation rate, the predominance of SMEs, the system of unemployment benefits, and the almost complete absence of legal or negotiated obstacles to firing workers. The legal protection schemes used elsewhere do not fit the Danish industrial structure dominated by SMEs who are not able to shield themselves from the short-run effects of world market changes and have to adapt the level of activity instead. Trade union efforts have been directed at protecting employees from income losses through high unemployment benefits and establishing of a well-functioning system of job mobility. Much of the temporary unemployment is by mutual consent. Workers are laid off when production schedules are slack and taken on again when the order book is more full which is accepted by the workers because of the relatively generous unemployment benefits.

The Danish labour market is not divided into a functionally flexible core and different layers of a numerically flexible periphery (Atkinson, 1984). Internal labour markets are of insignificant importance in Denmark. The incentives to develop human resources inside the firm are weak because of the predominance of SMEs. Functional flexibility is primarily developed through the formal system of vocational training. The important division on the Danish labour market is of another kind; between the flexible insiders and the inflexible outsiders. A large part of the labour force is both functionally and numerically flexible. However, there is also a hard core of long-term jobless who are not functionally flexible because of low skills or lack of employment experience. It is claimed that they are effectively not part of the numerically flexible workforce either; the incentives for employers to employ them are modest because of the highly compressed wage structure and the high negotiated minimum wage; in addition, the economic incentives for this group of jobless to seek jobs are modest, too, because of the low difference between wage incomes and unemployment benefits at the bottom of the pay scale.

The Political Development

The political development in Denmark reflects its specific history of industrialization. The farmers' movement and the small owners play an important role. Ownership and financial control is diffused and the importance of big capital is rather limited. Also labour is more fragmented than in countries which have a dominant core of semi-skilled workers organized at large firms in industry-based unions.

Consequently, the basic conditions for a social contract between big capital and big labour, as, for instance, in Sweden, have never existed. It has not been possible to establish stable corporatist compromises and long-term policies. Capital and labour have neither been strong nor homogeneous enough. They have always had to make unstable compromises with other social groups. Parliamentary politics have been difficult because of the fragmented structure of political parties. Governments have generally been weak and decision-making has been dominated by short-term political concerns.

Until the election in 1973, the structure of political parties was no more fragmented in Denmark than in other countries with similar proportional election systems. It had been rather stable since the 1930s. Social Democracy was the largest party with 35-45 per cent of the seats in parliament. The two big bourgeois parties were the Liberal Party (*Venstre*) and the Conservatives who, together, normally had a slightly larger share of the seats. A small party, the Social Liberal Party (*Det Radikale Venstre*), had 5-10 per cent of the seats but they have, traditionally, held the balance of power in parliament. The only challenge to this four-party system was the Socialist Peoples Party, originally a 'Titoist' offshoot from the tiny Communist Party. They managed, from the early 1960s, to create a permanent parliamentary platform to the left of the Social Democracy and even to become the junior partner of socialist parliamentary majorities in 1966-68 and 1971-73.

The 1973 election put an end to this structure. The four old parties won only 60 per cent of the parliamentary seats; they had 90 per cent before the election. Five new parties entered parliament with, together, 34 per cent of the seats. The largest and most spectacular newcomer was the 'poujadist' Progress Party. Also the other important newcomer, the Center Democrats, an outbreak from the Social Democracy, was a newly formed party. Obviously, the Progress Party was the parliamentary symptom of a tax revolt and petty bourgeois protest against the 'social democratic' policies of the former bourgeois government. However, the political message of the election was ambiguous. The Center Democrats represented rather different political ideals: the protection of Fordist consumption norms and traditional cultural values against the challenging values of the new left which they saw as becoming too influential in the Social Democracy.

The period since 1973 has been characterized by permanent parliamentary instability. Denmark is the western democracy which in the period 1974-90 has had most general elections (8), the largest number of parties in parliament (10-11 parties from 1973-81 and, since then, 'only' 8-9), and has for the longest time, been governed by minority governments (the whole period). Actually in this period, except from the years 1983-87, Denmark had 'extreme minority parliamentarism' (Nielsen and Petersen, 1989a, pp. 365-368; Rasmussen, 1989); governments had to base their policies on changing majorities behind single compromises in parliament; furthermore, they were often outvoted without stepping down.

The Social Democrats have not succeeded in dominating governments in Denmark to the same degree as they have done in Sweden or in Norway. Yet, they have had the upper hand in the sense that all governments without social democratic leadership were always replaced by social democratic government at all elections from the late 1920s till 1984. They also managed to stay in power in the troublesome period 1975-82. By then, the social democrats were worn-out and resigned voluntarily, and the Social Liberal Party tipped the scales in favour of a bourgeois government. Since then there have been four general elections (1984, 1987, 1988 and 1990) but the Social Democrats are still excluded from government. The conservative prime minister Poul Schlüter has succeeded in breaking the long-term pattern of a divided right by keeping together coalition governments with the Liberal Party and alternate junior partners (1982-88: the *Center Democrats* and the *Christian Party*; 1988-90: the *Social Liberal Party*; 1990: none). However, the bourgeois governments have depended on cooperation with parties outside government; in the period 1984-87 with the Social Liberal Party; since then also with either the Social Democracy or the *Progress Party*. Accordingly, the bourgeois governmental policy reflects the need for broad compromises.

The political turbulence since the mid 1970s has resulted in ad hoc policies often based on short-term political concerns. This has happened within a stable framework for government policies: strict formal barriers exist between public activities and private production; public owned enterprises are limited to public utilities and less frequent than in other western European countries; and industrial policies are entirely non-interventionist. To put it in other terms: in Denmark socialization has happened almost entirely in reproduction and through the welfare state while production is entirely in private hands.

Of course, trade unions have influenced the organization of work in private enterprises in various ways but their efforts have been very much directed at wage formation, public services and transfers. This is a consequence of the industrial structure, and the liberal attitude to employer discretion in hire-and-fire policies is only one example of the prevalence of demand for public services and transfers rather than requests for legal or negotiated constraints on employer decision-making in production.

Danish trade unions have, next to the Swedish, the highest membership rates in Europe and, just as in Sweden, but unlike other EEC countries, there has been no decline in membership since the mid 1970s. Until recently bargaining has been rather centralized. However, unlike Sweden, state intervention in collective bargaining has been rather frequent; the parties have not been able to manage industrial relations autonomously. Nor has solidaristic wage policy been pursued as systematically as in Sweden and active labour market policy has not been as developed as in the Swedish 'model case'. The Danish system of bargaining has left more room for bonuses related to the productivity of the workers at the level of single firms. Even so, strong egalitarian values have prevailed and the actual degree of solidarity in wage formation is on a par with the Swedish if measured by wage dispersion; the negotiated minimum wage is high and the wage structure is highly compressed even after 15 years with high unemployment rates (Rowthorn, 1991). The magnitude and the structure of public spending on labour market programmes in Denmark may be interpreted as another expression of the high degree of actual solidarity. Denmark spends a higher proportion of GDP on labour market programmes than any other OECD country (Reuterswürd, 1990). Income support for the jobless takes the lion's share: 4.5 per cent of GDP (the OECD average is 1.3 per cent) which is far higher than anywhere else although the unemployment rate is at about the average OECD level. However, Denmark is also a leading spender in relation to programmes which target unemployed and disadvantaged people and aim at ordinary jobs. Only Sweden (and Ireland) spend higher shares of GDP on such programmes and the share of total unemployed participating in such programmes is higher only in Sweden and Norway (Reuterswürd, 1990). The organizations of the labour market are involved in preparing and implementing public policies within many fields but they have only been able to dominate labour market policies - through an elaborate network of corporatist institutions. Tri-partite consultation in relation to wider issues have, of course, occurred (Pedersen, 1991) and it is not unreasonable to characterize Denmark as corporatist. However, to measure the actual forms of concerted action and mechanisms of coordination in Denmark in relation to an ideal-type corporatism (3) is in our view misleading. For mobilizing consensus and compromise Denmark has developed a specific set of institutions which is hardly comprehensible as corporatism. It involves not only state and corporatist institutions but non-corporarist structures as well. The coordination is less formal, more indirect and looser than presupposed in ideal-type corporatism. These forms of concerted action and mechanisms for coordination of behaviour are not unique Danish phenomena and I firmly believe that they will be become more common elsewhere, too, as a result of the gradual withering away of the (Fordist) preconditions for the concentration of power in (two- or three-party) corporatist institutions. At the same time I believe that these forms of coordination are more developed in Denmark than in most other countries because of its heterogeneous social structure and its wide dispersion of power in a culturally very homogeneous country dominated by communitarian, or even egalitarian values.

I shall shortly present our conception of these features under the heading of 'the negotiated economy'[2].

The Negotiated Economy

The essential characteristic of a negotiated economy is the interconnection of discursive and institutional features enforcing compromise and mobilizing consensus among a multitude of autonomous agents. Behaviour is coordinated through discursive as well as institutional means. It is not only a mechanism for regulation of disputes and mediation of conflicts but it also involves institutionalized mobilization of mutual understanding about problems, ends and means.

Several preconditions for the emergence of a negotiated economy exist: (1) an approximate symmetry relation of power among the major societal agents; (2) no exit alternatives (Hirschman, 1970) for any of them; (3) legalization and institutionalization of class conflict; (4) dispersion - or multi-centredness - of state authority; and (5) a certain measure of cultural homogeneity to make communication and consensus possible. These preconditions do not evolve over night. They are rather the result of a long historical development. Central in this process is the recognition of the coordination problems caused by the multi-centredness of societal power and state authority, the need for compromise caused by the 'symmetry' of power, and the possibility of consensus caused by cultural homogeneity. From this follows that coordination by legal administrative means appear impossible. Instead, a strategy for discursive coordination is developed and new institutions built to facilitate such coordination.

In the 'pure negotiated economy' allocation of resources is determined neither by individual agents adapting to market changes, nor through autonomous decision-making by public authorities. Instead, decision-making is conducted via institutionalized negotiations between interested agents who reach binding decisions typically based on discursive, political, or moral incentives rather than threats and economic incentives.

Denmark is not a 'pure' negotiated economy. However, discursive coordination is no doubt a central feature and a decisive part of the decision-making is actually conducted via institutionalized negotiations among autonomous actors. Such decision-making depends on the existence of many types of institutions with different functions. These institutions function as links in a specific process for developing ideals, tranforming them to discourses, and eventually to institutions and 'rules of thumb' in concrete decision-making. Important institutions are 'campaign institutions' (set up by interest organizations, private corporations, public authorities or even along corporatist lines, in order to influence the political agenda through formulating and propagating specific interpretations of problems and specific solutions), 'discourse institutions' (scientific or other institutions which test the consistency of the dominant conceptions and try to formulate these into analytically coherent language codes), and 'policy institutions' (public commissions or committees, often composed along corporatist lines, to formulate consensus on problems and specify steps to be taken).

Some institutions engage in ideological struggle and attempt to mobilize mutual understanding around an ideological (normative) framework for the actual decision-making. Within this framework the involved parties engage in institutionalized games developing compromises on themes and procedures for the negotiations. Then in other institutions negotiations take place on the basis of the agreed upon themes and procedures. The activity around the negotiating table is just one link in this overall process of discursive and institutional coordination.

The civilization of class confrontation is a decisive premiss for the development of a negotiated economy in postwar Denmark. As a result of the long lasting and deep going civilization of class conflict, state authority has been dispersed. It has been delegated into many different types of institutions where organizations are represented. State authority has been multi-centred, thereby creating coordination problems. The increased institutional diversification became an explicitly formulated political problem from the 1960s. Coordination, concertation, or planning, became the order of the day. The autonomy of the above-mentioned institutions were accepted as a basic premiss making coordination by legal administrative means impossible. Instead a strategy for discursive coordination was formulated and new institutions were erected to facilitate such coordination. The main objective in this process was the formulation and propagation of a 'socio-economic ideology', or a 'socio-economic frame of meaning', i.e. a normatively orientated understanding of society as an 'economic organism' where the behaviour of public administration, organizations, corporations and households is not automatically established, but only created if and when the agents observe a normative injunction to take macroeconomic questions into consideration when making microeconomic decisions. This incentive is being mobilized through a lot of institutions which formulate problems and designate ends, means and strategies in various policy fields within the overall normative socio-economic frame of meaning.

This is certainly not a smooth and fast process without tensions and conflicts. Elite consensus is being mobilized through a lengthy and conflicting process but popular support is not necessarily assured simultaneously. This may concentrate tensions at the parliamentary level, especially in periods with weak governments. Such tensions might hamper and delay the transformation of an elite consensus into state programmes and administrative action.

However, it has been possible, even in periods of extreme minority parliamentarism, to achieve consensus about long-term policies within various policy fields through the discursive and institutional processes of the negotiated economy. Or rather, this has probably been the only way to pursue long-term economic policies in the Danish context. I shall now give a brief account of the genesis of two of the most important instruments in the economic policy since the mid 1970s: wage policy and public-expenditure policy.

These were not developed overnight. Wage policy, for instance, originates from discursive processes in the 1950s. The need for coordination of wage agreements with socio-economic objectives was first described in various Green Papers (especially Green Paper (*Betænkning*) no. 154, 1956). A comprehensive process of institutional innovation in the Danish labour market took place in the 1960s and 1970s. As a result indirect steering and control of the formation of wages became possible from the late 1970s. Institutional cooperation between autonomous labour market organizations rather than discretionary intervention by the state made possible flexible adjustment of wages to the changing macroeconomic conditions.

A wage-policy discourse was formulated and propagated institutionally through campaign institutions. Most important is the Economic Advisory Council (*Det Økonomiske Råd*) that was set up in 1962 to deal specifically with this issue. It consists of representatives from labour market and other organizations and a board of chairmen who are independent economic experts. Since publishing its first report in 1962, the Council has given a high priority to wage policy in its recommendations.

The participants in negotiations have usually taken the Council's guideline as a point of departure, and since 1979 wage policy has come to be accepted as an economic political instrument to be applied for long-term redistribution of income from wages to profit. This did not happen without severe conflicts both between the big organizations and as a result of internal contradictions. However, by a slow process full of ruptures, an 'elite' consensus was formed about the necessity of such redistribution of income as a means of improving the international competitiveness of Danish industry. As a result, wage policy became very effective in the years following 1979. In the period until 1982 Danish international competitiveness improved as much as 20 per cent as an effect of the development of relative wage costs (Zeuthen, 1986).

Since 1988 the wage-policy discourse has been developed further. It has now become accepted that wage increases should be lower than in Denmark's main trading partners (Pedersen, 1991). This has been realized during the last two years and in the last round of collective bargaining in spite of the simultaneous change of the procedures of coordination which have become more decentralized to make possible more flexibility at the industry level.

It seems that wage policy has become an effective mechanism for flexible adjustment of wages in accordance with socio-economic necessities. The flexibility acquired did not originate from liberalization or revitalization of the labour market. Rather it was a result of discursive and institutional innovations.

The expansion of the Danish public sector did not proceed as a carefully planned process. On the contrary, it happened in a relatively short period, through distinct processes in each sector guided by disconnected specific motivations leading to pragmatic compromises between various interests without any reference to overall socio-economic considerations or necessities.

At the end of the 1960s, the unintended consequences of these processes became evident. Welfare state expenditures grew out of control. The economic and administrative consequences became still more unmanageable. Moreover, the widespread decentralization of authority and responsibility from the state to the municipalities from the early 1970s made the use of authoritative means of coordination impossible.

Efforts to construct a total 'planning machine' (Green Paper no. 723, 1975) were attempted but failed. From the abortive attempts, however, one of its elements - public expenditure planning - was soon given prominence. A public expenditure discourse was formed through a lengthy and pragmatic process similar to the process which formed the wage policy discourse. The need for coordination of public expenditures with socio-economic objectives was localized in a series of Green Papers, Commission reports and medium/long-term blueprints (*perspektivplaner*). The Ministry of Finance (*Budgetdepartementet*) played a major role as organizer of 'campaigns'.

Furthermore, new institutions were set up to deal with policy implementation. Simultaneously, a so-called budgetary cooperation has developed between the government and the independent organizations of the municipalities and the Counties (*amtskommunerne*).

In the late 1970s a rather comprehensive and detailed system for coordination and control of public expenditures was constructed both within central administration and between the state, the counties and the municipalities. By these instruments public expenditure policy was meant to curtail internal costs and demand as a major contribution to solve the macroeconomic imbalances. This was further stressed when the bourgeois government took over in 1982.

Public expenditure policy achieved rather remarkable results (Nielsen, 1988). In 1982 Denmark had an enormous public deficit (10 per cent of GNP). Only 4 years later this was transformed to a surplus (3 per cent of GNP), partly because of successful public expenditure policy which reduced the share of public expenditures (excluding interest payment) in relation to GNP almost 8 per cent. The process did include authoritative state decisions, but it was mainly achieved through institutionalized communicative coordination of independent decisions in local and regional authorities.

Post-Fordist Prospects

The Danish economic and political structure implies favourable opportunities in a post-Fordist perspective. Some of these are caused by the absence of 'sunset' industries and of the rigidities which are typical for Fordist mass production. The Danish industrial structure implies a high capacity for flexible adaptation of the product mix and the level of production. Furthermore, the labour force is highly mobile and its major part is also functionally flexible as a result of the formal education and training system.

The barriers between insiders and outsiders in the labour market are severe but nothing indicates that the labour force is being divided into a decreasing, functionally flexible core and growing layers of numerically flexible peripheral workers as in many other countries. The emergence of 'micro- or firm-corporatism' is not at all a realistic perspective apart from enclaves of a few (mainly foreign) big firms. The emergence of segmented forms of corporatism which exclude the permanently marginal groups is certainly a possibility but so far, at least, this has been counteracted by the seemingly still forceful solidaristic and egalitarian values. The partial decentralization of collective bargaining has not caused higher inequalities and support for the welfare state has not diminished. Furthermore, opinion polls and research results show a widespread willingness to share 'great sacrifices (decreases in real wages, etc.) to take the nation out of the crisis' (Petersen, E., 1989).

The welfare state has also shown capacity for flexibilization of programmes and forms of organization (see later), and the capacity of the apparatus and the employees for revitalization of the welfare state is probably relatively high. The welfare state might be revitalized through the application of new technology not only in order to reduce the amount of labour used on existing services but also to improve the quality of these services and to introduce new ones. Such changes are essential in order to counteract the pressures for marginalization, fragmentation, segmentation and weakening of solidarity. On the other hand, 'a strong solidaristic union movement can play a critical role in sparking the revitalization of the welfare state' (Mahon, 1987, p. 53).

The dispersion of authority and control, the heterogeneous social structure, and the relative weakness of big capital and big labour have hitherto been interpreted as disadvantages; the multi-centredness has apparently rendered impossible stable compromises based on corporatist interaction among a few privileged actors. However, this 'backwardness' will hardly remain a disadvantage in the future when the social structure and life patterns everywhere can be expected to become more heterogeneous than hitherto. The negotiated economy has developed in response to the need for coordination in a multi-centred system. In this way consensus and compromise have been mobilized in spite of fragmentation of the party system, extreme minority parliamentarism and unstable governments.

Denmark has apparently been able to maintain, at least partly, the ideals of welfare, equality, solidarity and consensus in spite of 'post-Fordist' cleavages and multi-centredness. It has already faced and coped with some of the tendencies of dissolution of unity and homogeneity that other countries will have to experience in the future.

However, it is evident that Denmark has to confront severe obstacles to a successful transition to post-Fordism as well: the absence of 'sunrise' or just growing industries, the low level of R&D, the labour market insider/outsider split, the pattern of international integration and, not least, the traditional neglect of the supply-side. Below we shall see how these 'obstacles' have been perceived and handled.

The Crisis of Fordism and the Danish Response

Three series of phenomena and different sequences of linked events must be distinguished in the present crisis: (1) those that have to do with the general crisis of Fordism and which can be found in more or less every country that has adopted this mode of development; (2) the sequence of events that amplify the interconnection between different socioeconomic formations; (3) the phenomena specific to each of the social formations involved (Lipietz, 1988, p. 29). While the general crisis of Fordism did not, from the beginning, imply particular problems Denmark was certainly influenced through its dependence on the international economic development; also some of the specific features of the Danish Fordism were seen to constitute problems. It was not before the mid 1980s that the structural changes elsewhere in response to the crisis of Fordism were recognized as something that required specific Danish responses.

Danish industry was not hit at the outset by the disturbances created by the rigidities of the Fordist production model. The absence of 'sunset' industries was one of the reasons. Moreover, the high capacity for flexible adjustment to changing niches on the international market implied relative advantages in the new economic environment of stagnant total demand, differentiation of consumer demand and industrial restructuring. In the period 1975-82, Danish exports developed more favourably than, for instance, Swedish exports (Mjøset, 1987, p. 442).

Of course, the long-lasting world-market stagnation did imply pressures on the Danish mode of development because of lower exports. Counter-cyclical Keynesian demand management was attempted for a brief period but from 1977 the increasing deficits on the current accounts and the budget forced the government to abandon this policy and replace it with pro-cyclical austerity measures. Ordinary macroeconomic demand management and exchange rate devaluations did part of the job, but austerity was mainly implemented through wage policy and public expenditure policy as described above. From 1977 until the mid 1980s intervention on the demand side through such measures was seen as not only necessary but also, by and large, as sufficient; not only in order to adjust internal demand and imports but also to boost exports through adjustment of relative wage costs.

Alongside the adjustment of costs and demand to the international conjunctures other policies confronted some of the specific rigidities of the Danish 'demand-side Fordism'. The generalization of the Fordist consumption norms were counteracted by some of the initiatives of the bourgeois government after 1982. The wage indexation system was abolished by law and a set of public transfers (unemployment and sickness benefits, social welfare, etc.) were frozen at the 1982-level until 1986. In the same period, however, they refrained from counteracting the credit financed private consumption boom effectively stimulated by the very favourable tax rules concerning deduction of interest payments on private debt. Tax deduction rules were not tightened until 1986.

More important have been the attempts to confront the rigidities in the large public sector. Alongside the political measures to steer the growth of the public expenditures an ambitious programme was launched for modernization of the public sector (Bentzon, 1988). The programme involved a budgetary reform which introduced more administrative discretion and economic responsibility at various decentral levels, the introduction of 'market-proxies' within the public sector, wide-scale introduction of new technology, strengthening of training and re-education and various other means to ensure higher motivation and capacity for adaptation and the development of a service-minded attitude among public employees.

The effects of the efforts are still uncertain and comparative research is not available but it appears probable that the motivation and adaptability of public employees in Denmark is relatively high. One indicator is the very fast, efficient and almost totally unproblematic introduction of new office technology in public administration during the 1980s.

As elsewhere the Danish welfare state has suffered from the economic 'scissors' effect due to decreased revenues and increased demand for transfers and services. It has also experienced problems as a result of the diversification of the needs for public services. When the welfare needs are more basic and homogeneous they are easier to satisfy through the welfare state in its rational-legal form and even if the Danish welfare state can hardly be characterized as the rational-legal bureaucratic stereotype (cf. Jessop, this volume) it was to a certain extent organized according to the Fordist ideal: delivering of standardized products in large series in bureaucratic organizations. However, the administration of all major welfare services has been highly decentralized since the early 1970s. The tax revolt and the protests against the expansion of the welfare state occurred early and, since the late 1970s, there has been broad political consensus about the need to flexibilize the public sector. It is probably because of the early attention to the problems of the public sector and the continued attempts to reform it in a consensual process that the welfare state has today wide support in the Danish population; this support even seems to have strengthened since the 1970s (Goul Andersen, 1988).

The Search for New Instruments

The expansion of the public sector involved far-reaching socialization of reproduction, or in the language of the regulation school, regulation of the wage-relation and generalization of the Fordist consumption norm. It did not, however, involve any significant direct intervention on the supply-side of the economy. Of course, education and labour market policies influenced the skills and the mobility of the labour force; and the material infrastructure and public procurement of private goods as well as environmental and other forms of regulation of standards and norms implied strong indirect influence on the supply-side. Apart from the constraints implied in the regulation of standards and norms the effects on the supply-side have been indirect side-effects. Direct and deliberate steering of the supply-side has been almost absent. Industrial and technological policies have been allocated only modest funds and the programmes have until recently been very general except from support for ailing industries such as shipyards.

The non-interventionist policies, of course, reflect the predominance of SMEs and the specific specialization pattern of Danish industry. This is also the reason why the trade unions have refrained from limiting employers' discretion in relation to hire- and fire-rules in exchange for welfare state compensation.

It has been considered impossible but also unnecessary to manage the supply-side. In this sense economic policies in Denmark were distinctly Keynesian. It was assumed that the supply-side adapts smoothly and rapidly to changes on the demand-side. Faith in the sufficiency of demand (and costs) management in the growth period as well as in the crisis predominated - at least until recently.

There are several reasons for the recent change. The continued macroeconomic imbalances - in spite of the relatively successful application of the preferred instruments of demand and costs management - is particularly significant. In the period 1982-86/87 the objectives as far as wages and public expenditures are concerned were actually met through the established mechanisms for coordination. However, severe macroeconomic imbalances remained. First and foremost, the balance of payments deteriorated further. To cope with these problems new instruments were needed. This need was further strengthened by the gradual elimination of monetary policy (because of full-scale liberalization of capital movements) and exchange-rate policy as instruments in economic policy. This is no doubt one of the major reasons why the bourgeois government abandoned its previous rejection of all measures which intervene directly on the supply-side. Another reason for the redirection was the growing recognition that the future 'internal market' and further EC economic integration imply a decreasing importance of traditional general instruments and simultaneously an increasing importance of structural intervention and supply-side measures.

Still another reason was the growing recognition that Denmark is not shielded from the international tendencies operating on the supply-side of the economy. Data on market shares and productivity revealed the fact that the international competitiveness of Danish industry is influenced by other features than relative unit costs of labour. The data seem to suggest that Danish industry is in a weak position to cope with the challenge of technological or structural competitiveness (Chesnais, 1986; Jessop, Nielsen and Pedersen, 1991). While the Danish industrial structure seemed to be relatively advantageous in the phase of structural crisis and defensive flexibilization (Boyer, 1988a, pp. 264-265) this is not so in the present phase of restructuring and offensive flexibilization. While specific measures to manage the supply-side may have been unnecessary in the former phase they appear urgent in the current one. The general crisis of Fordism did not influence Denmark very much but the structural adjustments originating elsewhere in response to the crisis of Fordism do now imply pressure for supply-side management. Neither wage policy nor public expenditure policy take account of the current restructuring of the technological base of capitalist production. A new structural policy has been designed to repair the deficiencies. Since 1986, this new policy has gradually been implemented but it has also been supplemented and at times challenged by other measures of a more neoliberal orientation. I shall briefly describe how the structural-policy discourse developed within the negotiated economy and how the new structural policy has been implemented.

The Structural-Policy Discourse

The structural policy has two main sources: (a) the development of a technology policy; (b) the reformulation of the socio-economic frame of meaning to take account of the need for an increased international competitiveness.

One of the most important actors in this process was the Technology Board which is a policy and campaign institution structured along corporatist lines. It was set up in 1973 and assigned the task of following and surveying technical and industrial development and taking or guiding action in order to promote technological development. It was expected to formulate and propagate a technology discourse, to design new institutions and to conduct experimental implementation. The long-term objective was to modernize the Danish economy and to contribute to elimination of the macroeconomic imbalances through promotion of technological progress.

During the first ten years, long-term plans for technological service were made, planning groups for various technical areas were erected, and a system of local information centres (*TIC's*) was established. A decisive step was taken in 1983, when a Program for Technological Development (*Det Teknologiske Udviklingsprogram* or 'TUP') was proposed by the Technology Board and followed by Parliament. Although the funds granted were rather meagre by international standards, the emergence of the programme signified a new phase. The programme covered promotion, development and application of information technology as well as financial support for R&D and technological service in microelectronics.

One of the reasons for the political consensus about this programme was the simultaneous reformulation of the socioeconomic frame of meaning. In the 1970s competitiveness was generally perceived as equivalent to RULC (relative unit labour costs).

However, after a long lasting debate among various campaign institutions the conception of the international competitiveness of the Danish economy has gradually changed. Over the period 1984-86 a consensus was established around an extended formulation. Reports from OECD and the Danish government played an important role in this process. They showed an astonishing industrial backwardness in relation to several of those new aspects of competitiveness. A new specialization pattern seemed to have developed. On international markets Denmark had increasingly become specialized in standardized goods with low technology content. Evidence showed that Denmark had net total import of both research and high technology.

The decisive formulation of the new consensus was produced by the Danish Ministry of Finance and further elaborated in contemporary documents from other government agencies and peak organizations. They pointed to the fact that the Danish economy suffered from the following structural problems: export products had an insufficient content of technology and Danish export markets had declining shares of international demand. Therefore, a structural policy should be applied to increase the level of technology, education and research, and to change the composition of exports as far as products and markets is concerned.

This formulation was further developed in important policy documents from the government in 1986 (Arbejdsministeriet et al., 1986; Industriministeriet, 1986), and in documents from the peak organizations. Further elaboration of the concept took place along these lines. A new consensus was formed around the formulation of a new socio-economic coordination problem (industrial structure and competitiveness) and the selection of technological renewal and restructuring as the solution to the problem.

The Structural Policy

The structural policy discourse implied recognition of specific rigidities blocking dynamic adjustment of the industrial structure as well as the selection of appropriate means to remove these rigidities (Nielsen and Pedersen, 1989a, pp. 355-360):

(a) The high proportion of SMEs has often been considered a relative advantage because of their capacity for flexible and dynamic adjustment to international market changes. They have maintained this capacity, according to new research (Jysk Teknologisk Institut, 1989). However, a new view has gained dominance. The absence of large firms is now considered a decisive disadvantage. The SMEs are considered unable to conduct research and development (R&D) of a sufficient measure and quality in an era of major changes. Furthermore, they are considered too weak as far as managerial and financial capacity is concerned to confront the challenges implied by the international specialization and integration. The formation of 'industrial locomotives' is seen as the primary cure to this structural disease. Larger concentrations of capital are needed through mergers of Danish (and later foreign) companies within selected branches: the food industries, environmental technology, etc. Besides, by strengthening inter-firm cooperation among the SMEs, some deficiences caused by the absence of large firms might be overcome. Mergers have been encouraged by public authorities and quite a few remarkable mergers have occurred since late 1988. Furthermore, inter-firm cooperation is supported by various means. A new programme for construction of inter-firm networks was implemented in 1989. Cooperation is encouraged in relation to marketing, application of advanced technology, administration, quality control, job training, use of knowledge and especially R&D.

(b) Too low R&D is now considered a central socio-economic problem but attention is also focused on the normative and institutional barriers between public research and commercial application. As a consequence, several large-scale R&D-projects, based on cooperation between private and public institutions, have been erected in recent years. Another important public-private initiative was the erection of a venture firm (*Dansk Udviklingsfinansiering A/S*) which substantially extended the supply of risk capital for development projects. In addition, various programmes have been elaborated by the Ministry of Education. They cover measures to improve the cooperation between universities and private firms in the field of research, development and education, restructuring of budgetary mechanisms and forms of financing and changes in recruitment and promotional systems.

(c) The legal barriers between public agencies and private firms are considered too rigid. They are seen as barriers for product innovation, modernization of the infrastructure, formation of new legal forms of enterprises and utilization of export opportunities. Many initiatives have been taken to make the relationship between public agencies and private firms more flexible. Cooperation in export of complex 'systems' (collective traffic systems, health systems, social institutions, administration of collective funds, etc.) has been strengthened. On the local level industrial development projects have been organized in cooperation between municipalities, trade unions, trade associations and private firms. As a result new combinations of public and private ownership develop.

(d) The established subvention schemes for ailing industries are considered a barrier to new industrial policy programmes as they take up resources within a tight budget. State subvention for shipyards has for long contributed a very high proportion of the total government subventions to trade and industries (more than 50 per cent). Now these subvention schemes are being dismantled and they will be totally liquidated in 1992. Other remaining subvention programmes are being reorientated from public grants to state guaranteed loans.

(e) The Danish capital market has for long been subject to detailed regulation and supervision. Financial security has been a primary objective. Now, these laws and institutional structures are considered obstacles to productive capital investment and to the formation of new financial institutions to promote venture capital and other new kinds of ownership and control. In this area major changes have happened already. The organization of the stock exchange has been changed by a major reform similar to the London 'Big Bang'. Financial control has been concentrated through mergers. New institutions are formed to promote productive investments of the huge collective pension funds. Wage earner funds have been assigned more room for manoeuvre on capital markets. Also, experiments with new types of relationship between ownership and management have taken place (Petersen, 1989a). As in Sweden institutionalized forms of investment through pension funds and wage earner capital still constitute controversial issues in the political debate. However, unlike Sweden, reforms have been implemented and new institutions have been erected while maintaining the traditional consensus.

(f) Labour market rigidities are seen as not only a potential cause for wage drift and unemployment but also as impediments to the restructuring of industry and the implementation of new technologies. The organized boundaries between the different crafts, and between skilled, semi-skilled and unskilled work are seen as one problem. The barriers between the insiders and the outsiders (the long-term jobless) is another. The investments of firms in developing human resources are considered insufficient as are the existing formal programmes for education, re-education and training. Furthermore, the public system of job assignments is seen as unable to promote mobility of the labour force and the system of unemployment benefits is seen to create other barriers to improvements in the mobility and training of the labour force. Until now, the consensus about the need for restructuring the labour market to strengthen mobility and training have only resulted in minor reforms. Major disagreement still remains concerning the financing of the reforms.

Opposing views come from the bourgeois government and the Federation of Danish Trade Unions (*LO*). The government rejects state subvention of the new programmes and stresses the need for some direct payment from the individuals concerned. LO will not accept individual financing, stresses the need for solidarity, and proposes collective financing by the labour market organizations (and the state).

(g) The internal organization of the state apparatus needs reorganizing in relation to structural policy. Rigidities have been localized in the established sectorization, in the internal ministerial coordinating procedures, and in the institutional interplay between central state, counties and municipalities. New forms of management are being applied and corporatist arrangements at the state level are reorganized. In the Ministry of Industry, for instance, this has been effeced through a major reform of the internal structure (Hansen and Søndergård, 1988). A corporatist institution (*Det Erhvervspolitiske kontaktudvalg*) has a strengthened position in relation to overall planning, survey and political counseling. At the same time, however, the influence of the trade associations has been reduced in relation to the administration of funds and programmes in order to simplify administrative procedures and remove barriers for reformulation of distribution principles. Simultaneously, industrial, technology and labour market policies being regionalized and new corporative structures constituted at the regional and local level.

(h) Most public agencies are not equipped with the necessary instruments for making a dynamic contribution to structural policy. They are often just capable of a re-active policy. Currently, various attempts are being made to strengthen the reflexive capacity of existing institutions for adaptation to new circumstances, their capacity for identification of development trends, and for formulation of problems and mobilization of consensus. Efforts to improve the reflexive capacity of the regional (corporatively constituted) labour market boards is a prominent example. The stated function of these boards have been deliberately changed from reactive administration into comprehensive investigation, planning and coordination of several policy fields. To accomplish this aim, the boards have been equipped with various new instruments. Regional econometric models and new information bases are developed. Information and campaign centres are formed, and new forms of planning are established.

Blockages and Implementation Problems

The Danish negotiated economy has shown capacity for: adjustment of its discursive foundation (through the conception of international competitiveness); formation of an (elite) consensus on a new overall policy (structural policy) to supplement wage policy and public-expenditure policy; and implementation of structural policy through identification of institutional rigidities and formulation of plans for action aiming at removing such rigidities.

However, these achievements ought not to divert our attention from the problems and ambiguities. The emergence of the structural policy is a very new phenomenon and it even appeared to run out of steam by late 1988 as traditional conflicts in Danish politics re-emerged.

Severe questions remain concerning policy implementation. The policy is still vague and a major reallocation of resources in accordance with the objectives of the structural policy still remains to be seen. The programme for support to inter-firm networks, for instance, has only meagre funding. Even so, it had to be compensated by cuts elsewhere within the budget of the Ministry of Industry in accordance with the tight budget policy followed by the bourgeois government. The priority of public-expenditure policy in relation to structural policy also surfaced when the 1989 state budget was passed in parliament. The appropriation for the last year of the Technological Development Programme was simply cut out from the budget as one of the last minute measures adopted to fulfil the targets for total expenditure.

The implementation of the structural policy seems to have provoked a confrontation between, on the one hand, export-orientated industry, big industry and big finance (by Danish standards) and, on the other hand, the smaller companies orientated towards the domestic market. The first group promotes the 'locomotive strategy' while the second group have united behind the so-called 'tax strategy'. This strategy attempts to lower charges on employers and corporate taxation as well as marginal income taxes. They propose large cuts in public budgets to finance the tax reductions. The overall purpose is to lower relative costs in comparison with foreign competitors on the domestic market.

The Social Democrats and the trade unions are in favour of full steam under the implementation of the locomotive strategy. The bourgeois government is split between representatives from each strategy. The Liberal Party advocates the tax strategy and a more confrontational attitude to the Social Democrats while the, at least until mid 1990, dominant group within the conservative party is in favour of the locomotive strategy and more consensual parliamentary policies.

The split between these two strategies was sharpened when the liberal Minister of Taxes and Duties from 1988 launched an ambitious attempt to challenge the position of the Ministry of Finance as the dominant governmental campaign institution. A neo-liberal supply-side policy has since been formulated and propagated in various campaign documents from the

Minister of Taxes and Duties in open opposition to the campaigning from the Ministry of Finance under the leadership of a centre-orientated conservative. It is argued that the high marginal taxes constitute the main problem as they are supposed to reduce the supply of labour, savings and risk taking, to create pressure for higher wages and to distort investments, including decisions on plant localization.

Since 1988, election results and opinion polls have strengthened the Liberal Party as opposed to its more centre-orientated partners in government. The policy of the government was pushed in a right-wing direction if not merely paralysed in the troubled waters of extreme minority parliamentarism. No major compromises have been made. In 1989 the government launched what was proclaimed to be a 'grand plan' for recovery of the Danish economy. The plan was simply a set of tax reductions and of means to counteract the loss of revenue and it included no structural policy measures. It represented a breakthrough within the bourgeois government of a neo-liberal supply-side approach. Protracted negotiations for a compromise ended without any results.

The implementation of structural policy suffered from this development. Only meagre funds have been allocated to the programmes, and the Budget of 1990 actually implied a true massacre against the major industrial policy programmes.

The current (1990) discourse on international competitiveness reflects the strategic splits and the parliamentary stalemate. A typical report from the Ministry of Finance (Finansministeriet, 1990) distinguishes between wage competitiveness and structural competitiveness. The development of interest rates, exchange rates and wage costs are considered decisive for short-run competitiveness but the former of these instruments are now regarded as technical parameters rather than variables. This leaves wage costs as the only remaining variable with short run effects on competitiveness. In the long run, however, competitiveness 'depends on factor conditions, especially R&D, and the institutional conditions (especially labour markets and capital markets) for adaptation of the structure of firms and industries'. The report applies the following factors as indicators for the structural competitiveness of Danish industry: R&D-intensity, investment ratios, profitability, and flexibility of the labour force.

The policy implications are evidently a continued policy for relatively lower wage increases than abroad, supplemented with measures to increase R&D and reforms of the labour market. The structural policy has been more sharply focused on R&D and the structural approach to the labour market has been mingled with a neo-liberal one. However, neither the intended promotion of R&D nor the search for labour market flexibility have yet been followed up by major government programmes.

The institutions of the labour market are still seen in relation to the requirements of new technology and restructuring of industry. However, labour market rigidities are now, in particular, identified as causes for structural unemployment. Excessive real wage levels, small wage differentials, the system of unemployment benefits and other institutional features are seen as responsible for 'classical unemployment' and excessively prolonged search activities (OECD, 1990b).

During 1989 and 1990 there were intense discussions and negotiations in both parliamentary and corporative forums about proposals for reform of the unemployment benefit system, the hire and fire rules and efforts to improve the education and training of the labour force. The traditional conflicts and the parliamentary stalemate has blocked any progress so far.

The relatively low R&D investment in Danish firms is often considered the most important structural problem. It is argued that R&D has become even more important than before:

> Traditionally firms in small European countries have only to a modest degree aimed at developing their own technology. Instead flexible adaptation and application of basic technologies developed elsewhere have been the (until now) rather successful strategy... However, this strategy is less attractive than it was. OECD research has shown that integration of technological development and commercial application have become still more important. As a result it has become still more difficult to use technology developed by others (IUI et al., 1990).

While it is no doubt true that Denmark has weaknesses in generic technologies and in relation to systematic technological change (Edquist and Lundvall, 1990, p. 26) it is misleading to focus exclusively on the importance of R&D and introduction of new technologies. Recent studies indicate that the late, but rapid introduction of new process technology in Danish firms in the mid 1980s was very difficult to absorb and these difficulties seem to explain the extraordinary absolute decline in productivity in the period 1984-87. The difficulties reflect, in particular, problems with qualifications and work organization in relation to introduction of new technology (Gjerding et al., 1990).

It is also often ignored that the structural problems of Danish industry are connected to the predominance of traditional industrial complexes with falling or stagnating world market demand; and the creation of new complexes requires much more deep-going changes than increased R&D. If this is ignored it is probable than promotion of R&D will result in the emergence of high-tech enclaves similar to the current situation in the Danish electronics industry. A recent report from the Ministry of Industry points at the importance of stimulation of new complexes in opposition to official government policy; the new industrial policy programme of the Social Democracy puts much emphasis on such measures; and the debate inspired by the publication of Porter (1990) has further strengthened this line of thinking. So far, however, it is not reflected in actual government policy.

In the absence of full-scale government implementation of the structural policy, private institutions have taken over. A wave of mergers among 'big' Danish firms, and, to a much lesser degree, acquisitions and strategic alliances involving foreign capital, has taken place. This implementation of the 'locomotive strategy' has been initiated by a group of big banks and insurance companies, wage earner funds and (collective) pension funds, trade unions and representatives of Danish big industry. This group has not just initiated mergers. It has also, among other things, made important investments in venture capital and basic research, attempted to force through a major restructuring of the Danish agro-industrial complex, and prevented hostile foreign take-overs of Danish firms. Furthermore, all these initiatives have been coordinated by common institutions which analyse and decide on issues which are normally the area of industrial policy. It might actually be designated a 'private industrial policy', formulated, propagated, and implemented within the institutions of the negotiated economy as usual - except from the absence of direct government or political involvement (Petersen, 1989b).

Conclusion

Recent events have made visible that the elite consensus around the socio-economic ideology is not always easily translated into a popular consensus. The parliamentary stalemate has blocked the implementation of the structural policy - as well as the adaptation of the Danish tax structure to the 'inner market' - and this has shown that parliamentary politics might disrupt the processes of the negotiated economy.

Other events, however, show the vitality of the negotiated economy. The events following the elaboration of the neo-liberal 'grand plan' in 1989 point to the strength of the discursive processes. As a means politically to legitimize the governmental proposal for tax reduction the macroeconomic models being used by the Ministry of Finance to predict the effects of proposed policies were restructured, at rather short notice, to take account of the proposed causal link between taxes and savings and between taxes and supply of labour. This was heavily criticized by other campaign and discourse institutions for being politically motivated and without any scientific basis (National-økonomisk Tidsskrift, no. 1, 1990). The subsequent report from the Ministry of Finance was much more carefully prepared in order to counteract their loss of legitimization in other discourse and campaign institutions.

It is another sign of the continued strength of the negotiated economy that the bourgeois government has leaned heavily on the established institutions of the negotiated economy, and has even strengthened and innovated them, in its attempts to overcome the parliamentary stalemate of 1989/1990. The Ministry of Finance has introduced a new procedure for the publication of its most important regular report. It has formally involved all the major interest organizations in a phase of consultation about all the major issues of economic policy, and it attempts to reformulate points of agreement into issues for further investigation in discourse institutions. In addition, a new institution has been erected: four-party negotiations (Pedersen, 1991). The parties are being side-stepped through negotiations between labour, capital, government and the association of local municipalities. In at least one case such negotiations have led to an agreement about issues which were until then blocked in parliament. These innovations are remarkable because the bourgeois parties in government have earlier expressed a dislike, in principle, of many of the institutions of the negotiated economy.

Another indicator of the continued strength of the negotiated economy in Denmark is the emergence of the 'private industrial policy'. Danish wage earner funds and (collective) pension funds have actually, as an effect, gained an importance in capital allocation which is level with that of the controversial Swedish wage earner funds, and they have been able to follow a more active investment policy than their Swedish equivalents. It is remarkable that this has happened in a consensual way. An absence of harsh ideological struggle is a general characteristic for Denmark in this era as compared with the current situation in Sweden. Ideological conflicts are contained within the discursive framework of the negotiated economy and they do not call into question the basic institutional structure.

Denmark has embarked on the process of learning how to manage the supply-side. It constitutes a major socio-institutional innovation in a country like Denmark with its Keynesian faith in automatic supply-side response and its traditional non-interventionist industrial policies This learning process is apparently full of obstacles and even relapses and the evidence is contradictory. It remains to be seen if the stability of the negotiated economy also in this area will ensure flexible adjustment of policies.

Notes

1. This is common for many small countries. Even so, they may be termed Fordist if Fordism is redefined in the following way: 'the virtuoso circle need not operate ... through a close coupling of mass production and mass consumption within national economies... Fordist expansion in a given national economy may not require that it produces complex mass consumer durables. It would be enough to have an industrial base which generates sufficient export earnings to finance their importation and a mode regulations which works to generalize mass consumption norms along with the income to realize them' (Jessop 1990, pp. 15-18).

2. The concept of 'the negotiated economy' has been developed in a Scandinavian context and up till now only used in the Scandinavian countries. It was launched about 10 years ago in connection with a long lasting and very ambitious Norwegian public research project (*Magtudredningen*) (NOU, 1982; Hernes, 1978). Since then theoretical discussions have taken place and also efforts have been taken to apply the concept in empirical studies in the different Scandinavian countries (Nielsen and Pedersen, 1988a; 1988b; 1989a; 1991; Berrefjord, Nielsen and Pedersen, 1989; Berrefjord and Nore, 1988; Midttun, 1988). Others have some similar lines of argument used similar concepts such as 'the negotiated order' (Moore and Booth, 1989), 'negotiated coordination' (Devine, 1988,) and 'negotiation, in a wider interactionist sense' (Clark, 1989). Lipietz and other regulationists designate as 'negotiated involvement' the forms of cooperation between employers and employees in 'a new compromise' in the post-Fordist era. See also Boyer (1988a, pp. 268-273).

16. Workplace Reform and the Stabilization of Flexible Production in Sweden

Mark Elam and Martin Börjeson

Introduction[1]

The underlying argument of this paper is that the current 'flexibilization' of Swedish capitalism has been ushered in by the transformation of the national politics of production and the formulation of a new shared language of workplace reform[2]. Rather than being a straightforward reflection of the pervasive diffusion of the new technological paradigm of 'flexible specialization' or 'flexible automation', the new hegemonic language of reform is playing an important constitutive role in the restructuring process; inscribing the imperatives of post-Fordist capitalist production in the Swedish context. Contemporary changes in the nature of Swedish working life are to be partly explained by crucial social and historical processes occurring within the national language of workplace reform. A central element of production politics in any nation is made up of struggles and disputes over language; over the meaning of keywords like 'democracy', 'efficiency', 'competence', 'management' and 'participation'[3]. Those organized interests with the ability effectively to appropriate the meaning of these keywords are in a position to create and orchestrate workplace demands and shape individual aspirations and processes of self-identification.

What we identify as the new shared language of workplace reform in Sweden is not exclusively concerned with the reorganization and revitalization of Swedish industry; it tends to address the broader issue of the qualitative renewal of Swedish capitalism per se. Although, it is the character of industrial work and the competitive performance of export industry which is addressed in the first instance, the new language of reform succeeds in raising a vision of a way of life under capitalism which has far-reaching implications for every sphere of the organized economy. It articulates the need for educational reforms, a new balance between 'free' time and 'work' time, a new system of taxation, a new ethics of business practice, a new brand of trade unionism and new modes of welfare provision. What is being offered is a coherent representation of the realities of capitalist life in an era of smart machines and globalized competition. Both the amended rights and extended responsibilities of the individual wage-earner are comprehensively outlined; the new opportunities and rewards she is entitled to demand and the new duties she is expected to perform as a consenting participant in a remodelled world of work.

In the following sections we commence by outlining the fate of the rival languages of workplace reform which have appeared since the end of the postwar 'Golden Age' of Swedish capitalism in the late 1960s. We link the reaching of the developmental limits of the Taylorist paradigm of work organization to the breakdown of the discursive hierarchy within the workplace. The discursive boundaries defining the national politics of production became exceptionally fluid at the beginning of the 1970s and the authority of the established political apparatuses of production was seriously challenged both from below and from other spheres of social life. The trajectory of the Swedish economy became uncertain and even the occasional poet was considered to have something worthwhile to say about the reform of working life! Many contending voices of workplace reform were vying to be heard and the 'proper' meaning of crucial keywords in production was the subject of an intense public debate. Throughout the 1970s, a prolonged process of elimination and settlement took place as the bearers of the different languages of reform used their varying power resources to disqualify or neutralize the rival authors of change.

Gradually, a preferred language of reform has appeared and its bearers have been widely accepted as experts; the new 'legislators' in the workplace with justified claims to authoritative social knowledge. During the 1980s, the discursive boundaries defining the politics of production have been extensively reconstructed around a rhetorical 'anti-Taylorism' which successfully accommodates demands for the 'democratization of working life' by strategically linking 'more challenging jobs for well-educated individuals' to a new paradigm of capital rationalization and 'total productivity' in Swedish industry[4] destined to improve its performance in global competition. Subordinate groups have begun to borrow the major terms of this new preferred language of reform and accept the meanings ascribed to them. This has enabled the reign of a smooth flow of consensual rhetoric to prevail within the political apparatuses of production and a measure of intellectual collaboration to take place between previously opposed interests. It is only with the coming of a new shared language of reform in the workplace that it has been possible to initiate 'fruitful' discussions and move towards a temporary, if still superficial, restabilization of the reciprocal expectations of capitalist enterprise in Sweden.

Having discussed the major features of the new politics of production in Sweden, we proceed in the second half of this paper by examining its unequal hold on different industrial sectors. By contrasting the steel industry with the printing industry we indicate the significant role played by exposure to international competition, technological configuration and established management-labour relations in shaping the propensity of the sector to receive and contribute to the new shared language of reform. The flow of consensual rhetoric is smoother, and the discursive boundaries more settled, in some sectors than in others. The aim is to show that although the perennial 'difficulties'[5] of capitalist production appear to have found an increasingly stable post-Fordist resolution in Sweden, fissures filled with divergent meanings still exist in the new landscape of reciprocity, and these may either continue to heal up or grow progressively wider into gulfs of contrariety.

Swedish Languages of Workplace Reform: 1969-1989

1969-1975: An Obstreperous Era

Historically, the fundamental objective of the 'Swedish Model' has been to unite a 'desirable' programme of social welfare with a 'necessary' one of economic growth (Elander, 1978). 'Solidaristic wages policy' has meant coordinated wage bargaining at the central level and the setting of standard wage rates based on the principle of 'equal pay for equal work'. These standard rates have been forced on employers regardless of varying profitability and ability to pay (Martin, 1984, p. 235). Consequently, only 'sufficiently' profitable firms have been able to survive in the longrun; those which have continually sought to modernize production. An 'active labour market policy' has been the essential complement to a solidaristic wages policy, ensuring that workers discharged from the technologically torpid back-waters of the economy are spared the pain of prolonged unemployment and quickly re-introduced at the high productivity frontier.

However, in the late 1960s the Swedish economy was experiencing the beginnings of a structural crisis which threatened to expose the institutionalized foundations of the Swedish Model to insuperable pressures. The Taylorist paradigm of work organization had reached its developmental limits and the further modernization of production along Taylorist lines was proving ineffective and counter-productive. The rationalization process was increasingly seen as injurious not only to those workers facing unemployment and cultural dislocation on the technological periphery but also to those employed at the technological frontier. Technical change was no longer synonymous with social progress and there was a widespread 'flight from work' (Palm, 1977).

Both the Swedish Confederation of Trade Unions (*LO*) and the Swedish Employers' Association (*SAF*) were generally confounded by the exhaustion of the Taylorist paradigm. Alienation at work had to be combatted but without the serious diminution of productivity levels. LO and SAF instigated a programme for 'deeper democracy' in the workplace and encouraged the joint 'Development Council' (*Utvecklingsrådet*)[6] to join in this venture by commissioning relevant research (Simonson, 1988). The primary obstacle to the democratization of working life was quickly identified as management's omnipotent powers in the workplace guaranteed by LO's continued acceptance of paragraph 32 in SAF's constitution. This paragraph stipulated that SAF's members must include a clause in all agreements with unions reserving the right of the employer to engage and dismiss workers at his own discretion; to direct and allot work and to avail himself of workers belonging to any organization whatsoever, or to none (Martin, 1984, p. 251).

During the autumn of 1969, the Development Council decided to commission a new programme of experiments on alternative patterns of work organization. Study trips were arranged to Norway, where Einar Thorsrud in collaboration with the Tavistock School of Human Relations had been experimenting with the idea of 'semi-autonomous work groups' (*självstyrande grupper*) since the beginning of the decade. Several of the Swedish sociologists commissioned by the Development Council, for example Bertil Gardell and Edmund Dahlström, were very enthusiastic about the 'Norwegian Experience' and lauded autonomy in groups as offering the key to the creation of more humane workplaces in Sweden (Karlsson, 1989, p. 30). However, the views of these aspiring experts on industrial democracy were almost immediately subject to intense criticism which questioned whether they had anything at all to say about 'real' democracy in the workplace. In a provocative book called; 'The art of habituating humans' (*Konsten att dressera människor*), which was published in four editions during the late 1960s and early 1970s, the official programme for 'deeper democracy' was condemned for failing to empower workers and for only offering them superficial involvement in decision-making procedures. In addition, the higher quality of working life arising from a deepening of democracy was linked to the search by management for 'higher qualities' within the labour force during an era of growing absenteeism:

> It is only good quality labour-power which is useful. There is a need for less muscle and more brain. Workers should be able to solve problems and be innovative. A good worker is one with the same objective as management - higher productivity (Flordh et al., 1971, p. 128 - our translation).

The possibilities for containing discussions of the democratization of working life within the established political apparatuses of production evaporated. On the 9th December 1969, a wild strike broke out at LKAB, the state-owned mining company in northern Sweden and soon approximately 5000 workers were on strike. A wave of unofficial strikes beyond anything experienced in Sweden in the postwar period followed in the wake of the LKAB strike. Immediately prior to, and in the aftermath of, this strike wave, well-known literary figures, such as P.C. Jersild, Sara Lidman and Göran Palm, temporarily abandoned literature in order to document and debate the powerlessness of workers in modern Swedish factories (Anshelm, 1990). Both SAF and LO were confronted with an inescapable crisis of authority. The situation was perhaps most unsettling for LO: by continuing to support solidaristic wages policy they were helping to intensify a Taylorist rationalization of work which condemned their members to what had been revealed to be a barbarous working life.

Paragraph 32 as a cornerstone in the postwar compromise between labour and capital in Sweden was in urgent need of replacement by a new 'democratic' framework for the regulation of working life and a new paradigm of work organization had to be found. By the spring of 1971, LO was demanding a new approach to workplace reform which relied on government legislation rather than formal agreements between themselves and SAF. Consequently, a special parliamentary committee was established to coordinate a programme for the reform of Labour Law. Between 1971 and 1976, a series of new laws was enacted covering such areas as health and safety at work, employment security and union representation on company boards. The culmination of this legislative programme came during the summer of 1976 with the Law of Co-determination (*MBL - Medbestämmandelagen*) which represented the symbolic legal nullification of paragraph 32.

1976-1981: Short-circuiting the Voice of Reform

At the point of MBL's enactment, the late Olof Palme described the comprehensive reform of Swedish Labour Law which had been carried out since 1971 as the 'greatest diffusion of power and influence since the introduction of universal suffrage' (Martin, 1984, p. 263). Such immoderation, however, is hard to justify. The legislation only provides the initial infrastructure for the construction of democratic routines in the workplace. Employers are now enjoined to provide information about changes in the organization of production and obliged to negotiate these changes with union representatives, if negotiations are requested, but are still able to reserve for themselves the right to decide if they so wish (Simonson, 1988,

p. 135). Only in one relatively minor instance does MBL offer union representatives the power actually to veto management decisions[7]. Therefore, although MBL significantly broadens unions' opportunities to participate in the decision-making process in the workplace, it does not guarantee them any significant rights to decide[8]. If any real change in the balance of power between labour and capital is to take place it must occur first in connection with the co-determination agreements (*medbestämmandeavtal*) which are to follow on from MBL.

After June 1976, the immediate pursuit of a co-determination agreement between SAF, LO and the central cartel of private sector white-collar unions, PTK, was effectively curtailed by both the Social Democratic Party's election defeat in September and the marked deterioration of the general economic climate. It was during 1976 and 1977 that structural crisis within the Swedish economy became painfully manifest (Mjøset, 1985b). Internationally, the competitive performance of Swedish export industry was extremely poor and a modern industrial structure which had first taken shape at the beginning of this century, during the 'age of steel and electrification' (Freeman, 1989; Landes, 1969), was in dire need of restructuring. Although much attention has been focused on an apparent 'wages explosion' in 1975-76 and excessive 'labour hoarding', the most immediate problem for Swedish industry at this time was probably the return of competitive pricing within central export markets (Mjøset, 1985b, p. 64).

Structural crisis was also followed by an acceleration in the trend towards the internationalization of the Swedish economy. The declining significance of domestic demand for development of Swedish industry as a whole had a clear effect on SAF's profile. The previous balance of power in the Association between domestic interests (mainly small and medium sized firms) and export interests (mainly large multinational firms) was tipped significantly in the latter's favour. A charismatic 'rough diamond' from ASEA, Curt Nicolin, took over as chairman in 1976 and transformed SAF's established routines. Despite his unpolished edges he was able to unite the Association with the promise of strong leadership and appease the domestic faction (Schiller, 1988, p. 138; de Geer, 1989, p. 228). SAF was ascendant.

A new look SAF was first to take the initiative in the quest for a co-determination agreement after MBL. Economic crisis and a change of government had given them the breathing space they required to devise a far-sighted approach to co-determination. SAF's Technical Department (*Avdelning T*) played an instrumental role in defining the strategic line to be followed. The basic idea was effectively to subordinate demands for greater democracy in the workplace to the question of industry's long-term survival in the new global competition. To achieve this subordination it would be necessary to 'short-circuit' (*kortsluta*) the sphere of union influence (Schiller, 1988, p. 154). This would, in turn, require a greater decentralization of managerial responsibilities for the planning of production to trustworthy section leaders who would be given the key task of maintaining a healthy 'team spirit' (*laganda*) on the shopfloor favouring the active, but informal, involvement of workers in the solving of routine production problems. Significant union involvement in the decision-making process was to be restricted to those areas of production where it could be most useful for the disciplining of individual workers and kept as far away as possible from the commanding heights of corporate power.

The clearest expression of SAF's strategic approach to co-determination is given in a booklet called 'Different factories' (*Annorlunda fabriker*), compiled by Stefan Agurén and Jan Edgren of Avdelning T and published in 1979. Two driving-forces are identified explaining the emergence of 'different factories' dramatically deviating from the Taylorist norm. Firstly, the need for a new paradigmatic approach to productivity able to guarantee survival under tougher competitive conditions, and secondly, the need to satisfy the justified demands of well-educated individuals for more challenging jobs (Agurén and Edgren, 1979, p. 8). These two imperatives, however, do not require separate attention as they are harmoniously inter-related. By attempting to meet one imperative we inevitably help to meet the other. A more flexible pattern of work organization emphasizing problem-solving activities leads to more challenging jobs and these more challenging jobs, when taken on by 'competent' and ambitious individuals, make a vital contribution to increased efficiency (ibid, p. 9). Allegedly, the decentralization of responsibility for routine production planning means work is organized on a more 'human-scale'; this encourages individual involvement and allows the growth of a team spirit which naturally arises when groups of people work closely together towards common goals (ibid, p. 96).

It is interesting to compare 'Different factories' with an earlier publication from Avdelning T which appeared in 1974. This previous publication called 'New patterns of work organization - Evidence from 500 experiments' (*Nya arbetsformer - Rapport från 500 försök*) was designed to respond to the major assault on managerial prerogatives by showing that despite all the hullabaloo about industrial democracy, the most competent and the most active reformers of working life remain the private firms themselves rather than the unions, the politicians or the academics. It also expresses the need for a good deal of caution in reforming workplaces and that 'small words and significant results are better than the opposite' (SAF Avdelning T, 1974, p. 31). Taylorism as a paradigm of work organization is, after a few qualifying remarks, still portrayed as a progressive force in the development of modern Swedish society. Functional specialization has obviously been taken too far in some cases but the essential problem remains one of finding 'a suitable balance' (*en lagom avvägning*) between Taylorism's undeniable advantages and unfortunate negative side-effects (ibid, p. 37). In 'Different factories', such a strategic defence of Taylorism is no longer considered necessary. SAF is now prepared to condone a definite break with an ugly Taylorist past. The attractions of a new paradigm of productivity and work organization emphasizing capital rationalization are now considered significant enough to allow a consistent tongue-lashing of Taylorism in the public arena. The general adoption by SAF of a rhetorical 'anti-Taylorism' was to prove of crucial importance for the identity of the belated co-determination agreement eventually drawn-up in 1982. The declamatory jacket for a new shared language of workplace reform had been found.

1982-1989: A New World of Efficiency and Participation?

The co-determination agreement signed by LO, PTK and SAF on the 15 April 1982 bears the name *'Utvecklingsavtalet'* (UVA). A literal translation is 'The Development Agreement', the official translation, however, is 'The Agreement on Efficiency and Participation'. This official translation is most informative as it clearly indicates the success of SAF's strategy to integrate demands for industrial democracy with the search for a new approach to productivity and an effective way of prevailing in global competition. In UVA's initial declaration of 'shared opinions' (*gemensamma värderingar*) the genuinely harmonious relationship between improved business efficiency and the protection/utilization of employees skills and occupational experience is identified. Co-determination has become primarily a matter of installing the efficient alternative to the Taylorist paradigm in the Swedish workplace. The implicit assumptions behind this expedient approach to co-determination are that if work organization is no longer Taylorist it must be better (i.e. democratic), and that if Sweden is unable to beat the world in competition it will not matter if work organization is Taylorist or not, as Swedish industry will cease to exist:

> ...there is no suggestion that, outside of the firm's commercial objectives, worker involvement in the planning and organization of production is of intrinsic value for democratic reasons alone' (Schiller, 1988, p. 211 - our translation).

In the negotiations leading up to UVA, SAF had been able to assimilate one of LO's established arguments for greater worker involvement in production and make it into one of their own. From the early 1920s, LO has persistently argued that greater worker involvement could, under the proper circumstances, lead to significant productivity gains: that management's principled refusal to assign workers a role in the detailed planning of production is irrational from a commercial point of view (Schiller, 1974, p. 109). Although, this 'sensible' argument for 'democratization' was pushed into the background at the beginning of the 1970s, when the dominant issue was the morality of management's exclusive control of the workplace, ten years on, in the face of a more hostile world of competition, it appeared to have renewed relevance for LO's membership and the protection of their jobs. SAF had recognized this fact and had grasped this long-standing argument of their opponents for a 'democratic' reform of working life and presented it as the only justified one and the only one they were now prepared to listen to. Thus, during the course of 13 years (1969-82), a vital moral dialect of industrial democracy and self-determination had been refined into a formal language of co-determination only to be eventually reduced to a sensible syntax of participation for efficiency. LO's efforts to win a co-determination agreement which preserved MBL's formal tone concerning the division of decision-making powers within the workplace proved fruitless. UVA is about relatively informal cooperation for the creation of new economic resources - about 'working together for a better business' (Agurén, 1988).

The regulative paragraphs in UVA concern the correct approach to 'Enterprise Development' (*Företagets Utveckling*). Three key areas of development in need of regulation are identified: work organization, technical development and business strategy/company finance. As far as work organization is concerned, it is considered important to build on employees' own expectations of work in the specification of job content. The gendering of specific jobs is taken up as something to be avoided. In relation to technical development, employees are to be given the opportunity to participate in the actual design of new process and product technology so that its introduction helps to make their working lives more stimulating and challenging. Regarding business strategy and company finance, local union organization is to be granted rights of access to information concerning the firm's economic situation and financial resources and, to be able to participate in strategic discussions concerning market trends, competitive situation, purchasing policy, product development and choice of machinery. Co-determination is no longer a potentially disruptive factor in the search for capitalist efficiency - it is now an important stabilizing factor.

As Schiller (1988) and Simonson (1988) point out, UVA can be seen as representing a return to the consensual 1960s and an almost blind faith on the part of LO in the advantages of efficient capitalist production and rapid restructuring for the maintenance of a healthy welfare state. While the old Taylorist paradigm for efficiency ultimately betrayed this faith; the emergent technological paradigm with its emphasis on capital rationalization rather than division of labour appears well-deserving of renewed fealty and less prone to contradiction because it offers workers such a stimulating role in its evolution. Apparently, the Swedish Labour Movement is once more highly predisposed to the idea that capitalist efficiency is equivalent to social progress: not only will it provide a constantly higher standard of living for the individual wage-earner but also the chance for self-realization at work.

The general propagation of the gospel of efficiency and participation contained in UVA has primarily taken place through two major national programmes both financed by the state through the Swedish Work Environment Fund (*AMF*) and each lasting 5 years: the Development Programme (1982-87) and the LOM Programme (1984-89)[9]. Representatives from SAF, LO and the central white-collar organization *TCO* have sat on the steering committees of both of these prestigious money-spinning programmes which have literally monopolized the official discourse of workplace reform in both the private and public sectors in the 1980s.

The Development Programme (cost: 55 million SwKr.) aimed to lead by example and sought to encourage and publicize 'showcase' projects which were deemed to be in the 'frontline' with regards to the renewal of technology, work organization and management practice. The 40 projects which were chosen were extremely varied and encompassed manufacturing industry (e.g. Volvo Components); process industry (e.g. Boliden Metall); service industry (e.g. SAS Information Systems); the small firms sector (e.g. printing and furniture firms); public enterprise (e.g. Swedish Telecom) and central, regional and local government (e.g. the National Housing Authority, the Regional Health Authority in Värmland and Malmö City Council's Technical Services Department). Collectively, these cases of excellence are presented as concrete evidence of the growth of a 'new world of work' (*en ny arbetsvärld*) and the continued relevance and vitality of a unique 'Swedish Model of industrial relations' (AMF, 1988).

The LOM (*Leadership-Organization-Medbestämmde*) Programme (cost: 50 million SwKr.) has aimed to initiate change rather than support/publicize it. The immediate ambition has been to start a 'democratic dialogue' in about one hundred different workplaces (e.g. a police district, a steel mill, a confectionery firm and a postal sorting office) in order to generate better leadership, new work organization and greater co-determination which will allow the satisfaction of consumer demand for higher standards of 'quality', 'flexibility' and 'service' (LOM, 1985). The development of 'effective' workplaces is considered to depend upon greater cooperation and decentralization of responsibility. About 50 'young and enthusiastic' researchers have been engaged under the LOM Programme as 'missionaries'.

Their job has been to go out into the world of work and set up a 'dialogue' between management, workers and the unions which can break down 'rigid' and 'undemocratic' organizational structures. It is considered crucial to establish such 'missionary work' as a legitimate area of research with a firm base in Sweden's universities and technical high-schools (LOM, 1989).

Both the Development Programme and the LOM Programme make the link between the need for a new world of work and the often negative attitudes of young Swedes (as well-educated individuals) to traditional forms of wage-labour especially in industry:

> All the studies show that young people today want to shape, and can shape, their work. They have a social ambition. When it is possible to unite this ambition with a firm's business objectives we have two strong forces moving in the same direction. It is then we have great opportunities for enterprise renewal (Anders Edström interviewed in LOM, 1989).

Apart from financing ventures like the Development and LOM programmes, an important task for the state in the continuing reform of working life would appear to be serious engagement with the problem of strategic 'labour shortages'. As was the case during the heyday of the Swedish Model in the 1950s and 60s, an 'active labour market policy' is identified by both SAF and LO as of great importance for the maintenance of levels of productivity and employment. In a nutshell, a new world of work cannot be generated and survive unless willing and competent participants are forthcoming. A recurrent question in Sweden today is 'who will do the work?' (Madsén, 1988; Bull, 1989). In addition to the capricious attitudes of young Swedes to traditional employment relations, the perturbing spectre of a severe 'population implosion' has been raised: allegedly the number of 'economically-active' Swedes will have shrunk drastically by the year 2000 and it is essential that key sectors of the economy do not lose out in the intensifying competition for labour[10]. Industrial workers are becoming a 'rare commodity' (*bristvara*) and it is therefore essential that they be treated as such and offered greater 'freedom' in the workplace. SAF and LO have gone on the offensive in schools to correct the perceptions of young people concerning the world of work and its future. A life of labour in industry need no longer be seen as something to be avoided (Lindgren, 1988); car plants and steel mills are now dynamic social environments which hold the promise of enormous opportunities for self-expression and creative practice (Ohlsson, 1988; Renström, 1988).

The crucial National Board for Employment-Training (*AMS*), with its local and regional training centres, which has been the institutional foundation for the execution of labour market policy in Sweden since the early 1950s, was significantly reorganized in 1986.

The new AMU Group is a 'market-orientated agency' whose aim is to 'educate adults for a working life in transition'. The intention is that the Group shall be self-financing and sell training services to its regional labour exchanges and directly to private industry. Rather than 'fitting' job-seekers to job vacancies, AMU's new philosophy is to act as a key resource for industry in their search for suitably competent employees who are equal to the challenge of industrial work today. As the level of unemployment remains low in Sweden, a complementary focus has been identified as the continuous development of the 'skills' of workers already in employment. During 1987-88, the Group's sales of personnel training to industry increased by approximately 30 per cent (AMU Gruppen, 1988). Regular clients now include, SKF, Volvo, IBM, Philips, Atlas Copco, SSAB, Electrolux, Ovako Steel and Sandvik. Efforts are being made to customize training to the individual needs of client firms. As well as concentrating on basic knowledge and occupational competence; AMU's pedagogues shall strive to develop 'social skills' and 'cooperative ability' (*social kompetens och samarbetsförmåga*).

Sector Experience: Steel and Printing

Having focused our attention on the increasingly detailed articulation of a new shared language of workplace reform at the national level it is informative to examine how questions of 'democracy' and 'efficiency' have been handled within different sectors of the Swedish economy. The new vocabulary of reform continues to be remarkably absent in some sectors while it has substantive roots in others. Unquestionably, those sectors which have figured most strongly in the making and raising of the new world of efficiency and participation have been those associated with export industry. It is within the large globalized firms which increasingly dominate the Swedish economy that there has been most interest in the establishment of a discursive link between notions of co-determination; the performance capacity of individual wage-earners and levels of productivity. It is no surprise that those who have sought to label Swedish post-Fordism have christened it 'Volvoism' (Boyer, 1989). In fact, not only have particular large firms played an important role in the making of the new language of reform but also specific workplaces. It would appear as though many of the authors of the new world of work have no trouble in giving a concise account of its evolution in terms of the move from Volvo Kalmar to Volvo Uddevalla (Agurén, 1985; Nilsson, 1987).

Clearly, a comprehensive survey of the unequal hold of the new shared language of workplace reform on different areas of the Swedish economy is beyond the scope of this paper. We have chosen to focus on the steel and printing industries because they provide a good illustration of the contrasts in approach to workplace reform still visible in Sweden today. Although our primary ambition remains description rather than explanation, as we have already mentioned exposure to international competition as a key factor influencing receptivity to the new language of 'efficiency and participation' we can introduce two additional factors which we also feel are of importance:

Technological configuration: Different industries are locked into different technological trajectories and display contrasting technological configurations. These contrasting histories of technological development shape the receptivity of the industry to any new discourse of restructuring. An industry which has proved technically impervious to Taylorist rationalization is unlikely to be very impressed by a rhetorical 'anti-Taylorism'. With reference to the Swedish steel and printing industries; SSAB's contemporary ('post-Taylorist') reorganization of its steelplants, emphasizing functional integration (e.g. continuous casting, 'hot-linking' and continuous annealing) for the improved synchronization of demand and supply and just-in-time deliveries of strip to 'hard to please' Volvo can be compared with the traditional organizational challenge facing Dagens Nyheter; Sweden's most famous daily newspaper - For Sweden's printers the 'new world' responsibilities of workers for 'quality', 'flexibility' and 'continuity' in production can seem rather familiar. Even within different industries important differences in technological configuration may exist affecting receptivity. Broadly speaking, general printing and commodity steel production have been more 'Taylorist' than newspaper printing and special steel production and are therefore likely to be more amenable to 'anti-Taylorist' rhetoric[11].

Traditional management/labour relations: Following on directly from above, a key factor determining receptivity is whether or not management has traditionally relied on labour to assume responsibility for the detailed planning and smooth running of production. In the Swedish printing industry, the established responsibilities of the print-workers and their union have extended into key areas such as recruitment, training and skill development. Historically, this has meant that the printers have been able to define more or less independently what a 'good job' is and what makes a 'good print-worker'. Therefore, while Swedish steelworkers, who have tended not to enjoy such definitional privileges, are encouraged to support with enthusiasm the contemporary commitments of their employers to 'co-determination', 'participation' and 'human resource development', it is apt for Swedish print-workers to view the same developments with suspicion and a measure of distrust.

With these factors in mind we will now follow the recent development of the workplace politics of steel and printing in Sweden more closely in order to examine the contrasting commitments and contributions made to the new shared language of reform. Special attention will be paid to the pursuit of divergent trade union strategies for restructuring in the two sectors.

Coping with Restructuring in the 1970s: MBL versus Technology Agreements

Both the Swedish steel and printing industries underwent significant structural changes during the 1970s. Steelworkers and printers alike generally accepted the need for major programmes of restructuring and the introduction of new technology. However, while the steelworkers relied on central MBL negotiations to protect their interests in the restructuring process, the printers consistently fought for local technology agreements.

MBL was given something of a baptism of fire when it was applied to the expedient restructuring of the Swedish steel industry in the late 1970s. Over-capacity and the return of competitive pricing in central export markets meant that the immediate agenda for local MBL negotiations was typically comprehensive merger plans and/or the imminent threat of closure. Consequently, the only visible option for local union organization unaccustomed to engaging with production issues usually appeared to be a request for central MBL negotiations in the hope that central union negotiators together with representatives from the government would be able secure a 'fair deal'. In many cases it is not clear that such a deal was won and, although MBL guaranteed the steelworkers a voice in the restructuring process it may ultimately have served mostly to quell their protests over large job losses and help convince them of the inevitability of the changes taking place:

> It may be possible to assert that a formalizing of negotiations speeded up and simplified restructuring within the industry. The time taken from the initiation of local MBL negotiations to the termination of central ones was rarely more than a couple of months. This was often equivalent to the time needed by the firms themselves to complete their programmes for change. If we also take into account that during this period (1977-82), approximately 10,000 jobs disappeared from the industry, it is somewhat surprising that restructuring was able to take place so rapidly without giving rise to the kinds of sweeping protest that arose elsewhere in Europe (Berglund, 1987, p. 250 - our translation).

The rise of local technology agreements in the Swedish printing industry in the early 1970s occurred in connection with the introduction of a new generation of technology encompassing photo-setting and offset printing. The established typographical union (*Typografförbundet*) readily accepted the need for comprehensive modernization and decided to try and develop their traditional involvement with production issues in order to prevent restructuring from taking place at their expense in terms of job losses and the routinization of the labour process (Börjeson, 1989; Ekdahl, 1988). Unlike their colleagues on London's Fleet Street, the Swedish print-workers have responded to new technology by committing themselves to the daunting and protracted task of translating their established skills into a new productive context. Technology agreements have been the key device for guaranteeing print-workers 'rights of access' (*betjäningsrätt*) to both the new technology itself and the retraining required to command it.

After having successfully won their first local technology agreement in 1972, *Typografförbundet* quickly recognized that because every occupational group in the industry was threatened by the introduction of new technology, a strategic readjustment of lines of union representation would have to take place in order to avoid divisive inter-union conflict. Consequently, *Grafiska Fackförbundet* (GF) was founded in 1973 with the merger of *Typografförbundet, Litografförbundet* (the lithographers' union) and the smaller *Bokbindareförbundet* (the bookbinders' union). Since its instigation, GF's self-proclaimed task has been to shape the future of 'graphical work' in Sweden.

GF has defended its tendency to 'go its own way' within the Swedish Labour Movement by maintaining that technology agreements are a more genuine and effective approach to workplace democracy than MBL negotiations. MBL has been interpreted by GF as inadequate legislation which does little to restrain management from rationalizing production on their own terms. When MBL negotiations have been initiated in the printing industry they have seldom resulted in consensus.

A 'Total Productivity' Programme versus 'Total Engagemnent in Production Issues'

The crisis of the steel industry in the 1970s was also a crisis for the steel communities: the cradles of industrialization in Sweden. The survival of the institutional fabric of these communities was quickly interpreted as dependent upon the joint efforts of employers and workers to respond to the new foreign competition. By the beginning of the 1980s a consensus had arisen encompassing the steel employers (*Järnbruksförbundet*), the metalworkers' union (*Metall*)[12] and the white-collar unions (*CF, SIF* and *SALF*) over the urgent need for productivity-enhancing measures. Traditional approaches to productivity were perceived as largely obsolete and unable to guarantee secure employment in the future. A Joint Productivity Committee was formed at the beginning of 1982 and in the initial statement of strategic guidelines the notion of a 'total productivity' approach is introduced implicating all areas of production and all employees in the search for improvements in productivity.

Inspiration has clearly been drawn from the Japanese emphasis on 'total quality control' and explicit reference is made to quality control circles as an interesting social innovation for Swedish steel producers, involving the assignment of significant responsibility to the individual worker for the organization of their own work situation (Jbf-Metall, SIF, SALF and CF, 1982, p. 4).

In the comprehensive study material and promotional films, the Productivity Committee has produced to encourage the widespread adoption of a total productivity approach throughout the Swedish steel industry, the new programme for efficiency is not only portrayed as a means of enhancing competitive performance but also of fulfilling the legal requirements for democracy in the workplace set out in MBL and developed in UVA. The protection of the 'democratic' character of a total productivity approach has led Metall to attack some employers for an opportunistic approach to quality circle activities. Allegedly, a number of employers have had a tendency to use quality circles as means for driving a divisive wedge between Metall and its membership. Union officials have been left on the periphery of circle activities which have taken up issues traditionally dealt with through union channels. In this way employers have betrayed the spirit of UVA by choosing to work against, rather than with, the unions in the battle for industrial progress[13] (Metallarbetaren, 1985, 1986). Such antagonistic management practice is taken as indicative of a persistent, irrational, 'lust for power' which is severely damaging to the Swedish steel industry's long-term chances of survival in global competition. A total productivity approach builds on voluntary cooperation between 'partners of equal merit' (*jämbördiga parter*) and, therefore, can only be seriously pursued after the age-old struggle for power in the workplace has been left on the wayside of history (Metallarbetaren, 1985).

GF perceived the introduction of a new generation of technology in the Swedish printing industry during the 1970s as a threat not only to employment security but also to the traditional involvement of print-workers in the detailed planning and organization of production. Rights of access to the new technology via technology agreements were crucial for the protection of employment but provided no guarantee that printers would be able to preserve their established grip on production. In addition, the provision of new training programmes was also seen as a necessary but still insufficient measure to assure printers continued mastery over their own skills (Börjeson, 1989). What was needed was a new 'total union engagement with production issues' for the faithful translation of print-workers traditional skills into the new productive context (Ekdahl, 1988).

In 1976, with the transition to photo-setting at one of Sweden's largest newspapers, Svenska Dagbladet, GF decided to seek assistance and advice from the newly formed Centre for Working Life (*Arbetslivscentrum*); a research centre for studies in co-determination established in conjuncture with MBL. Svenska Dagbladet was consequently included in a major research programme coordinated by Arbetslivscentrum called DEMOS. This programme involved study circles for workers and group discussion concerning alternative approaches to work organization in connection with the introduction of new technology. These new study circles which aimed to build on historical traditions of trade union engagement with production issues varied significantly from the Japanese-style quality control circles emerging elsewhere in Swedish industry at this time (Bengtson and Sandberg, 1987, pp. 61-62). According to the chairman of GF's Stockholm branch, quality circles have filled 'vacant spaces' which only arise in industries and firms where local union organization has been disinterested in production issues. Such union disinterest allows management to take the initiative and set the agenda for changes in technology and work organization. GF, however, has always strived to occupy the vacant spaces that quality circles invade and alternative study circles have been a contemporary sign of their continued tenancy. These study circles have been instrumental in developing 'the power of printers' words and thoughts' concerning the restructuring of production (Ring and Tillybs, 1988).

The Good Working Life versus Utopia

Metall produced two major reports in the second half of the 1980s which together form the most lucid and detailed statement made by any Swedish trade union on the contemporary era of industrial transformation. These reports are entitled; 'The good working life' and 'Solidaristic labour policy for the good working life' and were presented at Metall's National Congress in 1985 and 1989 respectively. Despite the notion of a 'good' working life the approach taken to rapid techno-economic change is unmistakeably pragmatic.

The two reports build on the assumption of the continuing centrality of efficient industrial production for the maintenance of the Swedish welfare economy. Post-industrialism is a myth; the knowledge and experience of dedicated industrial workers is more important than ever for the protection and improvement of national welfare (Svenska Metallindustriarbetare-förbundet, 1985, p. 14). The contemporary vulnerability of the Swedish economy is due to a fundamental imbalance: industrial production is too small to cover all the social needs which have to be satisfied in the type of welfare system which has been built up in Sweden since the 1930s. This problem of imbalance can only be solved by 'strong growth in the industrial sector' (ibid,

p. 17).

If 'strong growth in the industrial sector' is to be achieved both Swedish metalworkers and their employers will have to accept and accommodate the new global conditions of production which inevitably set the agenda for restructuring. Neither party should attempt to ignore or try to escape these new conditions as they are genuinely inescapable if industrial progress is to be made. They encompass capricious and fragmented markets which crave a flexible response from producers; sophisticated and expensive capital equipment which must be used continuously and well-educated workforces who demand active involvement in the planning and organization of their work (ibid, pp. 130-139). These new conditions will increasingly force employers to offer their employees more responsibility and control over their working lives and will inevitably lead to greater recognition of the mutual dependency of employer and employee:

> Firms depend on the skills and knowledge of workers...An employer can never free himself of this state of dependency. We are dependent on employers for our jobs. We need money - wages - to buy food, clothing and to pay all the expenses in life. We also rely on our work for our sense of pride and self-identity and cannot free ourselves from dependency on the firm. There exists, therefore, a state of mutual dependency in our society between employees and employers, between labour and capital. A long time ago, it was believed that this state of dependency would be abolished for ever (Svenska Metallindustriarbetareförbundet, 1989, p. 139).

Allegedly, both Swedish industry and the Swedish nation have rarely achieved any significant objectives through confrontation between different groups. Most progress has been made when different interests have cooperated (Svenska Metallindustriarbetareförbundet, 1989, p. 18). A rapid adjustment to the new global conditions of production is of benefit to all. Metall is not putting forward a strategy for the good working life for reasons of social justice alone. All theories that maintain that there might be a contradiction between the good working life and rational and efficient production can be dismissed without hesitation. The good working life is one of the essential foundations on which industrial development, competitive power and economic growth can and must be built for the future (Svenska Metallindustriarbetareförbundet, 1989). Solidaristic labour policy (*solidarisk arbetspolitik*) is to be the basis for a born again Swedish Model; well-adpated to the pressures of new times. The relationship between solidaristic labour policy and traditional solidaristic wages policy is complementary: together they can guarantee the smooth and continuous modernization of the Swedish economy into the next century. Metall wishes to present solidaristic labour policy as a policy objective for the Swedish Labour Movement in general and hopes to gain the support of a Social Democratic government for its rapid implementation (Svenska Metallindustriarbetarförbundet, 1989). Collectively, the unions can wield MBL and UVA in order to put pressure on recalcitrant employers to cooperate in the creation of the good working life but, ultimately, the state will still have to enforce new regulations and inflict new penalties if it is going to be made available for all employees as a right. In addition, major changes in labour market and education policy are inevitable if solidaristic labour policy is to be taken seriously. As has been the case with traditional solidaristic wages policy, those firms which do not fulfil their obligations to Swedish society will eventually have to be closed down and their employees retrained for a grant-worthy encounter with the good working life on the new high productivity frontier.

In comparison with Metall's full-blown manifesto for the reform of the Swedish welfare economy, GF's attempts to shape the future of the Swedish printing industry tend to pale into insignificance. This is unfortunate as GF's approach to restructuring is potentially far more ambitious than Metall's. Whereas Metall is prepared, even eager, to accept and accommodate the new global conditions of production, GF wishes to continue challenging them. For GF the 'facts of industrial life' are never given. Throughout the 1970s and '80s they have strived to develop and implement their own independent vision of what the future of 'graphical work' should be. This has been a vision encompassing the integration of different areas of production and the negotiated reallocation of work tasks between different occupational groups. The strengthening of this vision and the preservation of trade union solidarity has depended on the 'tearing down of both physical and psychological barriers' between different occupations in the workplace (Ekdahl, 1988, p. 159).

In the aftermath of the DEMOS Programme, a new research programme was initiated in cooperation with Arbetslivscentrum: the UTOPIA Programme. The scale of this programme was larger, encompassing print unions and researchers from Norway and Denmark as well as Sweden. Projects in all three countries during the 1970s had shown that attempts to influence the introduction of new technology were continuously thwarted by the 'built-in' qualities of the new technologies themselves. The opportunities for developing print workers' established skills and securing their continued centrality in the production process were limited by the design of the new technology available on the market. Therefore, the mighty ambitions of the UTOPIA Programme were formulated as follows:

...to contribute to the development of powerful tools to be used by skilled graphical workers...(To influence) both the development of technology and the development of human skills...(To offer) both quality in work and product' (UTOPIA, 1984, p. 6 - our translation).

Although, UTOPIA's hopes of finding commercially-viable alternatives to existing technology have largely remained unfulfilled, the Programme has succeeded in advancing trade union engagement with production issues into previously unexplored territory. After DEMOS and UTOPIA, GF now possesses such a wealth of knowledge concerning the properties and capabilities of new technology in the printing industry that their understanding of the future of graphical work is more or less invulnerable to any new discourses of restructuring bearing false managerial dreams or promises. By pursuing an active and offensive strategy in support of modernization GF has been able to largely safeguard the occupational identities of their members by reshaping them (Nilsson and Sandberg, 1988, p. 82). They have been aware of the dangers of a 'joint assessment' of the agenda for restructuring and have always insisted on the right to an independent vision of the future of the industry (GF Stockholm, 1988, p. 24)[14]. Old traditions have informed new challenges and GF's language of modernization has been filled with a self-confident blend of fresh and familiar terms challenging the voice of authority. As one of GF's leading figures warns:

Passive and submissive workers accept the word of authority. They lack the self-esteem to answer back; to think for themselves; to define their own interests. They fall prey to the myth of technological necessity and the inevitability of change decreed by the powerful (Ring, 1981, p. 303 - our translation).

Conclusion

In this paper we have focused on a 'new world of work' in Sweden as a discursive rather than ontological reality. Our primary aim has been to examine assertions, rather than make assertions, about the contemporary transformation of Swedish capitalism - we remain reluctant to join the ranks of 'expert opinion'. We believe such reluctance is justified because 'authoritative words' on the future of work are rarely innocent: they usually contain a desire to amplify the new realities of which they speak. Agreements like UVA and Metall's manifesto for the 'good working life' are not simply strategic responses to the new imperatives of capitalist production; they are partly constitutive of these imperatives and are playing an important role in the advance of their rule. As major contributions to a new and powerful discourse of workplace reform they represent concerted attempts to foreclose on the future of Swedish capitalism - to colonize an essentially open prospect with a new vision of capitalist common sense. They seek to legislate over how and why new technology should be adopted and claim to offer a strategy for prevailing in global competition which is both sensible and humane.

It has also been our aim to avoid implying that languages of workplace reform can be shared to the extent that all other modes of discourse defining alternative patterns of development cease to emerge. By referring to contrasting discourses of restructuring and trade union strategies within the Swedish steel and printing industries, we have sought to reveal a persistent measure of ambiguity and contingency in the identity of Swedish post-Fordism. Three factors have been put forward which we consider to be of importance in the explanation of the unequal hold of the new shared language of reform across different sectors of the Swedish economy: exposure to international competition, technological configuration and established management-labour relations. Steel and printing are both old industries in Sweden at the forefront of new worlds of work - two very different new worlds of work. The articulation of a 'total productivity' approach within the political apparatuses of steel was an early attempt to give concrete expression to the spirit of UVA and Metall's manifesto for the 'good working life' is of vital significance for the qualitative enlargement of the hegemony of the discourse of 'efficiency and participation'. The developmental trajectory of the printing industry is in stark contrast to that of steel because it continues to be guided by a resilient 'culture of resistance' amongst print-workers which has always repulsed 'joint assessment' and intellectual collaboration between labour and management over the agenda for restructuring. As yet the winds of 'efficiency and participation' have been unable to erase the print-workers' unorthodox words.

Despite the ambiguities and contingencies that remain in the identity of the post-Fordist world of work in Sweden, there can be no doubt that the range of competing discourses of workplace reform is much narrower today than in the 1970s, at the height of the crisis of Swedish Fordism. The gospel of 'efficiency and participation' is now sufficiently shared to allow us to talk of a return to the consensual 1960s and a restabilization of the reciprocal expectations of capitalist enterprise. Compared with the old-style Swedish Model, the foundations of the new variant appear to involve the granting of greater rewards to Swedish wage-earners in return for the acceptance of extended duties. UVA and solidaristic labour policy imply a much more intimate and intense cooperation between labour and capital in Sweden than in the past. In future, they shall not only enter into negotiations at the central level to decide the just division of the fruits of industrial progress; they shall also work together on a routine everyday basis for the simultaneous achievement of a 'good working life' and enhanced business efficiency. By launching the notion of solidaristic labour policy and encouraging the Swedish Labour Movement to abandon its historic struggle for power in the workplace, in favour of a new phase of sensible collaboration, Metall are clearly paving the way for a new 'business unionism' in Sweden, comparable with the brand of company unionism visible in Japan. Ultimately, however, the newly conceived Swedish Model may yet prove to be stillborn. Linking capitalist efficiency to what can be enduringly classified as the 'good working life' for the majority of the working population is an awesome task. As was the case with Swedish Fordism, the incoherencies and inconsistencies of Swedish post-Fordism will most likely make their first appearance in the workplace and probably in the not too distant future.

Notes

1. We would like to thank Hans Glimell, Charles Edquist, Klaus Nielsen, Sten Karlsson and Maureen McKelvey for their comments on earlier drafts of this paper. The authors are also grateful to the Swedish Council for the Planning and Coordination of Research (FRN) and the Swedish Work Environment Fund (AMF) for supporting the research on which this paper is based.

2. Burawoy distinguishes the politics of production as follows:
   '...the process of production is not confined to the labour process - to the social relations into which men and women enter as they transform raw materials into useful products with instruments of production. It also includes political apparatuses which reproduce those relations of the labour process through the regulation of struggles. I call these struggles the politics of production or simply production politics' (Burawoy, 1985, p. 122). A focus on 'language' as an important arena of struggle is inspired firstly by the 'languages of class' literature - e.g. Burke and Porter (1987); Gray (1986, 1987); Sonenscher (1984) and Stedman-Jones (1983).

3. For the meaning of keywords see, of course, Williams (1983). See also Williams (1989).

4. Whether or not the technological paradigm for the post-Fordist era in Sweden is best described as 'flexible specialization', 'flexible automation' or 'just-in-time production' is beyond the scope of this paper. However, we will take this opportunity to stress the importance of an indigenous 'capital rationalization movement' dating from the early 1960s and making its major breakthrough in industrial engineering circles in the mid 1970s. See Björkman and Lundqvist (1981), Edquist and Glimell (1989) and Helgeson (1986).

5. A central difficulty of capitalist production is identified by Burawoy as the continual translation of labour-power, the capacity to work, into sufficient labour and the necessary application of effort to provide both wages and profits for the survival of the firm (1985, 123).

6. Utvecklingsrådet was set up in 1966 with representatives from both LO and SAF to encourage greater cooperation in the solution of problems associated with the pace and direction of technological change. From the outset 'job satisfaction' and the 'mental health' of workers were identified as important issues (Karlsson, 1989).

7. This is in relation to whether or not areas of production should be contracted out to external sources. This exception can be largely explained by the fact that, in this one instance, union interests coincide with those of the state and the effective control of employers' abilities to avoid taxation and insurance payments (Simonson, 1988, p. 134).

8. Due to this paradox, MBL has been given the popular nickname 'the horn' ('tutan'). The jest usually proceeds as follows: 'Before, the boss use to drive right over us. Now he has to sound the horn first - before driving right over us.'

9. Another important medium is the new 'Efficiency and Participation Council' (*Rådet för Utvecklingsfrågor*) with a board of representatives from LO, SAF and TCO; highly reminiscent of the old 'Development Council' (Utvecklingsrådet). Like its predecessor (which fell victim to the radicalism of the '70s) the new Council shall commission research for the smooth resolution of the problems associated with rapid technological progress. An initial theme for investigation is the network given by the keywords - 'Technology - Economy - People - Business'.

10. Of course, the more severe the problem can be made to appear the more drastic the measures that can be demanded. There is a stark contrast between the sober reports provided by the Swedish Central Office of Statistics on the 'future supply of labour-power' and SAF and LO's sensational accounts of imminent crisis (SCB, 1989; Nilsson, 1989).

11. This encourages the question: what are we comparing? What sort of existence do economic sectors and industries have? Industries typically encompass a range of related production systems which are always in a constant state of flux (Storper and Walker, 1989). Is it meaningful to talk of a steel industry when the inter-industry links between steel users and producers are in many senses stronger than the intra-industry links between different steel producers themselves? All we can say here is that the first step towards coping with complexity is recognizing it.

12. Svenska Metallindustriarbetareförbundet (Metall), founded in 1888, on the eve of the breakthrough of modern industry in Sweden, are a crucial 'work-materia' union which have played a major role in shaping the historical identity of the Swedish Labour Movement. Although Metall's numerical strength is now matched by the public-sector union SKAF, they remain enormously influential with their membership concentrated in the most 'globalized' sectors of the Swedish economy; not only in steel firms but also in engineering giants like SKF, ABB, Electrolux, SAAB and of course Volvo.

13. UVA does refer to something similar to quality circles - 'workplace meetings' (*arbetsplatsträffar*) - as a possible form for employee participation in development work. The topics to be discussed in such meetings should ideally be relatively broad-ranging (UVA, para. 5, moment 3).

14. The most immediate threat to GF's grip on the industry comes from an expansive group of heterogeneous small firms offering specialized printing services, e.g. 'pronto printing', 'desktop agencies'. These firms rarely have more than 15 employees and are largely 'union free' (Börjeson, 1990).

References

Abrahamson, P. (1987), 'Dualisation of the welfare state - towards a claimants society?', Paper, The 14th Nordic Sociological Conference, Tampere.

Adamy, W. (1988), 'Deregulierung des Arbeitsmarktes - Zwischenbilanz des Beschäftigungsförderungsgesetzes', *WSI-Mitteilungen* 8, 475-482.

Adler, P. (1986a), When knowledge is the critical resource, knowledge management is the critical task, Mimeograph, Department of Industrial Engineering and Engineering Management, Stanford University, September.

Adler, P. (1986b), Automation and skill: new directions, Mimeograph Department of Industrial Engineering and Engineering Management, Stanford University, October.

Aglietta, M. (1974), *Accumulation et regulation du capitalisme en longue periode. Exemple des Etats-Unis (1870-1970)*, Paris, INSEE.

Aglietta, M. (1979a), *A Theory of Capitalist Regulation*, London, New Left Books (French edition 1976).

Aglietta, M. (1979b), 'Die gegenwärtigen Grundzüge der Internationalisierung des Kapitals' in Deubner, Ch. et.al., Hrsg., *Die Internationalisierung des Kapitals. Neue Theorien in der Internationalen Diskussion*, Frankfurt, Campus.

Aglietta, M. (1982), World Capitalism in the Eighties, *New Left Review*, 136.

Aglietta, M. (1986), *La fin des divises clé*, Paris, La Découverte.

Aglietta, M. and Brender, A. (1984), *Les métamorphoses de la société salariale*, Paris, Calmann-Lévy.

Aglietta, M. and Orlean, A. (1982), *La violence de la monnaie*, Paris, P.U.F.

Agurén, S. (1985), *Volvo Kalmar Revisited: ten years of experience*, Stockholm, Rådet för Utvecklingsfrågor.

Agurén, S. (1988), *Working Together for a Better Business*, Stockholm, Rådet för Utvecklingsfrågor.

Agurén, S. and Edgren, J. (1979), *Annorlunda Fabriker*, Stockholm, SAF's Förlagssektion.

Alestalo, M. and Uusitalo, H. (1986), 'Finland' in Flora, P. (ed.), *Growth to Limits*, Berlin and New York, Walter de Gruyter.

Allardt, E. (1989), 'Finland as a Nordic Country' in Engman, M. and Kirby, D. (eds), *Finland: People, Nation, State*, London, Hurst and Company.

Allen, J. and Massey, D. (eds) (1988), *The Economy in Question. Restructuring Britain*, London, Sage.

Altvater, E. (1987), *Sachzwang Weltmarkt. Verschuldungskrise, blockierte Industrialisierung, ökologische Gefährdung - der Fall Brasilien*, Hamburg, VSA-Verlag.

Altvater, E. and Hübner, K. (1986), 'Neokonservative Dilemmata', *Gewerkschaftliche Monatshefte*, Nr. 1.

Altvater, E., Hübner, K. and Stanger, M. (1983), *Alternative Wirtschaftspolitik jenseits des Keynesianismus. Wirtschaftspolitische Optionen der Gewerkschaften in Westeuropa*, Opladen, Westdeutscher Verlag.

Altvater, E. and Hübner, K. (1987), 'Ursachen und Verlauf der

337

Internationalen Schuldenkrise', in Altvater, E., Hübner. K., Lorentzen, J. and Rojas, R. (Hrsg.) *Die Armut der Nationen. Handbuch zur Schuldenkrise von Argentinien bis Zaire,* Berlin, Rotbuch Verlag.

Altvater,E., Hoffmann, J. and Semmler, W. (1979), *Vom Wirtschaftswunder zur Wirtschaftskrise,* Berlin, Olle and Wolter.

AMF (1990), *En Ny Arbetsvärld,* Stockholm, Utvecklingsprogrammet

Amin, A. and Dietrich, M. (1990) 'From hierarchy to "hierarchy": The dynamics of contemporary corporate restructuring in Europe', Paper to the EAEPE conference in Florence, November 15-17, to be published in Amin, A. and Dietrich, M. (eds) (1991) *Towards a New Europe. Structural Change in the European Economy,* Edward Elgar, Aldershot.

Amin, A. and Robins, K. (1990), 'The re-emergence of regional economies? The mythical geography of flexible accumulation', *Environment and Planning D: Society and Space,* 8, pp. 7-34.

Amoroso, B. (1990), 'Development and Crisis of the Scandinavian Model of Labour Relations in Denmark', in Baglione, G. and Crouch, C. (eds), *European Industrial Relations. The Challenge of Flexibility,* London, Sage.

AMU Gruppen (1988), *Verksamhetsberrättelse,* Stockholm.

Andersen, E.S. and Lundvall, B.-Å. (1988), 'Small national systems of innovation facing technological revolutions: an analytical framework' in Freeman, C. and Lundvall, B-Å. (eds), *Small Countries Facing the Technological Revolution,* London, Printer.

Andersson, J.O. (1987), 'The economic policy strategies of the Nordic countries' in Keman, H. et al. (eds), *Coping with the Economic Crises. Alternative Responses to Economic Recession in Advanced Industrial Societies,* London, Sage.

Andersson, J.O. (1989), 'Controlled Restructuring in Finland', *Scandinavian Political Studies,* 12, 4, 373-389.

Andersson, J.O. and Mjøset, L. (1987), 'The Transformation of the Nordic Models', *Cooperation and Conflict,* 22.

Anshelm, J. (1990), *Förnuftets Brytpunkt,* Stockholm, Bonniers.

Aoki, M. (1986), 'Horizontal vs Vertical Information Structure in the Firm', *American Economic Review,* 76. (5).

Aoki, M. (1987), A microtheory of the Japanese economy; information, incentives, and games, Mimeograph, Department of Economics, Stanford University.

Arbejdsministeriet et al. (1986), Debatoplæg om vækst og omstilling, Copenhagen, Arbejdsministeriet

Arrow, K. J. (1962), 'The Economic Implications of Learning by Doing', *Review of Economic Studies,* June.

Atkinson, J. (1984), *Flexibility, Uncertainty and Manpower Management,* IMS Report 89.

Atkinson, J. (1987), 'Flexibility or Fragmentation?', *Labour and Society,* 12 (1).

Ayres, R.U. and Miller, S. (1981), Robotics, CAM, and industrial productivity, *National Productivity Review,* 1, 42-60.

Baethge, M. and Oberbeck, H. (1985), 'Zur Entwicklung von Arbeit und Beschäftigung im Dienstleistungssektor' in Alvater, E. and Baethge, M., *Arbeit 2000. Über die Zukunft der Arbeitsgesellschaft,* Hamburg, VSA-Verlag.

Baethge, M. and Oberbeck, H. (1986), *Zukunft der Angestellten. Neue Technologien und berufliche Perspektiven in Büro und Verwaltung,* Frankfurt, Campus.

Barkin, S. (1987), 'The Flexibility Drive in Western Europe', *Relations industrielles,* 42 (1).

Barnes, R.M. (1980), *Motion and Time Study Design and Measurement of Work* (7. Edition), New York.

Barnett, C. (1986), *The Audit of War. The Illusion and Reality of Britain as a Great Nation,* London, Macmillan.

Barou, Y. and Keizer, B. (1984), *Les grandes économies,* Paris, Seuil.

Basle, M. Mazier, J. and Vidal, J.F. (1984), *Quand les crises durent...* Paris, Economica.

Bassett, P. (1986), *Strike Free. New Industrial Relations in Britain,* London, Macmillan.

Beck, U. (1986), *Die Risikogesellschaft. Auf dem Weg in eine andere Moderne,* Frankfurt/Main, Suhrkamp.

Becker, U. (1989), 'Akkumulation, Regulation und Hegemonie. Logische Korrespondenz oder Historische Konstellation', *Politische Vierteljahresschrift,* Heft 2, 230-253.

Bengtson, G. and Sandberg, Å. (1987), *Kvalitetscirklar - en översikt om bakgrund och erfarenheter,* Arbetsrapport, Sociologiska Institutionen, Uppsala Universitet.

Bentzon, K.H. (ed.) (1988), *Fra vækst til omstilling. Modernisering af den offentlige sektor,* København, Nyt fra Samfundsvidenskaberne.

Benyon, J. et al (1990), 'Opencast coalmining and the politics of coal production', *Capital and Class,* 40, 89-114

Berger, S. (ed.) (1981), *Organizing Interest in Western Europe: Pluralism, Corporatism and the Transformations of Politics,* Cambridge University Press, UK.

Berggren, C. (1988), 'New Production Concepts' in Final Assembly - The Swedish Experience', in Dankbaar, B. Jürgens, U., Malsch, T. (eds) *Die Zukunft der Arbeit in der Automobilindustrie,* Berlin, Sigma.

Berglund, B. (1987), *Kampen om Jobben,* Göteborg, Meddelanden från Ekonomisk-Historiska Institutionen vid Göteborgs Universitet 56.

Berrefjord, O., Nielsen, K. and Pedersen, O.K. (1989), 'Forhandlings-økonomi i Norden - en indledning' in Nielsen, K. and Pedersen, O.K. (eds), *Forhandlingsøkonomi i Norden,* København, Jurist- og Økonomforbundets Forlag.

Berrefjord, O. and Nore, P. (1988), 'Political and Economic Policy Planning - Exorcism and Laws of Gravity', *Scandinavian Political Studies,* 2, 103-114.

Beyleveld, D. and Brownsword, R. (1986), *Law as a Moral Judgment,* London, Sweet and Maxwell.

Birkinshaw, P. (1988), *Freedom of Information; the Law, the Practice and Ideal,* London, Weidenfeld and Nicolson.

Birkinshaw, P., Harden, I. and Lewis, N. (1990), *Government by Moonlight; the Hybrid Parts of the State,* London, Unwin Hyman.

BIS (1987), *Geschäftsbericht 1986/87,* Basel.

Bishop, M.W. and Kay, J.A. (1988), *Does Privatization Work?,* London Business School.

Bishop, M.W. and Kay, J.A. (1989), 'Privatization in the United Kingdom: Lessons from Experience', *World Development,* 17 (5), 643-657.

Björkman, T. and Lundqvist, K. (1981), *Från MAX till PIA,* Malmö, Arkiv Avhandlingsserie 12.

Blackburn, P., Coombs, R. and Green, K. (1985), *Technology, Economic Growth, and the Labour Process,* London, Macmillan.

Boje, T. (1991), 'Flexibility and fragmentation in the Labour market. Recent trends in the structuring of employment and industrial relations', Paper to the EAEPE conference in Florence, November 15-17, to be published in Amin, A. and Dietrich, M. (eds) (1991) *Towards a New Europe. Structural Change in the European Economy,* Edward Elgar, Aldershot.

Börjeson, M. (1989), 'Typograferna och Tekniken', *Arbetsnotat 48,* Tema T: Universitetet i Linköping.

Börjeson, M. (1990), 'Grafisk Industri, Teknik och Arbete', *Arbetsnotat 64,* Tema T, Universitetet i Linköping.

Boulding, K. E. (1985), *The World as a Total System,* Beverly Hills, Sage Publications.

Bosworth, B.P and Rivlin, A.M. (eds) (1987), *The Swedish Economy,* Washington D.C The Brookings Institution.

Bowles, S. and Edwards, R. (1985), *Capitalism,* New York, Holt Reinhart.

Boyer, R. (1983), L'introduction du taylorisme en France à la lumière de recherches rècentes. Quels apports et quels enseignements pour le temps présent? Mimeograph CEPREMAP no. 8313, *Travail et emploi,* no. 18, Octobre-Decembre.

Boyer, R. (1985), The influence of Keynes on French economic policy: past and present, in Wattel, H.L. (ed.) *The Policy Consequences of John Maynard Keynes,* New York, Sharpe.

Boyer, R. (ed.) (1986a), *Capitalismes fin de siècle,* Paris, PUF.

Boyer, R. (1986b), *La théorie de la régulation: une analyse critique,* Paris, La Découverte.

Boyer, R. (1987), 'Labour Flexibilities: Many Forms, Uncertain Effects', *Labour and Society,* vol 12, no. 1.

Boyer, R. (ed.) (1988a) *The Search for Labour Market Flexibility. The European Economies in Transition,* Oxford, Clarendon Press (French edition 1986).

Boyer, R. (1988b), 'Regulation', in Eatwell, J. et al. *Marxian Economics. The New Palgrave Dictionary of Economics,* London, Macmillan, pp. 126-128.

Boyer, R. (1988c), 'Technical change and the theory of regulation ', in Dosi, G. et al. (eds), *Technical Change and Economic Theory,* London and New York, Pinter.

Boyer, R. (1988d), 'New technologies and employment in the 1980s: From science and technology to macroeconomic modelling', in Kregel, J.A., Martzner, E. and Roncaglia, A. (eds), *Barriers to Full Employment,* London, Macmillan.

Boyer, R. (1989), *New Directions in Management Practices and Work Organization: general principles and national trajectories,* paper prepared for the OECD Conference 'Technological Change as a Social Process - Society, Enterprises and the Individual', Helsinki, December 11-13.

Boyer, R. and Coriat, B. (1986) (untitled), Paper presented to Conference on

Technology, Innovation, in Venezia, March.

Boyer, R. and Coriat, B. (1987), Technical flexibility and macro stabilization, in Arganceli F., David, P.A. and Dosi, G. (eds) (1988), *The Diffusion of New Technologies*, Volume 2, Advances in Modelling Technology Diffusion, London, Oxford University Press.

Boyer, R. and Coriat, B. (1987), 'Is a New Mode of Development Emerging? Technical Flexibility and Macro Stabilisation: A Tentative Analysis', in André, Ch., Boyer, R., Delorme, R., Leborgne, D. and Petit, P. (dir.) *Aspects De La Crise*, Paris, Tome I.

Boyer, R. and Mistral, J. (1982), *Accumulation, Inflation, Crises*, Paris, Presses Universitaires de France, 2e Edition.

Boyer, R. and Ralle, P. (1986), Croissances nationales et contrainte extérieure avant et après 1973 et L'insertion internationale conditionne-t-elle les formes nationales d'emploi?, *Revue Economies et Sociétés*, Tome XX, no. 1, série P29, janvier, pp. 117-144 et 145-168.

Briggs, A. (1961), 'The Welfare State in Historical Perspective', *Archives Europeennes de Sociologie, 2*, 221-58.

Briggs, A. and Spicer, J. (1986), *The Franchise Affair*, London, Century Hutchinson.

Brindley, T., Rydin, Y. and Stoker, G. (1989), *13 Remaking Planning: the politics of urban change in the Thatcher Years*, London, Unwin Hyman.

Bromley, S. (1988), *From Fordism to post-Fordism: Old Wine in New Bottles?*, Sheffield, unpublished typescript.

Bruno, S. (1987), 'Micro-Flexibility and Macro-Rigidity. Some Notes on Expectations and the Dynamics of Aggregate supply', *Labour, 1* (2), 127-151.

Buci-Glucksmann, C. and Therborn G. (1982), 'Formen der Politik und Konzeptionen der Macht', in *Neue soziale Bewegungen und Marxismus, Argument Sonderband, AS 78*, Berlin.

Buci-Glucksmann, C. and Therborn, G. (1983), *Le Defi Social Democrate*, Paris, Maspero.

Bull, M. (1989), *Ålderschocken*, Göteborg, RE-VÄST Seminarierapport 2.

Burawoy, M. (1985), *The Politics of Production*, London, Verso.

Burke, P. and Porter, R. (1987), *The Social History of Language*, Cambridge, Cambridge University Press.

Cairncross, A. (1985), *Years of Recovery*, London, Methuen.

Campinos-Dubernet, M. (1983), Productivité du travial et hétérogénéité sectorielle dans le BTP. Communication au Colloque organisé par le Plan Construction *Letravail en chantiers. Emploi, qualification, technologie*, 16-17, Novembre.

Cardif, B. (1985), Progrès technologique, mutations structurelles et emploi, *Economie Européenne*, no. 25, September.

Chan-Lee, J.H. and Sutch, J. (1985), 'Profits and rates of return', *OECD Economic Studies*, No. 5, Paris.

Chesnais, F. (1986), 'Science, technology and competitiveness', *STI Review*, no. 1, August.

Christiansen, N.F. (1984), 'Denmark: End of the Idyll', *New Left Review*, 144, March-April.

Clark, J. (1989), New Technology and Industrial Relations', *New Technology, Work and Employment*, 4 (1), 5-17.

Clarke, S. (1988), 'Overaccumulation, class struggle and the regulation approach', *Capital and Class*, 36, 36-62.

Coggan, P. (1988), *The Money Machine: how the City works*, Hamondsworth, Penguin.

Commons, J. R. (1931), 'Institutional Economics', *American Economic Review*, 21, December.

Coopers and Lybrand Associates (1984), *Streamlining the Cities. An Analysis of the Government's Proposals for Reorganising Local Government in the Six Metropolitan Counties*, London.

Coriat, B. (1979), *L'atelier et le chronomètre*, Paris, Bourgois, 2e édition (1982).

Crouch, C. (1986), 'Conservative Industrial Relations Policy: Towards Labour Exclusion?', in Jacobi, O. et al. (eds), *Economic Crisis, Trade Unions and the State*, London, Croom Helm.

Cummings, T.G. and Molloy, E.S. (1977), *Improving Productivity and the Quality of Worklife*, New York, Praeger.

Dahmén, E. (1988), '"Development Blocks" in Industrial Economics', *Scandinavian Economic History Review*, 1.

Daniel, W.W. (1970), *Beyond the Wage-Work Bargain*, London, PEP.

Dankbaar, B., Jürgens, U. and Malsch, T. (eds) (1988), *Die Zukunft der Arbeit in der Automobilindustrie*, Berlin, Sigma.

Davis, M. (1986), *Phoenix im Sturzflug*, Berlin, Rotbuch Verlag.

de Bernis, G. (1988), Propositions for an analysis of the crisis', *International Journal of Political Economy*, 18 2, 44-66.

de Cecco, M. (1979), 'Origins of the Post-War Payments System', *Cambridge Journal of Economics*, No. 3.

de Cecco, M. (ed.) (1987) *Changing Money. Financial Innovation in Developed Countries*, Oxford, University Press.

de Geer, H. (1989), *I Vänstervind och Högervåg*, Stockholm, Allmänna Förlaget.

de Vroey, M. (1984), 'A Regulation Approach Interpretation of the Contemporary Crisis', *Capital and Class*, 23.

Debier, J. C., Deléage, J.P. and Hémery, D. (1986), *Les Servitudes de la Puissance: une histoire de l'energie*, Paris, Flammarion.

Delorme, R. (1990), 'Economic Intervention in the History of the French and other European States: A Comparative Study', Paper prepared for the Conference on The Market and the State in the 1990s, University of Sao Paulo, October 25-26 1990.

Delorme, R. and Andre, C. (1983), *L'etat et l'economie*, Paris, Seuil.

Denisson, E.F. (assisted by Poullier, J.P.) (1967), *Why Growth Rates Differ?*, Brookings Institution, Washington D.C.

Dertouzos, M., Lester, R. K. and Solow, R. M. (1989), *Made in America*, Cambridge, Mass., The MIT Press.

Devine, P. (1988), *Democracy and Economic Planning*, London, Polity.

Donati, P. (1983), 'Natura, Problemi e limiti del Welfare State: un intepretazione', in Rossi, P. and Donati, P. (eds), *Welfare State: Problemi e Alternativi*, Milano, Franco Angeli.

Dore, R. (1986), *Flexible Rigidities. Industrial Policy and Structural Adjustment in the Japanese Economy 1970-1980*, London, Athione Press.

Dosi, G. (1987), Some notes on patterns of production, industrial organization and international competitiveness, Mimeograph prepared for the meeting on 'Production reorganization and skills', BRIE, University of California, Berkeley, September 10-12.

Dosi, G. (1988), 'Sources, Procedures and Microeconomic Effects of Innovation', *Journal of Economic Litterature,* XXVI (3), September.

Dosi, G. et al. (1988), *Technical Change and Economic Theory,* London and New York, Pinter.

Douglas, M. (1986), *How Institutions Think,* Routledge and Kegan Paul.

Drache, D. (1983), A note on regulation: il y a plein de choses qui clochent. Tant mieux!, Mimeograph.

Drouin, M.J., Ernst, M. and Wheeler, J.W. (1987), *Western European Adjustment to Structural Economic Problems,* Lanham, New York and London, Hudson Institute.

Dyson, K. (ed.), (1988), *Local Authorities and New Technologies: The European Dimension,* London, Croom Helm.

Edquist, C. and Glimell, H. (1989), *Swedish Frontiers of Change: a guide to the impact of new technologies, work designs and management practices,* A report prepared for the OECD, Draft.

Edquist, C. and Lundvall, B.-Å. (1989), 'Comparing Small Nordic Systems of Innovation', Paper presented at the Maastricht Seminar on National Systems Supporting Technical Progress, nov. 1989, Mimeo.

Edquist, C. and Lundvall, B.-Å. (1990), 'Comparing the Danish and the Swedish Systems of Innovation', Paper prepared for the Colombia University project on National Systems Supporting Technical Advance in Industry and presented at a Conference at Standford University, October 18-19.

Edwards, R. et al. (1986), *Unions in Crisis and Beyond,* Dover, Mass., London.

Ekdahl, L. (1988), *Den Fackliga Kampens Gränser,* Lund, Arkiv.

Elam, M. (1989), 'Puzzling out the post-Fordist Debate: Technology, Markets and Institutions', *Industrial and Economic Democracy,* 11 (1).

Elander, I. (1978), *Det Nödvändiga och det Önskvärda,* Stockholm, Arkiv Avhandlingsserie.

Eliasson, G. (1987), *Technological Competition and Trade in the Experimentally Organized Economy,* IUI, Research Report No. 32, Stockholm, Almqvist and Wiksell.

Erixon, L. (1985), 'What's wrong with the Swedish model? An analysis of its effects and changed conditions, 1974-1985', *Institutet för Socialforskning, Meddelande,* 12.

Esping-Andersen, G. (1985), *Politics Against Markets. The Social Democratic Road to Power,* Princeton, Princeton University Press.

Esping-Andersen, G. (1986), 'Power and Distributional Regimes', *Politics and Society,* 223-256.

Esser, J. and Hirsch, J. (1987), 'Stadtsoziologie und Gesellschaftstheorie. Von der Fordismus-Krise zur "postfordistischen" Regional- und Stadtstruktur' in Prigge, W., Hrsg., *Die Materialität des Städtischen,* Basel and Boston.

Evans, S. and Lewis, R. (1989), 'Destructuring and Deregulation in the Construction Industry' in Stehanie Tailby and Colin Whitson, *Manufacturing Change,* Oxford, Blackwell.

Fagerberg, J. (1988), 'Models of Accumulation and Models of Regulation in a Classic Model of Economic Growth', Paper for the Conference on Regulation Theory, Barcelona, June.

Ferner, A. (1985), 'Political Constraints and Management Strategies', *British Journal of Industrial Relations,* 22 (1).

Ferner, A. (1987), 'Public Enterprise and the Politics of "Commercialism"', *Work, Employment and Society,* 1 (2).

Finansministeriet (1990), *Finansredegørelsen 90,* København.

Flanders, A. (1964), *The Fawley Productivity Agreements,* London, Faber.

Flora, P. (1985), 'On the history and current problems of the welfare state', in Eisenstadt, S.N. and Ahimeir, O. (eds), *The Welfare State and its Aftermath,* London, Croom Helm, pp. 11-30.

Flordh, C. et al. (1971), *Konsten att Dressera Människor,* Stockholm, Prisma.

Florida, R. and Kenney, M. (1989), *High Technology Restructuring in the USA and Japan,* School of Urban and Public Affairs, Carnegie Mellon University, Pittsburgh, USA.

Forum for Industriel Udvikling (1988a), *Introduktion til foranalyse,* København, Forum for Industriel Udvikling.

Forum for Industriel Udvikling (1988b), *Har Danmark en fremtid som industrination?,* København, Forum for Industriel Udvikling.

Fox, A. (1985), *History and Heritage,* London, Allen and Unwin.

Freeman, C. (ed). (1983), *Long Waves in the World Economy,* Kent.

Freeman, C. (ed). (1984), *Design, Innovation and Long Cycles in Economic Development,* Richard Langdon, Department of Design Research, Royal College of Art, London.

Freeman, C. (1987), *Technology Policy and Economic Performance: Lessons from Japan,* London, Pinter.

Freeman, C. (1988a), 'Japan: A New National System of Innovation?', in Dosi, G. et al. (eds), *Economic Theory and Technical Change,* London and New York, Pinter.

Freeman, C. (1988b), 'Introduction', in Dosi, G. et al. (eds), *Economic Theory and Technical Change,* London and New York, Pinter.

Freeman, C. (1989), 'The Third Kondratieff: age of steel, electrification and imperialism', paper prepared for the conference on 'The Long Waves of the Economic Conjuncture', Vrije Universiteit, Brussels, January 12-14.

Freeman, C., Clark, J. and Soete, L. (1982), *Unemployment and technical innovation. A study of long waves and economic development,* Frances London, Printer.

Freeman, C. and Perez, C. (1984), 'Long Waves and New Technology', *Nordisk Tidsskrift for Politisk Ekonomi,* 17, 5-14.

Freeman, C. and Perez, C. (1988), 'Structural crises of adjustment: business cycles and investment behaviour' in Dosi, G. et al. (eds), *Economic Theory and Technical Change,* London and New York, Pinter.

Freeman, C. and Soete, L. (eds) (1987), *Technical Change and Full Employment,* Oxford, Basil Blackwell.

Friedman, G. (1974), *Industrial Society. The Emergence of the Human Problems of Automation,* Toronto, Ayer Co. Publishers.

Frøslev Christensen, J. (1980), *Erhvervsstruktur, teknologi og levevilkår. Del 1,* København, Lavindkomstkommissionen, Arbejdsnotat 12.

Galbraith, J.K. (1967), *The New Industrial State,* Harmondsworth, Penguin.

Gershuny, J. and Miles, I. (1983), *The New Service Economy,* London,

Frances Pinter.

Gertler, M. (1988), 'The limits to flexibility: Comments on the post-Fordist vision of production and its geography', *Transactions of the Institute of British Geographers*, 13.

Gewirth, A. (1978), *Reason and Morality*, Chicago, Chicago University Press.

GF Stockholm (1988), *Facket, Företaget och Solidariteten*, Stockholm, Federativ.

Gibbon, P. (1988), 'Analysing the British Miners' Strike of 1984-5', *Economy and Society*, 17 (2), 129-194.

Gibbon, P. and Bromley, S. (1990), 'From an institution to a business? Changes in the British coal industry', *Economy and Society*, 19 (1), 56-94.

Giedion, S. (1948), *La mecanisation au pouvoir. Contribution à l'histoire anonyme*, Traduction Francaise 1980, Denoël-Gonthier, Paris.

Gjerding, A. et al. (eds) (1990), *Den forsvundne produktivitet. Industriel udvikling i firsernes Danmark*, Jurist og økonomforbundets forlag, Copenhagen.

Glaser, E.M. (1976), *Productivity Gains Through Worklife Improvements*, New York, Harcourt Brace Jovanivich.

Goldsmith, M. and Newton, K. (1985), 'Central-Local Government Relations: the Irresistible Rise of Centralized Power', *West European Politics*, 216-233. Goldthorpe, J.H. (1966), 'Attitudes and Behaviour of Car Assembly Workers: A Deviant Case and a Theoretical Critique', *British Journal of Sociology*, 17 (3).

Goldthorpe, J.H. (1985), 'The End of Convergence: Corporatist and Dualist Tendencies in Modern Western Societies', in idem (ed.), *Order and Conflict in Contemporary Capitalism*, Oxford, Oxford University Press.

Goodman, G. (1986), *The Miners' Strike*, London, Pluto Press.

Gordon, D., Edwards, R. and Reich, M. (1982), *Segmented Work. Divided Workers: The Historical Transformation of labour in the United States*, New York.

Gough, J. (1986), 'Industrial Policy and Socialist Strategy', *Capital and Class*, 29.

Goul Andersen, J. (1986), 'Electoral trends in Denmark in the 1980's', *Scandinavian Political Studies*, 9 (2).

Goul Andersen, J. (1988), 'Vælgernes holdning til den offentlige udgiftspolitik', Bentzon, K.H. (ed.) (1988), *Fra vækst til omstilling. Modernisering af den offentlige sektor*, København, Nyt fra Samfundsvidenskaberne.

Gower, L. (1984), *Review of Investor Protection*, Report Part 1, London, HMSO, Cmnd. 9125.

Graham, I. (1986), 'Japanisation as Mythology', *Industrial Relations Journal*, 19 (1).

Graham, C. and Prosser, T. (1987), 'Privatising Nationalised Industries: Constitutional Issues and New Legal Techniques', *Modern Law Review*, 50, 16-51.

Graham, C. and Prosser, T. (1989), 'The Constitution and the New Conservatism', *Parliamentary Affairs*, 42 (3), 330-349.

Grahl, J. and Teague, P. (1989). 'Labour Market Flexibility in West

Germany, Britain, and France', *West European Politics,* 12 (2), 91-111.

Grahl, J. and Teague, P. (1990), 'A New Deal for Europe?', Paper to the EAEPE conference in Florence, November 15-17, to be published in Amin, A. and Dietrich, M. (eds) (1991) *Towards a New Europe. Structural Change in the European Economy*, Edward Elgar, Aldershot.

Grando, J.M., Margirier, G. and Ruffieux, B. (1980), Rapport salarial et compétitivité des économies nationales: analyse des économies britannique, italienne et ouest allemande depuis 1950, *Thèse Grenoble* 11.

Grant, W.P. (1989), 'The Erosion of Intermediary Institutions', *Political Quarterly,* 60 (1), 10-21.

Gray, R. (1986), 'The Deconstructing of the English Working Class', *Social History,* 11, 363-373.

Gray, R. (1987), 'The Languages of Factory Reform in Britain, c. 1830-1860' in Joyce, P. (ed.), *The Historical Meanings of Work,* Cambridge, Cambridge University Press.

Gretschmann, K. (1986), 'Social Security in Transition: some reflections from a fiscal sociology perspective', mimeo, Florence: European University Institute.

Gunst, J. and Heinesen, E. (1985), *Når staten skal sælges,* København, Jurist-og Økonomforbundets Forlag.

Gustavsen, B. (1986), 'Evolving Patterns of Enterprise Organization: The move towards greater flexibility', *International Labour Review,* 125 (4), 367-381.

Gustavsen, B. and Hethy, L. (1986), 'New Forms of Work Organization: A European Overview', *Labour and Society,* 11 (2), 167-188.

Habermas, J. (1979), *Communication and the Evolution of Society,* London, Heinemann.

Hack, L. (1987), '"Dienstleistungsgesellschaft" oder Strukturwandel der Industrie?', *Links* nr. 208/209, 35ff.

Hack, L. and Hack I. (1986), 'Gesamtarbeiter, aufgemischt und umgeforscht. Veränderte Strukturen industrieller Produktionssysteme', *PROKLA,* Nr. 64, 46ff., Berlin, Rotbuch Verlag.

Hadenius, A. (1986), *A Crisis of the Welfare State? Opinions About Taxes and Public Expenditure in Sweden,* Stockholm, Almqvist and Wiksell International.

Hansen, R. and Søndergård, J. (1988), Erhvervspolitikken og dens administration. Harmoni eller konflikt', *Nordisk Administrativt Tidsskrift,* 4, 488-509.

Harden, I. (1989), 'Regulated Autonomy and the Concept of "Public" and "Private": Organisational Accountability in Britain', TS, Sheffield.

Harden, I. and Lewis, N. (1986), *The Noble Lie: The British Constitution and the Rule of Law,* London, Hutchinson.

Harvey, D. (1987), 'Flexible Akkumulation durch Urbanisierung: Überlegungen zum "Post-Modernism" in den Amerikanischen Städten', *PROKLA,* Nr. 69, Berlin, Rotbuch Verlag.

Harvey, D. (1989), *The Condition of Postmodernity*, Oxford, Basil Blackwell.

Haslam, C., Williams, K. and Williams, J. (1987), *The Breakdown of Austin Rover,* Leamington Spa, Berg.

Häusler, J. and Hirsch, J. (1987), 'Regulation und Parteien im Übergang zum "Post-Fordismus"', *Das Argument,* Nr. 165, 651ff.

Hayek, F. (1960), *The Constitution of Liberty*, London, Routledge and Kegan Paul.

Helgeson, B. (1986), *Arbete, Teknik, Ekonomi*, Luleå, Högskolans Tryckeri.

Hernes, G. (1978), *Forhandlingsøkonomi og blandingsadministrasjon*, Oslo, Universitetsforlaget.

Herr, H. (1986), 'Weltgeld und Währungssystem', Discussion Paper, Wissenschaftszentrum Berlin.

Herr, H. (1987), 'Zur Stabilisierung ökonomischer Prozesse durch institutionelle Regelungen', Discussion Paper, Wissenschaftszentrum Berlin.

Hickel, R. (1987), *Ein neuer Typ der Akkumulation? Anatomie des ökonomischen Strukturwandels - Kritik der Marktorthodoxie*, Hamburg, VSA-Verlag.

Hirsch, J. (1985a), 'Fordismus und Post-Fordismus: die gegenwärtige gesellschaftliche Krise und ihre Folgen', *Politische Viertel-jahresschrift*, 26, Juni.

Hirsch, J. (1985b), 'Auf dem Weg zum Post-Fordismus?', Unpublished TS.

Hirsch, J. (1986), *Der Sicherheitsstaat. Das "Modell Deutschland, seine Krisen und die "neuen sozialen Bewegungen"*, Frankfurt/Main, 2. Auflage.

Hirsch, J. (1988), 'Regulation Theory and Historical-Materialistic Societal Theory. Remarks on a Shaky yet Necessary Relationship', Paper to the Conference on Regulation Theory, Barcelona, June.

Hirsch, J. and Roth, R. (1986), *Das neue Gesicht des Kapitalismus. Vom Fordismus zum Postfordismus*, Hamburg VSA.

Hirschman, A. (1970), *Exit, Voice and Loyalty*, Cambridge, Harvard University Press.

Hirschhorn, L. (1981), The post-industrial labour process, *New Political Science*, Fall, pp. 11-32.

Hirst, P.Q. and Zeitlin, J. (eds), (1988), *Reversing Industrial Decline*, Leamington Spa Berg.

HMSO (1984), *The Audit Commission, The Impact on Local Authorities' Economy, Efficiency and Effectiveness of the Block Grant System*, London.

HMSO (1988a), *Department of Enterprise*, London, DTI.

HMSO (1988b), *Employment for the Nineteen Nineties*, Cmnd. 540, London.

HMSO (1988c), *Improving Management in Government: The Next Steps*, Report to the Prime Minister, OMCS, London.

Hodgson, G. M. (1988), *Economics and Institutions, A Manifesto for a Modern Institutional Economics*, Polity Press.

Holland, S. (1982), *Out of the Crisis*, Frances Pinter, London.

Holloway, J. (1988), 'The Great Bear and Class Struggle', *Capital and Class*, 36, 93-105.

Horwitz, E.C. (1984), 'Export Performances of the Nordic Countires 1965-1982 - A Constant Market-Shares Analysis', in IUI, DØR, ETLA and IØI. *Economic Growth in a Nordic Perspective*.

Hounshell, D.A. (1984), *From the American system to mass production, 1800-1932*, John Hopkins University Press, Baltimore.

Hübner, K. (1989), *Theorie der Regulation. Eine kritische Rekonstruktion eines neuen Ansatzes der Politischen Ökonomie*, Berlin, Sigma Verlag.

Hübner, K. and Mahnkopf, B. (1988), 'Ecole du Regulation. Eine kommentierte Literaturstudie', *Discussion Paper*, Wissenschaftszentrum Berlin.

Hull Kristensen, P. (1989), 'Denmark - An Experimental Laboratory for New Industrial Models', *Entrepreneurship and Regional Development*.

Hull Kristensen, P. (1990), 'Denmarks Concealed Production Culture, Its Socio-Historical Construction and Dynamics at Work', in Borum, F. and Hull Kristensen, P. (eds) *Technological Innovation and Organizational Change - Danish patterns of knowledge, networks and culture*, New Social Science Monographs, Copenhagen.

Hunt, Sir N. (1982), *Report of the Inquiry into Cable Expansion and Broadcasting Policy*, Cmnd. 8679, London, HMSO.

Hyman, R. and Elger, T. (1981), 'Job Controls, the Employers' Offensive and Alternative Strategies', *Capital and Class*, 15.

Hyman, R. (1987), 'Strategy or Structure?' *Work, Employment and Society*, 1 (1).

Hyman, R. (1988), 'Flexible Specialisation: Miracle or Myth?', in Hyman, R. and Streeck, W., *New Technology and Industrial Relations*, Oxford, Blackwell.

Iden, P. (1988), 'Auffälligkeit als Konsequenz von Entscheidenheit', *Frankfurter Rundschau* 27.7., 11.

IG Metall (ed.) (1989a), *Wofür wir streiten. Solidarität und Freiheit*, Internationaler Zukunftkongreß 1988, Köln.

IG Metall (ed.) (1989b), *Solidarität und Freiheit. Leitlinien der IG Metall zur gesellschaftlichen und gewerkschaftlichen Reform*, Frankfurt/Main.

IMF (1987), *International Financial Statistics, Yearbook*, Washington DC.

Income Data Services (1986), *Flexibility at Work*, Study no. 360, April 1986.

Industriministeriet (1986), *Den industripolitiske redegørelse 1986*, København.

IUI, DØR, ETLA and IØI, (1984), *Economic Growth in a Nordic Perspective*, The Industrial Institute for Economic and Social Research, Stockholm.

IUI, ETLA and NØI (1990), *Growth and Integration in a Nordic Perspective*, The Industrial Institute for Economic and Social Research, Stockholm.

Jacobi, O., Jessop, B. and Kastendiek, H. (1985), 'Corporatist and Liberal Responses to the Crisis of Postwar Capitalism', in idem and Marino Regini, (eds), *Capitalist Crisis, Trade Unions, and the State*, London, Croom Helm.

Jbf-Metall-SIF-SALF-CF (1982), *Riktlinjer för Produktivitetsfrämjande Åtgärder*, Produktivitetskommittén'.

Jessop, B. (1982), *The Capitalist State*, Oxford, Martin Robertson.

Jessop, B. (1986), 'The Mid-life Crisis of Thatcherism', *New Socialist*, March.

Jessop, B. (1988), 'Post-Fordismus, Massenintegration, und der Staat: Eine Kritik an Joachim Hirsch', *Das Argument*.

Jessop, B. (1989a), 'Regulation Theory in Retrospect and Prospect', *Economy and Society*, 19 (2), 153-216

Jessop, B. (1989b), 'Polar Bears and post-Fordism. Much less than a self-criticism', University of Essex, Unpublished paper.

Jessop, B. (1989c), 'Neo-Conservative Regimes and the Transition to Post-Fordism: the cases of Great Britain and West Germany', Gottdiener, M. (ed.), *Modern Capitalism and Spatial Development: Accumulation, Regulation and Crisis Theory*, New York, St Martins.

Jessop, B. (1990), 'Fordism and post-Fordism. A Critical Reformulation',

COS Research Report, 16/1990, Center for Public Organization and Management, Copenhagen Business School, Copenhagen.

Jessop, B. et al. (1984), 'Authoritarian Populism, two nations and Thatcherism', *New Left Review*, 147, 87-101.

Jessop, B. et al. (1988), *Thatcherism: a Tale of Two Nations*, Cambridge, Polity.

Jessop, B., Nielsen, K. and Pedersen, O.K. (1991), 'Structural Competitiveness and Strategic Capacities in Scandinavia and Great Britain', *COS Research Report*, Center for Public Organization and Management, Copenhagen Business School, Copenhagen.

Jessop, B. and Stones, R. (1991), 'Old City and New Times: Economic and Political Aspects of Deregulation', in Budd, L. and Whimster, S. (eds), *Global Finamce and Urban Living*, London, Routledge.

Johansen, L.N. and Kolberg, J.E. (1985), 'Welfare State Regression in Scandinavia? The Development of the Scandinavian Welfare States Form 1970 to 1980', in Eisenstadt, S.N. and Ahimeir, O. (eds), *The Welfare State and Its Aftermath*, London and Sydney, Croom Helm.

Johnson, B. (1981), *Aktuelle Tendenser i den Økonomiske Politik under Krisen. Den Nyliberale Tendens*, Aalborg, Aalborg Universitetsforlag.

Johnson, B. (1985), '"Flexibility lost" eller marknaden som patentlösning. En kritik af nyliberalismen', in Persson, K. (ed.), *Utmaning för Norden: alternativ til nyliberalismen: om konkurrenskraft, strukturomvandling och teknisk utveckling i Norden*, Nordens Fackliga Samarbetsorganisation.

Jordan, B. (1985), *The State: Authority and Autonomy*, Oxford, Blackwell.

Jürgens, U., Dohse, K. and Malsch, T. (1985), 'Japan als Orientierungspunkt für den Wandel der industriellen Beziehungen in der US-amerikanischen und der europäischen Automobilindustrie', in Park, S.J. (ed.), *Japanisches Management in der Praxis. Flexibilität oder Kontrolle im Prozeß der Internationalisierung und Mikroelektronisierung*, Berlin, Express-Edition.

Jysk Teknologisk Institut (1989), *Tekniske Handelshindringer*.

Kaldor, N. (1977), The nemesis of Free Trade, in *Collected Writings*, Volume 6, Duckworth, London.

Kamenka, E. and Tay, A. (1975), 'Beyond Bourgeois Individualism: the Contemporary Crisis in Law and Legal Ideology', in Kamenka, E. and Neale, R. (eds), *Feudalism, Capitalism and Beyond*, London, Edward Arnold, p. 127.

Karlsson, S. (1989), 'Vem Älskar Arbetlivsforskare?', *Arbetsnotat* 50, Tema T, Universitetet i Linköping.

Kastendiek, H. (1985), 'The Politics of Industrial Relations - a Persistent Diversity of National Patterns', paper presented at Conference on Labour Exclusion or New Patterns of Cooperation, Institute for Social Research, December 12-15, 1985.

Katzenstein, P.J. (1984), *Corporatism and Change*, Ithaca, Cornell University Press.

Katzenstein, P. J. (1985), *Small States in World Markets*, Ithaca and London, Cornell University Press.

Kern, H. and Schumann, M. (1984a), *Das Ende der Arbeitsteilung? Rationalisierung in der industriellen Produktion*, Munich, Beck.

Kern, H. and Schumann, M. (1984b), 'Work and Social Character: Old and New Contours', *Economic and Industrial Democracy*, 5, 51-71.

Kosonen, P. (1985), 'Public Expenditure in the Nordic Nation-States - the Source of Prosperity or Crisis' in Alparu, R. et al. (eds), *Small States in Comparative Perspective*, Oslo, Norwegian University Press.

Kosonen, P. (1987), *Hyvinvointivaltion haasteet ja pohjoismaiset mallit (The Challenges of the Welfare State and the Nordic Models)*, Tampere, Vastapaino.

Kremp, E. and Mistral, J. (1985), 'Commerce Extérieur Américain: D'ou Vient, où va le Déficit?', *La Documentation Francaise*, No. 22, Paris.

Krieger, J. (1986), *Reagan, Thatcher, and the Politics of Decline*, Cambridge, Polity.

Krüger, A. (1988), 'Die Zukunft gestalten', *Der Arbeitsgeber* 11, 414-416.

Kuhnle, S. (1986), 'Norway' in Flora, P. (ed.), *Growth to Limits. The Western European Welfare States Since World War II*, Berlin and New York, Walter de Gruyter.

Kundig, B. (1984), 'Du taylorisme classique a la "flexibilisation" du systeme productif. L'impact macro-economique des differents types d'organisation du travail industriel', *Critiques de l'economie politique*, 26/27.

Labour Research Department (1989a), 'Attacks on Our Rights', *Labour Research*, May, 9-11.

Lachman, L. M. (1970), *The Legacy of Max Weber*, London, Heineman.

Landes, D. (1969), *The Unbound Prometheus*, Cambridge, Cambridge University Press.

Lash, S. and Urry, J. (1987), *The End of Organized Capitalism*, Cambridge, Polity.

Lash, S. and Bagguley, P. (1988), 'Arbeitsbeziehungen im disorganisierten Kapitalismus. Ein Vergleich von fünf Nationen', *Soziale Welt*, Nr. 3, 239ff.

Lawler, E. E. III (1978), 'The New Plant Revolution', in *Organizational Dynamics*, 6, (3), 3-12.

Lawler, E. E. III (1986), *High-Involvement Management, Participative Strategies for Improving Organizational Preformance*, San Francisco, Jossey-Bass.

Leborgne, D. and Lipietz, A. (1988), 'New Technologies, New Modes of Regulation: Some Spatial Implications', *Space and Society*, 6 (3).

Leborgne, D. and Lipietz, A. (1989), *Pour Eviter L'Europe a Deux Vitesse*, CEPREMAP, Paris

Leibenstein, H. (1987), *Inside the Firm: The Inefficiencies of Hierarchy*, Cambridge Cambridge University Press.

Lewis, N. (1981), 'Towards a Sociology of Lawyering in Public Administration', *Northern Ireland Legal Quarterly*, 32, 89.

Lewis, N. (1988a), 'Undemocratic Centralism and Neo-Corporatism: the New British Constitution', *Bulletin of the Centre for Constitutional Studies*, Alberta.

Lewis, N. (1988b), 'If you see Dicey, will you tell him? Regulatory Problems in British Constitutional Law', *Political Quarterly*, 59, 6.

Lewis, N. (1989), 'A Standing Administrative Conference', *Political Quarterly*, 60.

Lewis, N. and Wiles, P. (1984), 'The Post-Corporate State?', *Journal of Law and Society*, 11, 65.

Lewis, R. (1988), 'Strike-Free Procedures: Are they what they seem?', *Warwick Papers in Industrial Relations*, No. 20, January.

Leys, C. (1985), 'Thatcherism and British Manufacturing', *New Left Review,* 151, May-June, 5-26.

Lindbeck, A. (1986), 'Limits to the Welfare State', *Challenge,* Vol. 28, January-February.

Lindgren, A. (1988), 'Learning to Avoid Labour', *Forskningsrapport,* Tulea 88, 05, Tekniska Högskolan i Luleå.

Lipietz, A. (1979), *Crise et inflation, pourquoi?,* Paris, Maspero.

Lipietz, A. (1985), 'Le national et le regional: quelle autonomie face a la crise capitaliste mondiale?', CEPREMAP, Couverture Orange, No. 8521 Paris.

Lipietz, A. (1988), 'Accumulation, crises and the ways out. Some methodological reflections on the concept of "Regulation"', *International Journal of Political Economy,* 18 (2), 10-43.

Lipietz, A. (1989), 'The Regulation Approach and the Problems of the Current Capitalist Crisis', Paper prepared for an international conference on 'Marxism and the New Global Society', Seoul, Korea, October 25-27.

Listhaug, O. and Aardal, B. (1989), 'Welfare State Issues in the Norwegian 1985 Election: Evidence from Aggregate and Survey Data', *Scandinavian Political Studies,* 12.

Llewellyn, K. (1940), 'The Normative, the Legal and the Law-Jobs', *Yale Law Journal,* 49, 1355

LOM (1985), *Syfte-Bakgrund-Dialog,* Stockholm, ASF.

LOM (1989), *På Väg,* Stockholm, AMF.

Lower, M.D. (1987), 'The Concept of Technology within the Institutionalist perspective', *Journal of Economic Issues,* No. 3, September, pp. 1147-76.

Lundberg, E. (1985), 'The Rise and Fall of the Swedish Model', *Journal of Economic Literature,* Vol. 23, March.

Lundvall, B.-Å. (1988), 'Innovation as an Interactive Process', in Dosi, G., et al., *Technical Change and Economic Theory,* London, Pinter Publishers.

Lutz, B. (1984), *Der kurze Traum immerwährender Prosperität. Eine Neuinterpretation der industriell-kapitalischen Entwicklung im Europa des 20 Jahrhunderts,* Frankfurt, Campus.

Lybeck, J.A. (1986), *The Growth of Government in Developed Economies,* Aldershot, Gower.

MacInnes, J. (1987), *Thatcherism at Work: Industrial Relations and Economic Change,* Milton Keynes, Open University Press.

Madsén, T. (ed.) (1988), *Vem Skall Göra Jobben?,* Lund, Studentlitteratur.

Mahon, R. (1987), 'From Fordism to ? New Technology, Labour Markets and Unions', *Economic and Industrial Democracy,* 8.

Mandel, E. (1980), *Long Waves of Capitalist Development. The Marxist Interpretation,* Cambridge, Cambridge University Press.

Martin, A. (1984), 'The Erosion of the Swedish Model' in Gourevitch, P. et al. (eds), *Unions and Economic Crisis: Britain, West Germany and Sweden,* London, Allen and Unwin.

Mayhew, A. (1987), 'Culture: Core Concept Under Attack', *Journal of Economic Issues,* XXI (2).

Mazier, J. et al. (1985), *Quand Les Crises Durent,* Paris, Maspero.

MacRae, M. (1984), 'Health Care International',*Economist,* 28 April, 23-37.

McDowell, M. (1990), 'European Labour and the Politics of the American

Model', Paper presented at the VII International Conference for Europeans, Washington DC, March 23-25.

Meegan, R. (1988), 'A Crisis of Mass Production?' Allen, J. and Massey, D. (eds), *The Economy in Question. Restructuring Britain*, London, Sage.

Melnick, S. (1986), El desafio de la sociedad postindustrial, Futurion, Vol 1, Fundacion de Estudios Prospectivos, Planification Estrategia y Decisiones de alto nivel, Universidad de Chile.

Mensch, G. (1979), *Stalemate in Technology*, Ballinger, Cambridge, USA (German edition in 1974).

Messine, Ph. (1987), *Les saturniens. Quand les patrons réinventent la société*, Paris, La Découverte.

Metallarbetaren (1985), 'Metall kritiserar kvalitetscirklar', nr. 42.

Metallarbetaren (1986), 'Demokrati i cirkel', nr. 21-22.

Midttun, A. (1988), 'The Negotiated Political Economy of a Heavy Industrial Sector: The Norwegian Hydropower Complex in the 1970s and 1980s', *Scandinavian Political Studies*, 2, 115-144.

Milkovich, G.T. and Glueck, W. F. (1985), *Personnel/Human Resource Management: A Diagnostic Approach*, (4. Edition) Texas.

Mirowski, P. (1981), 'Is there a mathematical neoinstitutional economics?', *Journal of Economic Issues*, September 81, 593-613.

Mishra, R. (1984), *The Welfare State in Crisis,* Brighton, Harvester.

Mjøset, L. (1985a), 'Regulation and the Institutionalist Tradition', *Arbejdspapir fra NSU*, nr. 21, Nordisk Sommeruniversitet, Ålborg.

Mjøset, L. (1985b), 'Ekonomi och Politik i Norden', *Häften för Kritiska Studier*, 18, 4, 51-81.

Mjøset, L. (ed.) (1986), *Norden dagen derpå,* Olso, Norwegian University Press.

Mjøset, L. (1987), 'Nordic Economic Policies in the 1970s and 1980s', *International Organization*, 41 (3), 403-456.

Moore, C. and Booth, S. (1989), *Managing Competition: Meso-Corporatism, Pluralism and Negotiated Order in Scotland*, Oxford, Clarendon Press.

Moran, M. (1982), *The Politics of Banking. The Strange Case of Competition and Credit Control*, London, Macmillan.

Moran, M. (1987), 'A State of Inaction: the state and stock exchange reform in West Germany', *Manchester Papers in Politics*, Manchester University 6/87.

Murray, J. (1985), 'Benetton Britain', *Marxism Today*.

Møller, K. and Pade, H. (1988), *Industriel succes*, København, Samfundslitteratur.

Nelson, R. and Winter, S. (1982), *An Evolutionary Theory of Economic Change,* Cambridge, Mass.

Nielsen, K. (1988), 'Den borgerlige regerings styring af den offentlige sektors økonomi' in Bentzon, K.H., (ed.) *Fra vækst til omstilling - Modernisering af den offentlige sektor,* København, Nyt fra Samfundsvidenskaberne.

Nielsen, K. and Pedersen, O.K. (1988a), 'The Negotiated Economy: Ideal and History', *Scandinavian Political Studies*, 2, 79-102.

Nielsen, K. and Pedersen, O.K. (1988b), 'Fra blandingsøkonomi til forhandlingsøkonomi' in Klausen, K.K. and Nielsen, T.H. (eds), *Stat og marked. Fra Leviathan og usynlig hånd til forhandlingsøkonomi,* København, Jurist- og Økonomforbundet.

Nielsen, K. and Pedersen, O.K. (1989a), 'Is Small Still Flexible - An Evaluation of Recent Trends in Danish Politics', *Scandinavian Political Studies*, no. 4.

Nielsen, K. and Pedersen, O.K. (1991), 'From the Mixed Economy to the Negotiated Economy - The Scandinavian Countries', in Coughlin, R.M. (ed.), *Morality, Rationality and Efficiency: Perspectives on Socio-Economics 1990*, New York, M.E. Sharpe

Nilsson, J.-E. (1989), 'Ålderschocken - storm i ett vattenglas?', in Bull, M., (ed.), *Ålderschocken*, Göteborg, RE-VÄST Seminarierapport 2.

Nilsson, K.-E. (1987), 'Volvo i Rörelsens Frontlinjer' in Lundgren, N. et al. (eds), *Människan i Arbete*, Stockholm, Sveriges Rationaliseringsförbund.

Nilsson, T. and Sandberg, Å. (1988), *Rörelse över Gränser*, Lund, Arkiv.

Nobel, D.F. (1977), *America by Design*, Oxford University Press, Oxford.

Nobel, D.F. (1984), *Forces of Production. A social history of industrial automation*, Alfred A. Knopf, inc., New York.

Noel, A. (1987), Accumulation, Regulation and Social Change: an Essay on French Political Economy, *International Organization*, 41 (2), 303-333.

Nordisk Råd (1988), *Yearbook of Nordic Statistics*, København, Nordisk Råd.

NOU (Norwegian Public Reports) (1982), *Maktutredningen. Slutrapport*, NOU 1982, Oslo.

OECD (1983a), 'Eurocurrency banking: Alarmist concerns and genuine Issues', *OECD Economic Studies*, No 1, Paris.

OECD (1983b), *Positive Adjustment Policies: Managing Structural Change*, Paris, OECD.

OECD, (1984), 'Social Expenditure: Erosion or Revolution?', *The OECD Observer*, 126, January.

OECD (1985), *Social Expenditure 1960-1990. Problems of Growth and Control*, Paris, OECD.

OECD (1986), *Economic Outlook*, No 40, Paris, OECD.

OECD (1987), *Economic Outlook*, 41, June, Paris, OECD.

OECD (1988), *Reviews of National Science and Technology Policy: Denmark*, Paris, OECD.

OECD (1989), *Labour Market Flexibility: Trends in Enterprises*, Paris, OECD.

OECD (1990), *OECD Economic Surveys: Denmark*, Paris, OECD.

Offe, C. (1984), *Contradictions of the Welfare State*, London, Hutchinson.

Ohlsson, R. (1988), 'Ålderschocken är på väg!' in Madsén, T. (ed.), *Vem Skall Göra Jobben?*, Lund, Studentlitteratur.

Olson, M. (1982), *The Rise and Decline of Nations*, New Haven, Yale UP.

Olson, S. (1986), 'Sweden', in Flora, P. *Growth to Limits. The Western European Welfare States Since World War II*, Berlin and New York, Walter de Gruyter.

Ominami, C. (1986), *Le tiers-monde dans la crise*, Paris, La Découverte.

Page, A. (1987), 'Financial Services: the Self-Regulatory Alternative?', in Baldwin, R. and McCrudden, C. (eds), *Regulation and Public Law*, London, Weidenfeld and Nicolson.

Palm, G. (1977), *The Flight from Work*, Cambridge, Cambridge University Press.

Peacock, A. (1986), *Report of the Committee on Financing the BBC*, Cmnd. 9824, London, HMSO.

Pedersen, O.K. (1991), 'At first they were two, the three and now four.
Generalized Political Co-operation in Modern Danish History', Paper
prepared for ILO, Center for Public Organization and Management,
Copenhagen Business School, Copenhagen.

Pendleton, A. (1986), *Management Strategy and Labour Relations on British
Rail*, PhD thesis, University of Bath.

Perez, C. (1983), Structural change and assimilation of new technologies in
the economic and social systems, *Futures*, 15 (2), October.

Perez, C. (1985), 'Long Waves and Changes in Socioeconomic Organization',
IDS Bulletin, 16 (1), Institute of Development Studies, Sussex.

Perrons, D. (1981), 'The Role of Ireland in the New International Division
of Labour: A proposed framework for regional analysis, *Regional Studies*,
15 (2), 81-100.

Petersen, E. (1989), *De krisebevidste og offervillige danskere. Den politisk
psykologiske udvikling*, Psykologisk Institut, Århus Universitet.

Petersen, J. (1989a), 'Pensionsfonde som aktieejere. Nye institutionelle
muligheder for samfundsøkonomisk forhandlingsstyring på det danske
kapitalmarked', in Nielsen, K. and Pedersen, O.K. (eds),
Forhandlingsøkonomi i Norden, København, Jurist- og Økonomforbundets
Forlag.

Petersen, J. (1989b), 'Pensionskapital i erhvervslivet. Historiske
forudsætninger og institutionelle konsekvenser', unpublished manuscript,
Roskilde, Institut for Samfundsøkonomi og Planlægning, Roskilde
Universitetscenter.

Petit, P. (1984), *Slow Growth and the Service Economy*, Frances Pinter,
London.

Piore, M. (1985), Outline for a Research Agenda for 'The new industrial
organization', Mimeograph, M.I.T., Cambridge, December.

Piore, M. (1986), Corporate reform in American manufacturing and the
challange to economic theory, Mimeograph, M.I.T./ILO Geneva, March

Piore, M. and Sabel, C. (1984), *The Second Industrial Divide*, New York,
Basic Books.

Plender, J. and Wallace, P. (1985), *The Square Mile: a Guide to the New
City of London*, London, Centry.

Poggi, G. (1978), *The Development of the Modern State*, London,
Hutchinson.

Polanyi, K. (1957), *The Great Transformation*, Boston, Beacon Press,
(originally published in 1944).

Pollert, A. (1987), 'The "Flexible Firm": A Model in Search of Reality (or
a Policy in Search of a Practice)?', *Warwick Papers in Industrial Relations*,
No. 19, December.

Pollert, A. (1988), 'Dismantling Flexibility', *Capital and Class*, 34, 42-76.

Pollert, A. (1989), 'The "Flexible Firm": Fiction or Fact?', *Work,
Employment and Society*, 2 (3).

Pöntinen, S. and Uusitalo, H. (1986), 'The Legitimacy of the Welfare State:
Social Security Opinions in Finland 1975-1985', *Soumen Gallup Oy*, Report
No. 15.

Poulantzas, N. (1978), *State, Power and Socialism*, London, New Left Books.

Porter, M. (1990), *The Competitive Advantage of Nations*, New York, The
Free Press.

Prosser, T. (1988), *The Privatisation of Public Enterprises in France and Great Britain*, Working Paper 88/364, Florence, EUI
Przeworski, A. (1985), *Capitalism and Social Democracy*, Cambridge, Cambridge University Press.
Ramsay, I. (1987), 'The Office of Fair Trading: Policing the Consumer Market-Place', in Baldwin and McCrudden, *Regulation and Public Law*, London, Weidenfeld and Nicolson.
Ranta, J., Koskinen, K. and Ollus, M. (1988), 'Flexible Automation and Computer Integrated Manufacturing in Finland', *SITRA, Series A, No. 86*, Helsinki.
Renström, L. (1988), 'Den Goda Fabriken', in Madsén, T. (ed.), *Vem Skall Göra Jobben?*, Lund, Studentlitteratur.
Reuterswärd, A. (1990), 'A Flexible Labour Market in the 1990s', *OECD Observer*, 164, June/July, 29-32.
Rentoul, J. (1985), *The Rich get Richer*, London, Methuen.
Riddell, P. (1989), *The Thatcher Decade: How Britain has changed during the 1980s*, Oxford, Blackwell.
Ring, S. (1981), *Typerna och den Datoriserade Draken*, Stockholm, Marieberg.
Ring, S. and Tillybs (1988), *Har Facket Gjort Sitt?*, Stockholm, Tiden.
Ringen S. (1987), *The Possibility of Politics. A Study in the Political Economy of the Welfare State*, Oxford, Clarendon Press.
Robens, Sir A. (1972), *Report of the Committee on Health and Safety at Work*, Cmnd. 5034, London, HMSO.
Roobeek, A.J.M. (1987), The crisis in Fordism and the rise of a new technological paradigm, *Futures*, April, 129-154.
Rosenberg, N. (1982), *Inside the Black Box*, Cambridge, Cambridge University Press.
Rowthorn, B. (1991), 'Corporatism and the Labour Market Performance', in Pekkarinen, J., Pohjola, M. and Rowthorn, B., *Social Corporatism - A Superior Economic System*, Forthcoming.
Rowthorn, B. and Glyn, A. (1989), The diversity of unemployment experience since 1973, in Marglin, S. (ed.), *The Golden Age of Capitalism*, Oxford, Oxford University Press.
Sabel, C. (1989), 'The Reemergence of Regional Economics', Discussion Papers, Berlin, Wissenschaftszentrum.
SAF (Swedish Employers' Confederation) Avdelning T (1974), *Nya Arbetsformer: rapport från 500 försök, Stockholm*, SAF's Förlagssektion.
SAF-LO-PTK (1982), *Utvecklingsavtalet*.
SAF (1986), *Wages and Total Labour Costs for Workers. International Survey 1974-1984*, Stockholm, SAF's Förlagssektion.
Salvati, M. (1988), 'Rapport Salarial and Flexibility or: Regulation Theory and Political Economy', Paper to the conference on regulation theory, Barcelona, June.
Saunders, P. (1986), 'What Can We Learn from International Comparisons of Public Sector Size and Economic Performance?', *European Sociological Review*, (2), (1).
Saunders, P. and Klau, F. (1985), 'The Role of the Public Sector. Causes and Consequences of the Growth of Government' *OECD, Economic Studies*, No 4, Paris.

Sayer, A. (1989), 'Post-Fordism in Question', *International Journal of Urban and Regional Research*, 13 (4), 666-693.

SCB (1989), 'Det Framtida Arbetskraftsutbudet', *Information om Arbetsmarknaden* 4, Stockholm, SCB Förlag.

Schabedoth, H.-J. (1985), *Bittsteller oder Wegenmacht. Perspektiven gewerkschaftlicher Politik nach der Wende,* Marburg, SP-Verlag.

Schabedoth, H.-J. (1989), 'Modernisierungspolitik im Widerstreit, in Kißler, L. and Kreuder, T. (eds), *Der halbierte Fortschritt,* Marburg, SP-Verlag.

Schabedoth, H.-J. and Weckenmann, R. (1988), *Strategien für die Zukunft,* Marburg, SP-Verlag.

Schabedoth, H.-J. and Scherer, K.-J., (eds), (1990), *Ende der Wende? Konservative Hegemonie zwischen Manifestation und Erosion,* Marburg, SP-Verlag.

Scharpf, F. (1987), *Sozialdemokratische Krisenpolitik in Europa*, Frankfurt am Main, Campus.

Schiller, B. (1974), *LO, Paragraf 32 och Företagsdemokratin,* Stockholm, Prisma/LO.

Schiller, B. (1988), *'Det Förödande 70-talet': SAF och medbestämmandet 1965-1982,* Stockholm, AMF.

Schmid, J. and Tiemann, H. (1988), 'Rückschritt oder postmoderner Umbruch? Grundlinien der CDU-Politik', *Sozialismus*, Heft 9/1988.

Schmid, J. and Tiemann, H. (1989), 'Postmoderne CDU - Bastelei am christlichen Menschenbild und am politischen Profil der Union', *Die Neue Gesellschaft/Frankfurter Hefte*, 1, 62-67.

Schmitter, Ph. C. (1981), Interest intermediation and regime governability in contemporary Western Europe and North America, in Berger, S. (ed.) *Organizing Interest in Western Europe: Pluralism, Corporatism and the Transformation of Politics*, Cambridge University Press, Cambridge.

Schoenberger, E, (1988), 'From Fordism to flexible accumulation: technology, competitive strategies and international location', *Society and Space*, 6 (3), 254-262.

Schor, J., Gordon, D., Bowles, S. and Weisskopf, T. (1983), Conflict in the employment relations and the cost of job loss, Working Paper 6, Economic Institute of the Center for Democratic Alternatives.

Schumpeter, J.A. (1919), *Theorie der wirtschaftlichen Entwicklung*, English translation, *The Theory of Economic Development*, Cambridge, Mass., Harvard University Press., 1934.

Schumpeter, J A. (1928), 'The Instability of Capitalism', *Economic Journal*.

Schumpeter, J.A. (1942), *Capitalism, Socialism and Democracy,* New York, Harper and Row.

Schwerin, D.S. (1984), 'Historic Compromise and Pluralist Decline? Profits and Capital in the Nordic Countries', in Goldthorpe, J.H. (ed.), *Order and Conflict in Contemporary Capitalism,* Oxford, Clarendon Press.

Scitovsky, T. (1980), 'Can Capitalism Survive? - An Old Question in a New Setting', *American Economic Review,* Papers and Proceedings.

Scott, A. (1988), *Metropolis: From the Division of Labour to Urban Form*, Berkeley and Los Angeles, University of California Press.

Scranton, Ph. (1983), *Proprietary Capitalism. the textile manufacture at Philadelphia: 1800-1885*, Cambridge University Press.

Sethi, A.K. and Sethi, S.P. (1990), 'Flexibility in Manufacturing: A Survey',

The International Journal of Flexible Manufacturing Systems, 2, (4) 289-328.

Shell, D. (1988), 'The British Constitution 1987', *Parliamentary Affairs*, 41 (4).

Shonfield, A. (1965), *Modern Capitalism*, Oxford, OUP.

Siegel, T. (1988), 'Welfare Capitalism, Nazi Style', *International Journal of Political Economy*, 18, (1).

Simonson, B. (1988), *Arbetarmakt och Näringspolitik: LO och inflytande-frågorna 1961-1982*, Stockholm: AMF.

Singh, A. (1978), 'UK Industry and the world economy: a case of de-industrialisation?', *Cambridge Journal of Economics*, 1 (2), 113-136.

Skocpol, T. (1984), 'What is Happening to Western Welfare States?', *Contemporary Sociology*, 307-311.

Skouras, A. (1981), 'The Economics of Joan Robinson', in Shackleton, J.R. and Locksley, G. (eds), *Twelve Contemporary Economists*, London, Macmillan, 199-218.

Sonenscher, M. (1984), 'The Sans-Culottes of the Year II: rethinking the language of labour in revolutionary France', *Social History*, 9, 3, 301-328.

Sorge, A. and Streeck, W. (1987), 'Industrial Relations and Technical Change. The Case for an Extended Perspective', in Tolliday, S. and Zeit, J. (eds), *Between Fordism and Flexibility*, Cambridge, Polity.

Soskice, D. (1988), 'Industrial Relations and Unemployment: The Case of Flexible Corporatism', Kregel, J.A., Martzner, E. and Roncaglia, A. (eds), *Barriers to Full Employment*, London, Macmillan.

Späth, L. (1985), *Wende in die Zukunft. Die Bundesrepublik auf dem Weg in die Informationsgesellschaft*, Hamburg, VSA-Verlag

Späth, L. (1989), *Regierungserklärung von Ministerpräsident Lothar Späath zur Kunstkonzeption vor dem Landtag Baden-Württemberg am 13.12. 1989*, (ed.) by Staatsministerium Baden-Württemberg, Stuttgart.

Standing, G. (1986), 'Meshing Labour Flexibility with Security : an answer to British unemployment' *International Labour Review*, 125, 87-106.

Stedman-Jones, G. (1983), *Languages of Class*, Cambridge, Cambridge University Press.

Storper, M. and Walker, R. (1989), *The Capitalist Imperative*, Oxford, Basil Blackwell.

Strange, S. (1985), *Casino Capitalism*, Oxford, Blackwell.

Streeck, W. (1987a), 'The Uncertainties of Management and the Management of Uncertainty', *Work, Employment and Society*, 1 (3).

Streeck, W. (1987b), 'Industrial Relations in West Germany: Agenda for Change', *Discussion Paper IIM/LMP 87-5*, Wissenschaftszentrum Berlin für Sozialforschung, Berlin.

Streeck, W. and Schmitter, P.C. (1983), 'Community, Market, State - and Associations? The prospective contribution of interest governance to social order', in idem (eds), *Private Interest Government*, London, Sage.

Svenska Metallindustriarbetareförbundet (1985), *Det Goda Arbetet*, Huvudrapport från Programkommittén presenterad vid Kongressen, 1-7 September.

Svenska Metallindustriarbetareförbundet (1989), *Solidarisk Arbetspolitik för det goda arbetet*, Huvudrapport från Programkommittén presenterad vid Kongressen, 3-9 September.

Teubner, G. (1983), 'Substantive and Reflexive Elements in Modern Law', *Law and Society Review,* 17, 1667.

Therborn, G. (1986), *Why Some Peoples Are More Unemployed Than Other. The Strange Paradox Of Growth And Unemployment,* London, Verso.

Therborn, G. and Roebroek, J. (1986), 'The Irreversible Welfare State: Its Recent Maturation, Its Encounter with the Economic Crisis, and its Future Prospects', *International Journal of Health Services,* 18 (3).

Threakston, K. (1989), 'The Civil Service: Progress Report 1988/89', *Contemporary Record,* 2 (6), 16-17.

Tobin, A. (1984), 'On the Efficiency of the Financial System', *Lloyds Bank Review,* July.

Tonboe, J.C. (1988), 'Colonization of Urban Civil Society', *Acta Sociologica,* 31.

Treasury H.M. (1984), *Nationalised Industries Consultative Proposals,* London.

Trist, E. et al. (1963), *Organizational Choice,* London, Tavistock.

Tunstall, B. W. (1983), 'Cultural Transition at AT and T', *Sloan Management Review* 25/1, Fall 1983, 15 - 26.

Turnbull, P. (1988), 'The Limits to Japanisation', *New Technology, Work and Employment,* 3 (1).

UTOPIA (1984), *Informations blad* nr. 7, Stockholm, Arbetslivscentrum.

Vaccarini, I. (1984), 'La riflessione della sociologia germanica sul "Welfare State"', in Rossi, G. and Donati, P. (eds), *Welfare State: Problemi e Alternavi,* Milano, Franco Angeli.

Veblen, T. (1898), 'Why is Economics Not an Evolutionary Science?', *The Quarterly Journal of Economics,* vol. XII, July.

Wachtel, H.M. (1986), *The Money Mandarins. The Making of a Supra-national Economic Order,* New York, Pantheon.

Wachtel, H.M. (1987), *The Politics of International Money,* Amsterdam.

Walker, R.A. (1989), 'Regulation, Flexible Specialization and the Forces of Production in Capitalist Development', Paper to the Cardiff Symposium on Regulation, Innovation and Spatial Development, September 13-15.

Walton, R. E. (1985), 'From Control to Commitment in the Workplace', *Harvard Business Review* 2, 77-84.

Wass, Sir D. (1984), *Government and the Governed,* London. Routledge and Keegan Paul.

Weisskopf, T.E., Bowles, S. and Gordon, D.E. (1983) Hearts and minds: A social model of US productivity growth, *Brookings Papers on Economic Activity,* no. 2.

Widick, B.J. (ed.) (1976), *Auto Work and its Discontents,* Policy Studies in Employment and Welfare, No. 25, Bks. Demand UMI, Baltimore.

Wilensky, H.L. (1975), *The Welfare State and Equality,* Berkeley, University of California Press.

Williams, K., Cutler, T., Williams J. and Haslam, C. (1987), 'The End of Mass Production?, *Economy and Society,* 16 (3).

Williams, K., Williams J. and Haslam, C. (1989), 'Do Labour Costs Really Matter?', *Work, Employment, and Society,* 3 (3), 281-305.

Williams, R. (1983), *Keywords,* London, Fontana.

Williams, R. (1989), 'Mining the Meaning: keywords in the miners' strike', in *Resources of Hope,* London, Verso.

Williamson, O. (1975), *Markets and Hierarchies*, New York, Free Press.

Winkler, J. (1981), 'The Political Economy of Administrative Discretion', in Adler, M. and Asquith, S. (eds), *Discretion and Welfare*, London, Heinemann, 82.

Wood, S. (1988), 'The Transformation of Work?', in Wood, S. (ed), *The Transformation of Work*, London, Unwim Hyman, pp. 1-43.

Woodcock, L. (1977): 'Labor and Multinationals', in Banks, F. and Stieber, J. (eds), *Multinationals, Unions, and Labor Relations in Industrialized Countries*, Ithaca.

Zacher, (1985), 'Verrechtlichung im Bereich des Sozialrechts', in Kübler, F. (ed.), *Verrechtlichung von Wirtschaft, Arbeit und sozialer Solidarität*, Frankfurt, Suhrkamp.

Zeuthen, H. (1986), 'Perioden 1979-82: Indkomstpolitik, valutakurs-politik og twist-politik', in Det Økonomiske Råd, *Råd og realiteter*, København.

Index